Fabulous Vernacular

Fabulous Vernacular

Boccaccio's *Filocolo* and the
Art of Medieval Fiction

VICTORIA KIRKHAM

Ann Arbor
THE UNIVERSITY OF MICHIGAN PRESS

A CIP catalog record for this book is available from the British Library.

Library of Congress Cataloging-in-Publication Data

Kirkham, Victoria.
    Fabulous vernacular : Boccaccio's Filocolo and the art of medieval fiction / Victoria Kirkham.
        p.   cm.
    Includes bibliographical references and index.
    ISBN 0-472-11164-7 (alk. paper)
    1. Boccaccio, Giovanni, 1313–1375. Filocolo. 2. Fiction, Medieval—History and criticism. 3. Novelle—History and criticism. I. Title.
    PQ4270.F53K57   2000
    853'.1—dc21   00-08868

In memory of my parents,
Don and Betty Kirkham

Preface

Fabulous Vernacular is as much an expression of my identity as a scholar as a synthesis of my thinking about Boccaccio. This sense of professional identity, which has roots reaching back to a family background in Iowa where both parents were university professors, was something first cultivated in graduate school at Johns Hopkins University. There I found a rich intellectual environment at an American institution with proudly maintained connections to the German world of learning, from avatars of Romance philology to the dreaded public dissertation defense, an event anyone could attend to query candidates on our universal knowledge. Charles Singleton presided over our Gilman Hall seminars opposite two older worthies, spiritually with us in their portraits—a magisterial Wilhelm Meyer-Lübke towering in an oil painting high on the wall and, below him, in a large black-and-white photograph propped on the chalk tray, Leo Spitzer, intensely cerebral with his lighted cigarette. As Singleton spoke of the men in those pictures, he made us feel the power of academic continuities, for in this scene there was a succession of generations from the great nineteenth-century philologist, to his student Spitzer, to Singleton, and right on down to us. So, too, when our professor recited and explained the *Divine Comedy* in that long room with its battered oak conference table, we could envision ourselves as new links in a historical chain uninterrupted since the fourteenth century, when it started with Dante's own sons and his most passionate medieval reader, Giovanni Boccaccio.

Memorable for his teaching in the classroom, Singleton was a strong scholarly model for me as I began to find my own academic voice. No less important in my formation was the larger Hopkins community, inspirited by interdisciplinary ideals of study in the humanities and the history of ideas. Intellectual itineraries all take unpredictable turnings that push our research into new directions, and so it was with mine, thanks to several visits as a fellow at the Harvard Center for Renaissance Studies in Florence, Villa I Tatti, a haven imbued with the character of its remarkable maker, Bernard Berenson. As I knew them, both Hopkins and Harvard privileged the literary classics. Both settings nurtured a kind of scholarship cast in historical depth yet inclined to move freely across disciplinary boundaries. Both provided strong examples of scholars who had forged distinctive styles of writing, English prose bearing a personal imprint that it has also been my goal to craft.

Others in the field of literary studies have gone in directions different from mine, following successive waves of semiotics, deconstruction, new historicism, and cultural studies. Their work has touched and taught us all. Since I am a literary historian, I have not theorized the *Filocolo.* My lexicon is belletristic. My approach couples philology and criticism, a pairing for which the studies of Vittore Branca stand as paradigmatic. Here my curiosities converge on Boccaccio's notions of literary decorum, on the creative continuities that unify his corpus, and on the new "poetry" that emerges from his engagement with Latin and vernacular tradition.[1] To answer them, I have meditated on the provocative interplay between his poetic inventions and historical truth; on the autobiographical stamp of his fiction, especially as it reflects the author's formation in canon law; on "signature" themes to which he keeps returning, such as the story of his love for Fiammetta; on the kinds of compositional structures he prefers, typically symmetrical or "Gothic" arrangements around a center; and on the medieval esthetics of concealment, the practice of layering hidden meanings into a text for the delight of discovery that comes as we readers recognize its allegory and decode its symbolism, iconography, and numerology.[2]

---

1. I take the accommodating term *engagement* from Winthrop Wetherbee, *Chaucer and the Poets: An Essay on Troilus and Criseyde* (Ithaca: Cornell University Press, 1984), 9–11; Wetherbee writes of his subject's "engagement" with tradition, both Latin and vernacular, including Boccaccio. By *poetry* I mean imaginative literature in the widest sense, as Boccaccio would have understood the word.

2. Our categories of "fiction" and "nonfiction" only partially overlap with Boccaccio's notions of generic distinctions and the relationship between fiction and truth. Long-held critical convictions about his "realism," for example, rested on anachronistic assumptions. Their drift has found correction in such recent work as Millicent Marcus, *An Allegory of Form: Literary Self-Consciousness in the Decameron* (Saratoga, Calif.: Anma Libri, 1979); Giuseppe Mazzotta, *The World at Play in Boccaccio's Decameron* (Princeton: Princeton University Press, 1986); Pier Massimo Forni, *Adventures in Speech: Rhetoric and Narration in Boccaccio's Decameron* (Philadelphia: University of Pennsylvania Press, 1996). Most attention has gone to the *Decameron,* much less to the early fiction, and virtually none to the late Latin encyclopedias, which freely intermingle history and poetry. A classic and appealingly lucid treatment of these problems for medieval narrative fiction more broadly is Eugène Vinaver, *The Rise of Romance* (Oxford: Oxford University Press, 1971).

If the elegance of science lies in its capacity to reduce mysterious complexity to understandable simplicity, the virtue of the humanities is their tolerance of ambiguities, of conflicting points of view, and of endless possibilities of interpretation. The university, which in its medieval origins was quite literally "diversity coming together," ought to be an environment where different schools of thought can flourish, an intellectual chorus of many voices. Every humanist must speak in his own voice. Every author must write his own book. I have written mine.

Acknowledgments

The history of this book, which spans my career as an Italianist, had its origins thirty years ago when I wrote a dissertation on the *Filocolo* under Charles S. Singleton. That project sparked my first article, "Reckoning with Boccaccio's *Questioni d'amore*," *MLN* 89, no. 1 (1974): 47–59, here reproduced in updated form as chapter 4 by permission of the Johns Hopkins University Press. A portion of chapter 2, "Signed Pieces," overlaps in part with "Iohannes de Certaldo: La firma dell'autore," my contribution to the anthology *Gli zibaldoni di Boccacio: Memoria, scrittura, riscrittura,* ed. Claude Cazalé Bérard and Michelangelo Picone (Florence: Franco Cesati, 1998). I thank my European collaborators and Franco Cesati Editore for permission to reproduce parts of that article, originally presented as a paper at the conference they organized on Boccaccio's working notebooks. The rest of the material in this volume has never before been published. Portions of it have been presented over the years in talks for colloquia, occasions that pushed me to develop my ideas in writing and provided opportunities for a preliminary scholarly airing. I am grateful to those colleagues who invited my participation at such events, in particular Claude Cazalé Bérard, Pier Massimo Forni, Christopher Kleinhenz, Lucia Marino, Michelangelo Picone, Janet Smarr, and Elissa Weaver.

Others who have contributed enrichment from their fields of expertise, shared both in correspondence and conversations pleasant to recall, include Samuel G. Armistead, Susannah Baxendale, Pamela Benson, Renate Blumenfeld-Kosinski, Kevin Brownlee, Barbara Burrell, Allen Grieco, Tim Halliday, Sylvia Huot, and Georg Nicholas Knauer. I owe a particular debt to Paul F. Watson, a past collaborator and coteacher at Penn, for sharing from his wealth of knowledge on Boccaccio and the visual arts. Patricia Grieve was extraordinarily generous in making available to me photocopies of articles on the diffusion of the *Filocolo* source tale, as well as an early draft of her book manuscript, which takes welcome account of the Spanish prototype (a version of which was known to Boccaccio) and has now appeared as *Floire and Blancheflor and the European Romance* (Cambridge: Cambridge University Press, 1997). Both Vittore Branca and Robert Hollander provided important encouragement for completing this book when my own spirits were flagging. I especially thank Pier Massimo Forni, Millicent Marcus, Ronald Martinez, and Janet Levarie Smarr, those close colleagues in Italian studies who, with patient goodwill and judicious advice, scrutinized my manuscript as it was evolving.

Knowingly or not, many others have contributed to this book along the way, in friendship, generosity of spirit, and hospitality, among them Ann Arnaud and her family, Bianca Tarozzi, both Vittore and Olga Branca, Marco and Paola Frascari, Pietro Frassica, Rebecca West, Apostolos and Marina Condos, and Marco and Edda Vandini. Over the years, the University of Pennsylvania has assisted me with leave time and supported travel in Italy through the Henry Salvatori Fund of the Center for Italian Studies. I am especially grateful to Walter Kaiser, directory of the Villa I Tatti, for welcoming me twice as a visiting professor during the years of this project's long gestation. Finally, I have benefited for work on the final stages of the book from a grant at the Newberry Library in Chicago funded by the Rockefeller Foundation.

My mother, Mary Elizabeth Erwin Kirkham, always one of my best readers and boosters, read as much of the manuscript as had taken shape before she died. To her memory and to that of my father, a passionate traveler who first introduced me to Italy, I dedicate this book.

Contents

Fabulous Vernacular

Introduction

The *Filocolo:* Fabulous Vernacular

Raphael's *Parnassus,* frescoed for Pope Julius II in the Vatican *Stanza della Segnatura* (ca. 1511), envisions a universal gathering of poets from ancient to modern times. Oblivious to barriers of history, they connect with each other as poets are wont to do, through a common language Boccaccio had called "confabulation." On the peak of Parnassus stand those who practiced the art of poetry in its highest form, the epic. Blind Homer, Virgil, Statius, and Dante embody the heroic style, which in the hierarchy of genres still in the cinquecento ranked as most noble. Although Boccaccio, too, stands among the seventeen laurel-crowned worthies on the mount sacred to Apollo and the Muses, Raphael places him among a different group of men, suggesting that the writer will be remembered not for his early Italian epic-romance, the *Filocolo,* or even for his subsequent epic proper, the *Teseida* in twelve books of true verse, but probably for his *Decameron* and nymphals in the pastoral mode.[1] Yet had the *Decameron* not eclipsed his more youthful work, the *Filocolo* would surely have vindicated its author's dreams of recognition.

---

1. Boccaccio stands on the opposite side of Raphael's *Parnassus* from Dante and the other epic poets. Positioned farther down on the slope and at the rear fringe of the gathering, he seems to gaze off into the distance, absorbed in contemplation. How Raphael disposed the poets on Parnassus in groups by genre (epic, lyric, pastoral) has been described by Paul F. Watson, "On a Window on Parnassus," *Artibus et Historiae* 16 (1987): 127–48. He has advanced the notion that the poets are "confabulating," according to a definition from Boccaccio in *Genealogie deorum gentilium libri,* ed. Vittorio Zaccaria, in vols. 7–8 of *Tutte le opere* (Milan: Mondadori, 1998), 14.9. See Watson, "To Paint Poetry: Raphael on Parnassus," in *Renaissance Rereadings: Intertext and Context,* ed. Maryanne Cline Horowitz, Anne J. Cruz, and Wendy A. Furman (Urbana: University of Illinois, 1988), 114–41. For discussion of Raphael's Parnassus in the family of Boccaccio's early portraits, see Victoria Kirkham, "L'immagine del Boccaccio nella memoria tardo-gotica e rinascimentale," in *Boccaccio visualizzato,* ed. Vittore Branca (Turin: Einaudi, 1999), 1:85–144.

The first sustained work of prose fiction in Italy, it was the most ambitious prose narrative to its day in any European vernacular. As for literature in the Arno idiom, nothing would match it for length or art until the appearance in the nineteenth century of the nation's founding novel, Alessandro Manzoni's *Promessi sposi.* The "new author" proudly establishes his credentials, displaying his culture through links to Latin epic, Dante's *Vita nuova* and *Divine Comedy,* French romances, a Spanish source tale, Holy Scripture, hagiography, universal history, the literature of travel, canons in church law, and statutes of the Justinian Code. To assert his artistry in the vernacular, Boccaccio devises an epic plan, played out by gods and mortals in providential Christian history. Juno descends on her peacock-drawn chariot to set in motion his narrative machinery by visiting the pope (fig. 2); at her prompt, he calls into Italy a dynasty of Angevin kings. Against this elevated political setting and at the climax of the liturgical year, the narrator's own fantasy drama unfolds: first in San Lorenzo, the Neapolitan church consecrated to a saint martyred by fire, where his Flame-Lady, Maria, appears amid blazing paschal candles; and soon after within the walls of a convent famous for ladies who were "models of all virtues and talent combined,"[2] Sant'Arcangelo a Baiano, where Maria invites him to write the book.

What a shame, she confides to him at that nunnery, not to have Prince Florio's story "in the verses of any poet, but left only in the fabulous parlance of the ignorant" [ne' fabulosi parlari degli ignoranti]. She charges him to set about "composing a little booklet in the vernacular" that will recount how the two amorous youths Florio and Biancifiore were born and fell in love, everything right up to the end of their famous tale. "Some years" and several hundred pages pass before her admirer, occupied with the study of canon law, completes the lady's daunting commission. Speaking again for the first time since he had embarked on his labor of love, he bids his "little booklet" farewell and claims a place for its "verses" at a humble distance behind Virgil, Lucan, Statius, Ovid, and Dante.

---

2. So it was still remembered in 1864 by a Neapolitan nun who told a horrifying story of her imprisonment within convent walls, after suppression of the monasteries by the new national government enabled her to return to secular life. See Enrichetta Caracciolo, *Misteri del chiostro napoletano* (1864; reprint, Florence: Giunti, 1986). Caracciolo cites from an anonymous *Cronaca del Convento di Sant'Arcangelo a Bajano,* which states that during the reign of the Angevins, the ladies there "furono il modello di tutte le virtù riunite al talento, frutto d'un'educazione distinta." Later, during the reigns of Ferdinand the Catholic and Charles V, it changed much for the worse.

As his rhythmic words respectfully march after illustrious forebears, Boccaccio tropes their examples. Like Statius at the end of the *Thebaid,* who follows in the footsteps of Virgil's *Aeneid,* and like Dante in Limbo, "sixth among so much wisdom," Boccaccio modestly asserts his membership in the most elite family of letters. Prose is his medium, but he conspicuously calls it "verses" to emphasize the epic connection at the beginning of the *Filocolo,* at the end, and, to complete the symmetry, right at the center. There, deep in sixth-century fiction, Jove's oracle predicts future greatness for Giovanni of Certaldo, who in the fourth decade of the fourteenth century will make Filocolo's adventures "manifest to the ignorant" with his "memorable verses." Three times, at signal moments in the structure, the author comes forward to call us dynamically across the book with recurrent key words that announce a "picciol libretto" cast in "versi" for the benefit of "ignoranti."

This privileged vocabulary, purposefully reiterated, sends us back to Dante's *Vita nuova,* itself a diminutive vernacular "libello" and the context in which Boccaccio found the ready-made phrase *parlare fabuloso.*[3] Dante had used it to say why he omits some matters from his memoire, things having to do with the passions of youth, since to dwell on them would be "a sort of fabulous parlance" [alcuno parlare fabuloso]. As Boccaccio's Maria adopts the expression, shifting to plural, "fabulosi parlari degli ignoranti" comes to imply the "fables" or tall tales of unlettered folk. In both poets, there is a suggestion of subjects without serious meaning or artistic motivation. When the Dantism *parlare fabuloso* resurfaces in Boccaccio's prose, we could suppose that he refers to the romance of Prince Florio as it circulated orally, performed by minstrels or *cantastorie* for publics congregated in the *piazze.* In fact, Italian popular culture has bequeathed us the *Cantare di Fiorio e Biancifiore,* a simple version of the source tale in ottava rima roughly contemporary with the *Filocolo.* Nevertheless, as Boccaccio will later polemically maintain, the word *fable* and its etymological relatives are a family that need not have pejorative connota-

---

3. Dante calls his book of memory a "libello" [booklet] in the second sentence of the *Vita nuova.* The phrase "parlare fabuloso" occurs at the end of the second chapter. See Dante Alighieri, *Vita nuova,* ed. Domenico De Robertis, in *Opere minori,* ed. Domenico De Robertis and Gianfranco Contini (Milan: Ricciardi, 1984), vol. 1, pt. 1, 1–247. Michelangelo Picone has graphed the intertextual dynamics of Boccaccio's citation and his source, in "Tipologie culturali: Da Dante a Boccaccio," *Strumenti critici* 30 (1976): 263–74. See further Francesco Bruni, *Boccaccio: L'invenzione della letteratura mezzana* (Bologna: Il Mulino, 1990), 347–51.

tions. It is a mistake, he asserts at the close of his *Genealogies of the Gentile Gods,* to dismiss poets just as "fabulosos homines" [men who make fables] or, worse, to disparage them as "fabulones" [fabulators, lying babblers]. Boccaccio admits that poets are "fabulosos, id est fabularum compositores" [fabulous, that is, composers of fables], but he argues that theirs is an honorable art, for *fable* derives from the Latin *for, faris* [to speak], and from that we get *confabulation,* which simply means "talking together." Therefore, he concludes, "if it is a sin to compose fables, it is a sin to converse, which only the veriest fool would admit." Maria's expression "fabulous parlance of the ignorant" turns on an ambiguous signifier, *favola,* meaning loosely "fiction," alternatively either a way of confabulating (either speaking or writing) that may be superficial and false or a worthy discourse susceptible of fuller resonance in an allegorical dimension.[4]

For all his pretense at looking down on "low" culture, that fertile matrix is where Boccaccio found the most fabulous material. The "ignoranti" knew a good story when they heard it. They could appreciate his rip-roaring adventure story about a heartrending romance between a king's son and an orphan slave girl, twinlike Florio and Biancifiore, "flower children" with fabled names, born on the same Easter holiday and bonded in undying love. Cruel destiny, whose agents lurk at every turn, grinds relentlessly against them, in the forms of infernal furies, parental opposition, angered gods, diabolical pagans, violent Saracens, a villainous

---

4. Boccaccio *Genealogie* 14.9, trans. Charles G. Osgood, *Boccaccio on Poetry, Being the Preface and the Fourteenth and Fifteenth Books of Boccaccio's Genealogia Deorum Gentilium,* (1930; reprint, Library of the Liberal Arts, Indianapolis: Bobbs-Merrill, 1956), 47–48. I cite Osgood throughout but have sometimes modified his renderings to make them more literal. In this passage, Boccaccio goes on to define "fiction" *(fabula)* as allegory: "a form of discourse, which, under guise of invention, illustrates or proves an idea; and, as its superficial aspect is removed, the meaning of the author is clear." In the *Decameron,* "fable" will be one of the nuanced designations Boccaccio gives for the short stories ("novelle") he has decided to tell, which will be "fabule" or "parabole" or "istorie" (proem 13). The point has been noted by Margherita Heyer-Caput in "Le *questioni d'amore* del *Filocolo:* Tirocinio letterario di Giovanni Boccaccio," in *Studies in Honor of Dante Della Terza,* ed. Marilina Cirillo-Falzarano and Mei-Mei Akwai Ellerman (Cambridge: Harvard University Office of the University Publisher, 1996): 65–88. Roberta Morosini has suggested how specifically Boccaccio sought to improve on the "fabulous parlance" of his source tale with reference to what he himself says; see " 'Per difetto rintegrare': Il *Filocolo* di G. Boccaccio," *Bollettino dell'Accademia Lucchese di Scienze Lettere e Arti* 8, nos. 3–4 (1997):14–20. The passage in which Fiammetta invites Boccaccio to write can recall Chrétien de Troyes at the opening verses of *Erec et Enide,* where he announces his intention of drawing a very fine "conjointure" from an old adventure story. Vinaver (*Rise of Romance,* chap. 3), connects what the French poet says with Horace's *De arte poetica,* explaining "conjointure" as a new, more artistic treatment of the subject.

seneschal, a deathly harem, heartless judges, wicked jailers, gale-force weather, shipwreck, Jealousy, and hair-raising death sentences. Naturally, they will marry and live happily ever after. To frame all this romantic action, Boccaccio smilingly designs some "fabulous" discourse of his own, the motifs of a royal setting (King Robert's Naples); a beautiful virgin princess (the king's daughter, Maria), whose aura is enhanced by illegitimacy because she is a love child secretly royal (since her biological father wisely assigned her the name of another man); and a commoner and poor student in love with the princess, his heart pierced by Cupid's fiery arrow, with ardor coincidentally kindled at Eastertide. The poet cuts the frame to fit the tale.

The *Filocolo* does not, then, discard archetypes and conventions of popular fiction. Rather, it subsumes them into a new, more heterodox mix, simultaneously a vehicle for *translatio* of the classical epic, a platform supportive of Ciceronian prose, a medium friendly both to Ovid and to secular Romance models, and a language that can absorb as readily the Scholastic cadences of Aristotle as the *sermo humilis* of the Gospels. In the *Filocolo,* Boccaccio, indefatigably an innovator, aggressively measures himself against the best of the ancients as well as his most recent European predecessors. He rejects the option of writing in Latin, available to him through Guido delle Colonne's less than felicitous attempt at rendering the Trojan War, *Historia destructionis Troiae* (1287), a dispiriting and an inauthentic dead end. Maria's charge that he recompose a familiar old love story "volgarmente parlando" allows him the pretext of writing in the mother tongue because he is writing for a female audience, a pose he successfully kept for fiction to follow. Beyond the letter of the text, what the lady requests conveys the poet's decision to commit himself to the emerging Tuscan language and experimentally test its limits.

Fabulous Vernacular: Boccaccio's Filocolo and the Art of Medieval Fiction is a topology of the book that gave birth to Italy's great tradition of prose narrative, mapped within larger surrounding territories of literary activity in the Middle Ages. These stratified borderlands stretch from the classical heritage, with its epic and amorous models, to the French and Italian moderns—the troubadours, Chrétien de Troyes, Jacques de Longuyon, Giacomo da Lentini and the Sicilian poets, their successors in the *dolce stil nuovo,* and, above all, Dante. Central to the spaces that encircle the *Filocolo* and define by comparison its features are other writings by Boccaccio himself, from his first practice pieces to his most erudite encyclopedias. A landscape reconstructed to the years he composed the *Filo-*

colo (1336–39?), it is characterized by not only dominant presences but also telling absences. Fiammetta here makes her grand entrance into the poet's oeuvre, but Petrarch is barely in the picture. How did Boccaccio establish his claim to attention and respect in the world of letters beside those giants already firmly implanted there?

Although the *Filocolo* is not his first vernacular attempt, it far outweighs what had come before, a graceful little allegory in terza rima called *Diana's Hunt* and the relatively short *Filostrato,* its seductive ironies set in rhyming octaves. Boccaccio now more seriously broaches the business of asserting his authority, proclaiming his identity as a "new author" (*Filoc.* 1.2) in the grandest international traditions. In chapter 1 of *Fabulous Vernacular,* I show how he approached that end by providing himself with a poetic mistress—what John Addington Symonds called "necessary equipment"—a lady who incorporates countless old metaphors of amorous fire that merge into a single "New Flame" meant to remind us of perfect women from the Virgin Mary to Dante's Beatrice.

In chapter 2, I argue that Boccaccio, aware of the decorum governing authorial signatures from Virgil onward, exemplifies the most sophisticated practice in his signed pieces, taking cues for the *Filocolo* from recent antecedents in French and Italian vernacular. He who in his *congedo* designates the poets before him with epithets of geographic origin ("Sulmonan Ovid," "Tolosan Statius") understandably chooses to take his place in line after them as "Giovanni of Certaldo." This Certaldan John is both a typical medieval and a talented individual. Obvious as the facts are, scholarship long denied his ties to the trecento and kept shunting him forward into the Renaissance with anachronistic arguments all attached to the magnetic *Decameron,* read as a manifesto of modernity. A stirring address delivered in 1875 on the five-hundredth anniversary of Boccaccio's death by Italy's first Nobel laureate in literature, Giosuè Carducci, vaunts it as a triumph over the Middle Ages. Dante looked heavenward; Petrarch looked inward; Boccaccio looked worldward, as a new "Tuscan Ovid."[5] His manly identity, too, was conditioned by his masterpiece, extrapolated from the *Decameron* narrator and buttressed by other fictional doubles, the likes of Caleon, Idalogos, Palemone, Dioneo, the scholar Rinieri, and the risible canonist of the *Corbaccio.* What they all added up to was a male

---

5. Carducci's address, delivered in Certaldo on Dec. 21, 1875, was published under its title, *Ai parentali di Giovanni Boccacci in Certaldo* (Bologna: Zanichelli, 1876). The classicist-poet chose the unusual Latinate term *parentali,* a solemn commemoration of a celebrated deceased person.

obsessed by erotic passion in its unstable phases—anticipated, imagined, enjoyed, suffered, lost. Nevertheless, while scholarship of the last half century has mostly stripped the picture of those fanciful overlays, one important part of the poet's identity still hides in shadows. That is his status as a canonist, usually downplayed by those who have documented his life, because it has been assumed that he hated both the law and his father for forcing him to learn it.

I show in chapter 3 that Boccaccio himself planted the idea that he was a "reluctant canonist." In an autobiographical moment of his *Genealogies of the Gentile Gods,* he recalls how his father, Boccaccino, drove him into uncongenial careers, though all along, from his mother's womb, his true vocation had been poetry. Giovanni seems to be speaking God's truth in his own first-person voice, but the words that come out have a literary source. He is not speaking; he is citing. For the passage in question, he quotes Ovid, a ploy he elsewhere adopts to play the role of narrating "Author." Ovid complains in the *Tristia* how a tyrannical father pushed him toward the law, notwithstanding the fact that from childhood the lad had been quite spontaneously composing verse.

Law and poetry, irreconcilable opposites in the topos, cooperate in Boccaccio's writing, a fortiori in the *Filocolo,* composed during the years he was a church law student at the University of Naples. His studies as a canonist are perfectly consonant with major new directions in his reworking of the story, explored in the last three chapters of *Fabulous Vernacular.* If his writing is to answer and correct "fabulous parlance," it must move away from narrative that is reminiscent of fairy tales (cf. Italian *favoloso,* from *favola*) toward an opposite epistemological sphere. The fiction can no longer float through a timeless realm of make-believe but must be grounded solidly in the real march of history. Such history must conform to a providential plan, furnishing a structure that allows the characters to mature and advance morally. As the *Decameron* would be anchored to the Black Death that swept into Florence during March, 1348, so already in the *Filocolo* Boccaccio fuses creative writing with chronicle. He sets his tale in the age of Justinian, author of the Western legal code. Supreme jurist, Justinian guarantees an allegorical atmosphere of justice. Boccaccio's fictional narrator is Ilario, an interior double, but one far different from Idalogos or Dioneo and usually forgotten because he does not fit so conveniently the vita of an amorous fellow. Instead, Ilario is a priest and a preacher; his "temple" is the mother church of Christendom, San Giovanni in Laterano. He plays alter ego to the canonist, who is learning the laws of Christ's successors in the papacy when he conceives his epic with a proemial colloquy that features—who else?—the pope. Clement IV, responsible for summoning the Angevins into Italy to defeat the Imperialists, has within the historical fiction of the *Filocolo* a sixth-century counterpart in the chair of Saint Peter's, Pope Vigilius. Vigilius receives a good part in the plot, for after Ilario's religious instruction, straight out of the manual, Florio can progress to baptism, which that pope himself administers. The ritual takes place in the most solemn location possible for a pious Christian, none other than the Lateran Bapistry.

Justinian, popes, priest, catechism, Rome, the Lateran—all this only begins to account for the canonist's improvements on an old-fashioned fairy tale. He must have been drawn to it in the first place because a pilgrimage to Santiago de Compostela had launched the story of Florio and Biancifiore, which ended joyfully with the Spanish nation's conversion to Christianity. For him, the next logical step would have been to expand religious dimensions of the received romance. How he capitalizes on the liturgical calendar by shifting forward the children's birth date from Easter (which it had been in older versions) to Pentecost gives insight into his remodeling techniques. Easter remains, of course, as the date of the poet's enamorment in the frame tale, but the symbolic nexis for primary narrative motifs inside that frame is Pentecost, a feast that fulfills the paschal cycle and commemorates the original descent of the Holy Ghost in tiny flames on the apostles' heads, imparting to them the gift of tongues so they could carry the gospel throughout the world. Pentecost recurs in significant anniversaries for Florio and Biancifiore; in the flamelet that magically dances above Parthenopean Fiammetta, queen of the love debate; in Saint James's evangelical mission to the West; and in a final chain of conversions to the faith, starting with the prince of Spain and extending to his entire population. Boccaccio's *Pente*costal agenda explains, too, why the *Filocolo* contains just five books and why he describes his own enamorment in such "flamboyant" rhetoric.[6]

We should understand in the same light Maria's second appearance to

---

6. To my knowledge, nothing systematic has yet been written on the relationship between Boccaccio's literary corpus and his legal culture. Indicating an awareness of the connection, hints have been dropped but not developed. See, e.g., Fredi Chiappelli, "Discorso o progetto per uno studio sul *Decameron,*" in *Studi di Italianistica in onore di Giovanni Cecchetti* (Ravenna: Longo, 1988), 105–11. The starting point for such a study could be Pier Giorgio Ricci's biographical note of 1971 on the connection between Boccaccio's honorific title *dominus* and his preparation as a canonist; see "Notizie e documenti per la biografia del Boccaccio," pt. 5, "Dominus Johannes Boccaccius," *Studi sul Boccaccio* 6 (1971): 1–10.

him, at a convent named for the archangel Gabriel. A certain grumpy professor, back in 1918, belittled Boccaccio's "rather grotesque attempt to
turn his romance into an epic" and pointed to his repeated mention of the
Annunciation as an example of how he had "dragged" all kinds of scriptural allusions into the story "without any artistic justification whatsoever."[7] Ironically, his note overlooked the proemial episode that anticipates the others, Boccaccio's careful mise-en-scène of Maria at
Sant'Arcangelo a Baiano. From that grump's perspective, typical of
Romantics and Victorians, the Boccaccio who burdened his fiction with
Scripture had not yet hit his stride. According to that school of thought, it
was a mistake that a wiser man would rectify in his masterpiece the
Decameron, which makes religious practice a subject more of ridicule than
of reverence. Yet for the church law student at Naples hopeful of patronage from pious King Robert, whose hobby was writing sermons, literature
comports a Christian lesson. The Annunciation reminds us of another
major liturgical feast on March 25, an archetypical date of beginnings that
would return as the emblematic First Day in the *Decameron* calendar and
that in Florence for centuries marked the start of the new year. The same
season in which Dante had auspiciously begun his journey through the
Afterworld, it celebrates the moment when the Word became flesh, foun-
dational in the Gospels. In the *Filocolo,* gospel truth is absolutely central
to the poet's plan and to the canonist's art, which aims to historicize "fabulosi parlari."[8]

Critical times so long ago were not yet ripe for rediscovering programmatic iconography of the *Filocolo,* to which Janet Levarie Smarr and
Steven Grossvogel have alerted us in recent years. A single symbol can be
layered with meanings that encompass multiple connotations, secular and
sacred. One example, the focus of my fifth chapter, is Juno's bird, the peacock. Boccaccio calls on this colorful creature to pull Juno's chariot for
her initial epic descent and then, more surprisingly, to provide a royal banquet's pièce de résistance, dead and roasted on a platter. Boccaccio the
mythographer allegorizes this bird, just as he does Juno, along with the
other Greek gods and goddesses, figures essential to keeping in motion an

---

7. Olin Moore, "Boccaccio's *Filocolo* and the Annunciation," *MLN* 33 (1918): 438–40.

8. James H. McGregor, in *The Shades of Aeneas: The Imitation of Vergil and the History of Paganism in Boccaccio's Filostrato, Filocolo, and Teseida* (Athens: University of Georgia Press, 1991), 23–43, perceptively explores Boccaccio's programmatic application of an Orosian concept of history to the *Filocolo.* He counts allusions to at least ten successive empires and eras, all envisioned around the supreme and central moment of Christ's Advent.

elaborate plot mechanism. When it escorts Juno *Pronuba,* the peacock alludes to marriage, union that will bring a fictional happy ending to Florio and Biancifiore's love story. On the other hand, as drayfowl for the Olympian lady who conducts a diplomatic visit to the pope, its implications are quite naturally Christian. This epic Juno signifies the church, allied with the papacy; the bird in the care of Juno *Ecclesia* adumbrates eternal life, promised by baptism, awaited as the spiritual goal of Florio's quest and the sacrament that draws Spain into the Christian fold. Similarly resplendent, the peacock will make a triumphant return some twenty years later in Boccaccio's *Trattatello in laude di Dante,* as a shimmering apparition in Alighieri's mother's dream, prophetic of her prodigious son's long-lived masterpiece.

As much as Christian Scripture, pagan deities have their artistic rationale in the *Filocolo.* Boccaccio could have discussed with Paolo da Perugia, the librarian and mythographer at Robert's court, Isidore of Seville's views on poetry and the gods, along with those of Virgil's allegorizers, commentators like Servius and Fulgentius, who surely influenced his thinking. In the *Etymologies,* a seminal text of reference, Isidore states on the authority of the Christian lawgiver Lactantius, "The duty of the poet consists in transforming what has really happened into other things by means of oblique figures."[9] Here the key term is "obliquis figurationibus," which refers to fictional disguises, typically the veil of allegory. Thus Isidore explains "Mars" as "mas," meaning "masculine," and it is in just that capacity that the warrior god will assist Florio when he must gather his courage for a duel unto death with the king's wicked seneschal. So, too, in the classicizing code language of the *Filocolo,* "Jove" stands for God, our heavenly father, because his name (and hence function) derives from *juvans pater,* or "helpful father." Boccaccio so etymologizes it in his

---

9. Isidore of Seville, *Etymologiae sive origines,* ed. W. M. Lindsay (1911; reprint, Oxford: Clarendon Press, 1971), 8.7.10: "Officium autem poetae in eo est ut ea, quae vere gesta sunt, in alias species obliquis figurationibus cum decore aliquo conversa transducant." For what he says on Jove, see 8.11.34 and 50. See further the commentary by Katherine Nell MacFarlane, "Isidore of Seville on the Pagan Gods (*Origines* VIII.11)," *Transactions of the American Philosophical Society* 70, no. 3 (1980): 1–40. Through Paolo da Perugia, librarian to King Robert and Queen Giovanna, Boccaccio knew the allegorizing commentaries on the *Aeneid* by Servius and Fulgentius, as well as Isidore. See Francesco Torraca, *Giovanni Boccaccio a Napoli (1326–1339)* (Naples: L. Pierro e figlio, 1915), 82–98. Fulgentius was the first Christian grammarian systematically to apply the allegorical method to pagan poetry. As C. S. Lewis put it, in *The Allegory of Love* (1936; reprint, New York: Oxford University Press, 1958), 85, "When once the ancients are read in this way, then to imitate the ancients means to write allegory."

Genealogies, but he would have remembered the information from his youthful exposure to Isidore, whose alternate formula for the name's origin further reinforces the aptness of Jove's role in the *Filocolo:* "Iovis . . . a iuvando" [Jove . . . derives from helping].

In and of themselves, the myths that entranced Boccaccio throughout a lifetime of writing are "fables," but when properly understood in their deeper sense, the doings of the gods become vehicles for truth. Along these lines, he would early have encountered Macrobius, who in his *Commentary on the Dream of Scipio* distinguished fables that "merely gratify the ear" from those that "draw the reader's attention to a certain kind of virtue." The latter are called "narratio fabulosa, non fabula" [fabulous narrative, not fable].[10] Thus for Boccaccio there could be such a thing as "fabulous" diction in a positive sense, provided it carry a moral meaning. The literal must be susceptible of didactic allegory. Poetry, as he defends it whenever the subject arises, is not merely empty "favole" but conceals the "sweetest fruits of historical and philosophical truth." Precisely to answer the widespread false belief that poetry is nothing more than fabulous parlance (*fabuloso parlare*), he enters into the passionate defense of imaginative literature that forms the central core of his *Trattatello in laude di Dante.* From ancient times, he affirms, the mission of poets has been to please the prince, to delight his subjects, and to persuade men to behave virtuously: "Thus was born our custom of singing with high-sounding verse the battles and other notable deeds of men mingled with those of the gods" (*Filoc.* 1.136–37). Men and gods together, a mixed population from ancient epic, take root in medieval romance as Boccaccio recasts the genre. No longer "fabula" or "favoloso parlare," the *Filocolo* is in the distinction of Macrobius the better "narratio fabulosa." Recast as "favoloso e ornato parlare" [fabulous and adorned parlance], to borrow a phrase from Boccaccio's *Expositions on Dante's Commedia* (1.78), it is literature embellished with myth, and the myths are allegorically resonant in the service of goodness, virtue, and truth.

Entering the book, we find ourselves in a Gothic space, both awesome and reassuring, both novel and known. Much as a medieval church summons the visitor to its portal and orients spiritually whoever passes inside, so Boccaccio with quill and parchment creates a literary architecture to attract and hold the reader's attention. We can take our bearings from the

---

10. Ambrosius Theodosius Macrobius, *Commentarium in somnium Scipionis,* ed. J. Willis (Leipzig: Teubner, 1970), 1.2.9. A key statement for Boccaccio's understanding of ancient epic and myth occurs at his *Genealogie* 14.9, for which this passage in Macrobius is a source.

medieval Book of the World, echoed no less in the design of the *Filocolo* than in the great human artifacts raised by the cathedral builders. Here, too, order follows principles of hierarchy, symmetry, and analogy. The dynamics of the structure are ascensional, leading childish lovers to morally responsible adulthood, pagan society to Christian salvation. Its word space pulsates with symbols that draw their sense and power from the cultural unity of the Christian community. Pejoratively labeled by its modern editor "an armor" that "imprisons the text,"[11] these ubiquitous signs on the contrary vivify the literary landscape, where virtually everything "speaks"—names, colors, clothes, flowers, trees, birds, animals, numbers, seasons, planets, astrological signs, gemstones, the elements (especially fire), personifications, gods, saints, and mortals. Boccaccio's vernacular "booklet" is actually an encyclopedia, not because he was so impetuously eager to show off whatever he knew that he lacked the discipline to prune away uncontrolled patches of words, but because he designed it to be a summa. That is its strength, not a weakness. The poet's encyclopedic mentality, taught by authorities from Isidore to Aquinas to Dante, makes the *Filocolo* an album of universal history, from Genesis to the Judgment, from the coming of the Word in history to the establishment of the Angevins in Italy.

It begins with the poet at mass on Holy Saturday, at the Easter vigil, the most important of the year and the true celebration of Easter itself. In Augustine's words, this is "the mother of all vigils." Its solemnities, ritualized in fire dominated by the paschal candle as a symbol of the risen Lord, express our passing over with Christ from death in sin to new life in God. This service primarily celebrates the mystery of baptism with scriptural readings and baptismal rites for catechumens. Conditioned by such surroundings, Maria appears to the poet amid a burst of flame imagery, then reappears in another locale consonant with her name, a convent associated with Mary Annunciate. The stage is set for the framed tale, evangelical in its thrust toward the baptism of the protagonist and his kingdom. Catholic liturgy impresses narrative unity.[12]

In the *Filocolo,* all roads begin and end in Rome. Florio's point of arrival, the tale's spiritual center, is San Giovanni in Laterano. Giovanni Boccaccio, named for the same patron saint as the basilica, identifies that

---

11. Antonio Enzo Quaglio, in *Scienza e mito nel Boccaccio* (Padua: Liviana, 1967), 7, writes of the "spessa corazza di simboli in cui è imprigionato il testo del *Filocolo.*"

12. Augustine, *Sermo 219, Patrologia latina* 38:1088. See also *New Catholic Encyclopedia,* (New York: McGraw Hill, 1967), vol. 5, s.v. "Easter and its cycle."

sanctuary in one of those little rhetorical riddles he so favored, "the fairest of temples adorned with the fair name of him who in the desert first commanded sinners to repent." When Florio one day happens to walk in (*Filoc.* 5.52), lead at last by destiny to this holiest of sanctuaries, a great image captivates him. It is an effigy of "the man who was the salvation of the world." The picture of the Savior will prove thaumaturgic, for it makes Florio ask Ilario what the wounded figure means, and that curiosity in turn prompts the priest's religious instruction, a pocket catechism that covers the six ages of the world: it summarizes the Old Testament, reviews the life of Christ, recites a glossed Credo, and climaxes with a fervid invitation to rush to the Font. This scene, which portrays Ilario as a model of priestly conduct according to precepts of church law, may also be based on a personal memory. When the teenage Boccaccio and his father moved to Naples in 1327, they must have passed through Rome on their way southward from Florence. If the two Boccaccios stopped in Rome to visit the Lateran—and it is hard to imagine they would not have, given its towering importance as a pilgrimage goal and cult site from the time of Constantine—they could indeed have seen a monumental Crucifixion similar to the icon of Florio's conversion. The fresco, dating from the papacy of Honorius III (1216–17), survives in a drawing of the seventeenth century that records its primary features: a bearded Christ bearing a cruciform nimbus and held by four nails to the cross, elevated by a hillock (fig. 9). At its base are two smaller figures with arms upraised in worshipful reverence. To the left stands Pope Honorius III; to the right, his father confessor, a tonsured Fra Jacobus.[13] Just as the fictional episode of Florio's encounter with Ilario may reflect Boccaccio's remembered experience in the Lateran, so the *Filocolo* is replete with facts basic to his present religious curriculum. Were he truly as hostile to canon law as the legend has liked to paint him, he ought to have written a different book, one neatly purged of such allegedly otiose doctrine. Instead, he crafts his fiction to embrace Roman Catholicism. Study and poetry cooperate as Boccaccio daringly merges contradictory modes, transforming "fabulous parlance" into a creative new hybrid: prose verse, a historical fairy tale, a contemporary classic, Christian myth, a humanistic romance.

---

13. Stephan Waetzoldt, *Die Kopien des 17. Jahrhunderts nach Mosaiken und Wandmalereien in Rom*, Römische Forschungen der Bibliotheca Hertziana, vol. 18 (Vienna: Anton Schroll and Company, 1964), 26 and fig. 98. The Vatican Library copybook that preserves the image is in MS Barb. Lat. 4423, fol. 1. This manuscript is an untitled collection of 1672 with copies of mosaics, paintings, small objects, and antiquities.

After the *Filocolo*

A monumental feat for a fledgling author (1336–39?), the *Filocolo,* a flowing romance enfolded with the surprises of multiple internal *novelle,* marks two signal starting points in Italian literary history. Here begins Boccaccio's long and felicitous activity as one of Europe's most gifted prose narrators. Here, too, begins the fertile tradition of prose fiction native to Italy.[14] Mainly the province of academic curiosity seekers in modern times, it has been probed for its literary sources by generations of philologists, whose vigilance continues to uncover new secrets in Boccaccio's imaginative habits of borrowing. What has never been re-created, except in disconnected moments, is the history of the book's afterlife, its critical *fortuna.* By ancestry it descends from the beloved old medieval *Romance of Floire and Blanchefleur,* itself an offshoot of Europe's archetypical and fertile Charlemagne legends. The enormous popularity of Boccaccio's source tale, resung for centuries by minstrels and poets in tongues from Old Icelandic to Modern Greek, makes it hard sometimes to tell whether a version of the story from after the *Filocolo* depends on Boccaccio's version directly or filters down from a more archaic account. Certainly those narrative ingredients of adventure and love that propelled the Old French story to such long success also attracted Boccaccio and contributed to the appeal of his learned adaptation. Yet the *Filocolo's* reception also makes clear that not just plot but art carried the Tuscan book to its own measure of fame and fortune. From Catalonia to Bohemia, from Antwerp to Naples, it has touched a vast fellowship of European poets.

Boccaccio himself was the first to capitalize on what he had invented for the *Filocolo,* above all the marvelous device of the frame tale, which he later expanded from episodic status (in the interlude of Fiammetta's Neapolitan love court) to a fully rounded *cornice* encompassing the entire work, once in his *Ameto* and then again, of course, in the *Decameron.* For two tales in the latter (*Dec.* 10.4–5), he also mined the *Filocolo's questioni d'amore* (13 and 4, respectively). Before the end of the fourteenth century,

---

14. In his own eloquent style, John Addington Symonds salutes Boccaccio's innovation, in *Giovanni Boccaccio as Man and Author* (London: John C. Nimmo, 1895; reprint, New York: AMS Press, 1968), 31: "Italian prose . . . which had hitherto been practised with the dove-like simplicity of the 'Fioretti di S. Francesco,' or with the grave parsimony of the 'Vita Nuova,' is now made to march in sonorous periods. The language, no less than the stuff and manner of 'Filocopo,' proclaims the advent of Renaissance art."

the *Filocolo* echoes in writings by Boccaccio's epigones, among them Giovanni da Prato's *Paradiso degli Alberti,* a loose ensemble of stories set in 1389. During the next two centuries, the text enjoyed noteworthy diffusion, despite its formidable length. Surviving in fifty-five manuscripts (some partial), between 1472 and 1594 it went through thirty-four editions. By comparison, during the same period there were six editions for the *Amorosa visione,* seven for the *Filostrato,* ten for the *Teseida,* twenty-six for the *Corbaccio,* twenty-eight for the *Elegia di madonna Fiammetta,* and eighty-one for the *Decameron* (*Diana's Hunt* was not published until 1832).[15]

In the century following Boccaccio's, his *Filocolo* found its way into the welcoming hands of Giacomo di Giovanni di Ser Minoccio, a Sienese poet who singled out Fiammetta's love debate, the *questioni d'amore,* for a trial in terza rima. He christened his opuscule *Il libro delle difinizioni* (The book of definitions).[16] As a young book lover, the Venetian polymath and editor Lodovico Dolce set himself a much more ambitious goal, to rewrite the whole romance in ottava rima. Even though his limping *Amore di Florio e Biancofiore* bogged down along the way, Dolce did publish in 1532 the part that he had been able to finish. He clearly thought of it as an epic, since he chose the meter that Boccaccio himself had sanctioned for that form in the *Teseida,* and since his flirtation with the *Filocolo* dates to a decade when he was also editing Ariosto's *Orlando Furioso* and composing his own chivalric epics, *Stanzas on the African Victory of Charles V* and a *Sacripante.* He could know that the very masters would have approved his project, for both Boiardo, in the *Orlando innamorato,* and Ariosto, in the

---

15. Guido Traversari, in *Bibliografia Boccaccesca,* vol. 1, *Scritti intorno al Boccaccio e alla fortuna delle sue opere* (1907; reprint, New York: Burt Franklin, 1973), no. 200, cites the *Paradiso degli Alberti.* For lists of the manuscripts, see Vittore Branca, *Tradizione delle opere di Giovanni Boccaccio,* vol. 1, *Un primo elenco dei codici e tre studi* (Rome: Edizioni di Storia e Letteratura, 1958), 37–40; vol. 2, *Un secondo elenco di manoscritti e studi sul testo del Decameron con due appendici* (Rome: Edizioni di Storia e Letteratura, 1991), 31–32. The classic catalogue of printed editions of Boccaccio's works is Alberto Bacchi della Lega, *Serie delle edizioni delle opere di Giovanni Boccaccii* (1875; reprint, Bologna: Forni Editore, 1967), which should be consulted in conjunction with Francesco Zambrini, *Le opere volgari a stampa dei secoli XIII e XIV,* 4th ed. (Bologna: Zanichelli, 1878).

16. Notice of the *Libro delle difinizioni* in sixty-two *capitoli* of terza rima by Giacomo di Giovanni di Ser Minoccio (1417–ca. 1477) appears in Luigi Surdich, *La cornice di amore: Studi sul Boccaccio* (Pisa: ETS Editrice, 1987), 13. See also below, n. 27, for the nineteenth-century publication of an excerpt from Giacomo's book, which otherwise still exists only in its manuscript form.

Furioso, displayed their acquaintance with the *Filocolo.* So, too, had Sannazaro, as would Vida and Tasso.[17] Cinquecento editors of the romance,
men like Gaetano Tizzone da Pofi, who brought it out in 1527 and again
in 1538, predictably waxed rapturous in their prefaces, commending to
readers its marvelous peripeteias of plot, exemplary Tuscan style, and
uplifting moral advice for daily life.[18] From translators as well, naturally,
we hear why this is indeed a most worthy book, and through them we can
track its progress beyond the Alps and the Pyrenees. Separated from their
context as they had been by Ser Minoccio, the *questioni d'amore* were published as *Treize elegante demandes d'amour* at Paris in 1530 and reissued
there in 1541. At least twice, in 1542 and 1554, the work entire was rendered into French. Its 1542 translation by Adrien Sevin, *Le Philocope de
messire Jehan Boccace contenant l'histoire de Fleury et Blanchefleur,* went
through another eight Renaissance printings. On the Iberian Peninsula,
Catalan poets were quick to take up the *Filocolo,* and in 1512 the Spanish
translation by Juan De Flores appeared at Alcalà. Already in 1499 it had
been introduced to Germans at Metz, as *Florio und Biancefora: Ein gar
schone newe hystori der hochen lieb des kuniglichen fursten Florio unnd von
seyner lieben Bianceffora.* Among those familiar with that "fair new story"
was the sixteenth-century dramatist Hans Sachs, who composed a play
that counts among major offshoots of the *Filocolo.* The Metz translation
served as model for the Czech *Filocolo,* published at Prague in 1519 and
1600.[19]

17. Emil Hausknecht, in the edited volume *Floris and Blauncheflur: Mittelenglisches
Gedicht aus dem 13. Jahrhundert* (Berlin: Weidmann, 1885), 35–36, dismissed Dolce's halting
rhymes as a "recht unglücklichen Versuch," but not even the sixteenth century seems to have
had much patience with them, judging from what Girolamo Ruscelli wrote in his *Discorsi a
M. Lodovico Dolce* of 1553. For the biographical context, see Ronnie H. Terpening, *Lodovico
Dolce: Renaissance Man of Letters* (Toronto: University of Toronto Press, 1997), 167. Paolo
Savi-Lopez, in "La novella di Prasildo e Tisbina (*Orlando innamorato* I, XII)," in *Raccolta di
Studi dedicati ad Alessandro d'Ancona* (Florence: Barbèra, 1901), 54–57, notes the connection
in Boiardo's *Orlando innamorato;* Pio Rajna, in *Le fonti dell'Orlando furioso: Richerche e
studi* (Florence: Sansoni, 1876), reckons the *Filocolo* among sources for the *Orlando furioso;*
E. H. Wilkins, in *A History of Italian Literature,* rev. Thomas G. Bergin (Cambridge: Harvard University Press, 1974), numbers Sannazaro, Vida, Tasso.

18. E. H. Wilkins, in "Variations on the Name *Philocolo,*" in *The Invention of the Sonnet
and Other Studies in Italian Literature* (Rome: Edizioni di Storia e Letteratura, 1959), 139–45,
cites extensively from Gaetano Tizzone da Pofi's rave review, which, after listing the marvels
of its fictional inventions, praises the *Filocolo* for "un parlar d'alto stile con la perfetta lingua
volgare italiana" [speech in the high style with the perfect Italian vernacular language].

19. There are conflicting reports on the versions in French. Bacchi della Lega (*Opere di
Giovanni Boccaccii,* 107) somewhat skeptically lists an anonymous French translation published in 1485 at Venice; his inventory also registers a translation by J. Vincent of 1554. No

As copies multiplied and passed from reader to reader, another sure sign of the book's popular success were the zealous guardians of morality who rose up to condemn it. What doubtless sparked their disapproval were scenes like a lover's visit to his entombed lady and his mournful palping of her breasts, actually a moment of mistaken necrophilia (since she was not really dead), or Florio and Biancifiore's long night of erotic lovemaking in the Admiral's harem tower—without benefit of a church wedding. Writing in Bruges, Juan Luis Vives (d. 1540), the Spanish scholar and friend of Erasmus who tutored the future "Bloody" Mary of England, branded the *Filocolo* in his influential *Education of a Christian Woman* one of those "favorite books" to be avoided because they have been written by "lazy men given to vices and filth, in which I wonder what pleasure they give except that shameful passions attract us so much." We know, too, that in its French dress it was sought after in Flanders, for the good bishop of Antwerp saw fit to index it on April 16, 1621.[20]

Within Italy, this favored reading sprinkled traces of its passage from precincts as elite as the burgeoning academies to the crossroads of mass culture, and it even passed through thick convent walls to the pleasure of those isolated women who dwelt within. The Parmesan poet Jacopo Caviceo had Florio's vicissitudes of love in mind—separation, lover's quest, happy ending—when he designed his hugely popular *Libro del Pellegrino*. First published in his native city in 1508, *The Pilgrim's Book* went through numerous reprintings, prompting translations into French and Spanish. The title of its 1520 Milanese embodiment gives an insight into Caviceo's understanding of the *Filocolo,* a polemical response to the

incunabulum figures on Patricia Gathercole's list in "The French Translators of Boccaccio," *Italica* 46, no. 3 (1969): 300–9, but that list, by her own acknowledgment, is incomplete. For the Catalan echoes, Traversari (*Bibliografia,* no. 552) cites Otto Denk's classic *Einfürung in der Geschichte der Altcatalischen Litteratur, von deren Anfängen bis zum 18. Jahrhundert* (Munich: M. Poessl, 1893). Bacchi della Lega (*Opere di Giovanni Boccaccii,* 108) catalogues the Spanish version. The 1499 Metz edition as reprinted in 1500 has been recently reproduced (Hildesheim: Olms, 1975). The *Filocolo* reappeared at Strasbourg as *Ein schone history auf das französischer sprach in tütsch gebracht und sagt von herre Florio . . . unnd Bianceffora,* and it was printed again in Frankfurt am Main in 1559. Woodcuts adorned the 1519 Prague edition. Hausknecht (*Floris and Blauncheflur,* 14–19) reviewed the German and Czech fortunes of Boccaccio's romance.

20. On the condemnation of the *Filocolo,* see Vincenzo Crescini, ed., *Il Cantare di Fiorio e Biancifiore,* 2 vols., Scelta di Curiosità Letterarie Inedite o Rare dal Secolo XIII al XIX, vol. 89 (Disp. 233) and vol. 100 (Disp. 249) (1889; reprint, Bologna: Commissione per i Testi di Lingua, 1969), 1:47; Edelstand du Méril, ed., *Floire et Blanceflor: Poèmes du XIIIᵉ siècle* (Paris: P. Jannet, 1856), xliv–v; Hausknecht, *Floris and Blauncheflur,* 4, quoting the scandalized Vives.

moralists: "Book of mine, should you be disdained or rejected, you could say, 'Not the battles of Troy, not the fortunes of Rome, not the wanderings of Ulysses, but the history of a chaste love I bear and tell, and so I travel safely because love and piety are my escorts.'"[21] Pietro Bembo, in his watershed grammar of 1525, cites the *Filocolo* alongside the *Decameron* for model usage of the vernacular.[22] Around midcentury and in the climate of debates on language and literature that canonized the Three Crowns of Florence, Benedetto Varchi drew on the *questioni d'amore* for lectures on love and jealousy offered to the Florentine Academy.[23] A romance by genre, and one with such an active heroine as Biancifiore, the *Filocolo* was bound to attract female readers, too. The years 1548–49 saw a Florentine nun base her own "commedia spirituale" for performance in her convent on the *Filocolo,* by then a vernacular classic. Beatrice del Sera, who had taken the veil in the Dominican nunnery of San Niccolò at nearby Prato, found in this story of star-crossed love a romance that would resonate with her cloistered audience, both as women of flesh and blood forever shut away from the company of men and as wimpled brides of Christ: *Amor di virtù: Opera fatta da una donna fiorentina sopra il Filocolo nella consideratione d'uno animo valoroso nelle virtuose imprese, il quale deliberatamente cercando il fine dell'aurata beatitudine, perviene alla cognitione di Dio* (Love of virtue: a work by a Florentine lady based on the *Filocolo* concerning the virtuous undertakings of a worthy soul, who, seeking with determination the goal of golden beatitude, comes to the awareness of God].[24] Two centuries afterward, the Enlightenment luminary Apostolo Zeno of Venice could reaffirm its uplifting force, noting with approval that in the *Filocolo* Boccaccio

---

21. Adolfo Albertazzi, in *Romanzieri e romanzi del cinquecento e del seicento* (Bologna: Zanichelli, 1891), 12–47, points out Caviceo's debt to Boccaccio. His *Libro del Pellegrino,* reprinted in Italy in 1513, 1514, 1520, 1526, 1533, 1547, and 1559, saw a Spanish version in 1527 and French adaptations in 1528 and 1535.

22. Pietro Bembo, *Prose della volgar lingua,* in *Prose della volgar lingua. Gli Asolani. Rime,*ed. Carlo Dionisotti (Turin: UTET, 1966), 3.39.

23. Vincenzo Crescini, *Contributo agli studi sul Boccaccio* (Turin: Loescher, 1887), 76n. See Benedetto Varchi, *Due lezzioni di M. Benedetto Varchi, l'una d'Amore, et l'altra della Gelosia, con alcune utili et dilettevoli quistioni da lui nuovamente aggiunte* (Lyons: Rovillio, 1560).

24. It survives in a single copy in Florence in the Biblioteca Riccardiana, MS Ricc. 2932, copied by a scribe and dated 1555. For discussion in the context of convent literature, see Elissa Weaver's introduction to her edition of Beatrice del Sera, *Amor di Virtù: Commedia in cinque atti, 1548,* (Ravenna: Longo, 1990).

"speaks at length and salubriously of the Christian religion."[25] Still in the nineteenth century, it could speak to Alessandro Manzoni and do service in another rectitudinous setting, that of those bygone Italian *libretti* that celebrated the occasion of a wedding. One such booklet of 1880, the *Ammonizioni del Re Felice di Spagna al suo figliuolo,* found a perfect set piece in King Felice's admonishments to his son Florio, dying words delivered in sermonlike cadences that recall Shakespeare's Apollonius. An 1887 marriage offering reprinted one of the questions raised at Fiammetta's love debate in its Sienese verse adaptation, *Un capitolo delle definizioni di Jacopo Serminocci.*

Although the first full English *Filocolo* did not appear until 1985, it was abroad in Britain from the fourteenth century. Chaucer must have encountered it, for it seems to have impinged on works of his bearing an Italian stamp—the *Parliament of Fowles, Troilus and Criseyde,* the *Legend of Good Women,* and the *Franklin's Tale.* Milton seems to have recalled the infernal convocation of demons who fuel Felice's violence against the Christians (*Filoc.* 1.9) in his *Paradise Lost.* As late as the Romantic period, Keats could return to the Tuscan romance for his *Eve of St. Agnes.*[26] Its most famous episode, Fiammetta's love debate, has a long history in our language that begins with the Elizabethan translation by "H.G." of 1567, *A Pleasaunt Disport of Divers Nobel Personages.*[27] Twentieth-century editors have several times repackaged that quaint prose. The first to do so was

---

25. Giusto Fontanini, *Biblioteca dell'eloquenza italiana di Mons. Giusto Fontanini . . . con le annotazioni del signor Apostolo Zeno,* 2 vols. (1706; reprint, Venice: G. B. Pasquali, 1753), 2:162.

26. David Wallace, in *Chaucer and the Early Writings of Boccaccio* (Woodbridge, Suffolk: D. S. Brewer, 1985), 41–60, intelligently maps lines of connection between the early Boccaccio and Chaucer in an analysis that takes good account of the *Filocolo.* Thomas G. Bergin, in *Boccaccio* (New York: Viking, 1981), 92 and xiii, mentions the authors from Sannazaro to Keats. He draws the information from Wilkins, *History,* 103. More on its English outreach was documented by Emil Koeppel, *Studien zur Geschichte der Italienischen Novelle in der Englischen Literatur des sechzenten Jahrhunderts* (Strasbourg: K. J. Trübner, 1892), for which see Traversari, *Bibliografia,* no. 534. For Manzoni and the *Filocolo,* see further Ausonio Dobelli, *Figure e rimembranze dantesche nel Decamerone* (Modena: Namias, 1897), cited in Traversari, *Bibliografia,* no. 622.

27. According to Bacchi della Lega (*Opere di Giovanni Boccaccii,* 108), the 1567 translation was reprinted in 1571 and 1587. Its original title page reads: "A pleasant disport of divers nobel personages, written in Italian by M. Iohn Bocace, Florentine and poet laureat, in his boke which is entituled Philocopo, and nowe Englished by H. G. Imprinted at London, in Pater Noster Rowe, et the signe of the Marmayd, by H. Bynneman, for Richard Smyth and Nicolas England, 1567." The Da Capo Press reproduced this edition in 1970.

a scholar of impeccable credentials, Edward Hutton, who in 1927 faithfully reproduced his source. A degraded copy, simplified for a more popular public and seasoned with a pinch of prurience, followed in 1931, *The Most Pleasant and Delectable Questions of Love.* Accompanying black-and-white illustrations starkly emphasize figures with bare female curves and protuberant breasts, their male lovers close by. Thomas Bell, who signs the introduction, reminds readers that this book, which was to be reissued at least twice in varying formats, comes from the same amorous author who created the spicy tales of the *Decameron.* As part of its series on early English printed books, in 1970 the Da Capo Press (Amsterdam and New York) reproduced the 1567 edition. My own translation of the *questioni d'amore,* framed by introduction and commentary, was completed as a doctoral dissertation at Johns Hopkins University in 1971. In 1974, Harry Carter "refashioned" the Elizabethan translation and added another set of illustrations for a dignified edition complete with brief explanatory notes.

Although interest in the romance waned in Italy after the Renaissance, it was sufficient to justify renewed press runs in 1612, 1723–24, and 1832 (when it joined Moutier's pioneering first series of Boccaccio's complete Italian works), as well as an excerpt of the two *questioni* that returned as *novelle* in the *Decameron.* Our own century has brought important revivals. Ettore De Ferri's 1927 edition was followed by a much improved version from Salvatore Battaglia in 1938. In 1967 Antonio Enzo Quaglio's long-awaited text appeared in the Mondadori series of Boccaccio's complete works, *Tutte le opere,* ten volumes carried to completion in 1999 by their general editor, Vittore Branca.[28]

---

28. See Traversari, *Bibliografia,* no. 203, for Giovanni Papanti, ed., *Due novelle di messer Giovanni Boccaccio che non si leggono nel suo Decamerone* (Leghorn: Tipografia di P. Vannini e figlio, 1868). Quaglio's edition, an invaluable contribution, does not grapple with the problem of the rubrics, which characterize one entire textual family. Were they intended by the author? As I argue (see especially chap. 3, below), it is clear that Boccaccio was counting chapters. We know, moreover, from his autograph of the *Teseida* in the Laurentian Library that there the rubrics were integral to the author's intentions. The next new edition of the *Filocolo* will be the task of a future generation.

CHAPTER 1

A New Flame

Once among all his fictions and rhymes, Boccaccio spelled his full name
into the fabric of his work. That unique signed piece is his *Amorosa visione,*
a rebus imbued with all the sophistication of its Gothic era. Cupid, it
seems, late one night unfurled a "marvelous fantasy" to the dreaming
poet, who captured the escapades of his imagination in a gigantic acrostic.
The world's longest, it extends through fifty cantos for 4,403 verses of
terza rima, those chain metrics not long before invented by Dante
Alighieri to honor the Christian Trinity. Three "tailed" sonnets preface the
lover's allegorical vision, a body of words (sometimes a bit quirky) whose
letters rescripted march down the manuscript folios in colorful columns of
capitals, successive initials for 1,481 tercets. The first sonnet, the Author's
dedication to his mistress, allows him to couple sentimentally on the page
with her, his "Flame." They come together, so to speak, in the concluding
triplet.

Adunque a voi, cui tengho donna mia
et chui senpre disio di servire,
la raccomando, **madama Maria;**
e prieghovi, se fosse nel mio dire
difecto alcun, per vostra cortesia
correggiate amendando il mio fallire.
Cara **Fiamma,** per cui 'l core ò caldo,
que' che vi manda questa Visione
Giovanni è **di Boccaccio da Certaldo.**

[Thus to you, whom I hold as my lady, and whom I always wish to
serve, I commend it, **Lady Maria;** and I beg you, if my verse contain

21

some defect, in your courtesy correct it, amending my failings. Dear
Flame, through whom my heart takes heat, he who sends you this
Vision is **John of Boccaccio from Certaldo.**]

About the woman who warms him with love, he reveals only a Christian
name, Maria, and a poetic *senhal,* or "sign name," Lady-of-the-Fire. But
speaking for himself, he is more specific and states his identity according to
the custom of the times, by patronymic and by toponymic. He is Giovanni,
son of Boccaccio, from the town of Certaldo.

Both "John" and "Flame" will return verbatim in the *Amorosa visione,*
as required by chiastic logic. "Giovanni" steps into vertical reading at
canto 15, where he finds himself as Dreamer inside a castle before a fresco
of Cupid, enthroned over a mob of famous lovers. We begin to reconstruct
his name, just as he had signed it at the end of the sonnet, stretching down
eight *terzine* that trace Dreamer's gaze across the mural. From the endless
multitude, he singles out a laurel-crowned lady, privileged to sit beside the
god.

> **G** aio e giocondo vi ne vidi alcuno . . .
> **I** o che mirava . . .
> **O** rnata [li scorsi allato una donna] . . .
> **V** aga negli occhi . . .
> **A** ngela mi pareva . . .
> **N** on so quel che 'l cuor mio così percosse . . .
> **N** é sanz'a lei pensar fu poi [l'alma mia] . . .
> **I** n fronte a cui [due occhi lucean]. . . .

> [**G** ay and jocund I saw some of them there . . .
> **I** kept looking about . . .
> **O** ne I noticed adorned at his side, her
> **V** ery eyes filled with desire . . .
> **A** ngel she seemed to me . . .
> **N** o, I know not what struck so my heart . . .
> **N** or from then on did my soul cease thinking of her . . .
> **I** n her forehead two eyes sparkled. . . .]

> > > > (*Am. vis.* 15.40–61, my trans.)

Not by accident, the letters that spell the name of "Giovanni" enter the
narrative precisely where our hero first catches sight of his "angel."

Graphic propinquity allows them another tryst on the page; now they embrace acrostically (figs. 1a–b).[1] So far, however, she remains nameless. Wonderstruck at the triumph of Cupid, Dreamer does not know what she is called. For that, he must wait until her second appearance, when he views her on a riverbank with other beauties. Even then, the information is oblique, in a riddle. We are told that she bears the same family name as "the man from Campania who followed the Spaniard in wearing the cape," that is, Thomas Aquinas, follower of Saint Dominic in donning the robes of the Dominican order (canto 43, vv. 46–49). We are also told that she shares a given name with "the woman in whom He who ennobled our nature was compressed," the Virgin Mary (canto 43, vv. 55–57). Conjoining the clues, we deduce that our poet's Lady-of-the-Flame, intimate object of his passion, lives her public life as "Maria d'Aquino." She whose acquaintance Giovanni progressively makes while dreaming—first in a painted icon, then in a landscape—reappears once more near the end of the poem, quite literally in the flesh. This time their kissing is as real as can be, nude and erotic in the shady Venerean recess of a rose privet (canto 49). Taken serially, Fiammetta's three appearances in the *Amorosa visione* mark an amusing anti-Platonic progression, from abstract image to carnal body. The sequence has a significant center. At that midpoint, the second sighting, Boccaccio discloses her two names.[2]

Of course, this fiery Mary is not a newcomer to Boccaccio's fiction. She had made her debut in his oeuvre with the *Filocolo* (ca. 1336–1338/39), an

---

1. Giovanni Boccaccio, *Amorosa visione,* ed. Vittore Branca, in *Tutte le opere,* vol. 3 (Milan: Mondadori, 1974); trans. Robert Hollander, Timothy Hampton, and Margherita Frankel (Hanover, N.H.: University Press of New England, 1986). I cite these texts throughout. The three prefatory sonnets are all of supernumerary length, respectively seventeen, sixteen, and twenty-five verses. Technically, each of the first two is a *sonetto caudato* (a sonnet in the usual fourteen-verse scheme plus a "tail" of three verses). The third is both *rinterzato* (with extra internal verses, here four lines inserted in the octave and two in the sestet) and *caudato* (a five-verse "tail"). Such formal variations are unusual, especially the elaboration of the third sonnet. They announce the virtuoso performance of the poet in the *Amorosa visione.* The text survives in only eight copies, none an autograph. MS 1066 in the Biblioteca Riccardiana, Florence, carrying a date of 1433, displays the acrostic in its typical graphic layout. Figs. 1a–b reproduce folios 16v–17r, which correspond to 15.40–61, the verses with the poet's signature "Giovanni di Boccaccio di Certaldo." A hand in the margin points to the name.
2. Despite the seemingly retrograde movement by which Giovanni reaches Maria, she personifies Wisdom in the allegory. Janet Levarie Smarr first made the argument, calling attention to the progression in her triple appearances, in *Boccaccio and Fiammetta: The Narrator as Lover* (Urbana: University of Illinois Press, 1986), 124–27. See further Victoria Kirkham, "Amorous Vision, Scholastic Vistas," in *The Sign of Reason in Boccaccio's Fiction* (Florence: Olschki, 1991), 55–116.

encyclopedic romance conceived a half dozen years before the *Amorosa visione*. Not until more than two hundred chapters into the story does Florio, the protagonist, a Spanish prince of the sixth century, happen on Fiammetta. To search the world incognito for his lost Biancifiore (sold into slavery by stepparents, shipped off to Egypt, and imprisoned inside a harem tower), Florio changes his name to "Filocolo," a coinage from the Greek that Boccaccio explains as "labors of love" (*Filoc.* 3.75). Shipwreck forces him to winter at "old Parthenope" (4.9), and one day the next spring, as he and his companions are strolling the shore not far from Virgil's tomb, they meet a party of Neapolitan nobles merrily secluded in a countryside garden. All pass the warm afternoon together, protected by cool walls in a well-shaded circle, debating questions concerning love. Queen-for-the-day and case arbiter is a lady whose "eyes filled with fiery rays scintillant like the morning star" had sparked Florio's curiosity about her identity. Caleon, her adoring lover, obliges with the answer.

Il suo nome è da noi qui chiamato Fiammetta, posto che la più parte delle genti il nome di Colei la chiamino, per cui quella piaga, che il prevaricamento della prima madre aperse, richiuse. Ella è figliuola dell'altissimo prencipe sotto il cui scettro questi paesi in quiete si reggono, e a noi tutti è donna: e, brievemente, niuna virtù è che in valoroso cuore debbia capere, che nel suo non sia.

[Among us she is known as Fiammetta, although most people call her by the name of the woman through whom that wound, which the first mother's prevarication opened, was closed. She is the daughter of the most high prince under whose scepter these lands are peaceably ruled, and she is mistress of us all, and in brief, no virtue that a valorous heart should hold is not in hers.] (*Filoc.* 4.16.4–5)[3]

Nicknamed Fiammetta, she is officially a Maria. For his roundabout onomastic rhetoric, Boccaccio took inspiration from Dante's *Paradiso,* where Mary presides as queen of heaven, with Eve positioned at her feet. The hierarchical union of Mary and Eve mimes the medieval *Ave-Eva*

---

3. Giovanni Boccaccio, *Filocolo,* ed. Antonio Enzo Quaglio, in *Tutte le opere,* vol. 1 (Milan: Mondadori, 1967). All translations from the *Filocolo* are my own. A full text is now available in English, in *Il Filocolo,* trans. Donald Cheney with Thomas G. Bergin (New York: Garland, 1985). Although serviceable, the translation by Cheney and Bergin is not without shortcomings. For a review, see Victoria Kirkham, "Two New Translations: The Early Boccaccio in English Dress," *Italica* 70, no. 1 (1993): 79–89.

palindrome. It telescopes a reverse symmetry between Eve's fault in Genesis, responsible for our "wound," and Mary's mission of healing, proclaimed at the Annunciation in Luke 1:28 when Gabriel saluted her with
one of the most famous greetings of all literature, "Ave, gratia plena"
[Hail, full of grace]. Biblical typology binds Eve and Mary. As he guides
Dante's gaze in the Empyrean, outermost sphere of fiery light, Saint
Bernard intimates the figural connection.

> La piaga che Maria richiuse e unse,
> quella ch'è tanto bella da' suoi piedi
> è colei che l'aperse e che la punse.

[The wound which Mary closed and anointed, that one who is so
beautiful at her feet is she who opened it and pierced it.] (*Par.*
32.3–6)[4]

Maria, styled as Fiammetta, wise queen of a secular love court, descends
via "father" Dante from the supreme model of womanhood, exemplar of
absolute perfection. Why, then, is the princess from Parthenope not just
Mary pure and simple, the *nec plus ultra* of female denominations? How
did she acquire her lambent nickname?

Fire is a time-honored metaphor for love's fervor, embedded in commonplaces of language that describe "burning" desire, "ardent" yearning.
Whoever carries a torch may also trace that heat to its amorous source
and, by the license of poetry, transfer his "ardor" to a pyrobolic agent.
One of Boccaccio's favored Latin poets, Ovid, had long before done so
and gone as far as to imagine the metamorphosis of female into fire. In a
passage of his *Amores,* often cited by medieval commentators because it
contains an autobiographical reference that names his hometown and
happily paints the surrounding region, Ovid complains of missing his lady.
Despite the beautiful, fertile countryside around Sulmona, where he
dwells, he cannot be content, because he feels alone.

> At meus ignis abest. verbo peccavimus uno!—
> quae movet ardores est procul; ardor adest.

---

4. Dante Alighieri, *La Commedia secondo l'antica vulgata,* ed. Giorgio Petrocchi (Milan:
Mondadori, 1966–67); *The Divine Comedy,* trans. Charles S. Singleton, 6 vols., Bollingen
Series 80 (Princeton: Princeton University Press, 1970–75). I cite Petrocchi and for the trans-
lation rely on Singleton throughout, with occasional departures.

[But my fire is not here. I was wrong in one word!—she for whom I burn is afar; the burning is here.] (*Amores* 2.16.11–12)

Boccaccio could have associated such seductive calorific sexuality with the dangerous element that, in misogynistic terms, defines "female" for the medieval lexicographer Isidore of Seville. Since women "burn" with lust more hotly than men, the second of the two etymologies he propounds for *femina* derives from the Greek word for "fire."

Alii Graeca etymologia feminam ab ignea vi dictam putant, quia vehementer concupiscit. Libidinosiores enim viris feminas esse tam in mulieribus quam in animalibus.

[Others think that by a Greek etymology female comes from fiery vigor, because she is more vehemently concupiscent. The female is more libidinous than the male, both in women and animals.][5]

Ovid's polish and Isidore's science reach Boccaccio via the powerful mediating influence of Dante, who knows fires of love both profane and sacred. His first vision in the *Vita nuova* fades in as "una nebula di colore di fuoco" [a cloud the color of fire]. It sheathes Amore, personified as an awesome man, who displays the poet's burning heart and feeds it to Beatrice, naked except for a bright red drape (3.3–5). Later in the love story, as Dante's spiritual eyesight improves, he perceives that Beatrice emits a beneficent, Christian flame.

Dico che quando ella apparia da parte alcuna, per la speranza de la mirabile salute nullo nemico mi rimanea, anzi mi giugnea una fiamma di caritate, la quale mi facea perdonare a chiunque m'avesse offeso.

---

5. Ovid, *Heroides and Amores,* trans. Grant Showerman, Loeb Classical Library (Cambridge: Harvard University Press, 1963). I have modified the translation to a more literal reading. This and other echoes of Ovid in Boccaccio's *Rime* are briefly reviewed by Rosario Ferreri in *Innovazione e tradizione nel Boccaccio* (Rome: Bulzoni, 1980), 42–50. Isidore of Seville (*Etym.* 11.2.24) gives this explanation as an alternative to the possibility that *femina* derives from *femur,* the word for the upper leg bone, which is in the body area where one can distinguish male from female sex.

[I say that wheresoever she appeared, in the hope of her marvelous salutation, I no longer held anyone my enemy; rather, I felt a flame of charity that made me forgive whoever had injured me.] (11.1)[6]

Shortly before Beatrice reenters Dante's life, this time from her home in the Kingdom of Glory, Dante lies dreaming on Purgatory beneath the planet of Venus, twinkling in the sky dome as the dawn star. In anticipation of the day's events, which lead to his lady's epiphany, he attaches a fiery epithet to that goddess, "che di foco d'amor par sempre ardente" [who seems always burning with the fire of love] (*Purg.* 27.96). He had just transited the uppermost ledge of penance in Purgatory, walled in with a blast-fire that "refines" the lustful, where "la ripa fiamma in fuor balestra" [the bank shoots out flame] (*Purg.* 25.113). At first he balks, mortally terrified, but Virgil reminds him that Beatrice awaits on the other side, and he assures Dante of his invulnerability: "se dentro a l'alvo / di questa fiamma stessi ben mille anni, / non ti potrebbe far d'un capel calvo" [if within the belly of this flame you should stay full a thousand years, it could not make you bald of one hair] (*Purg.* 27.25–27).

These and similar images—a whole stock-house of them from the poets of antiquity, troubadours, Sicilian sonneteers, and *stilnovisti*—fixed fire as one of love's most conventional attributes. Out of the old repertoire, Boccaccio creates a new flame, recognizable for her traditional features, yet remarkably individual. With typical eclecticism, he conjoins ancient and modern, Ovid and Dante. He merges a "flame of charity" with a suggestion from Ovid's *Amores,* a work considered so prurient that it was known in the Middle Ages as *The Book without a Title,* and transforms the pyrotechnic lady into a Venus ("foco d'amor") of Christian love.

His "Maria," alias "Fiammetta," inherits another part of her fiery personality, as she does her contrariness to Eve, from the Virgin Mary herself.

---

6. Dante, *Vita nuova,* ed. De Robertis; *Vita nuova,* trans. Barbara Reynolds (Harmondsworth: Penguin, 1971). I have consulted Reynolds for translations but have not adhered to her strictly, in order better to retain Dante's literal sense. Gordon Silber, in *The Influence of Dante and Petrarch on Certain of Boccaccio's Lyrics* (Menasha, Wis.: George Banta Publishing Company, 1940), 30–34, assembled a useful inventory of references to the "fire of love" in his commentary on Boccaccio's *Rime* 5, the poem that introduces the *senhal* "Fiammetta." He did not, however, see any point in trying to sort out which may have been most important for Boccaccio: "References to love and passion by metaphors having to do with fire, and phrases such as *foco d'amore,* are commonplace in classical and medieval literature and it is not necessary to look for a source or sources for Boccaccio's use of them."

Remember how, at Saint Bernard's invitation, Dante had looked up as he approached his final vision and had seen Maria lighting the heaven like the rising sun.

> Io levai li occhi; e come da mattina
> la parte orïental de l'orizzonte
> soverchia quella dove 'l sol declina,
>   così, quasi di valle andando a monte
> con li occhi, vidi parte ne lo stremo
> vincer di lume tutta l'altra fronte.

[I lifted up my eyes; and as at morning the eastern parts of the horizon outshine that where the sun declines, so, as if going with my eyes from valley to mountaintop, I saw a part on the extreme verge surpass with its light all the rest of the rim.] (*Par.* 31.118–23)

To borrow a phrase from the trecento commentator Benvenuto da Imola, she is the "dawn of the world" [aurora mundi], more luminous than any other arc in the Rose because she receives most from the "eternal sun."[7] On her throne, just above Eve, she "flames" thrice over with Christian ardor; that is, a rhetorical *figura etymologica,* or *adnominatio,* three times frames her in homographic rhymes with forms of the word *fiamma.* "Flame" first occurs in rhyme position as a verb, last as a substantive. Between these occurrences, at the center of the terza rima, Dante mounts the most eye-catching word-gem, a compound noun that appears here as hapax legomenon in the *Comedy,* where it couples "gold" with "fire" in an object allusive to French monarchic power.

> E come quivi ove s'aspetta il temo
> che mal guidò Fetonte, più s'infiamma,

---

7. Benvenuto da Imola, *Comentum super Dantis Aldigherij comoediam* (Florence: Barbèra, 1888), 5:482: "sicut enim pars orientalis nostri coeli est serenior et lucidior parte occidentali, quia plus et principalius recipit de lumine soli sensibilis, cui est vicinior; ita pars suprema coeli empyrei ubi est Maria, aurora mundi, est luminosior et splendidior reliqua parte, quia plus et principalius recipit de lumine solis aeterni cui est vicinior" [as the eastern part of our sky is more serene and luminous than the western, because it receives more of and chiefly the light of the sensible sun, to which it is nearer; so the highest part of the empyrean heaven where Maria is, dawn of the world, is more luminous and resplendent than the other part, because it receives more of and chiefly the light of the eternal sun, to which it is nearer].

e quinci e quindi il lume si fa scemo,
   così quella pacifica oriafiamma
nel mezzo s'avvivava, e d'ogne parte
per igual modo allentava la fiamma.

[And as the point where we await the pole that Phaethon misguided
is most aflame, and on this side and on that the light diminishes, so
was that pacific oriflamme quickened in the middle, on either side in
equal measure tempering its flame.] (*Par.* 31.124–29)

The epic simile turns on a myth, the tenor of which is to declare Mary's
incredible brightness. She outshines all the other souls in a spot of
intense light like the sun, whose chariot-pole Apollo's boy Phaethon
failed to keep hooked to his team of horses. The image calls to mind a
solar burst too huge and powerful for containment, a godly light source
triumphant. Triumph and conquest carry into the central metaphor, that
of the "oriflamme." Mary, in the midst of hovering angels, makes a burst
of red and gold comparable to this ancient battle standard of French
kings, said to have been given by Christ to Charlemagne, the emperor
who was the legendary founder of their dynasty. Borne on a gold pole, it
was woven of red cloth decorated with a golden flame at the center and
gold stars scattered in the field. Not war but peace now prevails under
the fire banner in the serene realm of heavenly love. In Dante's simile,
Mary, the soul closest to Christ, appears *like* the sun exploding over the
horizon; in his metaphor, she actually *is* the oriflamme. Brought more
precisely into focus, the flag embraces Mary as well as her accompanying
angels, and since she is at the center of the scene, she must be equated
with the center of the billowing oriflamme—that is, the smaller emblematic flame sewn into the middle of the starry battle standard. "Maria"
and "fiamma" are one.

   The character called Maria-Fiammetta whom Caleon presents in Boccaccio's *Filocolo* is the target of a daring *contaminatio*. Literally, she at
once relives the Mother of God and the most banal of erotic clichés, a
metaphor that Ovid had playfully tapped. Her double name converts passion fires of secular lyric to ardor with sacred connotations. They fuse an
attribute of Beatrice ("flame of charity") and Dante's dawn star Venus
("fire of love") with definitions of the Queen of Heaven from the final cantos in *Paradiso*. A new flame, Fiammetta reincarnates Dante's "gentilis-

sima," the goddess of love, the Virgin Mary (not Eve), and Mary the Oriflamme of French monarchy.[8]

As a Marian flamelet, Caleon's Fiammetta has a key double in the *Filocolo,* none other than the lady who commissioned it. She is the Author's personal flame, apart from and outside the story he recounts of Florio and Biancifiore's love. With a bloodline no less romantic than illustrious, this other Maria in the frame tale is an illegitimate daughter of King Robert of Naples.

E avanti che alla reale eccellenza pervenisse, [Ruberto], preso del piacere d'una gentilissima giovane dimorante nelle reali case, generò di lei una bellissima figliuola, . . . e lei nomò del nome di colei che in sé contenne la redenzione del misero perdimento che avvenne per l'ardito gusto della prima madre.

[And before he ascended the royal throne, Robert was taken with desire for a most noble young woman dwelling in the royal household, and by her he fathered a most beautiful little daughter, . . . and he named her with the name of the woman who contained in herself redemption for the miserable loss that befell for what the first mother dared to taste.] (*Filoc.* 1.1.15–16)

Clearly Boccaccio means us to remember his "Maria," daughter of the contemporary French Angevin king, when 215 chapters later we encounter her fictional congener, a princess "Maria" who had lived seven hundred years before. He names neither of his two fictional Marias openly, substituting for each instead the same periphrasis drawn from Dante's *Paradiso,* where it alludes to the vessel of our salvation. In so doing, Boccaccio's narrator sets up a parallel between his Maria and her earlier fictional counterpart, between the "historical" frame of the *Filocolo* and the fiction it encloses.

By association, Robert's daughter must also be a Fiammetta, even though Boccaccio never so designates her in the *Filocolo.* But from the moment he first glimpses her and is smitten, fire of some sort always seems

---

8. Modern commentators vary somewhat in their descriptions of the oriflamme. It is not certain how exactly Dante pictured the details of the device. Mosaics at the Lateran document the legend that Christ gave it to Charlemagne. See Dante Alighieri, *La divina commedia,* ed. Umberto Bosco and Giovanni Reggio, 3 vols. (Florence: Le Monnier, 1987), *Par.* 31.127.

to flare in her vicinity. Sign of her amorous nature and the ardor she kindles, it accompanies her inevitably, much as the number 9 could not help but turn up wherever Dante's Beatrice did. Hence it was fitting that their initial encounter at Naples should have occurred in the Franciscan church of San Lorenzo, a trecento sanctuary still standing today, consecrated to the martyr roasted on a grate, whom artists depicted in his fire-licked death.[9] Boccaccio sees her a second time, not coincidentally among virgins in a convent named after the heavenly messenger of the Annunciation, Sant'Arcangelo a Baiano. The archangel's greeting, "Ave, gratia plena," invokes the Virgin in her role as Eve's opposite, a polarity that likewise defines the poet's antilapsarian Maria. The settings in which he places her for her two first appearances in the *Filocolo,* San Lorenzo and Sant'Arcangelo, are frames becoming the identity of this lady, known both by her fiery *senhal* and her Marian name.

It is curious that in these first pages of his book, although Boccaccio christens Maria with a powerfully allusive loop of rhetoric and enfolds her in symbols of her dual nomenclature, he never so much as hints at his own name. Instead, he remains an anonymous first-person "composer" ("io, della presente opera componitore"). Referring to himself as "il nuovo autore" (1.2), the young writer releases only one other detail for our prelim-

---

9. Saint Lawrence, who died in the Roman church that bears his name, became one of the most famous early Christian martyrs. Tradition has it that he was roasted on a gridiron after he refused to surrender the church valuables to the city prefect, pointing to his poor congregation and saying, "Here is our treasure." Boccaccio may have visited San Lorenzo fuori le Mura, one of Rome's seven pilgrimage churches, on his way from Florence to Naples in 1327. If so, he would have seen depictions of the saint's life on its walls. Drawings made during the seventeenth century preserve some of its early mosaics and medieval frescoes. See Waetzoldt, *Die Kopien des 17. Jahrhunderts,* 44–46 and figs. 200 and 224, for cycles on the portico and the entrance wall. Boccaccio's possible route from Florence to Rome and the dating of that trip are discussed by Vittore Branca in *Giovanni Boccaccio: Profilo biografico,* 2d ed. (Florence: Sansoni, 1992), 12–17. The Neapolitan Duomo of San Lorenzo, rebuilt by Charles I and Charles II of Anjou, beginning late in the duecento, on ruins of a sixth-century paleo-Christian church, was completed in 1324. Favored by the Angevin kings, who had close ties to the Franciscan order, it was embellished with Giottesque frescoes by Tuscan artists and would doubtless have included images similar to the ones at San Lorenzo in Rome. Boccaccio's friend Giovanni Barrile seems to have been responsible for commissioning the decoration of his family chapel, dedicated to Saint Lawrence, in the period 1334–41. Descriptions of San Lorenzo Maggiore in Naples and its decorations can be found in Ferdinando Bologna, *I pittori alla Corte Angioina di Napoli* (Rome: U. Bozzi, 1969), 210–11. See further, for basic historical background, the standard encyclopedia of reference, *Storia di Napoli,* 10 vols. (Naples: Società Editrice Storia di Napoli, 1967–71), 3:499–512, 704–10. Virginia Brown documents examples of the Angevin-Franciscan alliance, in "Boccaccio in Naples: the Beneventan Liturgical Palimpsest of the Laurentian Autographs (Mss. 29.8 and 33.31)," *Italia Medioevale e Umanistica* 34 (1991): 41–126.

inary information: he is studying canon law (1.1). Much later, at the beginning of book 4, he finally discloses the clues we need to deduce both his
name and his surname. The delay, we shall see, is deliberate. Meanwhile,
since he floodlights Maria-Fiammetta center stage as the *Filocolo* opens, we,
before knocking at the location of his signature, should linger to make better acquaintance with his partner-in-poetry, the Flamelet of Naples.

No one, I suppose, any longer believes in the existence of a real Maria
d'Aquino, née Mary of Anjou, holder of the keys to Boccaccio's heart. Her
name has never been found in any archive, nor does it figure in a genealogy of the Angevin dynasty that Boccaccio himself transcribed into one of
his working notebooks, a three-generation registry with thirty-three
names.[10] Fiammetta is an absentee as well from the early biographies of
the Certaldan, which praise him for writings in Latin but have little to say
about the vernacular pieces. The oldest, Filippo Villani's *Lives of the
Famous Florentines* (ca. 1380; 2d ed., ca. 1390), takes care to record each of
Boccaccio's Latin compilations and then refers belittlingly, in a lump sum,
to "many lesser works [opuscula] composed in the vernacular language,
some modulated in rhyme, some written in prose, where the genius of las-
civious youth disported a bit too freely, and which, as Boccaccio grew
older, he himself thought best to pass over in silence." Villani continues,
"but he could not, as he would have wished, summon back to his breast
the word once spoken, nor use willpower to extinguish a fire that had been
aroused by fanning the flames."[11] Never quite snuffed out in the poet's
maturity—as the biographer would have it—the burning passion of youth
flickers metaphorically in his portrait, but without any awareness of a *sen-*

---

10. Boccaccio compiled a genealogy of Charles I of Anjou in his *Zibaldone magliabechiano* (Florence, Biblioteca Nazionale, MS B. R. 50 [II.ii.327], fol. 162v). The thirty-three generations are mentioned by Giuseppe Billanovich in *Restauri boccacceschi* (Rome: Edizioni di
Storia e Letteratura, 1945), 83. It became the basis for Boccaccio's chapter on Charles of
Anjou in *De casibus*, book 7. See Aldo Maria Costantini, "Studio sullo Zibaldone magliabechiano," *Studi sul Boccaccio* 7 (1973): 21–58. The totals must reflect as much the poet's
fascination with numerology as his interest in history. See discussion later in this chapter for
the combination of 3 and 33, which are significant as the numbers of Christ's age at his death.
They return in the probable date of Boccaccio's enamorment with Fiammetta and as a date
of reference in Petrarch's *Familiares* 4.1.
11. Filippo Villani, *De origine civitatis Florentiae et de eiusdem famosis civibus,* ed. Angelo
Solerti, in *Le vite di Dante, Petrarca e Boccaccio scritte fino al secolo decimosesto,* Storia letteraria d'Italia scritta da una Società di Professori, vol. 4 (Milan: Dottor Francesco Vallardi,
n.d.), 675: "Extant et quamplura eius opuscula vulgari edita sermone, plereaque rythimis
modulata, pleraque continuatione prosaica, in quibus lascivientis iuventutis ingenio paulo
liberius evagatur, quae, cum senuisset, ipse putavit silentio transigenda: sed non potuit, ut
optaverat, verbm emissum semel ad pectora revocare, neque ignem quem flabello excitaverat,
sua voluntate restinguere." Solerti reprints the second edition of Villani's vita.

hal. Still, whatever Villani's official position, he and members of his circle must have been happily dipping into those Tuscan "opuscules," at least the *Filocolo* and *Comedia delle ninfe fiorentine.* They are the sources of the information on his subject's illegitimate and foreign birth. It seems that Boccaccio's father, "readily inclined to love," conceived him during a business trip to Paris, where he was stricken by a "most burning passion" for a French woman—"so say those who cultivate Giovanni's works" [ut cultores operum Iohannis volunt].[12]

With the second edition of his biography, written some ten years after the first, Filippo Villani inaugurated Boccaccio's cult. He was authoritative for his connection with the most famous clan of Florentine chroniclers, he was copied, and what he wrote became codified. Brief notice in *Fountain of the World's Memorable Things,* the encyclopedia that for many years occupied Domenico Bandini di Arezzo (d. ca. 1415), echoes Villani closely on the amorous vulnerability that allegedly ran in the Boccaccio family. Although Bandini adds that not everyone agreed with "Giovanni's admirers" [diligentes Johannem] about his father's Parisian affair and its aftermath, he disappoints by not going on to say what people "more commonly" believed.[13]

At midquattrocento and more solidly grounded, Giannozzo Manetti restores Boccaccio's birth to Certaldo, the hilltop village south of Florence signed in the *Amorosa visione* and named "patria" in the poet's autoepitaph. Concerning Giovanni's *amores,* Manetti the humanist makes no mention of any particular woman. He concedes to the subject just a single sentence, nearly lost in a lengthy, admiring analysis of the poet's Latin and Greek scholarship: "Still as an older man he had that proclivity."[14]

---

12. Ibid, 672: "[pater] in quamdam iuvenculam Parisinam, sortis inter nobilem et burgensem, vehementissimo exarsit amore et, ut cultores operum Iohannis volunt, illam sibi in coniugem copulavit, ex qua ipse genitus est Iohannes." Cf. *Filoc.* 5.8; Giovanni Boccaccio, *Comedia delle ninfe fiorentine,* ed. Antonio Enzo Quaglio, in *Tutte le opere,* vol. 2 (Milan: Mondadori, 1964), 23.21–38. Villani gives two differing accounts of Boccaccio's birth. In his chronicle of 1380, he says Boccaccio was born in Certaldo, but in the second version, dating from the early 1390s, he changes the poet's birth to Paris. See Branca, *Profilo biografico,* 7. Aldo Francesco Massèra collected the early biographies of Boccaccio in "Le piú antiche biografie del Boccaccio," *Zeitschrift für Romanische Philologie* 27 (1903): 298–338.

13. *De viris claris,* in *Aedilium ecclesiae florentiae (Fons memorabilium universi),* in Solerti, *Le vite,* 677: "[pater] amavit vehementer quandam iuventulam Parisinam, quam, prout diligentes Johannem dicunt (quamquam alia communior sit opinio), sibi postea uxorem fecit; ex qua genitus est Johannes." Solerti (91) gives a brief notice identifying Bandini.

14. Solerti, *Le vite,* 689: "In amores usque ad maturam fere aetatem vel paulo proclivior." Manetti (1396–1459) was the first to anthololgize the lives of the Three Crowns of Florence. His *In vita et moribus trium illustrium poetarum florentinorum* is a literary triptych analogous to the men's first appearance as a threesome in Domenico Castagno's *Uomini famosi* of the midquattrocento.

By the last quarter of the fifteenth century, about a hundred years after the poet's death, the temper of these profiles begins to shift. They wax more fanciful, and as passing time allows more space for biographers to flex their imagination, Fiammetta becomes a fixture in the literature about Boccaccio's life. At first, she appears tentatively and in competing company. Girolamo Squarciafico, in an inventive and garbled vita that accompanies one of the two earliest editions of the *Filocolo* (1472),[15] has a longish section with quite a lot to say about Boccaccio's libidinous nature.

> He was much given to lusting after women and was in love with a good number of them, one being a Florentine who was called Lucia, but he always refers to her as Lia. Although it was unsuitable for him on account of his low station, he let himself be so bold as to love the natural daughter of the most serene King Robert, who was called Lady Maria. . . . And for love of her he composed the *Filocolo* and *Fiammetta*.

What came of this affair? Opinions vary, Squarciafico acknowledges. Still, he wonders how on earth Fiammetta could have been swayed by an upstart poet's scribblings.

> In my ignorance, I do not wish to pass judgment on this particular thing. Neither, though, can I believe that the daughter of such a high

---

15. Bacchi della Lega (*Opere di Giovanni Boccaccii*, 101–2) gives as the first edition a volume with the incipit "COMINCIA IL PHILOCOLO DI: M. G. BOCCHACH [sic]" and with the following on fol. 266: "Magister iouannes petri demagontia scripsit hoc opus floretiae Die: XII: nouembris: MCCCCLXXII." The date, however, has been contested by some scholars. In contrast, a Venetian imprint of the same year sports colors of Squarciafico's arrival on the scene: at the beginning, it reads, "INCOMENCIA ILLIBRO PRIMO: DI FLORIO: ET DI BIANZafiore chiamato Philocolo che tanto e a dire quanto amorosa faticha Composto per il clarissimo poeta miser Iohanne Boccaccio da certaldo ad instancia di la illustre: et generosa madonna Maria. figluola naturale delinclito Re Ruberto"; at the end, "Il libro del Philocolo di mesere iohanne boccatio da certaldo poeta illustre qui finisce: Impresso per maestro Gabriele di piero et del compagno maestro Philipo: in l'alma Patria Venetia nelli anni del signore. M. CCCC. LXXII. a giorni XX di novembre: Nicolo throno duce felicissimo imperante" and "Vita di miser Iohanne boccatio composta per Hieronymo Squazzafico de Alexandria; la quale finisce coll'epitaffio del Boccaccio: Hac sub mole jacent . . ." Of eight incunabula listed by Bacchi della Lega, all but one after the first contain Squarciafico's vita, and the exception (Milan, 1478) has at the beginning an "Epistola di Geronimo Squarciafico Alessandrino a Luigi Marcello." In other words, Squarciafico became part of the standard apparatus in the earliest editions. That he is absent only from the 1472 Florentine edition is another argument in favor of its position as editio princeps.

lord would compromise her honor like that, either for verses or for
epistles. Yet the truth is that for love of her he resided many years in
fair Parthenope.

Poor Squarciafico is hard put to reconcile the overriding evidence with his
status-conscious repugnance of it. But he finds an out by blaming young
Boccaccio's persistence on an irresistible force: "Ah, *amore*! What don't
you drive mortal souls to do!" That is why Boccaccio, the Tuscan, spent all
those years down in Naples. It was love! Signor Squarciafico closes his
meditation with an impersonal construction, grammar that argues no less
than absolute verity: "Vero è che per amore di lei parecchi anni si dimorò
in la bella Partenope."[16]

Here we have a situation not so different from what spurred Florio to
become Filocolo and persevere year after year until he won Biancifiore—
allowance made for a sex-role switch. In the *Filocolo* Biancifiore is the
commoner (so her stepparents thought) and Florio the prince. Squarciafico calls attention to the reversal of their relationship in the upsetting
love story of the frame tale: a male commoner loves a king's daughter. For
Squarciafico, the Author's explanation of how he came to compose the
Filocolo is true. And why not? Who would write a romance, he must have
asked, if not a romantically minded fellow? It seems not to have occurred
to him to suspect that Boccaccio, motivated by ambition for patronage at
Robert's court, could have crafted his love story as a mirror image of Florio's—paying all due respect to a courtly convention that commended
pedestaled ladies to aspiring poets—or that Fiammetta, like Biancifiore,
could be a fiction characterized to encompass all virtue, with Boccaccio's
purpose in the pretense being not to laud the lady but to flatter her
"father." From one fictional field of passion springs another.

The 1472 Venetian *Filocolo* marks an important new phase in the history of Boccaccio's reception. It was the first time one of his works had

---

16. Solerti, *Le vite,* 697: "Fu molto dato alla libidine delle donne, et de diverse fu
inamorato, e tra l'altre d'una fiorentina, la quale era dicta Lucia, dove lui Lya sempre
l'apella. Ancora che non gli era già convenevole per la sua bassa condizione, se lassò spingere
ad amare la figliola naturale del serenissimo re Roberto, la quale madonna Maria era chiamata. O amore, ad che non spingi l'animi di mortali! . . . Et per amore de costei compose il
Filocolo et la *Fiammetta.* . . . Io, come ignorante, questa tale cosa non la voglio determinare,
né ancora non posso credere che una figliuola d'uno tanto signore cosí per versi né per epistole se andasse a sottoponere del suo onore. Vero é che per amore di lei parecchi anni si
dimorò in la bella Partenope." Ameto, protagonist of the *Comedia delle ninfe fiorentine,* loves
Lia, who has congeners in the Emilias of the *Teseida* and *Decameron.*

been packaged for publication together with a vita of the author. Not coincidentally, the biographical tradition begins to couple Boccaccio and Fiammetta in a vita attached to the *Filocolo,* where Boccaccio himself had written Fiammetta into his oeuvre. Incarnate in print, Fiammetta gains title-page status: "INCOMENCIA ILLIBRO PRIMO: DI FLORIO: ET DI BIANZafiore chiamato Philocolo che tanto e a dire quanto amorosa faticha Composto per il clarissimo poeta miser Iohanne Boccaccio da certaldo ad instancia di la illustre: et generosa madonna Maria. figluola naturale delinclito Re Ruberto" [Here begins the first book of Florio and Bianzafiore called Philocolo, which is as much to say as labor of love, composed by the most distinguished poet Messer John Boccaccio of Certaldo at the request of the illustrious and generous Madonna Maria, natural daughter of the glorious King Robert]. The fiction inside the book has migrated "outside" to posture as bibliographical documentation. Once integrated into the title page, side by side with the author's name and his hometown, "Madonna Maria" naturally acquires authority. With a simple editorial decision, making for a much more salable title than the stark, mystifying *"Filocolo,"* fantasy is history; the make-believe character turns into an actual human being. Typography as a technology, readily adaptive to the ancient and medieval practice of publishing the author's vita with his work, would assure rapid-fire spread of Boccaccio's reputation as her romancer.

Eventually, Romantics, abetted by their allies the Victorians, would weave to perfection the fabulous stuff of Giovanni's affair with Maria. Their project could claim validity from the modern methods of a discipline that had been founded around 1800 and that had reached its heyday toward the end of the nineteenth century, Romance philology. Confident and prolific, the philologists saw themselves on the side of science as they practiced their new literary history, which sought to understand texts in cultural contexts, as products of an author's life and times. Historical background was fundamental to their research, and their approach led to significantly improved editions. The drawback was, they liked to call factual much that we have reclassified fictional. For instance, to grace the maiden issue of *Studi di Filologia Romanza,* a scholarly forum launched in 1885, Camillo Antona-Traversi contributed "Historical Notices" pertaining to Boccaccio's Neapolitan period. With rhetoric quite like the poet's, he asserts unequivocally Maria's control over her young man's affections. He wrote that she "kindled Messer Giovanni with true love that drove him

out of his mind," concluding, "But who can impose laws on the heart?"[17]
By a decade later, across the Channel John Addington Symonds was feeling the tug of some sensible doubts. The straitlaced scholar in him, though,
stifled the more judicious connoisseur:

> Dealing with this famous romance [*Filocolo*], one is tempted to won-
> der whether the young man who had now resolved on literature, did
> not set up a mistress as part of his necessary equipment. To do so,
> however, would be inconsistent with sound criticism. A certain ele-
> ment of ideality and indistinctness must be acknowledged in Dante's
> Beatrice, Petrarch's Laura, and in Boccaccio's Fiammetta. Yet we
> are bound to accept these heroines of fame as real women, who pow-
> erfully influenced the hearts and minds of their three poet lovers.[18]

Symonds had inherited a legend four hundred years strong, reauthenti-
cated by Romance philologists in a climate of philosophical positivism.
Willy-nilly, the Anglo-Saxon went along with the Mediterraneans.

If Fiammetta began by conquering Boccaccio, her fire swept seduc-
tively over many generations of the man's biographers and critics. More
convinced by the century that she dominated his existence, they seized a
myth he had tailored to the *Filocolo* and amplified it to remap his entire
career. Although Maria-Fiammetta did not appear in works before the
Filocolo, philologists backdated her dominion to his first Italian fiction,
Diana's Hunt, pronouncing her its Mystery Lady. They proceeded as well
to impose her on the early *Filostrato,* notwithstanding that the lover who
narrates it had addressed a woman "more than pleasing" with the *senhal*
"Filomena."[19] Looking ahead from the *Filocolo* to the *Teseida, Ameto,*

---

17. Camillo Antona-Traversi, "Notizie storiche sull'*Amorosa visione," Studi di Filologia
Romanza* 1 (1885): 425–444: "Maria d'Aquino, figlia naturale di re Roberto, tenne per molto
tempo le chiavi del cuore di messer Giovanni: ella lo accese di amore vero, forsennato. . . . Ma
chi può imporre leggi al cuore?" This scholar made quite a platform of his conviction. Cf.
"Della realtà dell'amore di M. G. Boccaccio," *Il Progpugnatore* 16 (1883): 57–92, 240–80,
387–417.

18. Symonds, *Giovanni Boccaccio,* 23.

19. Fiammetta was surely the anonymous lady of the *Caccia* for Francesco Torraca, who
could not believe that her insignificant predecessors, "Pampinea" and "Abrotonia," could be
given such an important role. See his *Giovanni Boccaccio a Napoli.* Billanovich (*Restauri boccacceschi,* 87–89) also assumed she was the *Caccia* heroine. The story of how she came to
replace "Filomena" in the *Filostrato* is told by Pier Giorgio Ricci in "Per la dedica e la
datazione del *Filostrato," Studi sul Boccaccio* 1 (1963): 333–47.

and *Amorosa visione,* diligent investigators fixed the phases of Boccaccio's affair with Fiammetta—dated by years, months, and even days of duration. Those temporal divisions, deduced from clues in the fiction, then served to articulate the stages of his development as a writer and to erase deep uncertainties about the dating of his works. In default of documentation, creative jugglers were not lacking, and they rearranged chronological order with little regard to the obvious internal textual evidence. For instance, once Fiammetta had been pinpointed as the femme fatale of the *Filostrato,* then that romance in ottava rima of the Neapolitan period could be advanced to a slot after the very substantial *Teseida,* an epic not completed until after 1341, when Boccaccio returned to Florence after twelve or so years in the south. No matter what her status in a given text—patron, dedicatee, narrator, character—or whether she was named at all, Fiammetta did not merely regulate his life, she tyrannized it in that marvelous vita fed by fancy and philology.[20] It died hard. The mythopoetic construct came to a late acme in 1969, when it was bizarrely skewed into the service of Boccaccio's "psychoanalysis": youth let him enjoy carefree love, which he hymned in *Diana's Hunt;* then it dawned on him that love can be difficult to acquire, an éclaircissement imparted in the *Filocolo;* then he lost his love but clung to hope, thinking to regain his lady by doing the *Teseida;* then he suffered total disillusionment and confided the failure in the *Filostrato;* then, back in Florence from Naples, feeling "empty of love, weary of spirit, and sad in family," he took refuge in classical culture and immersed himself in the *Ameto;* then a sudden desire for glory inspired him to write the *Amorosa visione;* and finally, disguised as a woman for a "posthumous" diary of his feelings, he set down the *Elegia of Madonna Fiammetta.*[21]

By the logic of such nonsense, Boccaccio's life in its broadest contours fell into two main parts, one before and one after the lady's death. These are, of course, the same periods posterity assigned to Petrarch—"in vita di madonna" and "in morte di madonna"—extrapolating them from the "true confessions" of his *Rime sparse.* But for Boccaccio the dichotomy

---

20. In the *Teseida* she was said to go by the name "Emilia," in the *Ninfale fiesolano* she was veiled as "Mensola," etc. A good reconstruction of Boccaccio's supposed history with Fiammetta, based on his fiction, appears in Torraca, *Giovanni Boccaccio a Napoli.* The first systematic deconstructions were undertaken by Vittore Branca in "Schemi letterari e schemi autobiografici" (1944), in *Boccaccio medievale e nuovi studi sul Decameron,* 6th ed., rev. (Florence: Sansoni, 1986), 193–249, and by Billanovich in *Restauri boccacceschi,* 81–101.

21. Salvatore Galletti, *Patologia al Decameron* (Palermo: S. F. Flaccovio, 1969), 78 and 87.

conveniently amounted to a basic critical taxonomy. The first half of his life, biographers found, was ruled by Fiammetta, the second by Petrarch. To put it another way, young Boccaccio was amorous and Ovidian, "much more immature in his reason than in his heart."[22] Only with the *Decameron,* the apogee of his lifelong output, did they think he had achieved a mature balance and artistic perfection: everything before was trial and error; everything after was dry and academic. As soon as Fiammetta had joined Boccaccio's literary vita on the same plane of authenticity as Petrarch and Ovid, that isometry could justify all sorts of editorial decisions. Thus when Francesco Corazzini anthologized Boccaccio's letters in 1877, the Author's dedicatory epistle "To Fiammetta" in the *Teseida* could take a place right alongside correspondence Mr. Boccaccio sent to living recipients—among them his Tuscan friends Niccolò Acciaiuoli, Zanobi da Strada, Mainardo Cavalcanti, and, naturally, Francesco Petrarca.[23] Fiammetta is so real, in fact, for the first twentieth-century editor of the *Filocolo* (1927) that she alone certifies the merits of his task. As Ettore de Ferri pens an introduction for his two-volume project, a late but recognizable descendant of the 1472 Venetian *Filocolo,* he bluntly asserts, "love for Fiammetta was the most important fact in Boccaccio's life; therefore it is enough to say that the *Filocolo* was composed at her invitation to show the importance of this youthful work."[24]

Less than twenty years away, at the great divide of a second world war that tragically destroyed the archives of Naples, two new philologists would demolish the myth of Giovanni's subservience to an arsonous passion. Actually, Vittore Branca and Giuseppe Billanovich were set less on a demolition operation than on a restoration. Like an art conservationist,

---

22. Silvio Segalla di Arco, *I sentimenti religiosi nel Boccaccio* (Bern: F. Miori, 1909), 76: "il suo razocinio è molto piú immaturo del suo cuore." Cf. Edward Hutton, introduction to *The Decameron,* by Giovanni Boccaccio, trans. J. M. Rigg, Everyman's Library (New York: Dutton, 1930).

23. Francesco Corazzini, trans. and comm., *Le lettere edite e inedite di messer Giovanni Boccaccio* (Florence: Sansoni, 1877). The letter to Fiammetta was removed from the epistles as published in Boccaccio's *Opere latine minori,* ed. Aldo Francesco Massèra (Bari: Laterza, 1928). Branca calls attention to its inappropriateness in Boccaccio's epistolary canon in "Schemi letterari e schemi autobiografici." It is, admittedly, difficult to separate Boccaccio's real epistles from the purely rhetorical. The latter are still classified with the rest in the most recent text, *Epistole,* ed. Ginetta Auzzas, in Giovanni Boccaccio, *Tutte le opere,* vol. 5, pt. 1 (Milan: Mondadori, 1992).

24. Giovanni Boccaccio, *Il Filocolo,* ed. Ettore De Ferri, 2 vols. (Turin: Unione Tipografico-Editrice Torinese, 1927), 1:xi: "l'amore di Fiammetta costituisce il fatto più importante della vita di B. [sic]; quindi basta dire che il Filocolo fu composto dietro suo invito per mostrare l'importanza di quest'opera giovanile."

they lifted away accumulated encrustations and uncovered a different looking Boccaccio, someone colored much less by yens for palace romance than by concern for his repute as a poet.[25] Boccaccio's fiction reflects a strong fidelity to literary models and a personal sense of artistic mission. To accomplish that mission, Fiammetta was definitely "necessary equipment." Untraceable by all who ever scoured those archives before they vanished in bombing, she does indeed powerfully influence Giovanni's life in his literary self-portraits as Author-in-Love.

Many of Boccaccio's literary self-portraits survive in an album of sorts, more than one hundred sonnets that span the whole arc of his career. Although profound uncertainties of dating and attribution bedevil the *Rime* we call Boccaccio's, editors have imposed a quasi-chronological order. It re-creates memories from a lifetime of love not so different from Dante's in the *Vita nuova* (sometimes also the *Rime petrose*) and Petrarch's in the *Rime sparse*.[26] The sonnets are like so many alphabet tiles in a Scrabble romance, each one marked with a lyrical moment that can be set into the mosaic of an ideal narrative. In sonnet 5, he recalls how at the sound of a blond angel singing, "nel petto entrommi una fiammetta" [a flamelet entered my breast], and he says that "m'accese il cor in più di mill'ardori" [it kindled my heart with more than a thousand fires]. Some people mock him while others pity him for this love, a mad derailment, which he describes further in sonnet 11: "That splendid flame, whose lightning first opened the amorous way to me, so inflames me that whenever my spirit flies to where Love calls it, the overbright light blinds the feeble power of my eyes and drives me away from the rightful path." With "sparks" in his eyes from her "amorous light" (12), his heart "flaring into fire" (13) and his "breast inflamed" (16), he prays for the gift of a sigh from her to "mitigate the fire that undoes me" (19); alternatively, he hopes,

---

25. Branca, "Schemi letterari e schemi autobiografici"; Billanovich, *Restauri boccacceschi,* 81–101, but cf. passim.

26. The anthology was constructed in Aldo Francesco Massèra, ed., *Rime di Giovanni Boccaccio* (Bologna: Romagnoli, 1914). For convenience, it has been retained by Vittore Branca, who, since his first edition of the *Rime* (Bari: Laterza, 1939), has continued to gather information about them, reevaluating the textual tradition with important new findings and commentary; see, e.g., "Nuove testimonianze manoscritte e nuove rime," in *Tradizione delle opere,* 1:243–86. I cite Branca's most recent edition of the *Rime,* in Giovanni Boccaccio, *Tutte le opere,* vol. 5, pt. 1 (Milan: Mondadori, 1992); see especially Branca's "Nota al testo" (195–205). Numbers in parentheses in my text refer to poem numbers in Branca's 1992 edition.

"burning, to be renewed in fire like the phoenix" (23).[27] To underscore the spreading conflagration, the octave of sonnet 27 is constructed entirely of "ardent fire" in both rhyme words (*rima identica,* a form inherited from the sestina) and homonymic rhyme (*rima equivoca*). At the sestet, "fire" then leads to "tears," and those in turn announce the outcome of his ardor. What came of them is encased in the last word of the poem, which recapitulates the medieval *amor-mors* connection as it comes to rest in the finality of "death."

> Quando s'accese quella prima fiamma
> dentro da me, che 'l cor mi munge e arde,
> io solia dir talor: "Questa non arde
> come suol arder ciascun'altra fiamma;
> anzi conforta, sospigne e infiamma
> a valor seguitar chiunque ella arde:
> per che de esser contento, in cui ella arde,
> di più fin divenir in cotal fiamma."
> Ma il cor, già carbon fatto in questo foco,
> senza pace sperar, in tristo pianto,
> ha mutata sentenzia e chiede morte.
> E non trovando lei in cotal foco,
> ora rovente e or bagnato in pianto,
> si sta in vita assai peggior che morte.

[When inside me was kindled that first flame, which milks and burns my heart, I was sometimes wont to say, "This woman does not burn as every other flame is wont to burn; no, she encourages, presses, and inflames whomever she burns to pursue valor, so that he in whom she burns must be content to become more refined in her flame."

But my heart, reduced already to charcoal in this fire, without hoping for peace, weeping sad tears, has altered its opinion and asks for death. And not finding it in her fire, now red-hot and now bathed in tears, it lingers in life far worse than death.]

---

27. All translations of the *Rime* are my own. "Quella splendida fiamma, il cui fulgore / m'aperse prima l'amorosa via, / m'incende sí, qualor l'anima mia / vola colà dove la chiama Amore, / che 'l troppo lume el debile valore / degli occhi abbaglia sí, che la si svia / dal debito sentier" (11); "Quell'amorosa luce, il cui splendore / per li miei occhi mise le faville, che dentr'al cor andando a mille a mille" (12); "Il folgor de' begli occhi, el qual m'avampa il cor" (13); "'l petto infiammato" (16); "mi facciate d'un sospiro dono, / il qual mitighi il foco che mi sface" (19); "ardendo spero / nel fuoco rinovar come fenice" (23).

Ever "quella fiamma" (35), the lady keeps burning him even in winter, as Petra had Dante, and so badly that by comparison Vulcan's "fire" is only one "spark" (37). In 40, he blames for his suffering not God, Love, or the lady but his eyes, since they were the "doors to the amorous flame." In 45, he seems to hear "Fiammetta" chide him in his heart, and he hurts to hear that she cares less for his sorrow than for her womanly honor.[28]

On it goes. Wondering when he can expect mercy for his "searing ardor," Boccaccio marks the fifth year of his love with the sonnet that begins "If I could believe that in five years" (47).[29] The only anniversary poem we have by him, it turns on the same number he assigned Fiammetta in the *ternario*, "Content—almost—in thoughts of love." There Cupid presents her allusively among twelve ladies of Naples and Florence, all the rest honored in the roll call by having their real names recited—"monna Itta," "Meliana," "la Lisa," "la Pecchia," "monna Vanna," "Filippa," "monna Lottiera," and so forth. Fiammetta, uniquely, is named by her *senhal* alone. (Guido Cavalcanti's lady "Primavera" appears in the list too, but she is first introduced by Cupid as "Vanna.") Secret identity in this *sirventese* heightens the special lady's aura. It is a sign of her privilege, just as it had been for the Mystery Lady in the feminine catalogue of Boccaccio's first fiction, *Diana's Hunt*. "Fiammetta" falls fifth in the *ternario* and, fittingly, on verse 41 (4 + 1 = 5): "A nostra danza *quinta* è il tuo sole, / cioè quella **Fiammetta,** che ti diede con la saetta al cor" [*Fifth* in our dance is your sun, **Fiammetta,** that is, she who struck you in your heart with an arrow].[30] The number 9 had miraculously accompanied Dante's Beatrice,

---

28. "E io, dolente, solo ardo e incendo / in tanto foco, che quel di Vulcano / a rispetto non è una favilla" (37); "agli occhi miei / ogni mia doglia appongo, che fur porte / all'amorosa fiamma che mi sface" (40); "Cosí Fiammetta par talor nel core / mi dica; ond'io mi doglio e hommi il danno" (45).

29. "Se io potessi creder ch'in cinqu'anni" (47). Dante also has one anniversary sonnet in the *Vita nuova*, commemorating the first year after Beatrice's death. Boccaccio, of course, knew that, but at the time he wrote the *Filocolo* he could hardly have had any idea of the more elaborate anniversary scheme with returns of April 6 in Petrarch's *Rime sparse*. That has been magisterially described by Thomas Roche in "The Calendrical Structure of Petrarch's *Canzoniere*," *Studies in Philology* 71 (1974): 152–72. In any event, this "fifth anniversary" of Boccaccio's is purely conventional, not historical, as Branca recognizes in his commentary.

30. For text and translation of the *ternario*, as well as discussion, see Anthony K. Cassell and Victoria Kirkham, eds. and trans., *Diana's Hunt, Caccia di Diana: Boccaccio's First Fiction* (Philadelphia: University of Pennsylvania Press, 1991), 6–11 and appendix, 220–23. Most names in the *ternario* are compound forms, either a patronymic or a husband's family name together with the woman's Christian name, which is sometimes in the form of an affectionate diminutive. It is the same technique Boccaccio uses in *Caccia di Diana* and repeats, but more obliquely, in *Amorosa visione*, cantos 40–44. Each is a catalogue of women modeled on the *sirventese* mentioned by Dante in *Vita nuova* 6. Boccaccio himself must have anthologized these three *sirventesi* in terza rima, as discussed below, in chap. 2.

and Fiammetta can be no less qualified as a poetic mistress; she, too, must have a number. It was acquired at her birth, so to speak, at the same time and in the same place as her names "Maria d'Angiò" and "Fiammetta." Boccaccio's "Lady 5" first sees the light of the world in the *Filocolo,* a romance in *five* books whose sacred theme is *Pentecost.*

Anniversaries, uncounted, must have long continued. At sonnet 97 enough have passed that Fiammetta's death can be presaged. She seems to transmute from woman to spirit as the poet imagines an angel perched on a cloud puff that condenses from flames encircling her rosy cheeks and blond locks.

> Sovra li fior vermigli e' capei d'oro
> veder mi parve un foco alla Fiammetta,
> e quel mutarsi in una nugoletta
> lucida più che mai argento o oro.
> E qual candida perla in anel d'oro,
> tal si sedeva in quella un'angioletta.

[Above vermilion flowers and golden hair, I seemed to see a fire on Fiammetta, and it turned into a cloudlet, brighter than ever silver or gold. And like a pure pearl in a ring of gold, just so a little angel upon it was sitting.]

By sonnet 99, her "veil" has disintegrated to "ashes," while she herself has been made "a goddess." Finally, the woman with "flaming eyes" now "sainted" (100) draws her poet's thoughts to heaven, but not to Dante's soaring heights or to a place where he can meditate on man's salvation.[31] Boccaccio's mind climbs only as high as the third sphere, pulled less by a wish to imitate Saint Paul's *raptus* than by a yearning for the planetary dwelling of Venus. There he seeks colloquy with Dante and Petrarch, fellow Florentines who have passed beyond to the spirit world. At sonnet 102, Boccaccio affectionately calls up to Dante "in the amorous sphere," asking him to intervene with Fiammetta.

> Io so che, infra l'altre anime liete
> del terzo ciel, la mia Fiammetta vede
> l'affanno mio dopo la sua partita:

---

31. "Dormendo, un giorno, in sonno mi parea / . . . quella, il cui bel velo / cenere è fatto, e ella è fatta dea" (99); "Se la fiamma degli occhi, ch'or son santi" (100).

pregala, se 'l gustar dolce di Lete
non la m'ha tolta, in luogo di merzede
a sé m'impetri tosto la salita.

[I know that, among the other blithe souls of the third heaven, my
Fiammetta sees how I struggle since she departed; beg her, if the
sweet tasting of Lethe has not snatched me from her, that as a sign of
mercy she soon grant me ascent to her.]

An answer is heard from a flame flying across the night sky: "a flame
brighter than day, as I was gazing upon things supernal, it seemed I saw on
streets eternal." Fiammetta, translated to the awesome light of a comet,
advocates those very qualities once emanant from Beatrice's magic circle
of moral perfection. Her voice instructs him in the virtues necessary for
their reunion: "Whoever desires to be with me, must needs be kindly and
obedient and clothed in humility" (103).[32]

In the end, Boccaccio entreats Petrarch, newly arrived in heaven, "Or
sei salito, caro signor mio." He asks, "You my lord, you who now behold
'Lauretta' and can look upon my 'bella Fiammetta,' you who are at peace
with the other poets Sennuccio, Cino, and Dante, help lift me there, too"
(126). He echoes a late sonnet in the *Rime sparse*, "Sennuccio mio benché
doglioso et solo," in which Petrarch had asked his departed friend Sennuccio del Bene to greet Guittone, Cino, and Dante "in the third sphere"
and to tell Laura how wildly her mourning lover weeps.[33] But although the
scene here is literary, the fictional end of Boccaccio's love story coincides
with the real end of his life, when he was a man alone in painfully failing
health. It is now his last year, after Petrarch's lamented death in July, 1374.
At the fourteenth verse of the sonnet, one last time, Giovanni embraces his
Flame. The poem comes to rest—dies out, one might say—on the verb
that all along had best described her effect, *accendere,* "to turn on, light,
kindle, set on fire."

Deh, s'a grado ti fui nel mondo errante,
tirami drieto a te, dove gioioso
veggia colei che pria d'amor m'accese.

---

32. "Era sereno il ciel, di stelle adorno, / . . . quand'una fiamma piú chiara che 'l giorno /
. . . / veder mi parve per le strade eterne. / . . . 'Chi meco esser desia, / benign'esser convien e
ubidiente / e d'umiltà vestito" (103).

33. Robert M. Durling, ed. and trans., *Petrarch's Lyric Poems* (Cambridge: Harvard University Press, 1976), no. 287.

[Pray, if ever you loved me in the errant world, pull me up after you, that there I may joyfully see the lady by whose love I first was kindled.]

The sonnet sequence closes with a fantasy of poetic community. On earth as in heaven, Boccaccio aspires to the highest Tuscan literary society. Even though Boccaccio did not order his *Rime* into the kind of perfected whole that Dante framed in the *Vita nuova* or that Petrarch fused in his *Canzoniere,* his sonnets freeze scenes that reappear, variously recombined, in book after book of his Tuscan fiction. Starting with the troubadours and still today in Harlequin novels, these are the classic moments in Occidental romance:[34] when time is ripe, love is born; first sight of the beloved is an *éblouissement;* love enters the eyes and pierces the heart; time passes—days and nights, seasons and years—with alternating emotions and returning anniversaries; the love is secret and difficult; love is awarded, delayed or denied, answered or discontinued—always at the beloved's will; the beloved dies; a ghost lingers.

Boccaccio personalized the romance paradigm, impressing on it motifs and variations of his own. Whereas Beatrice was a lady of Florence, Maria is an ethnic mix. Provençal by descent as a princess of Anjou, by birth she is Italian, burning with the southern warmth of Naples and its neighbor Baia, whose baths were ancient haunts of Venus.[35] While Beatrice stood alone, so to speak, propped by neither a noble title nor a family name, patronymic, or toponymic, the courtly Maria is much richer nominally.

---

34. Whereas Boccaccio refers with pride to some of his Italian works and took an active personal interest in their publication, his *Rime* fall under a veil of silence, except for what we know from correspondence with Petrarch about his decision to burn some of the earliest ones (an episode, perhaps inspired by the ancient *Life of Virgil,* that may have been more symbolic than real). From the manuscript tradition, Branca has reconstructed several minisequences (of three to seven poems each) that could possibly go back to an order imposed by the author, but scholars now agree that Boccaccio himself did not arrange them into the kind of corpus that Petrarch decided to shape for his *Canzoniere.* See Vittore Branca, "L'atteggiamento del Boccaccio di fronte alle sue *Rime* e la formazione delle più antiche sillogi," in *Tradizione delle opere,* 1:287–329. A classic discussion of the traditional "love story" is Denis de Rougement, *L'Amour dans l'Occident,* trans. Montgomery Belgion, *Love in the Occident* (New York: Pantheon, 1956). C. S. Lewis articulates the courtly topoi in *The Allegory of Love,* chap. 1.

35. On the Baths of Venus at Baia, see Cassell and Kirkham, *Diana's Hunt,* 63 and 93n. Boccaccio, probably in imitation of Ovid, refers to them in his *Rime* as places of dangerous erotic activity motivated by Venus: "Se io temo di Baia e il cielo e il mare / . . . / havvi Vener sì piena licenza, / che spess'avvien che tal Lucrezia vienvi, / che torna Cleopatra allo suo ostello" [If I fear the sky and sea of Baia . . . Venus has such license there, that it often happens that a woman comes as Lucretia and returns home as Cleopatra] (55).

She belongs to the aristocracy, to royalty at that. Daughter of a king, Maria d'Angiò will emerge in her fuller identity as the *Filocolo* and later works unfold, as Maria-Fiammetta, Maria d'Aquino, and Lady Fiammetta of Sulmona. Beatrice appears to Dante at calendrical times and intervals of nine; he conceals his love with a "screen lady" espied in church. Boccaccio begins trembling for Maria in the Franciscan church of San Lorenzo at Naples, at mass on Holy Saturday under the sign of Aries, amid great rejoicing.

Avvenne che un giorno, la cui prima ora Saturno avea signoreggiata, essendo già Febo co' suoi cavalli al sedecimo grado del celestiale Montone pervenuto, e nel quale il glorioso partimento del figliuolo di Giove dagli spogliati regni di Plutone si celebrava, io, della presente opera componitore, mi ritrovai in un grazioso e bel tempio in Partenope, nominato da colui che per deificare sostenne che fosse fatto di lui sacrificio sopra la grata; e quivi con canto pieno di dolce melodia ascoltava l'uficio che in tale giorno si canta, celebrato da' sacerdoti successori di colui che prima la corda cinse umilemente essaltando la povertade e quella seguendo. Ove io dimorando, e già essendo, secondo che 'l mio intelletto estimava, la quarta ora del giorno sopra l'orientale orizonte passata, apparve agli occhi miei la mirabile bellezza della prescritta giovane

[One day, ruled by Saturn in the first hour, after Phoebus with his horses had already reached the sixteenth degree of the celestial Ram, when people celebrate Jove's son's glorious departure from the despoiled realms of Pluto, it came about that I, composer of the present work, found myself in a graceful and lovely temple in Parthenope, named after him who, to become deified, suffered himself to be sacrificed on the grate; and there I was listening to the office, a song filled with sweet melody as it is sung on that day, celebrated by sacerdotal successors of him who first humbly girded the rope, exalting and following poverty. Where, as I was dwelling, and when, according to my mental estimate, the fourth hour of the day had already passed over the eastern horizon, there appeared to my eyes the amazing beauty of the aforesaid young lady]. (*Filoc.* 1.1.17–18)

Boccaccio's first Tuscan prose is at once most precise and intriguingly elusive. Astrology indicates the position of the sun in the zodiac (sixteen days, or "degrees," into the sign of Aries), and it names the day of the week

(Saturday, sacred to Saturn, the planet that rules the first of its twenty-four hours). A solar circumlocution tells the time of day (it is the hour after the fourth—in other words, the fifth hour). Counting from an ideal dawn at 6:00 A.M., that puts it between 11:00 A.M. and noon. Why does Boccaccio choose this particular configuration? Well-taught in the science of the stars by his master Andalò del Negro, he presents a horoscope appropriate to the event.[36] The zodiacal year and the season of spring begin when the sun enters Aries, an archetypal sign of beginnings: Dante had begun his journey in the *Comedy* then, when the sun returns to its position in the Beginning of the universe; life is then renewed on earth; in this vernal season, new love matches are born. As for the day of the week, two points count. First, it is "Not-Friday"; it is not the day of the Crucifixion, which "gave the wound" and marked the onset of Petrarch's suffering for love of Laura.[37] Boccaccio's choice, distinct from but presumably related to

36. Boccaccio's keen interest in astrology, which he studied with the Genoese master Andalò del Negro, has been demonstrated most extensively by Quaglio in *Scienza e mito nel Boccaccio*. See also Janet Levarie Smarr, "Boccaccio and the Stars: Astrology in the *Teseida,*" *Traditio* 35 (1979): 303–32. Boccaccio explains how diurnal hours and planets are matched in his *Genealogie,* ed. Zaccaria, 1.34: "Sed cum longe alius sit ordo planetarum quam in nominibus dierum habeatur, est sciendum secundum planetarum ordinem successive unicuique diei hore dari dominium, et ab eo cui contingit prime hore diei dominium habere, ab eo dies illa denominata est, ut puta si diei dominice Veneri secundam horam tribues, que Soli immediate subiacet, et Mercurio terciam, qui subiacet Veneri, et Lune quartam, que subiacet Mercurio, quintam autem Saturno, ad quem convertendus est ordo cum in Luna defecerit, sextam Iovi, et sic de singulis XXIIII°ʳ horis diei dominice, sub nomine vel dominio Mercurii invenietur hora XXIIIIᵃ et XXVᵃ que prima est diei sequentis sub nomine vel dominio Lune." The passage is translated as follows in Victoria Kirkham, "'Chiuso parlare' in Boccaccio's *Teseida,*" in *The Sign of Reason,* 17–53, especially 31: "Since the order of the planets is quite different from that of the names of the days, it must be understood that the planets, according to their order, are given dominion successively over the hours of each day, and the one that has dominion over the first hour of the day is the one from which that day takes its name. So, for example, if you attribute the second hour of the day Sunday to Venus, which lies immediately below the Sun, and the third to Mercury, which lies below Venus, and the fourth to the Moon, which lies below Mercury; and the fifth to Saturn (to whom the order must revert because it runs out at the Moon), the sixth to Jove, and so on for each of the 24 hours of the day; the 24th hour of Sunday will appear under the name or dominion of Mercury, and the 25th, which is the first of the following day, will be under the dominion of the Moon."

37. Billanovich, *Restauri boccacceschi,* 88n, quotes Geoffrey of Vinsauf, *Poetria nova* (ca. 1200), 375–77: "Veneris lacrimosa dies . . . dedit vulnus." It occurs in an example of *amplificatio* under the heading of grief: "O tearful day of Venus! O bitter star! . . . That day inflicted the wound." See Margaret F. Nims, trans., *Poetria nova of Geoffrey of Vinsauf* (Toronto: Pontifical Institute of Mediaeval Studies, 1967), 29. The *Poetria nova* is listed in the "little library" of Santo Spirito, mostly comprised of Boccaccio's personal library, which he bequeathed to that Augustinian institution. See Ginetta Auzzas, "L'inventario della 'Parva libraria' di Santo Spirito e la biblioteca del Boccaccio," *Italia Medioevale e Humanistica* 9 (1966): 1–74.

Petrarch's, is antiphrastic. By the same rhetorical technique of antiphrasis, he denominates the woman he loves, she who is "Not-Eve," that is, not the mother of our race responsible for "opening the wound." Through Eve's counterpart, Maria, we were healed when the Redeemer arose and harrowed hell, a miracle commemorated at the Easter vigil, on Holy Saturday. In the second place, therefore, Boccaccio privileges "Saturn's day" not because of its saturnine connections in mythography but as a great celebration of Christian redemption, a Saturday mass that is the most joyful service of the liturgical year. Similarly, since the sun is no longer in the fourth hour, the meaningful solar time marker is "not-four," or, better, "just-after-four," that is, "five." Rather than 11:00 A.M., a likely enough hour to be in church, it is this 5 that matters in Boccaccio's rationale of numbers. We should not be surprised to see the poet's own lady turning up in the fifth hour, "on five." She is, after all, that same "sun" of his who falls "fifth" in the *ternario* and for whom he records the fifth anniversary of his love.

But whereas we can easily tell season, day, and hour, other temporal coordinates require decoding. Setting aside zodiacal reckoning and clicking into conventions of historical and legal mensuration, can we say what year it is? Can we discern the month? Should we understand it to be March or April, since Aries extends through both? Boccaccio scholars of generations past emptied endless brainloads of energy in efforts to find the answers. In his biographical study of 1910, Edward Hutton summed up the challenge of figuring exactly the date when Giovanni first caught sight of Fiammetta: "this is the most difficult question in all the difficult history of the youth of Boccaccio."[38] To complicate calculations, Boccaccio kept spinning off variant accounts of his love story in later Italian fictions. These included an alternate version of his enamorment, written into an episode of the *Ameto*. There Boccaccio's interior double, Caleon, who says he was born in France, tells the story of his love for King Robert's illegitimate (French) daughter, Fiammetta: it was six years plus sixteen months after he had moved as a boy from Florence to Naples and first saw her in a prophetic dream (35.100–103).

Perhaps Boccaccio does reveal the year he fell in love by inviting us to play one of his favorite clue games. The solution would depend on when he thought the sun entered Aries and on which year(s) during his Neapolitan

---

38. Edward Hutton, *Giovanni Boccaccio: A Biographical Study* (London: John Lane at the Bodley Head, 1910), 35. Hutton summarizes the state of the question on Boccaccio's enamorment in his appendix 1, 319–24.

sojourn Holy Saturday coincided with the sixteenth day following. Among the dates proposed have been March 30, 1331, assuming spring begins on March 14 (but that seems to put his arrival in Naples, during his "puerizia," at an unacceptably early date). Next, in chronological order, April 3, 1333, has been argued, based on the March 18 inception of spring; March 30, 1336, gauging spring from March 14; April 11, 1338, putting spring ahead to March 25; and April 7, 1341, after spring on March 14.[39] If you ask most critics today, all these conjectures simply confirm how futile the whole quest has been. Nevertheless, from the semihidden data implied in Boccaccio's combination of degrees in the Ram and day lorded by Saturn, we are entitled to decipher a day, a month, and a year. Most appealing of all the possibilities, I find, is April 3, 1333.

Starting with Boccaccio's first fiction, 3 is the number of Venus, goddess of the third planetary heaven, where love poets and their ladies gladly gather after death. What would be a better time, then, for Cupid's arrows to pierce Giovanni's heart than in the spring season, which Venus oversees, and on a date so maximally vibrant with her special symbolic number? No other admissible date produces such a delightful coincidence. During the decade between 1330 and 1340, the only year when Holy Saturday fell on the third day of April was 1333.[40]

In a calendar year with Holy Saturday on April 3, 1333, the sun would have entered Aries sixteen days before, on March 18. Among the possible options for the onset of spring, March 18 has unusually solid support. It was sanctioned by the Venerable Bede, as authoritative on the subject of chronology as was Isidore of Seville on lexicography. King Robert of

---

39. Another useful review of theories is in Francesco Torraca, *Per la biografia di Giovanni Boccaccio* (Milan: Società Editrice Dante Alighieri, 1912), 7–35. The date March 30, 1331, had proponents in Arnaldo Della Torre, *La giovinezza di Giovanni Boccaccio (1313–1341): Proposta di una nuova cronologia* (Città di Castello: S. Lapi, 1905), and Hutton, *Giovanni Boccaccio;* April 3, 1333, in Francesco Torraca, op. cit. (Quaglio singles out Torraca for citations in his commentary in his 1967 edition of the *Filocolo*), and Ettore De Ferri, *Il Filocolo,* introd.; March 27, 1334, in Marcus Landau, *Giovanni Boccaccio: Sua vita e sua opere,* trans. Camillo Antona-Traversi (Naples: Dalla Stamperia del Vaglio, 1881); 30 March, 1336, in Henri Hauvette, *Etudes sur Boccace (1894–1916)* (Turin: Bottega d'Erasmo, 1968), 87–146; 1 April, 1338, in Vincenzo Crescini, *Contributo agli studi sul Boccaccio* (Turin: Loescher, 1887); 7 April, 1341, in Francesco De Sanctis, "Il Boccaccio e le sue opere minori," *Nuova antologia* 14 (1870): 221–52, and Francesco Corazzini, *Le lettere edite e inedite,* xx. Boccaccio says he arrived in Naples in his "puerizia" (*Ameto* 35.99).

40. See Christopher R. Cheney, ed. *Handbook of Dates for Students of English History* (London: Offices of the Royal Historical Society, 1945). For connections between 3 and Venus in Boccaccio's first fiction, see Cassell and Kirkham, *Diana's Hunt,* 25–27; for such connections in the *Amorosa visione,* see Kirkham, *The Sign of Reason,* 105–9.

Anjou cited Bede in his sermons, and Boccaccio refers to him in his *Genealogia*. Villani's *Cronica* accepts the March 18 spring, as do Brunetto Latini and at least two of Dante's early commentaries, the *Ottimo commento* and *Anonimo fiorentino*. Francesco Torraca, Boccaccio's turn-of-the-century biographer and builder of this argument, reconstructs the sequence: assuming the sun enters Aries on March 18, Boccaccio would have arrived in Naples in December, 1325, when he was twelve and one-half years old, seven years and four months before he met Maria. Impeccable in his arithmetic, Torraca missteps when it comes to symbols. Boccaccio devised this scheme not as a problem in math but as a pastime in *arithmosophia*. Let us then rephrase the story: Boccaccio arrived in Naples in his thirteenth year, when he "previewed" Fiammetta in a dream, six years and sixteen months (eighty-eight months all told) before he turned eighteen in a spring that began on March 18 and that saw him fall in love with her on the date of April 3, 1333.[41]

At issue here is an ideal timetable that Boccaccio embellishes with variations each time he rewrites the story. The frame tale of the *Filocolo* communicates the day, month, and year when he fell in love; one of the narratives in the *Ameto* then expands the story by filling in background. In much the same way, medieval cycles of epic poetry grew not only with continuations in the form of sequels but also with new material that explained antecedent events, such prequels as a hero's family history. (The tale of Florio and Biancifiore itself falls into this category, since they belong to the genealogy of Charlemagne.) While Boccaccio's chronology of Fiammetta may be fairly close to true dates in his real history, we cannot take it literally as reliable testimony.

To begin with, the numbers in question have a calculated, interlocking design. The 3 in the key date April 3, 1333 is an aliquot part, or factor, of both 6 and 18: $6 = 3 \times 2$ or $3 + 3$; $18 = 3 \times 6$, or three 3s twice $[3 + 3 + 3] + [3 + 3 + 3]$. The numbers 18 and 88 are numerological variants of 8. So the whole numeric cluster (3, 13, 6, 60, 18, 88) can be reduced to 3 and 8.[42]

41. Torraca, *Per la biografia di Giovanni Boccaccio*, 7–35. Boccaccio refers to Bede's *De temporum ratione* in *Genealogie* 2.4: "eo in eo quem De temporibus scripsit," and again at 6.24. See Attilio Hortis, *Studj sulle opere latine del Boccaccio con particolare riguardo alla storia della erudizione nel Medio Evo e alle letterature straniere* (Trieste: Libreria Julius Dase Editrice, 1879), 484.

42. Similar examples of how Boccaccio uses numbers and their numerological variants are discussed in Kirkham, "Amorous Vision, Scholastic Vistas," in *The Sign of Reason*, 105–9. Needless to say, Torraca believed that he was reconstructing a chronology that was historical, not poetical. We do not know the year that Boccaccio really reached Naples. Branca conjectures 1327 in *Profilo biografico*, 12–15.

Further, the make-believe dating and setting of Boccaccio's enamorment follow a literary model, Dante's love story in the *Vita nuova*. According to what Boccaccio says in the *Ameto*, he has a first view of Fiammetta in boyhood, and next he sees her at eighteen, the same age Dante was when he had his second encounter with Beatrice. In the *Vita nuova*, Dante does not reveal what year in the Christian calendar he fell in love, since the events in his narrative date not "from Christ" but "from Beatrice." The only date in the story, its chronological fulcrum, is the year of her death, 1290. Boccaccio, a storyteller fond of realistic detail, rectifies the omission with reversed information in the *Filocolo*, anchoring the birth of his love to the season of Venus in a particular chronological year, 1333. The multiple 3s in this date connect it to Dante's explanation of 9's affinity for Beatrice. That beatific lady, a "miracle," found close company throughout the *Vita nuova* in the number whose root was 3, sign of the miraculous Trinity. Rephrasing, we could say that Boccaccio pulls his life fiction into alignment with Dante's. They are parallel lives. In much the same way, his *Trattatello in laude di Dante* had (re)composed Alighieri's biography, to accentuate its amazing similarities with the vita of Virgil.[43]

Usually, when Boccaccio's fiction refers to numbers, openly ("quinta è il tuo sole") or obliquely ("the fourth hour of the day had already passed"), that means we must adjust them to a symbolic value. So when he says in *Ameto* 35 that "six suns" and "sixteen moons" had elapsed from his prophetic dream of Fiammetta until he loved her in San Lorenzo, it will not do to restate that as "seven years and four months," as used to be the critics' wont. It is a time reference like "11:00 A.M. on Holy Saturday," realistic but irrelevant. Whoever transposes "6 + 16" to "7 + 4" strips Boccaccio's figures of their figurative sense, which is the sense that most matters. With "six suns" and "sixteen moons" the poet has the rhetorical delight of counting both in solar and lunar units, and he underlines the day-night symmetry with variations on a number that is a multiple of 3. Otherwise combined, his "six" and "sixteen" produce a total of eighty-eight months.

Boccaccio's age of eighteen at his enamorment, which has a significant point of contact with Dante's chronology in the *Vita nuova*, reiterates the March 18 onset of spring and is related symbolically to the lover's waiting

---

43. Dante explains why Beatrice is a 9 in *Vita nuova* 29. In *Diana's Hunt*, the Mystery Lady is the thirty-third huntress, and as number 33 on the list she is a sister to Beatrice (3 x 3 = 9). See Cassell and Kirkham, *Diana's Hunt*, 23–27. Ideal analogies in two poetic biographies are discussed in Victoria Kirkham, "The Parallel Lives of Dante and Virgil," *Dante Studies* 110 (1992): 233–53.

period (after the presage in his thirteenth year) of eighty-eight months. The digit 8, one beyond 7 in the seven-day week of Creation, had strong and positive meanings. It marked a new cycle outside of earthly time—hence rebirth, baptism, and eternal life. Boccaccio understood the possibilities of the number. Thus when Arcita dies in the *Teseida,* the Theban knight's ghost ascends to the eighth heaven (11.1–3), a height that opens a spiritual retrospective on the vanities of our puny earth, much as it had for Dante (*Par.* 22.133–55) and Scipio Africanus before him. The *Filocolo,* plotted to carry its pagan protagonist toward conversion, is paced so that Florio's baptism, with the pope officiating, occurs in a chapter of the last book tagged with the number "8."[44] Not implausibly, then, the 8s implicit in his love schedule could herald Boccaccio's own "new life" with Fiammetta and imply her salvific, redemptive power.

The numeric sequence in the year 1333, a ready-made symbol hard to resist, would later be seized on by Petrarch for an amorous nexus in his *Familiares* 4.1. That famous letter to his father confessor, Dionigi da Borgo San Sepolcro, carries a date of May, 1336. It is apocryphal. Evidence both internal and external betrays a much later period of composition, 1352–53. Petrarch, we comprehend, situates his ascent of Mont Ventoux in a time frame on which he can capitalize allegorically. One part of his strategy is an *imitatio Christi.* A factitious date of 1336 puts him still only in his thirty-second year (he was born in July, 1304), implying that he falls short of Christian maturity, defined by the perfect age of thirty-three at which Christ was crucified. Petrarch also measures his moral insufficiency against Saint Augustine, whose conversion from an oracular book comes when he is just one year older than Petrarch would be the day he opened the *Confessions* atop Mount Ventoux. But Cupid, as well as Christ, figures in the mountain climber's calculations. While the poet meditates on his troubled situation, he realizes that three years have passed since one part of him began combating his fleshly desires for a lady unnamed (whom we recognize as Laura): "The third year has not yet passed since that perverse and worthless inclination, which held sway over me and ruled over my heart without opponent, began to be replaced by another inclination which was rebellious and reluctant. Between these inclinations a very insistent and uncertain battle for control of my two

---

44. See below, chap. 6; Victoria Kirkham, "Painters at Play on the Judgment Day (*Decameron* VIII,9)," in *The Sign of Reason,* 215–35 (first published in *Studi sul Boccaccio* 14 (1983–84): 256–77. The number 88 seems to be significant for Boccaccio, since he chose that sum as the regular number of verses per canto for his *Amorosa visione.*

selves has been going on for a long time in my mind." If the composer of the *Filocolo* fell *in* love in 1333, Petrarch dates to that year the beginning of his cure, when he starts falling *out of* love. So, at least, he would have us believe from a fictive chronology of his spiritual progress. What matters is not the date of 1336 in itself but another hidden number that is contingent on it, 33: *in saeculo* Petrarch has been resisting love since 1333, as he distances himself from that amorous juncture; *in spiritu* he has not yet arrived at the maturity of Christ in his final year, the age of thirty-three. Much like the protagonist of the *Rime sparse,* he presents himself between two poles on a moral path, still *in via,* still struggling toward the better life.[45]

Like Boccaccio, Petrarch alludes to 1333 as a number encoded with the power of Venus, goddess of the third planetary heaven. Her astrological address was public information, prominent in a canto beginning in the *Paradiso* that coincides with Dante's arrival at "la bella Ciprigna . . . volta nel terzo epiciclo" [the fair Cyprian, wheeling in the third epicycle] (*Par.* 8.2–3). Steeped in that amorous atmosphere, the pilgrim will meet one of his Italian precursors in the business of making love verse, the Genoese known as Foulquet de Marselha. When Petrarch confesses to a mind-battle ongoing for three years since 1333, he harks back as well to an earlier verse by Dante, also in high relief, "Voi che 'ntendendo il terzo ciel movete" [You who with understanding move the third heaven]. The incipit of the first canzone of the *Convivio,* it sets precedent for a mental struggle between two contending forces—one amorous and one more rational. Dante's commentary on the canzone enumerates the heavens with their resident deities and explains that Venus dwells in the third: "terzo è quello dove' è Venere." From that elevation, the goddess several times enters Petrarch's *Rime sparse,* at first as an enemy agent, but later in friendlier guise. In his sestina 142, her rays threaten to sear the young man, who must run for cover under a laurel : "A la dolce ombra de le belle frondi /

<hr>

45. Francesco Petrarca, *Epistole,* ed. Ugo Dotti (Turin: Unione Tipografico-Editrice Torinese, 1978), 4.1 (p. 128): "Nondum michi tertius annus effluxit, ex quo voluntas illa perversa et nequam, que me totum habebat et in aula cordis mei sola sine contradictore regnabat, cepit aliam habere rebellem et reluctantem sibi, inter quas iandudum in campis cogitationum mearum de utriusque hominis imperio laboriosissima et anceps etiam nunc pugna conseritur"; Francesco Petrarca, *Rerum familiarium libri I–VIII,* trans. Aldo S. Bernardo (Albany: State University of New York Press, 1975), 177. Giuseppe Billanovich has demonstrated that the 1336 date cannot be the real date in "Petrarca e il Ventoso," *Italia Medievale e Umanistica* 9 (1966): 389–401. Petrarch vis-à-vis Saint Augustine at the time of his conversion (*Confessions* 8.12) is an intertextual problem probed by Robert Durling in "The Ascent of Mt. Ventoux and the Crisis of Allegory," *Italian Quarterly* 18, no. 69 (summer, 1974): 7–28.

corsi fuggendo un dispietato lume / che 'n fin qua giù m'ardea dal terzo cielo" [To the sweet shade of those beautiful leaves I ran, fleeing a pitiless light that was burning down upon me from the third heaven]. Years afterward and when Laura is dead, a now aging lover turns upward in thought to the same place. He commemorates Sennuccio del Bene among the dear departed, directing his message to that circle of heaven whose status as a last home for love poets had been established ever since Dante's meeting there with the troubadour Foulquet. Petrarch's sonnet 287 describes Sennuccio's company as a "schiera," the same word Dante had used at *Inferno* 5.85 for Dido's flock ("la schiera ov' è Dido"): "ben ti prego che 'n la terza spera / Guitton saluti, et messer Cino, et Dante, / Franceschin nostro et tutta quella schiera" [I beg you to salute all in the third sphere: Guittone and messer Cino and Dante, our Franceschino, and all that band]. It is this sonnet of poetic fellowship that Boccaccio will cite in a final rhyme when he addresses Petrarch, only lately arisen to repose with Sennuccio, Cino, and Dante, "Or sei salito, caro signor mio."[46]

Perhaps it is only coincidence that like Boccaccio in the *Filocolo,* Petrarch, at *Familiares* 4.1, alludes to 1333 as a love year, mutatis mutandis. On a more important parallel of chronology, however, it is hard to suppose that their work could be unrelated. One man falls in love on Holy Saturday; the other's schedule of anniversaries dates from Holy Friday and April 6, 1327. Of these two myths, each connected to Easter weekend in the liturgy, which came first? Scholars tend, I think, to assume that the dominant author in that literary friendship was always Petrarch, who announces Good Friday as the fateful day he first saw Laura in *Rime sparse* 3.

> Era il giorno ch'al sol si scoloraro
> per la pietà del suo fattore i rai
> quando i' fui preso. . . .
> . . . onde i miei guai
> nel commune dolor s'incominciaro.

---

46. On the Italian Peninsula, from Dante onward, the "third heaven" is part of a vernacular love poet's stock in trade. See Dante Alighieri, *Convivio,* ed. G. Busnelli and G. Vandelli, rev. Antonio Enzo Quaglio (Florence: Le Monnier, 1968), 2.2.2–4. Petrarch elsewhere speaks of the third heaven. For example, *Rime sparse* 31 refers to Venus as "terzo lume"; in 177 Cupid gives his followers wings so they can fly to the "terzo ciel."

[It was the day when the sun's rays turned pale with grief for his Maker when I was taken. . . . and so my misfortunes began in the midst of the universal woe].

Nevertheless, in what Branca has called their "game of mirrors," influence often flowed the other way. Here evidence gives priority to Boccaccio, whose joyful Saturday surely conditioned Petrarch's injurious Friday.[47]

Branca tentatively dates the conception of Boccaccio's *Filocolo* to 1336. Bidding his book farewell (*Filoc.* 5.97), the young student of canon law speaks of a project that occupied him during "several years" [più anni], probably until 1338 or 1339. We are informed by Wilkins that Petrarch had begun composing lyrics by 1327 and did occasionally send them to other poets. One of these correspondents could have channeled them to Boccaccio, the poet-jurist Cino da Pistoia, who professed civil law at the University of Naples from 1330 to 1332. A stanza of the *Filostrato,* composed before the *Filocolo* (1335?), incorporates one of Cino's sonnets, verses that Branca believes could only have come into Giovanni's possession through direct contact with the admired senior poet, a personal friend of Dante's. Petrarch's early canzone 23, "Nel dolce tempo della prima etade" (In the sweet time of my first age), seems to hark back to Boccaccio's first fiction, *Caccia di Diana* (1333–34?), which begins, "Nel tempo adorno . . ." Both are allegories of young love; both present a narrator who has been transformed into a stag. Similarities reverberate more diffusely between the same canzone and Boccaccio's *Filostrato,* but as Marco Santagata has persuasively reasoned, in that case Boccaccio, not Petrarch, is the prior author. Data still being accumulated indicate that as of the mid-1330s, Boccaccio's acquaintance with Petrarch's lyrics was still minimal and could not have included the crucial prologue sonnets of the *Canzoniere* (1–5), composed long after the fictional date of Petrarch's enamorment, in the decade between 1340 and 1350. In fact, the key sonnet that tells how Petrarch first saw Laura on Holy Friday, *Rime sparse* 3, must have been written as late as sometime after 1348.[48]

---

47. The complex and uncertain relationship between the two poets—their "game of mirrors"—is the subject of Vittore Branca's "Implicazioni espressivi, temi e stilemi fra Petrarca e Boccaccio," in *Boccaccio medievale,* 300–32.

48. Branca dates the *Filocolo* to 1336–38 in his *Profilo biografico,* 44; so also does Quaglio in his introduction to his edition of the *Filocolo,* 47. Carlo Muscetta's chronology of Boccaccio's life, in *Boccaccio,* 2d ed. (Bari: Laterza, 1974), 3, gives the years 1336–39. Contacts between Boccaccio and Cino are documented by Vittore Branca and Pier Giorgio Ricci in "Notizie e documenti per la biografia del Boccaccio," pt. 4, "L'incontro napoletano con Cino

Outside his poetry, the first word we have from Boccaccio concerning his awareness of Petrarch comes from the summer of 1339, from a rhetorical Latin epistle with the salutation "Mavortis milex extrenue" [Worthy Soldier of Mars]. Structured by the trope of antithesis, this exercise piles hyperbolic adulation on its unnamed recipient and diminishes the sender's worth to an abject level of clumsy nonentity. Boccaccio's copybook missive hints that the poet to whom he pays tribute has a reputation for vernacular lyrics. The narrator—and we should call him a narrator, since Boccaccio is really spinning a tale, not drafting a letter—says that when the blows of Fortune had clobbered him into complete misery after a disastrous love affair, a friend appeared and told him how he could end his unhappiness by reading the "copious words" of a new author. The anonymous friend goes on to describes this author.

I met him at Avignon in the bosom of the Muses, trained by the hand of Jove, tutored by philosophical milk, and tonicized by divine sciences, and there, as if he were a disciple of the Chosen Vessel, once rapt up to the third heaven, he openly preaches to everyone things recondite and arcane. He is the same man whom winged Fame announces by word of her spokesmen; fair manners adorn him, and virtues surround him.

Under all the rampant metaphors and an irritatingly dense layer of literary allusions, what Boccaccio seems to be saying is that someone has told him

da Pistoia," *Studi sul Boccaccio* 5 (1968): 1–18. For the dating and diffusion of Petrarch's lyrics, see Ernest Hatch Wilkins, "Petrarch's First Collection of his *Rime*," "The Circulation of Petrarch's *Rime* during His Lifetime," "Notes on Certain Poems," and "A Chronological Conspectus of the Writings of Petrarch," in *The Making of the Canzoniere and Other Petrarchan Studies* (Rome: Edizioni di Storia e Letteratura, 1951), 81–92, 287–93, 300–301, and 348–58, respectively. Cassell and Kirkham note the apparent connection between *Caccia di Diana* 1.1 and *Canzoniere* 23, in *Diana's Hunt*, 153–54. See Marco Santagata, *Per moderne carte: La biblioteca volgare di Petrarca* (Bologna: Il Mulino, 1990), 166n, 250–58. Wilkins argued that two other poems by Petrarch (61 and 112) unquestionably influenced the *Filostrato*, but that dependency was challenged by Silber (*The Influence of Dante and Petrarch*, 25–26). The parallel verses could simply be independent examples of widespread motifs as old as Ovid. Going by the "chronological conspectus" that Wilkins charted for Petrarch's writings, a total of seventy-nine poems date from the decade 1326–36. The American scholar further dates Petrarch's first lyric anthology to 1336–38, which makes it exactly contemporary with Boccaccio's composition of the *Filocolo*. Yet even if Boccaccio could have seen it, which seems most unlikely, that collection does not contain the foundation sonnets about the poet's enamorment (*Rime sparse* 2 and 3), categorized by Wilkins among verses not datable to any specific period during the making of the *Canzoniere*, and dated by Santagata to after 1348. In fact, none of the poems that Wilkins assigns to the first decade of Petrarch's creative activity, including the canzone of metamorphoses, make it obvious that the protagonist of the *Rime sparse* fell in love on April 6 and Holy Friday.

about Petrarch and that he is excited by the knowledge. He seems not to have much specific information, since his praise is so formulaic: the subject is a poet; he is learned, courteous, and virtuous. Why does Boccaccio liken him to Saint Paul, the Chosen Vessel? A strange detail in an otherwise generic portrait, the source is 2 Corinthians 12:2: "I know a man in Christ who . . . was caught up to the third heaven—whether in the body or out of the body I do not know, God knows—and he heard things that cannot be told, which man may not utter." Petrarch's Tuscan compatriot, far away in Naples, must be identifying him not literally with a biblical third heaven but allegorically with that other third heaven where Venus dwells and where love poets congregate, at least in spirit.

For explicit declarations from Boccaccio concerning Petrarch's love story we must wait until the next decade. They appear toward the end of his *De vita et moribus Domini Francisci Petracchi de Florentia* (Concerning the life and manners of Lord Francis Petrarch of Florence), composed after he had learned of the Aretine's coronation in Rome but before the two men had met (1341–42? 1348–49?). Acknowledging that Petrarch was tormented by the pull of the flesh, the laudatory biographer exempts him from any weakness on that score with respect to Laura, whom he takes as an allegory for the laurel crown ("Laurettam illam allegorice pro laurea corona . . . accipiendam existimo"). Although Boccaccio met Petrarch briefly in Florence in 1350, his first real visit with the great expatriate took place in Padua in March, 1351, when he traveled as an ambassador on behalf of his city with an invitation for Petrarch to return as a citizen and professor at their new university. During this fertile encounter, they surely discussed informally their vernacular love stories, alongside such venerated Latin classics as Cicero's *Letters to Atticus,* recently rediscovered by Petrarch.[49]

Did the *Filocolo* at some point intersect with the sonnet sequence of the *Canzoniere*? If so, when and how? Negative parallels liken the two stories, which are analogous yet disjunctive. Both begin in a Franciscan religious

---

49. Boccaccio *Epistolae* 2.9: "Avinioni Musarum alvo iuvenem Iovis manibus alupnatum, lacte phylosophyco educatum, ac divinis scientiis roboratum cognovi, ibique velud discipulus sacri Vasis iam rapti ad tertium celum gloriosum, in aperto abscondita predicat et archana. Ipse enim est quem fama pennata gerulonum ore notificat, exornant mores et virtutes quempiam circumspectant." Renata Fabbri has edited the text of Boccaccio's *De vita et moribus Domini Francisci Petracchi de Florentia secundum Iohannem Bochacii de Certaldo,* with introduction, in Giovanni Boccaccio, *Tutte le opere,* vol. 5, pt. 1 (Milan: Mondadori, 1992), 881–88, 898–911. For the passage with Boccaccio's opinion that Laura is allegorically the laurel, see pp. 988–89. Branca discusses Boccaccio's 1351 trip to Petrarch in Padua in his *Profilo biografico,* 87–89.

establishment in the culminating days of Paschaltide, and each man is
unprepared for Cupid's sudden attack. But while for Petrarch the lady
announces soul-searching pain and guilt, for Boccaccio her advent is a
wondrous epiphany. Although he is shaken emotionally by the experience,
she comes into his life with all the hopeful promise of the Resurrection. In
fact, he thanks the worthy lord Love for setting before his eyes his "beatitude" ("Valoroso signore . . . io ti ringrazio, però che tu hai dinanzi agli
occhi miei posta la mia beatitudine" [*Filoc.* 1.1.20]). Laura is, true enough,
capable of harboring fire, but it smolders in her only exceptionally, as happens in the metrically atypical ballad (55): "Quel foco ch' i' pensai che
fosse spento / dal freddo tempo et da l'età men fresca / fiamma et martir ne
l'anima rinfresca" [That fire, which I thought had gone out because of the
cold season and my age no longer fresh, now renews flames and suffering
in my soul]. By nature elusive and cold, she descends from a mythological
forerunner, Daphne, the nymph vowed to chastity who took root as a tree.
Allegorically, so Boccaccio saw her, she is the laurel of poetic success.
Fiammetta's names, in contrast, mark her as a warm, nurturing creature.
Whereas Laura will never speak to Petrarch in any "real" conversation,
Fiammetta readily chats with her poet from their second meeting, when
she asks him to write the *Filocolo.* Her roots are in present political reali-
ties, for she is related to a specific court and its dynasty, a family closely
affiliated with the Franciscans. She signifies less fame than patronage for
her poet.

If we turn from motifs to style, we notice that Boccaccio's encounter
with Fiammetta—down to her names—owes much to Dante's *Vita nuova*
and *Comedy,* but it does not resonate Petrarchan. The composer of the
Filocolo sees his "beatitude," suffers much the same physiological effects
as Dante, and, like Dante in *Vita nuova* 2, deals with it by engaging in an
inner dialogue (although not with a Latin speaker). Later, Fiammetta asks
her poet to rescue the story of Florio and Biancifiore from the "fabulosi
parlari degli ignoranti" [fanciful parlance of the ignorant], a phrase that
repeats the end of *Vita nuova* 2, where Dante's narrative advances from
boyhood to events nine years after his enamorment, "però che soprastare
a le passioni e atti di tanta gioventudine pare alcuno parlar fabuloso"
[because to dwell on the passions and actions of such youth seems a sort of
fanciful parlance]. Examples could be multiplied of the Dantesque language lying thick in *Filocolo* 1.1. Even the church setting, which to be sure
has a parallel in Petrarch, conflates *Vita nuova* 2 with 5, the episode that
explains how Dante acquired a "screen lady" because she sat in his line of

vision while, during a Marian Mass, he gazed on his "most gentle one." At a linguistic level, the entire scene of Fiammetta's first impact on Boccaccio can be explained without any recourse whatsoever to Petrarch. Most striking about Boccaccio's meeting with Fiammetta—its setting and her naming—is how heavily he imbued the occasion with Dante's vocabulary of love for Beatrice and Mary. He composes his scene as a literary *contaminatio* that appropriates language and imagery running from the opening chapters of the *Vita nuova* to the final cantos of *Paradiso*.

Around 1336, when he began composing the *Filocolo,* Boccaccio had seen little of Petrarch's lyric output, perhaps only a handful of fragments. He could not possibly have known the timetable by which Laura was supposed to have captivated her lover, because Petrarch did not invent it until the 1340s. Not until after 1348 did Petrarch write the sonnet "Era il giorno ch'al sol si scoloraro" (It was the day when the sun's rays turned pale), which announces that he was "captured" on the day of the Crucifixion. But if Boccaccio was ignorant of a laurel romance yet to be plotted when Fiammetta was born, the reverse was not true when Petrarch scheduled his passion in synchrony with the Crucifixion. In 1341 he had gone to Naples to be examined and certified fit for his laureation by King Robert. That trip was just a few months after Boccaccio had left the city and returned to his native Tuscany. The time and place were right for Petrarch to encounter Boccaccio, not in person—that would have to wait another decade—but as an impressive new literary presence who had begun writing in Naples in a Tuscan voice. Santagata argues the scenario persuasively: "Boccaccio had been one of the animators of cultural and social life in that city; he had only very recently left it; he was Petrarch's compatriot and admirer; he was a friend and disciple of friends and teachers of Petrarch: in sum, it seems to me that we have all the elements for thinking that someone laid Boccaccio's writings before the eyes of the poet who was about to be laureated."[50] Parallel motifs, positive and negative, between Boccaccio's ideal love story and Petrarch's can be explained by Petrarch's acquaintance with the *Filocolo* and his programmatic borrowings from

---

50. Santagata, *Per moderne carte,* 269. Vittore Branca has found it prudent to approach the relationship between Boccaccio and Petrarch not in terms of demonstrable "influence and dependence" but as a "convergence" of shared "tastes and sensitivities." See his essay "Implicazioni espressivi, temi e stilemi fra Petrarca e Boccaccio," 305. Luigi Sasso, who briefly discusses the *senhal* "Fiammetta" in "L'*interpretatio nominis* in Boccaccio," *Studi sul Boccaccio* 12 (1980): 129–74, takes it for granted—wrongly, it would now seem—that Boccaccio's Fiammetta is inspired by Petrarch's Laura, even though he rightly saw the connections between Boccaccio's love lyrics and Dante's praise of Beatrice in the *Vita nuova.*

that love story. Its tie to the liturgy was the fantasy of a poet enrolled as a university student in a canon-law curriculum.

In surpassment of Dante, Boccaccio elevates his lady's social rank, designates her natal city, and manifolds her names: she becomes Princess Maria-Fiammetta d'Angiò d'Aquino da Sulmona. Each element of her name has emblematic import, and each serves the larger narrative motifs of the fiction for which it was invented. As an Anjou in the *Filocolo,* Maria represents the Angevins, allies of the Catholic Church, and their political claims on the former Ghibelline territory of the Italian Peninsula. Her associations with Dante's oriflamme—metaphorically Mary, Queen of Heaven—now assume their fuller resonance in that battle standard of French monarchs to whose genealogical line King Robert of Anjou belongs. Associated with combustion sparked by Venus and burning arrows shot by Cupid, Fiammetta evolves from earlier females in Boccaccio's fiction whose generic attributes were fire and light.[51] But as a "flamelet"—rather than a raging inferno—she is Venus ("foco d'amor") tempered by Diana, the goddess of chastity whose fire burns "cold" (*Filoc.* 2.1 and 2.4). In other words, her love is chaste and virtuous. When Giovanni meets her, it is Easter Saturday in the church named for a saint martyred by fire. Mass that day would have begun in darkness, broken by the lighting of the paschal candle, from which each member of the congregation would have lit a taper of his own until the whole church glowed with light from the spreading flame. In this setting, as Janet Smarr writes, the "narrator is set on fire like a candle from the luminous Fiammetta."[52] Eastertide, from Ash Wednesday through the forty days of Lent, ends fifty days after Paschday with Pentecost, another feast of fire. Pentecost, the liturgical holiday central to the allegory of the main story in the *Filocolo,* celebrates the inception of the universal Church, with the descent of the Holy Ghost onto the twelve Apostles in tonguelets of flame. As the *Filocolo* opens, the "composer" communicates his lady's unspoken name, "Maria," with reference to verses at the close of Dante's *Paradiso,* and both passages allude to an *Ave-Eva* palindrome. Since King Robert gave his girl-child "the name of the woman who contained in herself *redemption*" (*Filoc* 1.1), her attribute, chiefly, is "salvation from sin." She commissions Boccaccio to write the book about Florio and Biancifiore's great

---

51. Cf. *Caccia di Diana* 4.11–12, 13.26–30.
52. Smarr, *Boccaccio and Fiammetta,* 50–51.

personal love in a church named for the archangel Gabriel, a setting that frames her as "Mary Annunciate" and rightly so in the *Filocolo*, a romance that announces the coming of Christianity in western Europe. This is a "Maria" not born to the stage of history but fleshed to dwell in the folios of Boccaccio's first prose fiction.[53]

"Fiammetta" and "Maria" dovetail in their likeness to the "morning star." That image comes to Filocolo's mind the moment he catches sight of Caleon's Fiammetta, a beauty who resembles his missing Biancifiore: "he saw her eyes filled with fiery rays scintillant like the morning star [come matutina stella]." Stock rhymes had already prompted another of Boccaccio's amorous characters to the same comparison, namely, Troiolo, who yearned for his departed Criseida: "O luce bella, o stella mattutina" (*Filost.* 5.44). Formulaic simplicity typical of oral narrative rings in the Trojan knight's melancholy sighs. But when "stella mattutina" gravitates into Fiammetta's field of attraction for the more learned *Filocolo*, Boccaccio surely takes the simile on written authority. Twice it appears in the *Divine Comedy*, once as we glimpse the face of the angel of Purgatory, and again as Dante calls our attention to that comely saint who presents him the Queen of Heaven. Bernard "abbelliva di Maria, / come del sole stella mattutina" [drew beauty from Mary, as the morning star from the sun] (*Par.* 32.107–8).[54] The morning star, which for Dante conveys the glow of divine love, has in astrology a proper name, Lucifer, literally "Light-bearer." Actually Lucifer is not a star but the planet Venus when she appears in the sky at dawn. After Dante disembarked Easter morning on the shores of Purgatory, that astral deity was the first light in the vault of heaven to reassure him.

---

53. Billanovich, *Restauri boccacceschi,* 83: "[Fiammetta] non fu creatura che quaggiù soffrisse e facesse soffrire; ma va solo recercata tra chi per pura grazia dei carmi convive in società cogli spiriti che 'intendendo' muovono il terzo cielo" [[Fiammetta] was no mortal woman who suffered and caused suffering down here; we should look for her in the company of those who by the grace of poetry dwell together with those spirits whose "understanding" moves the third heaven]. Billanovich suggests (89) that her name becomes *Maria* "per la semplicità grande e la tanto usuale frequenza in testi religiosi (più ancora che 'Eva' o 'Adam') e amorosi" [for its great simplicity and such frequent use in religious and amorous texts (even more than *Eve* or *Adam*)].

54. The text cited is *Filostrato,* ed. Vittore Branca, in Giovanni Boccaccio, *Tutte le opere,* vol. 2 (Milan: Mondadori, 1964). Cf. *Purg.* 12.88–90: "la creatura bella, / biancovestito e ne la faccia quale / par tremolando mattutina stella" [the fair creature . . . clothed in white and such in his face as seems the tremulous morning star].

> Lo bel pianeto che d'amar conforta
> faceva tutto rider l'orïente,

[The fair planet that prompts to love was making the whole East smile]. (*Purg.* 1.20–21)

She will again shine benevolently on another dawn, just before Dante passes through the wall of passion fires on the seventh terrace of Purgatory. By the end of the *Comedy,* dawn and Maria have become one. When Dante raises his eyes to the Virgin in the Rose, she appears as a Christlike sun bursting over the horizon. "Dawn of the world" [aurora mundi] Benvenuto had called her.

As it happens, the Italian words *stella mattutina* reproduce a Latin epithet familiar from the Bible. Both Job and the Book of Revelation speak of the matutinal star. Because it is visible at daybreak as night dissipates, commentators understood an analogy between the rising sun of Christ and this bright celestial body, which they invested with the meaning of "redemption." The standard medieval gloss on the Book of Job, Gregory the Great's *Moralia,* affirms that the beleaguered prophet should have not been ungrateful for his ghastly suffering. Gregory argues that, the object of a contest between God and the devil, Job lived a life like night, lit by the Old Testament stars, until there arose "the bright morning star," which signifies the Redeemer, herald of the eternal morning.[55] An exegesis on the Apocalypse attributed to Augustine concurs, glossing "stellam matutinam" as "resurrection, which comes because of baptism." The morning star "flees the night and announces the light"; that is, "it takes away sin and bestows grace."[56]

Although Fiammetta's meanings can shift with context—in the *Ameto* she personifies Hope, whereas in the *Decameron* she resonates as Temperance[57]—in the *Filocolo* she is both an agent of Venus and a flame of Char-

---

55. Cf. Job 3:9 and 38:7 and Gregory the Great, *Morals on the Book of Job,* trans. J. Bliss, Library of the Fathers of the Holy Catholic Church Anterior to the Division of East and West, vols. 18, 21, 23, 31 (Oxford: John Henry Parker, 1844–50), vol. 1, pt. 1, 212–13; and vol. 3, pt. 6, 288–89.

56. Cf. Rev. 2:28 and Pseudo-Augustine, *Expositio in Apocalypsim B. Joannis, Patrologia latina* 35:2419.

57. Fiammetta is identified as Temperance in Victoria Kirkham, "An Allegorically Tempered *Decameron,*" in *The Sign of Reason,* 131–71. Smarr, in *Boccaccio and Fiammetta,* perceptively reconstructs multiple Fiammettas, citing many additional Marian attributes in her *Filocolo* appearance.

ity. Romantic readings of Boccaccio's early fiction emphasized her secular identity. But her ethical nature and sacred connections, lifting her above received conventional imagery of courtly love, are more powerful. Connected with the Virgin at the Annunciation and the Queen of Heaven, with the Resurrection, Easter, and Pentecost, she is love, purity, humility, the Good News, faith triumphant, and a female counterpart to Christ. In a word, Giovanni's Maria-Fiammetta means "Redeemer."

Her surname "d'Aquino" is a later acquisition. Boccaccio bestows it—while refusing to speak it—in the *Ameto* (35.31) and *Amorosa visione* (43.46–48). In the *Ameto,* Fiammetta claims as her forebear a soldier who was lord of "Juvenal's ancient citadel." We must supply the toponymic, *Aquino,* omitted so that we can have the fun of a riddle and so that Boccaccio can doff his cap to a fellow poet. The name *Aquino,* furthermore, grafts Fiammetta to a family illustrious for its intellectuals. Some d'Aquinos were of a lyrical bent, notably the poets Rinaldo and Iacopo, active in the Sicilian school at the court of the emperor Frederick II. Their most famous member was Saint Thomas Aquinas, the Angelic Doctor, who professed theology at Paris and was briefly associated with the Dominican *studium* in Naples. It is he, robed as a Dominican monk, whom Boccaccio remembers when he endows Maria with her last name in the *Amorosa visione* (canto 43), again by circumlocution: she belongs to the family of the man from Campania who followed the Spaniard (Saint Dominic) in wearing the cape. Silently christened "Aquinas" when she makes her central appearance in the acrostic dream vision, Maria d'Aquino plays "sister" to the Guide (alias Reason) and symbolizes *Sapientia.* Together the two women educate the recalcitrant Giovanni, whose attraction to Maria develops morally into a love of Wisdom.[58]

Even before she was attached to Juvenal or claimed her status as a kinswoman to Saint Thomas, Boccaccio's Flame Lady had achieved other distinguished literary connections. Through one of them we learn that she had origins (or lived) not far from Naples and its court, in the town of Sulmona. But young Boccaccio, who would much rather tiptoe around names than trumpet them outright, certainly will not be so unsubtle as to hand us this fact straightforwardly, like some chronicler reeling off one more sta-

---

58. Thomas Aquinas visited the Dominican *studium* in Naples in 1272. See Cassell and Kirkham, *Diana's Hunt,* 5. Boccaccio's own Dominican sympathies and the sapiential allegory of the *Amorosa visione* are discussed in Kirkham, *The Sign of Reason,* especially introd. and chap. 2. Billanovich (*Restauri boccacceschi,* 94) connects Maria d'Aquino with Rinaldo and Iacopo d'Aquino as well as with Juvenal.

tistic. Poets are not so fast and crisp. They want us to read through their word currents slowly, ready for depths and attuned to ambiguities, so they complicate and amplify the communication, calling one thing by the name of another, saying this when they mean that.

Soon before "Fiammetta," formally so named as a character, joins Boccaccio's fiction early in the fourth book of the *Filocolo,* the hero recounts a strange dream, its actors all birds (4.13). He dreamed he saw a merlin fly southward from an oak grove ("cerreto") and capture a fair pheasant, flushed "by no means far from the natal site of our poet Naso." Converting these avian takeoffs and landings to human doings, we can say that a man from Certaldo (a place whose name derives from *cerreto* in Boccaccio's folk etymology) wins the love of a female from the vicinity of Sulmona. How we know that "cerreto" translates to "Certaldo," an equivalency our poet coins in the first chapter of book 4, is a matter to which I shall soon return. Meanwhile, we need not doubt that Boccaccio personally is Certaldo's black-plumed traveler, because he was its most famous citizen. Metonymy establishes his identity. Why, though, is his colorful "bird" Sulmonese? Luckily, the Tuscan poet's oneiric logic is not impossibly deep. He makes things clear enough when he closes in circuitously on the long-feathered female's place of origin by referring to its favorite son, Ovidius Naso. Sulmona was Ovid's hometown, as Ovid's own verse professed: "Sulmo mihi patria est." This is the same tactic Boccaccio will repeat in the *Ameto,* whispering the town Aquino by pronouncing out loud the satirist Juvenal. In allegory, the *Filocolo* "lovebirds" enact Boccaccio's conquest of Ovid, a Latin poet of whom he was fond when young.[59]

Not long after reminding us of Ovid's birthplace, Boccaccio summons into his narrative another poet, this time by reference not to city of birth but to burial site. Stranded at Naples, Filocolo and his little band of travelers chanced on Fiammetta's *brigata* the day they strolled out of the city in the direction of Virgil's tomb: "they directed their steps toward that place where the revered ashes of the consummate poet Maro lie resting."[60]

---

59. *Filoc.* 4.13: "non guari lontana dal natale sito del nostro poeta Naso." Quaglio's commentary in his edition says that this literary birthplace is either Sulmona or Aquino. Billanovich (*Restauri boccacceschi,* 91) sees it clearly connected to Ovid. Cf. Ovid, *Tristia ex Ponto,* trans. A. L. Wheeler, Loeb Classical Library (Cambridge: Harvard University Press, 1965), 4.10.3: "Sulmo is my native place." In later life, one of Boccaccio's literary friends and correspondents was Barbato da Sulmona. See Boccaccio, *Epistole,* ed. Auzzas, epistle 12 of 1362 to Barbato and epistle 13 of 1363 to Francesco Nelli. The wanderings of Fileno in *Filocolo* 3 (see below, chap. 3) are related to the same Ovidian matter.

60. *Filoc.* 4.14: "verso quella parte ove le reverende ceneri dell'altissimo poeta Maro si posano, dirizzano il loro andare."

Doubtless their aim was to pass the time on a pleasant excursion to the legendary shrine venerated ever since antiquity and still visited by tourists in the trecento (among them Petrarch, who saw it when he went to be certified by King Robert of Anjou for his coronation as poet laureate). Under Boccaccio's quill, however, the locale is also most definitely a literary locus.

Filocolo may think it was mere chance that beached him in "old Parthenope" (4.9) and brought him to Fiammetta's circle (4.15), but we know that their intersection was scheduled by an omniscient Author who planned her propinquity to Virgil. Her origins in Sulmona are tied up with Ovid; her continuations in the *Ameto* link her to Juvenal; and when she matures as an Aquinas in the *Amorosa visione,* it is the theology of Saint Thomas for which she speaks. But the connection most powerful in her background, against a Neapolitan setting in the *Filocolo,* could only be Virgil. Greatest talent of them all, he had honored Naples by keeping a villa there during his life and choosing its environs for a final resting place.

These facts are reported in the *Life of Virgil* by Suetonius, which Boccaccio knew in an augmented form attributed in the Middle Ages to Donatus, a fourth-century grammarian. Two verses in the vita, said to be Virgil's autoepitaph, compress the history of its subject, from his birth in a village near Mantua to his death from sunstroke at Brindisi. This distich unites enduringly the poet and "Parthenope."

Mantua me genuit, Calabri rapuere, tenet nunc
Parthenope; cecini pascua rura duces.

[Mantua gave birth to me; Calabria snatched me away; Parthenope has me now. I sang flocks, tillage, heroes.]

Since much of the *Vita virgiliana* is legend or later interpolation, the epitaph may be spurious. But even if Virgil himself did not pen it, whoever did was aware of the indelible association between Virgil and "Parthenope." The Poet himself had already referred to Naples by that more esoteric designation in a key passage at the close of the *Georgics.* There, for the only time in all his works, he signed his name.

Illo **Vergilium** me tempore dulcis alebat
Parthenope, studiis florentem ignobilis oti,
carmini qui lusi pastorum audaxaque iuventa,
Tityre, te patulae cecini sub tegmine fagi.

[In those days I, **Virgil,** was nursed of sweet **Parthenope,** and rejoiced in the arts of inglorious ease—I who dallied with shepherds' songs, and, in youth's boldness, sang, Tityrus, of thee under thy spreading beech's covert.][61]

Why does Virgil refer to Naples as "Parthenope" in his rustic song? Boccaccio will do the same in his *Ameto,* a pastoral fiction. Composed after his return to Florence from Naples, it allows him to perpetuate the bond he had welded between his Maria and Parthenope in the *Filocolo,* when Florio's shipwreck in "Parthenope" interrupts his quest for Biancifiore and deflects him to Fiammetta's circle at a spot near Virgil's grave. In *Ameto,* he sets the lady who had entered his art in Naples against a new Tuscan background and endows her with a legendary genealogy much older than the Angevins, an origin remote in the prehistoric mists of Campania. Surrounded by Florentine nymphs, Fiammetta recounts how her ancestors (including the lord of Juvenal's citadel, Sulmona) attempted to settle "Parthenope" but were warded off when they unearthed an ill-omened marble sarcophagus with an inscription they took to mean "sterility and mortality": "Qui Partenopes vergine sicula morta giace" [Here lies the dead Sicilian virgin Parthenope]. Later they returned, after reinterpreting the message as a favorable sign of fertility, since on a second reading they decided it meant that both virginity and death had been buried with the maiden.[62]

The oracle inscribed on the tomb in *Ameto* exploits a pun in the etymology of the name *Parthenope* that Boccaccio knew from Isidore of Seville. In the section of his *Etymologies* with a geographical gazetteer, Isidore lists the root of *Parthenope* as "virgin."

---

61. Virgil *Georgics* 4.563–66, in *Eclogues, Georgics, Aeneid,* trans. H. R. Fairclough, Loeb Classical Library (Cambridge: Harvard University Press, 1974), 1:79–237. For the text of the *Vita virgiliana* by Suetonius (attributed in the Middle Ages to Donatus), see Colin Hardie, ed., *Vitae virgilianae antiquae* (Oxford: Clarendon Press, 1966). Which version(s) Boccaccio knew are discussed by Charles Osgood in "Boccaccio's Knowledge of the Life of Virgil," *Classical Philology* 25 (1930): 27–36. Virgil's famous burial site is the subject of a superb monograph by J. B. Trapp, "The Grave of Vergil," *Journal of the Warburg and Courtauld Institute* 47 (1984): 1–31. I adapt Dryden's translation of the epitaph, cited by Trapp. Boccaccio must have had access to a manuscript compilation of Virgil's works from his earliest years in Naples. On the typical appearance and apparatus of such compilations, see the *accessus* to Virgil by Conrad of Hirsau, in *Medieval Literary Theory and Criticism, c. 1100–c. 1375: The Commentary Tradition,* ed. Alastair J. Minnis and A. B. Scott, with David Wallace (Oxford: Clarendon Press, 1988), 62–64. I find the first trace of Virgil's *Georgics* (3.419) in *Caccia di Diana* 12.30, for which see Cassell and Kirkham, *Diana's Hunt,* 181.
62. Boccaccio *Comedia delle ninfe* 35.15–18.

Parthenope a Parthenope quadam virgine illic sepulta Parthenope
appellata; quod oppidum postea Augustus Neapolim esse maluit.

[*Parthenope* comes from Parthenope, a certain virgin called
Parthenope buried there, which town afterward Augustus preferred
to call Naples.] (*Etym.* 46.1.60)

In other words, *Parthenope* is the ancient, mythic name for Naples. Virgil
appropriately invokes it in the context of his agrarian world, a simple,
idyllic realm removed from the onrush of history, and Boccaccio follows
suit, when "old Etruria" becomes the pastoral background for Fiammetta's narrative in *Ameto,* with its many allusions to the Neapolitan city.
    Perhaps the connection between Virgil and Parthenope, so conspicuous
at the close of the *Georgics,* was reinforced in Boccaccio's mind by the
closing passages of Statius's *Thebaid,* an epic that left a clear imprint on
the final page of the *Filocolo.* Like Statius, Boccaccio dismisses his "little
book" with instructions to keep a respectful distance behind the peerless
Virgil (*Filoc.* 5.97). But just before Statius makes his farewell, the *Thebaid*
culminates with a triple lament for "the Arcadian," an ally of Theseus who
had died in the war of the Seven against Thebes. Here unnamed, he was
the king of Arcadia, Parthenopaeus. As Rachel Jacoff has suggested, the
allusion seems to be a silent tribute to Virgil, implicit in the phonic pun on
Parthenopaeus and *Parthenope.* Just a few verses later, apostrophizing his
poem, Statius honors Virgil explicitly.

vive, precor; nec tu divinam Aeneida tempta,
sed longe sequere et vestigia semper adora.

[O live, I pray! nor rival the divine *Aeneid,* but follow afar and ever
venerate its footsteps.][63]

Parthenope is a magnet word. It recalls by association *Parthenopaeus.*
Into the same field gravitates a third term, the epithet *Parthenias.* That
had come Virgil's way in the vita by Suetonius, augmented by Donatus,
and embroidered by medieval scribes: he was so chaste, his reputation

    63. Statius *Thebaid* 12.816–17, in *Statius,* trans. J. H. Mozley, Loeb Classical Library
(Cambridge: Harvard University Press, 1961). See Rachel Jacoff, "Intertextualities in Arcadia: *Purgatorio* 30.49–51," in *The Poetry of Allusion: Virgil and Ovid in Dante's Commedia,*
ed. Rachel Jacoff and Jeffrey T. Schnapp (Stanford: Stanford University Press, 1991),
131–44.

polishers asserted, that he earned the nickname "Parthenias." Their "correction" counters a statement about the poet's pederasty, probably part of the genuine core of the vita by Suetonius. Virgil's medieval and Renaissance imitators naturally preferred to think of him as a model of virginity, which is why Petrarch names the shepherd in his eclogues who recites with a Virgilian voice "Parthenias." Boccaccio himself will have a good deal to say about Virgil's amazing chastity in the "Defense of Poetry" at the end of his *Genealogie deorum gentilium.* Plato, he argues, surely would not have excluded from his Republic such a model of propriety as Virgil, "who withal was so pure that he blushed in mind as well as in countenance when he overheard an indecent remark among his coevals or others and thus won the nickname 'Parthenias,' that is, 'virgin,' or more correctly 'virginity.'"[64]

Virgil's ghost inhabits Boccaccio's poetry from first to last, from the forest of "Parthenope" where "nymphs" from of the court of King Robert of Anjou assemble for the *Caccia di Diana,* to the tomb bust in "Parthenope" near Fiammetta's love court in the *Filocolo,* to the "virgin Parthenope" in the history of Fiammetta's ancestry from the *Ameto,* to that "Parthenias" who towers as an ideal citizen-poet in the *Genealogie.* We take it for granted that the Tuscan poet's writings of the early period all "belong" to Naples because he was living there when he wrote them. They are all Neapolitan by setting, either in the fiction (*Caccia di Diana*) or in the frame that explains how the fiction came to be (*Filostrato, Teseida*) or both (*Filocolo*). But Boccaccio, resident in Naples, could perfectly well have conjured for his plots fictional backgrounds from more distant lands, as he would later in the *Decameron* with a geographic range from England to Cathay, from mercantile Paris to the anchorite-dotted deserts of North Africa. The young writer's constant allegiance to Naples and its court—as opposed, say, to mythic Greece or Asia Minor—transcends realistic detail. It is a poetic as well as a political choice. Interweaving his own writings, set in Angevin Naples, with the name *Parthenope,* he consciously places himself in Virgil's sphere. Fiammetta's "birth" in this environment is no accident.

Fiammetta's close connection with Virgil finds corroboration in another document, contemporary with the *Filocolo,* the aforementioned

64. *Genealogie,* ed. Zaccaria, 14.19: "Quid insuper de Virgilio nostro? <qui>, ut reliqua sinam, tanto frontis rubore et mentis verecundia inter coevos et quoscunque minus decentia queque audiebat, ut ob hoc iuvenis adhuc vocaretur parthenias, quod Latine virgo seu virginitas sonat"; trans. Charles Osgood, *Boccaccio on Poetry,* 14.19 (p. 91). For more commentary on Parthenope, see Cassell and Kirkham, *Diana's Hunt,* 70 n. 7; see also commentary on 1.12 at ibid., 155–56.

Latin exercise of 1339 in the form of an epistle, addressed to a "Soldier of Mars" and signed "Data sub monte Falerno apud busta Maronis Virgilii" [Written at the foot of Mount Falerno by Virgil Maro's bust]. The "bust" must be a sculpture mounted at the urn that was thought to hold Virgil's mortal remains. The dedicatee, "Mavortis milex," we have already met as Petrarch. Although Boccaccio would not meet him until 1350, the Aretine poet's renown had already journeyed from "the Muses" in Avignon to Giovanni in Naples. This pseudoautobiographical statement, clanking with rhetoric copied from Dante, reports how when the sender was in "Virgilian Naples," taking a morning constitutional by Virgil's tomb, he was blitzed by a living lightning bolt.

> . . . once I arose before daybreak, clumsy and half asleep, and after unlatching the door of my hovel, I went out and found my way along the damp shore. And just as night was turning to day, and I, carelessly feeling safe, was perambulating near Maro's bust, suddenly there appeared, I know not how, a bright lady who descended like lightning, the answer to my desires both in manner and appearance. O, how that apparition stupefied me! So much so that I seemed to pass beyond myself; nay, I felt as if I had become a ghost. . . . Then my stupor ceased with the terror of the thunderclap that followed. As celestial lightning flashes are succeeded by thunder, so once I had gazed on the flame of that beauty, I was seized by a terrible and imperious and fierce love.[65]

We have no trouble recognizing the scenario in this *coup-de-foudre*. Timed like the morning star, Lady-of-the-Fire strikes again. But she is subsidiary to another person, someone preconditional to the enslaving apparition and whom Boccaccio honors by naming, "Virgil." He intends an allegory, of course. Literally, as he nears Virgil's funerary bust, he falls under the

---

65. Boccaccio *Epistolae* 2.2–5: ". . . commodum semel antelucio, dum marcidus et semisopitus surgerem, reseratis postibus gurgustiolum exivi, carpens iter litora super uda. Sed cum iam nox iret in diem, et ego penes busta Maronis securus et incautus ambularem, subito suda mulier, ceu fulgur descendens, apparuit nescio quomodo, meis auspitiis undique moribus et forma conformis. O! quam in eius apparitione obstupui! Certe tantum quod magis aliud videbar esse quam ego, ymmo quod admodo larvale simulacrum me sciebam. . . . Tandem stupor subsequentis thonitrui terrore cessavit. Nam sicut divinis corruscationibus illico subcedunt tonitrua, sic inspecta flamma pulcritudinis huius, amor terribilis et imperiosus me tenuit atque ferox." The passage is taken almost verbatim from Dante's letter to Moroello Malaspina, as Branca has shown in "Schemi letterari e schemi autobiografici," in *Boccaccio medievale,* especially 219–20.

sway of a lightning-lady. Allegorically, cause and effect are the other way around: the letter writer comes under Virgil's influence, and as a consequence, he adopts a mighty flame-mistress.

She is a New Flame, as contrasted with the Old Flame in the grand romance from Virgil's epic. There Dido reacts to the arrival of Aeneas at her city of Carthage with deep stirrings of passion, the first she has felt since she lost her husband. She, who had sworn never to marry again after the death of Sychaeus, confesses her secret desire to her sister, Anna.

> . . . adgnosco veteris vestigia flammae.

> [. . . I recognize the traces of the old flame.]⁶⁶

Anna's reply fans the widow's already lighted fire: "incensum animum inflamavit amore" [she inflamed her kindled heart with love]. Love-stricken, Dido is consumed as by a feverish, wasting disease: "est mollis flamma medullas. . . . uritur infelix Dido" [the flame devours her tender heart-strings. . . . unhappy Dido burns]. All this metaphorical fire at the beginning of *Aeneid* 4, poetic fuel for Dido's forthcoming affair with the Trojan exile, finds tragic fulfillment in her funeral pyre after Aeneas has abandoned her, at the end book 4. She goes up in a devastating conflagration, compared in Virgil's epic simile to an entire city torched by an invading army and engulfed in wild flames.

> . . . non aliter, quam si immissis ruat hostibus omnis
> Karthago aut antiqua Tyros, flammaeque furentes
> culmina perque hominum volvantur perque deorum.

> [. . . even as though all Carthage or ancient Tyre were falling before the inrushing foe, and fierce flames were rolling on over the roofs of men, over the roofs of gods.] (*Aen.* 4.669–71)

Queen Dido's unchaste, uncontrolled lust—an "old flame" that flares up when Aeneas sails into her life—undergoes a major reversal in the *Filocolo,* where the royal flame is new, constructive as an inspirational literary patron, and diminutive. Not-Eve, she is also Not-Dido.

---

66. Virgil *Aen.* 4.23, in *Eclogues, Georgics, Aeneid,* trans. H. R. Fairclough, 1:239–571; 2:1–365.

The allegorical letter to a "Mavortis milex" describes a situation that corresponds perfectly to the *Filocolo,* where hallowed Virgilian ground heralds Maria-Fiammetta. Filocolo's shipwrecked party expect the "Virgil" tour as they stroll along the shore, but instead they are received by Fiammetta. Caleon's mistress and a secondary character, she is an interior double dependent for her existence on the Author's Maria d'Angiò, a lady vested with the power of the Angevin kingdom. Boccaccio assembles the two Fiammettas, Robert, and Virgil to convey a message of solemn import: the Neapolitan *Filocolo* is a Virgilian work furnished with an appropriate dedicatee—for purposes of the fiction, "Maria" and "Fiammetta," but in keeping with epic tradition, a new Guelf "caesar" who is the Angevin king. By composing an epic romance "in Parthenope," Boccaccio emulates his Roman mentor, who he believed had written the *Aeneid* at his villa in Naples.[67]

Virgil and Naples, Ovid and Sulmona, Juvenal and Aquino, Boccaccio and Certaldo—they are all synonymous couples. In the rhetorical epistle to a "Mavortis milex," the precincts of Virgil's tomb are haunted, possessed of conjuring powers. It is the locale of an apocalyptic love experience, sacred ground with thaumaturgical qualities, magic like that of which Virgil himself was capable in medieval imagination.[68] Fiammetta's apparition at Virgil's tomb implies that she, like Laura (whom Boccaccio would call an "allegory" in his *Life of Petrarch*), is a purely literary woman. A mistress sired no less by Virgil's specter than by Robert's power, she will serve her Author as partner in his poetic persona. Half a century later, tellingly, Filippo Villani gives his version of what happened to Boccaccio at Virgil's tomb. He leaves out the lady to reassert the activity that she embodies symbolically: poetry.

---

67. Boccaccio states that Virgil wrote his *Bucolics* and *Georgics* in Naples, and he cites the *Saturnalia* as his authority for the information that Virgil also composed the *Aeneid* at his villa there: "sì come Macrobio in libro Saturnaliorum scrive, mostra, mentre che scrisse l'Eneide, si stesse in villa; il dove non dice, ma per quello che delle sue ossa fece Ottaviano, si presumme che questa villa fosse propinqua a Napoli e prossimana al promontorio di Posilipo, tra Napoli e Pozuolo." See his *Esposizioni sopra la Comedìa,* ed Giorgio Padoan, in *Tutte le opere,* vol. 6 (Milan: Mondadori, 1965), 1.1.62, Charles Osgood (*Boccaccio on Poetry,* 180 n. 5) said he was unable to find that statement in Macrobius.

68. Domenico Comparetti, *Virgilio nel medioevo,* ed. Giorgio Pasquali (1943; reprint, Florence: La Nuova Italia, 1981), especially pt. 2, "Virgilio nella leggenda popolare." Cf. Giovanni Boccaccio, *Trattatello in laude di Dante,* ed. Pier Giorgio Ricci, in *Tutte le opere,* vol. 3 (Milan: Mondadori, 1974), 1.96–97, for examples of the important ties between Homer, Virgil, Ovid, Horace, and Juvenal and their cities. In this list, Boccaccio links Virgil with his birthplace, Mantua.

As Boccaccio was gazing on Virgil's tomb, with soul suspended, while he admiringly meditated at length on what was enclosed inside it and on the fame of those bones, suddenly he began to accuse and lament his fortune, by which he was violently constrained to give himself to business, hateful to him. Wherefore, touched by a sudden love of the Pierian Muses, he returned home, and, scorning business completely, he gave himself with most ardent study to poetry, in which, before long, conjoining his noble intellect and ardent desire, he made amazing progress.[69]

With the ellipsis of Fiammetta from Boccaccio's bouleversement, Villani draws us back into the mode of the chronicler, one officially uninterested in his subject's vernacular literary inventions. Suppressing the lady, he gives all the credit for Boccaccio's conversion to a more imposing male, Virgil immortal, "the Poet" by antonomasia.

Lady-of-the-Flame will keep returning to Boccaccio's Tuscan fiction. Her duality in the *Filocolo,* a split that makes her the composer's mistress and Caleon's, anticipates her ubiquity in later pieces. Sometimes she maintains frame-tale territory; sometimes, simultaneously or alternatively, she can play her role for a story told inside the frame(s). Boccaccio's framing, of course, need not be one single containment structure that occupies only the outermost limits of a text. If anything, he has a preference for plural frames—both frames within frames (*mise-en-abîme*) and frames eccentrically reduplicated to articulate a narrative in linear sequence. The most complex examples of these multiple boxing and nesting techniques are the *Ameto* and the *Decameron.*[70] But boundaries are always permeable for him, whose Gothic writing habits are more consonant with an anticlassical, or mannerist, aesthetic. Without that "classical" sense of sharp distinctions between "inside" and "outside" a frame, he can politely break into the enclosed, pastoral world of his *Decameron brigata* and, with a sud-

---

69. Solerti, *Le vite,* 673: "El cui sepolcro ragguardando Giovanni, e con ammirazione lungamente quel che dentro chiudea, e la fama di quelle ossa con animo sospeso meditando, cominciò subitamente ad accusare e lamentarsi della sua fortuna, dalla quale violentemente era constretto a darsi alle mercatanzie a lui odiose. Onde da un súbito amore delle Pieridi muse tócco, tornato a casa, sprezzato al tutto le mercatanzie, con ardentissimo studio alla poesia si dette; nella quale in brevissimo tempo, congiungendo insieme el nobile ingegno e l'ardente desiderio, fe' mirabile profitto."

70. A recent meditation on Boccaccio's framing techniques with focus on the *Decameron* is Franco Fido, "Architettura," in *Lessico critico decameroniano,* ed. Renzo Bragantini and Pier Massimo Forni (Turin: Bollati Boringhieri, 1995), 13–33 .

den change of both narrative voice and register, defend himself from detractors that we had no idea were out there mobilized against him, stirring up trouble. (In fact, they sound as fictional as the stories.) Earlier, when "Giovanni di Boccaccio di Certaldo" doubles as protagonist of the *Amorosa visione,* he exists simultaneously outside in the front matter and inside in the fiction; he is master at the controls of the gigantic acrostic on his desk but a childish adolescent who stumbles from one silly mistake to another in the labyrinth of his sleepwalk. At first it seems that there is no contradiction in this *dédoublement,* since the second Giovanni is only a dream character. But what are we to think when he awakens to find Lady Reason, she who had been his dream Guide, standing in broad daylight beside his bed with a promise that soon they will be seeing Fiammetta? How can a personification cross so easily from sleep to conscious awareness? The surprise ending blurs borderlines between life and art. Boccaccio playfully breaks with convention, established in such powerful literary models as the dream vision of Boethius, whom Lady Philosophy consoled, or the *Romance of the Rose,* which despite its internal rupture and dual authorship, never violates the pretense of Amant's sleep but makes the end of the poem coincide with the end of the dream.

Flame is privileged to receive his epic, sent with an introductory cover letter "To Fiammetta." Hers, too, is the honor of naming it *Teseida delle nozze d'Emilia,* an epistemological act that occurs after the epic ends, recorded in a sonnet exchange between the poet and the Muses. Again as dedicatee, she is the "Cara Fiamma" to whom he affectionately alludes in the triple-sonnet preface to his *Amorosa visione,* and at the same time she is the goal within the dream that the sonnets frame. Among the frame narrators in the *Decameron,* Fiammetta, loved by Dioneo, is privileged by virtue of her placement as queen at the center, on Day 5. (Needless to say, no other day could have been so suitable to Fiammetta in the Florentine *brigata* as the fifth.) Her foremother was another Fiammetta, a nymph coupled with Caleon and symbolic of Hope in the *Ameto,* the pastoral inspired by an unnamed lady whose traits are too generically those of the dolce stil nuovo to call her Fiammetta or any other specific name. This frame lady is probably pushed back into anonymity by the intervention, for the first time in Boccaccio's corpus, of a real dedicatee, fully named, Niccolò di Bartolo del Buono di Firenze. Before Boccaccio set down Fiammetta's adultery with Caleon in the pseudoautobiography and miniallegory of his *Ameto,* he had already conceived a homonymous pair for his *Filocolo.* They are characters in counterpoint to the protagonists Flo-

rio and Biancifiore as well as to the "new author" and Maria d'Angiò—
Giovanni di Certaldo is at the hopeful beginning of his affair, but Caleon
will come bitterly to the end of his. This Caleon and Fiammetta belong
properly to the framed story, not the frame tale; Filocolo, not the "composer" of the romance, encounters them. With *Madonna Fiammetta's
Elegy,* Fiammetta will take over an entire fiction, speaking as first-person
protagonist. Although after the *Decameron* Fiammetta disappears from
Boccaccio's fiction, her flame will continue to light his poetry to the end of
his life, shining through the lines of the *Rime.* Featured in the *Filocolo,
Teseida, Ameto, Amorosa visione, Elegia di madonna Fiammetta,
Decameron,* and *Rime,* Fiammetta is a most versatile figure. She may take
her place in the frame as the woman the narrator loves (*Filocolo, Teseida,
Ameto, Amorosa visione*), or she may be in the frame as the woman he
loves not (*Decameron*), or she may be in a frame and loved by one of Boccaccio's interior doubles (*Ameto, Decameron*), or she may be inside the
story as a character named Fiammetta (*Filocolo, Amorosa visione, Elegia*)
or as another female character whom she is supposed to resemble
(Biancifiore in the *Filocolo,* Emilia in the *Teseida*).

She does not dominate Boccaccio. Quite the contrary, her tyranny is an
amusing pretense. We may be disconcerted when she chains him literally
into the flesh of her breast in the *Amorosa visione,* but that can only be a
momentary startlement. Catching the drift of the allegory, we realize that
Fiammetta is acting as Wisdom when she firmly takes him to heart. And
beyond that, we see the controlling hand of the poet, he who unchains her
from his imagination to let her in and out of his fiction. His Fiammetta is
a free-moving persona who travels to settings frequently refurnished. Like
a detachable building block or a playing card the poet can deal out to any
new hand, she fits adjustably into every genre of creative writing in the vernacular (epic, lyric, romance, pastoral), into their frames, and into their
internal framed sectors. At the same time, she herself is subject to incre-
mental modification. As Boccaccio's corpus grows, so does she. Starting
already in the *Filocolo,* her names multiply from "Maria d'Angiò," more
familiarly "Fiammetta," to embrace associations from Venus to the kings
of France, from Ovid to Beatrice, from Virgil to Aquinas. It is a mistake to
think of her as one person, which she would have to be were she a real
woman. Rather she is an emblem of her author's evolving allegiances,
both in poetry and in politics. In that sense, there are many Fiammettas, as
many as there are Giovannis.

With all the similarities between the two of them, Boccaccio and

Fiammetta might almost be twins. In the *Filocolo* both are royal, illegitimate, and motherless. Both are progeny of a Gallic king. His connection is
maternal in Île-de-France, hers paternal in Provence.[71] Even in sacred
semantics their names seal their bond, for both are "full of grace." Gabriel
had flown to Maria with the greeting "Ave gratia plena." In Hebrew the
name *Giovanni* means "full of grace," and it is the name of John the Baptist, who, like Gabriel, brought word of Christ's Advent. Together they are
John and Mary, a perfect Christian couple. Maria, alias Fiammetta, is an
ideal feminine partner for Giovanni of Certaldo, a new flame for a modern
Virgil.

---

71. Later, in the *Ameto,* Fiammetta is derived from *fomans,* in reference to the blood of
Aeneas's men, while "French" Giovanni descends from Trojan exiles. See Billanovich,
Restauri boccaceschi, 94.

CHAPTER 2

Signed Pieces

Whatever we choose to call her—Maria, Fiammetta, Anjou, Aquinas, da Sulmona, Venus, Stella, Beatitude, Charity, Hope, Prudence, Wisdom, Redemption, King Robert, Juvenal, Ovid, Virgil—in her many-faceted existence Fiammetta reconfirms Giovanni di Boccaccio da Certaldo. But where are his own names? Although he unabashedly displayed his signature in the virtuoso acrostic of the *Amorosa visione,* most often in his vernacular fiction Boccaccio is more reticent about his name. Preferring instead to invent a pose, Giovanni vanishes behind one mask after another, cloaked anonymously as "the Author."

Never, for instance, does he otherwise refer to himself in the *Decameron.* He is always simply "the Author," as is plain beginning with the caption of the First Day.

Comincia la prima giornata del Decameron, nella quale, dopo la dimostrazione fatta dall'autore per che cagione avvenisse di doversi quelle persone, che appresso si mostrano, ragunare a ragionare insieme, sotto il reggimento di Pampinea si ragiona di quello che piú aggrada a ciascheduno.

[Here begins the First Day of the Decameron, wherein first of all the Author explains the circumstances in which certain persons, who presently make their appearance, were induced to meet for the purpose of conversing together, after which, under the rule of Pampinea, each of them speaks on the subject they find most congenial.][1]

---

1. Giovanni Boccaccio, *Decameron,* ed. Vittore Branca, in *Tutte le opere,* vol. 4 (Milan: Mondadori, 1976), introd., rubric. Unless otherwise specified, I cite this edition for Branca's commentary. For translations, I have consulted both *The Decameron,* trans. G. H. McWilliam

Although his book is loaded with literary conventions that signal beginnings, none of them communicates the name of the person who wrote it—
not the title rubric, not the Author's proem, not the rubric (just quoted)
before the introduction to Day 1, not the introduction to Day 1, not the
rubric before the first novella, not the first novella, not Day 1. In case we
had not noticed by the end of the Third Day and three decads of tales that
our Author is still anonymous, his interruption of the storytelling rhythms
with a defense in the introduction to the Fourth Day makes a point of
stamping this an *unsigned* work.

Addressing the "dearest ladies," those sweet lovesick creatures locked
in their chambers whom he gallantly entertains, he complains of being buffeted by blasts of envy, and most unfairly, since he has not sought lofty
heights. Lying low, a safety measure adopted by others before, ought to
have protected him from jealous enemies. Did he not know perfectly well,
from his own observations and from reading "wise men," how "the
impetuous and ardent wind of envy should not strike anything but tall
towers and the most elevated tree tops"? One poet wise enough to rate as
a model of precaution was the Frenchman Alan of Lille, a twelfth-century
Neoplatonist whose encyclopedic epics had appeal for Boccaccio. Alan
launched his *Anticlaudianus,* a Latin allegory that describes the making of
a "good and perfect man," with dramatic antitheses to underline the limits
of his small effort and to forestall stinging criticism.

The lightning's bolt does not deign to spend its force on the twig but
dislodges the proud outgrowths of full-grown trees. The mighty rage
of the wind does not waste its anger on the reed but . . . against the
highest of high things. The glare of envy does not flash through our
flawed and lowly book.[2]

Imitating Alan's prologue, Boccaccio invokes a modesty topos as he
begins his defense. Not only has he kept to the plains, but he has even tried
to walk in the "deepest valleys." That much should be manifest to anyone
who looks at the present novelle: "in fiorentin volgare e in prosa scritte per
me sono e senza titolo, ma ancora in istilo umilissimo e rimesso quanto il

---

(Harmondsworth: Penguin, 1972), and *Decameron,* trans. John Payne, revised with commentary by Charles S. Singleton, 3 vols. (Berkeley: University of California Press, 1982), but I have
modified them freely.
    2. Alan of Lille, *Anticlaudianus or the Good and Perfect Man,* trans. James J. Sheridan
(Toronto: University of Toronto Press, 1973), prologue, 39.

piú si possono" [written by me not only in Florentine vernacular and in prose and without a title but also in a most humble style and as unassuming as they possibly could be] (4, introd. 2–3). Italian, not Latin; prose, not poetry; the self-effacing style of comedy, not the assertive grandeur of serious drama—those traits constrain the book within modest proportions, as does its lack of "title."

The hierarchy of literature is here clear. Poetry, Latin, and tragedy outrank prose, vernacular, and comedy. Most noble is Latin poetry; most common is vernacular prose. Dante makes these distinctions in his *Vita nuova* 25, a mini *ars poetica* sketched from the perspective of a Tuscan writer. Those who wrote "verse" in Latin he calls "poets"; their vernacular epigones, relative latecomers to the scene who have been active only for about 150 years, he designates with a term that implies a lower level of inspiration, *rimatori* (rhymesters). Nevertheless, these modern Romance rhyme makers are due the same privileges as their classical counterparts, and whoever "speaks" in the more aristocratic form of poetry should be allowed greater license than is permitted to prose writers. Poets, in the samples of license that Dante then offers, can use personification, but whatever rhetorical figures they may employ, they are under an obligation to be able to "denude" their inventions, that is, explain them in plain language. The main reason that poets began to use the vernacular, Dante assumes, was to make themselves understood by women: "E lo primo che cominciò a dire sì come poeta volgare, si mosse però che volle fare intendere le sue parole a donna, a la quale era malagevole d'intendere li versi latini" [And the first man who began to write as a vernacular poet was motivated because he wanted to make his words understood by a woman, who found it difficult to understand Latin verses]. Read against Dante's definition of the vernacular as a female form, reiterated in his *De vulgari eloquentia*, Boccaccio's dedication of the *Decameron* to women in love, announced in his proem, is on one level an affirmation of an art form in Tuscan, not Latin. Women and the vernacular go together, as he will again remind us in his conclusion, where he returns to the defense of his prose novelle by remarking that they were not for scholars at Athens, Paris, or Bologna but rather for females with time on their hands. In addition to his target audience, his use of prose as the vehicle for his *Decameron* contributes another major element to its supposedly unassuming character. (Of course, the book does not completely lack the adornment of verse, since a ballad rounds off each narrative day.) Would our Author then not have been safe enough from the horrible assaults of envy simply by targeting females in Italian prose? Why does he include yet another disclaimer in the cluster of his book's modest features, calling attention to the fact that it is "senza titolo"? And what does he mean by the phrase "without a title"?

Although a public today would think this last phrase a reference to a name for the book, clearly it cannot be that here. On the contrary, the *Decameron* itself is amply endowed with titles, bearing not only a name but the surname "Prince Gallehault." They are conveyed in the title rubric, before the Author's proem: "COMINCIA IL LIBRO CHIAMATO DECAMERON COGNOMINATO PRENCIPE GALEOTTO, NEL QUALE SI CONTENGONO CENTO NOVELLE IN DIECE DÌ DETTE DA SETTE DONNE E DA TRE GIOVANI UOMINI." The *Decameron,* Boccaccio's "ten days" of storytelling, is a calendrical sequence designed as an ideal cycle, since 10 is a number of unity and totality both in Neoplatonic numerology (from the Pythagorean decad, which contains all things) and in the Judeo-Christian tradition (from God's Law in ten parts, the Decalogue).[3] *Gallehault* echoes the name of Galeotto, the knight who pandered to Lancelot and Guinevere in an Arthurian romance that captivated Dante's Francesca da Rimini, seducing her into a fateful embrace with Paolo: "Galeotto fu 'l libro e chi lo scrisse" [Gallehault was the book and he who wrote it] (*Inf.* 5.137). "Galeotto," like the *Decameron,* is both an object to be read and the man responsible for writing it. We could say, then, that this is the book called "Decameron," also known as "Boccaccio." The Author *is* his book. But the Boccaccio who is Prince Gallehault, pandering amusement to amorous females, still remains a figure cloaked in fiction. He is quite a different character from Giovanni di Boccaccio da Certaldo, who so conspicuously signed the *Amorosa visione.*

The "*Decameron* surnamed *Prince Gallehault*" cannot be "senza titolo" in the sense of "untitled." How else could Boccaccio mean the epithet of demurral? His *Little Treatise in Praise of Dante,* written during the same years as the *Decameron,* casts light on the question. Contexts in which he uses the Italian verb *intitolare* reveal how versatile it was. Three applica-

---

3. Vittore Branca points to the connection between the *Decameron* and hexameral treatises in his commentary (976 n. 1). For the implications of the two-week sequence of the *Decameron,* a secular departure from the week of Genesis, see Victoria Kirkham, "Morale," in *Lessico critico decameroniano,* ed. Renzo Bragantini and Pier Massimo Forni (Turin: Bollati Boringhieri, 1995), 249–68. More on the symbolism of the number 10 can be found in Victoria Kirkham, "Eleven is for Evil: Measured Trespass in Dante's *Commedia,*" *Allegorica* 10 (1989): 27–50.

tions pertain to authorship: books, their makers, and their dedicatees are all possible objects of the verb "to (en)title." All three occur in proximity toward the end of his biography, when he finds it opportune to make an orderly record of Dante's works "acciò che né alcuno delle sue s'intitolasse, né a lui fossero per avventura intitolate l'altrui" [so that no one else claim title to his, nor titles of those by others be signed over perchance to him]. He continues, "Egli primieramente, duranti ancora le lagrime della morte della sua Beatrice, quasi nel suo ventesimosesto anno, compose in uno volumetto, il quale egli intitolò *Vita nuova,* certe operette . . ." [Firstly, while still weeping for the death of his Beatrice, close to his twenty-sixth year, he composed in a little volume, which he entitled *Vita nuova,* certain short works . . .] (1.175). Whatever Dante wrote, let that—and nothing else—be attributed to Dante. No other authors should take the credit for what Dante has done, since they would be undeserving. Neither should Dante be credited with what they have done, because those other works would demean his name. Soon after, speaking of the masterwork, Boccaccio reports:

> Questo libro della *Comedia,* secondo il ragionare d'alcuno, intitolò egli a tre solennissimi uomini italiani, secondo la sua triplice divisione, a ciascuno la sua, in questa guisa: la prima parte, cioè lo 'Nferno, intitolò a Uguiccione della Faggiuola . . . ; la seconda parte, cioè il *Purgatoro,* intitolò al marchese Moruello Malespina; la terza parte, cioè il *Paradiso,* a Federigo III re di Cecilia. Alcuni vogliono dire lui averlo intitolato tutto a messer Cane della Scala.

> [He entitled this book the *Comedy,* according to what some say, to three most dignified Italian men according to its triple division, each man his part, in this fashion: he entitled the first part, that is, *Hell,* to Uguiccione della Faggiuola . . . ; he entitled the second part, that is, *Purgatory,* to the marquis Moroello Malaspina; the third part, that is, *Paradise,* to Frederick III king of Sicily. Some incline to think that he entitled it all to Messer Cane della Scala.] (1.193–94)[4]

---

4. *Trattatello,* ed. Ricci. The triple dedication may echo what Boccaccio knew of Virgil's three principal dedicatees from the ancient vita of Virgil by Suetonius-Donatus. See Kirkham, "The Parallel Lives of Dante and Virgil." Whether Dante intended the *Paradiso* for Frederick III or for Can Grande della Scala has provided loads of grist for scholarly mills. Hollander lays out the polemic in lively fashion in *Dante's Epistle to Cangrande* (Ann Arbor: University of Michigan Press, 1993).

Thus we could render *intitolare* in English as "to attribute (authorship)," "to title (a book)," or "to dedicate (a book)." It conveys the idea of naming as well as a related proprietary concept that we might call "entitlement." Based on these examples, we can say that the *Vita nuova* is a title, that Dante is "entitled" to the ownership of the *Comedy,* and that, in similar fashion, the trio of dedicatees (or Can Grande) are "entitled" to have their names attached to its three parts in honorific tribute.

Boccaccio gives us a better insight into his notion of what a title was in the *accessus,* or introduction, to his *Expositions on the Comedy of Dante.* Among the several topics he blocks out to define in these preliminaries, he includes "what the title of the work is." Some say, he reports, that the title of the *Divine Comedy* is "Incomincia la *Comedìa* di Dante Alighieri fiorentino" [Here begins the *Comedy* of Dante Alighieri the Florentine]. Others prefer an alternate form because it implies the division into three parts: "Incominciano le cantiche della *Comedìa* di Dante Alighieri fiorentino" [Here begin the canticles of the *Comedy* of Dante Alighieri the Florentine] (*Esposiz., accessus* 13). For Boccaccio, the author's name was just as normal a part of the title as was the name of the book. In fact, it is in the context of explaining the "title" in his *accessus* that Boccaccio considers how Dante left his name inscribed in the *Comedy.* The title as a whole was synonymous with what we call the title rubric.

But why is the *Decameron* deprived of an author with a name more historical than "Prince Gallehault"? Perhaps Giovanni di Boccaccio da Certaldo declines to identify himself because that suits the part he is playing as a "valley walker," a modest vernacular writer determined to duck the buffets of envy. By the rules of medieval rhetoric, for the sake of humility an author should not call attention to himself—at least, not without a "necessary reason," as Dante had explained in his *Convivio* (2.2.3). That exception to the rule, we can suppose, opens a space for Dante's name in the *Comedy* when he comes face-to-face with Beatrice and must stand up to her stern reckoning. His name, he says, "di necessità qui si registra" [is registered here by necessity] (*Purg.* 30.63). Unlike Dante at that moment of rebuke, Boccaccio was under no constraint to break silence and register his name in the novelle. There was no "necessaria cagione." Far from being a "sacred poem" like the hundred cantos, these hundred tales are secular female entertainment, nor could their Author be more deferential about their merit. Declining to state his name in the *Decameron,* he distances himself from Dante.[5]

---

5. The tension between recognition and denial of a source text is well summed up in Hollander's oxymoron "imitative distance." See his "Boccaccio's Dante: Imitative Distance

At the same time, he nudges another poet, one to whom he had been partial from his first literary projects. Through his strategy of silence, Boccaccio couples himself to Ovid, whose *Amores* were known to medievals as the book *Liber sine titulo* that is, *the Book without a Title.* An eleventh-century manuscript at Saint Gall accounts for this peculiarity with two explanations that found their way into almost all later commentaries: either Ovid was not seeking fame for himself but wanted only to please his beloved, or, alternatively, Augustus was so angry with Ovid for having written the racy *Art of Love* that the poor poet dared not sign the *Amores.* One *accessus* in the second family lays out the possibilities of why Ovid might personally have squelched the name of his *Amores.*

> Various reasons are given as to why this book is entitled *without a title.* One is that he [i.e., Ovid] feared those enemies who habitually criticized his writings lest, having read the title, they would denigrate the work. Another is that he feared Augustus Caesar who he knew had taken offence at the *Art of Love,* because in that book Ovid had fictitiously placed the Roman matrons in the setting of a brothel. He knew that he would be even more offended if he read this title. For here too some of the subject-matter relates to love.

Boccaccio, not surprisingly, was on most familiar terms with the *Amores.* In fact, confirmation of his close tie to that poem by Ovid comes from one of his own *Zibaldoni* (Florence, Biblioteca Laurenziana, MS 33.31), where it appears transcribed in his hand. Prefixed to the text is the title "**Publii Ovidii Nasonis Sine titulo**" [Without a title by Publius Ovidius Naso].[6]

While leaving the book anonymous, the rubric nonetheless openly

(*Decameron* I 1 and VI 10)," *Studi sul Boccaccio* 13 (1981–82): 169–98, reprinted in the useful *Boccaccio's Dante and the Shaping Force of Satire* (Ann Arbor: University of Michigan Press, 1997), 21–52.

6. Robert Hollander, arguing that Boccaccio as "Galeotto" is "Ovid," sketches a picture of the powerful affinity felt by the Tuscan for his Roman predecessor in the art of amorous poetry, in *Boccaccio's Two Venuses* (New York: Columbia University Press, 1977), 112–16. See further "The Proem of the *Decameron,*" in *Boccaccio's Dante,* 89–107. The eleventh-century *accessus* belongs to Saint Gall MS 864. The *accessus* I cite appears in Minnis et al., *Medieval Literary Theory and Criticism,* 27. Cf. also a second type of *accessus* to the *Book without a Title* in ibid., 28: "The reason why this book [i.e., the *Amores*] has no title must be understood as follows. Before he wrote it, he had written *On the Art of Love* and had made adulteresses of almost all the married women and maidens. This had made the Romans hostile towards him, and so, in case this book should incur even greater disfavour, he did not give it a title, and we readers call it Ovid's *Book without a Title.*" We know from the *Tristia* that the emperor's displeasure with Ovid caused him to exile the poet to the Caucasus, where he died. It is only speculation that the erotic nature of the *Ars amatoria* was to blame. See

attributes it to Ovid. From that Latin formula, Giorgio Padoan concludes, the *Decameron,* too, must have circulated from the beginning with the Author's name. Yet we cannot tell what Boccaccio originally intended. A copy survives that he personally transcribed late in life, around 1370 (Berlin, Staatsbibliothek, MS Hamilton 90). It lacks the first gathering, however—folios that would have contained the title, the summaries of the *novelle,* the proem, and the first part of the introduction to Day 1. As Vittore Branca speculates, these pages were probably a bifolium handsomely decorated with a dedicatee's coat of arms, or they may have boasted the signature of some prominent owner, tempting a later marauder to remove them from the manuscript. Franca Petrucci, on the other hand, doubts that the codex could have been a presentation copy. Its parchment is of poor quality, coarse in texture, with bumps, hair follicles, and holes. Uncharacteristic of Boccaccio, who copied elegantly his gift books, the size of the lettering in this manuscript is not uniform but shrinks as the text advances. Presumably the transcriber wanted to save the expense of another entire parchment gathering, so he crowded the script toward the end; the number of lines increases from fifty-three per page in the first eighty folios to as many as sixty-five in the last thirty. Perhaps, as Petrucci thinks, the first folios and two other quinterns missing today from the autograph fell away from the rest when the manuscript was unbound for printing in a typesetter's workshop late in the quattrocento or early in the cinquecento. If so, the imprint made from the autograph has yet to be discovered.[7]

Fausto Ghisalberti's classic "Medieval Biographies of Ovid," *Journal of the Warburg and Courtauld Institutes* 9 (1946): 10–59. Boccaccio's characterization of the *Decameron* as "without a title" is connected by Vittore Branca to Ovid's *Sine titulo* in his commentary to the text (1197 n. 4). See also Giorgio Padoan, "Sulla genesi del *Decameron,*" in *Boccaccio: Secoli di vita,* ed. Marga Cottino-Jones and Edward F. Tuttle (Ravenna: Longo, 1977), 143–76. Speculating on the complicated question of the different periods in the composition of the *Decameron,* he notes the passage in Boccaccio's *Zibaldone laurenziano* (Florence, Biblioteca Medicea-Laurenziana, MS 30.31) that refers to Ovid's untitled book.

7. It could well have been thrown away by the publisher, as was the custom with manuscripts once they had been set in the more enduring medium of print. For the manuscript history and a description of its graphic features, see Vittore Branca and Pier Giorgio Ricci, *Un autografo del Decameron (Codice Hamiltoniano 90)* (Florence: Olschki, 1962). Branca, *Tradizione delle opere,* vol. 2, provides an essential update with new information. See in particular 215 and 236 for discussion of the missing folios, 226 for the size of the script. Cf. Giovanni Boccaccio, *Decameron: Edizione diplomatico-interpretativa dell'autografo Hamilton 90,* ed. Charles S. Singleton, with Franca Petrucci, Armando Petrucci, Giancarlo Savino, and Martino Mardersteig (Baltimore: Johns Hopkins University Press, 1974). Franca Petrucci there argues (647–61) that its features are more characteristic of a working copy. It contains Boccaccio's final revisions.

For information of provenance, the last folio of a medieval book is often the single most important since it contains the closing rubric, or colophon, the "tail that speaks." Here, typically, the scribe signs his name (together with the author's) and the date when he was lucky enough to finish his transcription, giving thanks to God. Fortunately, the last gathering of Hamilton 90 survives. Boccaccio finished copying it a bit ahead of schedule, as parchment space went, so he left the last folium blank. Although he would have had room for an ample colophon, our authorial scribe still, even now, will not tell who he is. Instead he reiterates the wording of his title, writing his Italian book's twin names: "**Qui finisce la decima et ultima giornata del libro chiamato decameron cognominato prencipe galeotto;**" [Here ends the tenth and last day of the book called Decameron surnamed Prince Gallehault;]. The final mark Boccaccio put in his manuscript was the semicolon after "galeotto." What does it mean? He uses the same punctuation after other rubrics throughout the book. Thus the rubric between Days 3 and 4 reads: **Finisce la terça giornata del decameron et Incomincia la quarta. Nella quale sotto il reggimento di phylostrato si ragiona di coloro li cui amori ebbero infelice fine; rubrica;** [Here ends the third day of the Decameron and begins the fourth, wherein, under the rule of Filostrato the discussion turns on those whose love ended unhappily;]. For us a semicolon implies and requires that more will follow. That was not true for Boccaccio, who used it to indicate a full stop. In other words, the semicolon at the end of the explicit, attached to "galeotto," is the equivalent of a period.[8] It is another way of saying, "The end." Lest there be any question, thereafter the page is blank. Consequently, if Boccaccio did put his name to this autograph, it would have had to be at the beginning. Was this transcription a present for an illustrious friend, or was it a working copy for his final revisions? If the former, it could have had a complete rubric similar to the dedications of his Latin compilations, one that gave full names of the author, book, and dedicatee. The inferior parchment and graphic irregularity could be accounted for by Boccaccio's poverty and poor health. He may not have had the money or the physical

---

8. According to Franca Petrucci (in Boccaccio, *Decameron: Edizione diplomatico-interpretativa,* 645) the semicolon had for Boccaccio the value of a "long pause," as did the colon. In other words, it was like a modern period. As for the rubrics, Boccaccio inserted them without leaving a blank line immediately after the end of each story; to fill out the last line of the rubric, making a more even appearance on the page, he sometimes wrote the word *rubrica,* as in the introduction to Day 4. See Branca, *Tradizione delle opere,* 2:217. See also, for an excellent more general discussion, Malcolm B. Parkes, *Pause and Effect: An Introduction to the History of Punctuation in the West* (Berkeley: University of California Press, 1993).

strength to achieve a codex as aesthetically satisfying as the many he had earlier penned. If the manuscript were a personal draft, however, he would have no need to sign. Whatever the case, it is evident that *inside the text,* beginning from the title rubric, the person who had written the book was to be known only as "the Author."

So far as the maker of the *Decameron* stresses that he has written a "book without a title," he is telling us for one thing that it is "unentitled" by authorship. For another, this cue likens his book to Ovid's *Amores,* which were "sine titulo," or "titleless." Not only the two texts but also their poets emerge from comparison as look-alikes. Holding to the low ground of vernacular prose, the Tuscan writer claims that he seeks anonymity to forestall "blasts of envy." But from where would such cutting winds have been blowing? From the desk of Francis Petrarch? From a host of second-raters whose small-minded squibs have all been lost? Do not these attackers sound suspiciously like the people who plagued Ovid in legends transmitted by his medieval vitae, "enemies who habitually criticized his writings"? Whether or not Boccaccio's early novelle scandalized readers in fourteenth-century Florence—and there is no hard evidence that they did—his defense at the introduction to the Fourth Day is a classic Ovidian pose. Chances are, he is not answering a current public outcry but setting up dialogue in his "book without a title" with a silent partner from ancient Rome.[9]

Boccaccio's own rationale for the double identity of Ovid's erotic Latin book, offered in the vita of that poet he composed for his commentary on Dante's Limbo, gives another insight into the similarities.

. . . il quale alcun chiamano *Liber amorum,* altri il chiamano *Sine titulo:* e può l'un titolo e l'altro avere, per ciò che d'alcuna altra cosa non parla che di suoi inamoramenti e di sue lascivie usate con una

---

9. Janet Levarie Smarr makes this suggestion in "Ovid and Boccaccio: A Note on Self-Defense," *Mediaevalia* 13 (1987): 247–55. Her essay focuses on the echoes of Ovid's *Tristia* in Boccaccio's conclusion as "Author" to the *Decameron.* Ovid's voice in the proem, from the *Heroides,* marks a point of departure for Victoria Kirkham, "Boccaccio's Dedication to Women in Love," in *The Sign of Reason,* 117–29 (first published in *Renaissance Studies in Honor of Craig Hugh Smyth,* ed. Andrew Morrogh, Fiorella Superbi Gioffredi, Piero Morselli, and Eve Borsook [Florence: Giunti Barbèra, 1985], 1:333–43). See also Hollander, "The Proem of the *Decameron.*" Although Padoan (cf. above, n. 6) and others have argued that Boccaccio's introduction to Day 4 responds to real criticism of the novelle, which had begun to circulate independently, I prefer to think that the break for the Author's defense after the first three days of storytelling was planned from the beginning of the work. See Kirkham, *The Sign of Reason,* 131–71.

giovane amata da lui, la quale egli nomina Corinna; e puossi dire similemente *Sine titulo,* per ciò che d'alcuna materia continuata, dalla quale si possa intitolare, favella, ma alquanti versi d'una e alquanti d'un'altra, e così possiam dir di pezi, dicendo, procede.

[. . . which book some call *Liber amorum;* others call it *Sine titulo.* And it can have one title as well as the other, because it does not speak of anything except his amours and his dalliance practiced with a young woman loved by him, whom he names Corinna. And it can likewise be called *Sine titulo* because it does not talk of any matter continually by which it can be titled, but quite a few verses deal with one thing and quite a few with another, and so we can say that it proceeds, in telling, piecemeal.] (*Esposizioni* 4.1.119)

What this long-reeled prose communicates is that it you read the book's theme as love, you can fair enough entitle it *A Book of Love.* But if you recognize that it skips about from one subject to another, so that it stays with none continuously, then you had best label it *Titleless.* Each description fits the *Decameron.* Mostly it is a book about love. At the same time, it is a collection whose tales the compiler took care to vary.

Boccaccio's allusion to *Sine titulo* in the introduction to Day 4 complements other Ovidian connecters planted at the beginning and end of his volume. The proem, which dedicates the *Decameron* to idle women in love, echoes Hero's letter to Leander in Ovid's *Heroides.* For the Author's conclusion and a second defense, as Janet Smarr has shown, he relies conspicuously on Ovid's poems of exile, the *Tristia.* In other words, for the *Decameron* the absence of an authorial signature seems not to be an accident of manuscript transmission. To support this hypothesis, the *Decameron* provides strong internal evidence, especially in the *cornice,* where Boccaccio's Ovidian strategy is constant and obvious. As is often the case, he reverses his model: Ovid's *Amores* had a known author but were *Sine titulo;* Boccaccio's amorous tales come in a book blessed by two names, including a princely title, but they are unentitled by author. The humble, anonymously authored volume ("senza titolo") is a deliberate ploy on the part of the poet, calculated to align his anthology of love stories with those of his Latin predecessor. It was not the *Metamorphoses* alone, so influential for Boccaccio's enthusiasms as a mythographer, that earned him his nickname as "the Tuscan Ovid."

If it surprises us to realize that the book we remember as Boccaccio's masterpiece was purposely constructed to be anonymous, we must wonder no less at his strategy vis-à-vis the *Teseida delle nozze d'Emilia* (Thesead of Emilia's nuptials), offered with pride as the first epic in Tuscan vernacular. It, too, lacks a signature, despite the fact that it survives in an autograph embellished with a glossolary apparatus by the poet himself that surely ought to have announced the "Author's" name. Eclectic like all Boccaccio's works, this one was composed about 1339–41, ten years before the *Decameron.* It straddles times and styles—begun in Naples but completed in Florence; true to the Virgilian tradition but a response to Dante, whose *De vulgari eloquentia* (2.2) regretted that no one yet had written on "arms" in the Italian language.

While it was Boccaccio in his persona as new lover who composed the *Filocolo,* for purposes of the *Teseida* he has lived long enough to learn the pains of emotional attachment. Feeling especially miserable, because, no less than Francesca da Rimini, he remembers bygone happiness, he indicts an epistle to Fiammetta, whose flame went dead when she disdainfully withdrew her favors.[10] Time has passed since that Saturday morning in San Lorenzo, the day when he, "young in years and in sense," became her subject. Nonetheless, although Fortune is his enemy, he will never tire of faithfully serving. And because he well knows how much Fiammetta used to like love stories, to please her he will tell her "a very old one," in which she will recognize their own romance. Which one of the two male protagonists plays his part, he will not give away; she can see for herself. Has he disguised himself as Arcita, the exile hopeful of Emilia's hand who expired from wounds in a tournament, or Palemone, a luckier knight protected by the goddess Venus?

What mainly matters is that he is being mysterious. It is a ploy to attract curiosity, to pull Fiammetta (and the rest of us) into the body of his text. The Author retains his stance as riddler by next setting a challenge for his lady in her reading. Unlike most members of her sex, she is a cultured woman, and so he confidently adopts "closed speech"; that is, he promises the intellectual pleasure of a discourse that must be deciphered. As if on cue, to help in that process and explain the hard parts, once we enter the

---

10. Giovanni Boccaccio, *Teseida delle nozze d'Emilia,* ed Alberto Limentani, in *Tutte le opere,* vol. 2 (Milan: Mondadori, 1964), "A Fiammetta": "Come che a memoria tornandomi le felicità trapassate, nella miseria vedendomi dov'io sono . . ." [Since past happiness returns to memory, as I see myself in such a wretched state . . .]. Cf. *Inf.* 5.121–23: "Nessun maggior dolore / che ricordarsi del tempo felice / ne la miseria" [No greater sorrow than to recall, in wretchedness, the happy time].

epic, who should step up but a Glossator. He does not record his name, either when he signs on or off. But we are meant to recognize, or at least suspect, who is there smiling behind the mask. Boccaccio, after all, is hardly a fugitive from his public, so the disguise as Glossator need not and should not render him unidentifiable. That would spoil the fun, just as masquerades and Halloween costumes fail when they totally veil. When that happens, we cannot appreciate the humorous contrast between the character underneath and whatever startling personality he now pretends to be. Similarly, Boccaccio's *dédoublement* as Author and Commentator amounts to a witty game whose success requires that we recognize each face and the amusing ironies of their juxtaposition.

Whereas we can understand why this Commentator is reticent about his own name, it is more perplexing that he never tells us the Author's. True enough, by referring to the *Teseida*'s compiler only as "l'autore," he anticipates the strategy for self-effacement that will be elected by the writer of the "untitled" *Decameron*. Nevertheless, his refusal to name the Author violates the decorum of commentary, since as everyone knows, a proper apparatus opens with an *accessus,* and one of the main parts of "accessing the author" is registering his name—the name integral to a work's "title." What kind of commentator is this then? Not a real one, clearly. Here is Boccaccio in yet another mask, one with large enough eyeholes for us to catch his wink. As Virgil had a Servius to gloss the *Aeneid,* as Statius had Lactantius Placidus for notes on the *Thebaid,* so this modern Author of the first epic in Italy's vernacular must be published together with a colingual commentator. The latter figure gives his *Teseida* what Robert Hollander calls "instant classic" status when he spreads explanations all over the manuscript folios, in interlinear as well as marginal locations, as if this were information that had accrued through centuries. One of his chief concerns is to underline his Author's fidelity to epic forms as practiced by earlier authors. Thus the first thing he writes has nothing to do with the usual medieval glossolary preliminaries—who wrote the work, its title, to which branch of philosophy it belongs, and so forth—all the items that Boccaccio himself systematically broaches in the *Expositions on the Comedy of Dante.* Rather this commentary denies scholasticism and prefers a stance indicative of the early Renaissance. When it glosses the opening verses, "O Castalian sisters who dwell content on Mount Helicon, around the sacred Gorgonean font," it certifies their Author's authority by highlighting those parts of his compilation that repeat modes consecrated from antiquity: "In the beginning of his book the Author, according to the ancient custom of composers, makes an invocation, and he calls the Muses to help him in the present work; . . . 'Castalian' he calls them for a font in Boeotia, which is named Castalian, consecrated to the said Muses."[11]

The elusive *Teseida* poet is really a plurality. He still carries his torch, but by now frustration and fatigue have set in. Unhappy in love, he resembles either Arcita or Palemone; that is for Fiammetta, who is his target reader, to decide. Side by side with the narrator steps a scholarly twin who does duty as his Commentator, a man versed in the best rhetorical techniques of classical antiquity. This Author, a dejected lover straight from courtly romance, undergoes a final apotheosis at the end of the epic to become, in a transcending image, "vate" [bard]. When he takes leave of his work, Fiammetta, once responsible for his sentimental anxieties, has melted into the background, taking second place to new mistresses, the Muses.

> O sacre Muse, le quali io adoro
> e con digiuni onoro e vigiliando,
> . . . .
> io ho ricolte della vostra mensa
> alcune miche da quella cadute,
> e come seppi qui l'ho compilate.

[O sacred Muses, whom I adore and honor with fasting and vigils, . . . I have collected from your board some crumbs fallen from it, and I have compiled them as best I could.]

In Boccaccio's farewell invocation to the Muses, we seem to hear again Dante atop Purgatory as he girds his powers to describe his meeting with Beatrice, the solemn occasion for his self-naming: "O sacrosante Vergini,

---

11. *Tes.* 1.1–2 and gloss.: "O sorelle castalie, che nel monte Elicon contente dimorate"; "Nel principio del suo libro fa l'autore, secondo l'antico costume de' componitori, una sua invocazione, e chiama le Muse in suo aiuto alla presente opera; . . . 'castalie' le chiama per una fonte che è in Boezia, c'ha nome Castalia, consecrata alle dette Muse." Robert Hollander has written insightfully on the commentary in "The Validity of Boccaccio's Self-Exegesis in his *Teseida*," *Medievalia et Humanistica*, n.s., 8 (1977): 163–83. Jeffrey T. Schnapp focuses on tension between the "antiquity" of Boccaccio's epic and the "modernity" of the commentary, in "Un commento all'autocommento nel *Teseida*," in *Boccaccio 1990: The Poet and His Renaissance Reception*, ed. Kevin Brownlee and Victoria Kirkham, *Studi sul Boccaccio* 20 (1992): 185–203. See also Susan Noake's now basic chapter on the *Teseida* in her *Timely Reading: Between Exegesis and Interpretation* (Ithaca: Cornell University Press, 1973).

se fami, / freddi o vigilie mai per voi soffersi . . ." [O most holy Virgins, if
hunger, cold, or vigils I have ever endured for you . . .] (*Purg.* 29.37, 38).
At the same time, now that Boccaccio has completed the inaugural epic in
Italian vernacular, fulfilling a need mentioned in the *De vulgari eloquentia,*
he recalls the very opening of Dante's philosophical encyclopedia, *Convivio,* a banquet of learning that aspires to serve crumbs of wisdom collected under a high table: "O beati quelli pochi che seggiono a quella
mensa dove lo pane de li angeli si manuca!" [O blessed those few who sit at
that board where they eat the bread of the angels!] (*Conv.* 1.1.7) Boccaccio's learned Muses, more human in their impulses than Dante's heavenly
commensals, will rise from the table to run an important errand for him.
They deliver his poem to Fiammetta so she can save it from the obscurity
of anonymity. Not the Author but his Lady-of-the-Flame gives the book a
name, *Thesead of Emilia's Nuptials,* in a licensing ceremony that recalls the
rite of baptism. Precisely at the moment of informing him what name she
has chosen, the Muses address the Author as "vate" [bard], then sprinkle
the newly christened story with water from their "holy font"—that same
"Gorgonean font" of which Author and Commentator had spoken at the
start of the *Teseida*—and send it on a journey through all the ages.

This elaborate ritual for naming the epic, like the Commentator's reti-
cence at the beginning, underscores the absence of an authorial name.
Why, for all his pride of accomplishment, couched in language that points
back to Dante, can Boccaccio not sign the *Teseida*? Author and Commentator both conspire to withhold the name of the man who should be credited for this ambitious creation. Their silence—perhaps also Filostrato's in
turning as narrator to the Trojan War—is Boccaccio's homage to the master in the genre of epic as he then knew it, Virgil. Virgil had left a signature
in his *Georgics,* but he had not so signed the *Eclogues* or the *Aeneid.*[12] Thus
Boccaccio will not name himself, nor will he permit his Commentator to
name him, because that would violate the protocol of heroic poetry, epit-
omized by the Mantuan. It would not be "according to the ancient custom
of composers."

Boccaccio's first work after returning to Florence from Naples during
the winter of 1340–41 has a title that asserts its Tuscan provenance, *Comedy of the Florentine Nymphs.* As in the *Teseida,* a certain disjunction sep-

---

12. Virgil's signature (and its absence) are noted in the useful summary of examples by
Ernst Robert Curtius in "The Author's Name in Medieval Literature," in *European Literature and the Latin Middle Ages,* trans. Willard Trask, Bollingen Series 36 (Princeton: Princeton University Press, 1973), 515–18.

arates the voice who speaks at the start from the person who takes his leave. At first, discarding his title of poet, our Author steps back into his chivalric boots as the man content to admire a mistress: "Non poeta, ma piuttosto amante, quella, di cui io sono, aiutandomi, canterò" [Not as a poet, but rather as lover, helped by that lady to whom I belong, her I shall sing] (1.12–13).[13] Yet at the end, when the moon rises over the Ganges and stars adorn the sky, he must take his leave as witness to Ameto's story from the leafy spring bower where he had spent the day. Now he sheds the swain's happy cape and admits to envy of his rustic hero, contrasting the joys of pastoral Etruria with a loveless atmosphere that awaits him at home.

> Lì non si ride mai, se non di rado;
> la casa oscura e muta e molto trista
> me ritiene e riceve, mal mio grado;
>   dove la cruda e orribile vista
> d'un vecchio freddo, ruvido e avaro
> ognora con affanno più m'atrista,
>   sì che l'aver veduto il giorno caro
> e ritornare a così fatto ostello
> rivolge ben quel dolce in tristo amaro.
> . . . .
>   Io mi tornai, dolendo de' miei mali,
> al luogo usato; e attendendo peggio
> per la sua fine, ho già pennute l'ali
>   al volare alla morte, la quale cheggio
> la notte e 'l dì per men doglia sentire.

[There one never laughs, or rarely; and the house, dark, mute, and exceedingly sad, receives me and keeps me against my will, where the crude and horrible sight of a cold old man, rough and miserly, ever more burdens me with sadness, so that having seen the cherished day, returning to such a hostel indeed changes that sweetness into sad bitterness. . . . Sorrowful with afflictions, I took myself back to the usual place; and awaiting a worse end, I already have my wings

---

13. Giovanni Boccaccio, *Comedia delle ninfe fiorentine,* ed. Antonio Enzo Quaglio, in *Tutte le opere,* vol. 2 (Milan: Mondadori, 1964). I have also consulted *L'Ameto,* trans. Judith Serafini-Sauli (New York: Garland, 1985).

plumed to fly toward death, which I implore day and night, the less
to feel my grief.] (49.78–98)

Traditionally, this passage has been taken as an allusion to family tensions
at Boccaccio's house, an unhappy place where money was tight, dominated by an unloving father, and chilled by an intrusive stepmother.[14] Cut
off from old friends, youthful freedom, and privileges of his Neapolitan
years, he found himself trapped in a city provincial by comparison with
the sparkling southern court and gripped by deepening financial crisis. His
first months there were a lonely, sobering time. Then, in August, 1341,
more with "tears" than with "ink," he wrote his old friend Niccolò
Acciaiuoli, hoping to elicit an invitation that would give him an excuse to
escape back to Naples.

Yet clearly, although a difficult adjustment for Boccaccio, the move
north was not a dislocation that stopped him from soon resuming his writing. He returned to a vein he had mined in Naples, where it must have
served him well. *Diana's Hunt,* his first work in Italian from the Neapolitan period, provided inspiration for the first work in the Florentine period.
The *Hunt* is a fiction in which court ladies of Naples are disguised as
nymphs; thanks to Venus, beasts they track and capture are transformed
into lovers. The *Comedy of the Florentine Nymphs* replays this plot, except
that Boccaccio has revised it to suit his new Tuscan circles. Hence the
nymphs are mostly Florentine, from prominent families of that mercantile
milieu, and they hunt not in mythic "Parthenope" but in prehistoric
"Etruria." After each one tells how she has "tamed" a lover, all together
transform the protagonist Ameto from an animallike rustic to a perfect
gentleman. In allegory, both nymphals describe a triumph in the soul of
reason over beastly appetite, followed by baptism and conversion to
Christianity.

In practical terms, Boccaccio conceived these fantasies to win patronage by naming female members of wealthy dynasties. For his début in
Naples, he had cast a wide net and invoked fifty-eight, all designated outright with both Christian and family names—Zizzola Barrile, Cecca Boz-
zuto, Principessella Caracciola, and so on. For his entry into the literary

---

14. Raffaello Ramat, in "Boccaccio, 1340–1344," *Belfagor* 19 (1964): 17–30, speaks of the
striking "autobiographical violence" in these verses at the end of the *Ameto.* He believes that
they undoubtedly describe "his [Boccaccio's] father's house," depicted in terms that reflect
"Boccaccio's black mood." Ramat sees in the description of this house a new realism, which
is also symbolic: he argues that it "stands for" the opposite of what a true city should be, as
defined in the ideal-city myths of the *Ameto.*

scene in Florence, he plays a more subtle game. Now the women are only seven, we must reconstruct their names from clues, and each stands for one of the cardinal and theological virtues. Naturally, Boccaccio's flattery would be lost if symbolic names entirely concealed the ladies' real clans. It is another kind of masking, like the Author's, only successful when it is sufficiently transparent. The first nymph to tell her story is "Wisdom," whom the poet calls "Mopsa." Mopsa identifies herself by attributing an etymology to her paternal grandfather's name that recalls a shift in the surname of the line to which Dante had belonged. At a certain stage in his ancestry, so explains Boccaccio in his *Trattatello,* Dante had a female progenitor who gave her son her maiden name, *Aldighieri,* from which the *d* later dropped to leave simply *Alighieri.* Such was his valor that those descended from him decided to abandon their own family name ("titolo"), *Elisei,* and adopt his. Similarly, according to Mopsa, she had a grandfather who belonged to the Visdomini family, but he fell so in love with the woman he married, Cotrulla, that he discarded his own name and took hers. Going by imperfect Greek, Boccaccio intended for the name *Cotrulla* to mean "she whose hair is shorn." Its verb, "to sheer" or "to cut," would correspond in Italian to *tosare,* from which we derive the family name *Della Tosa.* The second nymph whose story we hear symbolizes Justice. She is an Emilia, granddaughter of a wool-guild member, and she says she married a man "il cui nome grazioso mi piacque" [whose gracious name pleased me]. In other words, like Boccaccio, he was a "Giovanni." Piecing together the clues, Boccaccio's biographers have discerned in this couple Emilia de' Tornabuoni and her husband, Giovanni di Nello. And so it goes for the other nymphs. Boccaccio manages to multiply his inventory not only by referring obliquely to the virtue-lady at hand, as she tells her story, but by letting her likewise hint at the famous names in her family tree. In that way the poet can deliver himself of an impressive Florentine list: beyond Visdomini, Della Tosa, and Tornabuoni, he invites us to recognize Gianfigliazzi, Peruzzi, Strozzi, and Regaletti. Who exactly each of these women was historically we can no longer always piece together; our best identifications remain partial. When the *Comedy of the Florentine Nymphs* began to circulate, though, people must have caught the allusions readily enough.[15]

There is in the conclusion of his *Comedy of the Florentine Nymphs* a new

---

15. *Trattatello* 1.15–16: "in uno [figlio], sì come le donne sogliono essere vaghe di fare, le piacque di rinovare il nome de' suoi passati, e nominollo Aldighieri; come che il vocabolo poi, per sottrazione di questa lettera 'd' corrotto, rimanesse Alighieri. Il valore di costui fu cagione a quegli che discesero di lui, di lasciare il titolo degli Elisei, e di cognominarsi degli

consciousness of literature's warming, life-affirming embrace. His book becomes metaphorically a rose, the flower that blooms among thorns of a harder, colder world around. This rose, coaxed from the pricklings of his adversity, Boccaccio gives to Niccolò di Bartolo del Buono di Firenze. Niccolò will stand in as his Caesar, his Herennius, his Maecenas.

> prendi questa rosa, tra le spine della mia avversità nata, la quale a forza fuori de' rigidi pruni tirò la fiorentina bellezza . . . . E questa non altrimenti ricevi che da Virgilio il buono Augusto o Erennio da Cicerone, o come da Orazio il suo Mecena, prendevano i cari versi.

> [take this rose, born among the thorns of my adversity, forced into bloom by Florentine beauty from the stiff brambles. . . . And receive this not otherwise than the good Augustus took the dear verses from Caesar and Herennius from Cicero, or as Horace did from his Maecenas.] (50.3–4)

Niccolò takes his place in an illustrious line: to Augustus Caesar Virgil had dedicated the *Aeneid;* Herennius was the recipient who had given his name to *Rhetorica ad Herennium,* a core manual on rhetoric attributed to Cicero; Maecenas was the contemporary of Augustus whose support of Horace and others made him "the Patron" by antonomasia. Who was Niccolò? In 1360, nearly twenty years after Boccaccio dedicated to him his pastoral allegory, Niccolò entered a political conspiracy with Pino de' Rossi, another of Boccaccio's friends, and he was put to death. Apart from that passing reference to his violent end, which Matteo Villani notes in his chronicle of Florence, we know little about this prominent citizen. Neither can we then guess what Boccaccio's particular motives would have been for offering him this piece, beyond the obvious hope of patronage from a burgher of wealth and culture. This gesture, however, is something new in the Certaldan's corpus. For the first time, his dedicatee is not a Mystery

---

Alighieri; il che ancora dura infino a questo giorno." Later in the *Comedìa delle ninfe,* when Boccaccio gets to Fiammetta-Temperance, he attributes to her one of the same Roman ancestors from whom he says in the *Trattatello* Dante was descended, the Frangiapani. Fiammetta calls them the "Fresapani" (*Com. ninfe* 35.30). For historical glosses on the women who have been identifed, see Quaglio's edition of the *Comedia delle ninfe fiorentine,* especially 18.4–6 and notes, 21.1–11 and notes. Close parallels in the allegory of the *Caccia* and the *Ameto* are identified in Cassell and Kirkham, *Diana's Hunt,* 30–33.

Lady or a Filomena or Fiammetta; it is a real person.[16] The literary impli-
cations are clear enough: if this Niccolò del Buono is the new Augustus,
Herennius, and Maecenas, then Giovanni Boccaccio is the new Virgil,
Cicero, and Horace.

We have to wait until the *Teseida*'s closing verses for Boccaccio to
unveil its full title, but even then he still will not name himself. Similarly, at
the end of the *Comedia delle ninfe* he highlights the name of "Niccolò di
Bartolo del Buono di Firenze" but suppresses his own. Here, as in the epic,
he must be following the example of Virgil, who did not leave a signature
in his *Eclogues*. How carefully Boccaccio choreographed his bucolic fantasy to follow the rules of the genre in other ways has been shown by
Giuseppe Velli. It is not just personal unhappiness but also poetic discipline that dictates that sudden autobiographical intrusion into the last
chapter. The abrupt shift there from third-person to first-person narrative
respects a convention of pastoral literature. Nightfall marks a melancholy
return to everyday reality, which ruptures the Arcadian boundary around
a primordial, timeless, and utopian world.[17] Emblematic of universal life
cycles, the pastoral day is a paradigm that was particularly suited to Boccaccio's current circumstances. The golden years of his youth behind him
in Naples, he could retreat in imagination to the sunny, idyllic realms of an
Arcadia on the Arno. As every story must unwind to an end, so, finally,
must we all troop back to daily routines with their troublesome demands.
The ultimate reality we shall have to confront is death, but as long as there
is fiction to read and write, we can keep postponing our departure.

Given Boccaccio's bent toward self-effacement—from the absence of
signatures in epic and pastoral to an "untitled" *Decameron*—what makes
him sometimes decide to sign at all? Why does he announce himself with
such fanfare in the *Amorosa visione*? And what is his intention in the *Filocolo,* the only work from the Neapolitan period to disclose its composer's
real name? Actually, the *Filocolo* falls somewhere in between the alterna-
tives of signing or not, since there he has it both ways. In the opening
pages, focused on Fiammetta, he is noticeably reticent about himself; only

---

16. Giuseppe Velli, commenting on Boccaccio's return to a first-person narrator at the
end of his *Ameto,* identifies the shift as a convention of the genre of pastoral; see "L'*Ameto* e
la Pastorale, il significato della forma," in *Boccaccio: Secoli di Vita,* ed. Marga Cottino-Jones
and Edward F. Tuttle (Ravenna: Longo 1977), 67–80, reprinted in Giuseppe Velli, *Petrarca
e Boccaccio: Tradizione, memoria, scrittura,* 2d ed. (Padua: Antenore, 1995), 195–208.

17. Branca, *Profilo biografico,* 60 and 121.

later does he declare his identity, and even then he speaks in a riddle. Why? Poetics of medieval vernacular art require "the composer" to wait his turn patiently on the sidelines, until it is time for him to step forward.

A clock ticks until the *Filocolo*'s fourth book. Its opening marks a new departure in the narrative, for there the hero initiates his love quest, having just at the end of book 3 assumed his *nom de voyage, Filocolo.* No sooner has Florio hidden behind an alias, than the Author peeks out of the page with the clues to his name. At this juncture in the plot, Filocolo and his companions have reached an oak grove in Tuscany, not far from Pisa. Since we are, fictionally, in the sixth century and among pagans—a background animate with all manner of gods, goddesses, omens, and prodigies—it should come as no surprise that here stands no ordinary forest. The wood is sacred and, as such, is appropriately possessed of a working oracle. True to form for an oracle, this one speaks from the ruined temple of Jove where it quarters, in a good and proper riddle. From the crumbling walls of its ghostly structure flows forth a command to Filocolo: "Onora questo luogo, però che quinci ancora si partirà colui che i tuoi accidenti con memorevoli versi farà manifesti agli ignoranti, e 'l suo nome sarà pieno di grazia" [Honor this place, because from here will also depart he who with memorable verses shall make manifest to the ignorant your fortunes, and his name shall be full of grace] (4.1).

The word for "oak grove" in Italian is *cerreto.* From *cerreto* we derive the homologous place-name *Certaldo,* as we learned in chapter 1 when analyzing Filocolo's dream about the blackbird from Certaldo who caught a well-feathered pheasant in Sulmona (4.13). According to the primeval oracle, murmuring its message from the oaks, the native of this place whose "verses" will unforgettably educate posterity to Filocolo's life bears a name "full of grace." Why does the voice speaking for Jove refer to the prose fiction of the *Filocolo* as verse? Perhaps, as Francesco Bruni suggests, Boccaccio here recalls Dante's distinction in the *Vita nuova* (chap. 25) between "writing in verses in Latin" and "writing in rhymes in vernacular." Coming from the king of the Greek gods, no less, the solemn pronouncement in the *Filocolo* authorizes Boccaccio's project on a high, classical register, a plane reinforced by the term "versi," which seems to hint at the Latin models that inspired the new author for his epic treatment of the legendary medieval lovers, Florio and Biancifiore—Virgil's *Aeneid,* Statius's *Thebaid,* and Lucan's *De bello civile.* As for the epithet "full of grace," from the Hebrew for "John," that had been privileged by Dante in *Paradiso* 12.80–81, when he praised the mother who would be blessed by bearing Saint Dominic: "Veramente Giovanna, / se, interpretata val come si dice!" [Truly Giovanna, if this, being interpreted, means as is said!]. Dante's lines conform to the medieval dictum concerning word origins, "Nomina sunt consequentia rerum" [Names are the consequence of things]. Both Dante and Boccaccio would have known the etymology for *Giovanni* (and hence its feminine variant, *Giovanna*) from Isidore of Seville, under his rubric on the apostles: "Iohanna autem interpretatur Domini gratia" [Now *John* is interpreted as "grace of the Lord"]. When Benvenuto da Imola glosses Dante's "Giovanna," he explains it a bit differently, "Johanna enim interpretatur gratia plena" [*Giovanna* means "full of grace"]. His Latin synonym for the proper noun of Hebrew origin is the same phrase as Gabriel's greeting at the Annunciation, "Ave, gratia plena." Boccaccio then scripts his oracle to predict that a poet will emerge from Certaldo to write in the Latin epic tradition. Prophesying that "his name will be full of grace" [e 'l suo nome sarà pieno di grazia], he alludes to Dante's little vita of Saint Dominic in *Paradiso* 12, as well as to an important passage on the art of poetry and allegory in the *Vita nuova*. He whose Christian name is "full of grace" [gratia plena] is, we could say, "truly John" [veramente Giovanni], that John of Certaldo who by "God's grace" [domini gratia] will realize a great literary opus.[18]

Restoring Boccaccio's narrative order of events in the *Filocolo,* we see how close after the oracle in the oak grove (4.1) he inserts the ornithological dream (4.13). He puts two autobiographical episodes in close proximity, early in book 4, and they are the first we have heard of him since the prologue scene of book 1. Actually, Boccaccio had already seeded Certaldo as the "cerreto" back in book 3, chapter 33. As we might expect from the numbers marking this place in the text, its subject is an amorous char-

---

18. Bruno Porcelli's analysis of the narrative structure of the *Filocolo* corroborates the importance of the juncture at 4.1, which he sees as the beginning of the third of three "macrosequences" that articulate the plot of the romance (the first two are books 1 and books 2–3); see "Strutture e forme narrative nel *Filocolo,*" *Studi sul Boccaccio* 21 (1993): 207–33. Francesco Bruni speculates on the rationale for the word *versi* in Boccaccio's prophecy at 4.1 in his compendious *Boccaccio: L'invenzione della letteratura mezzana* (Bologna: Il Mulino, 1990), 187–88. In studying Florentine archival documents of the sixteenth century, I have found *versi* still in frequent usage in nonliterary contexts, with the broad sense of "prose writing." On the meaning of the names *John* and *Giovanna,* see Isidore *Etym.* 7.9.5; Benvenuto da Imola, *Comentum super Dantis,* 5:80. Boccaccio, in bidding his book farewell, acknowledges his debt to Virgil and Statius (5.97) but does not declare Lucan's name, although conspicuous borrowings from that poet have been identified in the *Filocolo*. See, e.g., Quaglio's commentary in his edition and, for a lucid recent statement on the subject, Giuseppe Velli, "Cultura e 'imitatio' nel primo Boccaccio," in *Petrarca e Boccaccio,* 77–117.

acter, aptly named Fileno. Fileno has fled into the wilderness after losing a bid for Biancifiore's love. Eventually, he finds his way to the very grove that houses Jove's temple, and there, on a grassy meadow, he weeps himself into a liquid state. After receiving the oracle, Filocolo engages sympathetically in conversation with those gurgling waters that hide the sufferer (4.2), and then, on a subsequent visit to the same woodsy intersection, he witnesses Fileno recover his former human self. When, after its appearance at 3.33, the "cerreto" returns to open book 4, it is the place of departure for a writer in the high style who is graced by heaven. Thirteen chapters later, at 4.13, the "cerreto" reappears, again as city of origin, but this time there is more to the story: the Certaldan travels to southerly climes and loves a lady from Sulmona. Of these three references to the oak grove (3.33, 4.1, 4.13), the first centers on a figure who functions by antithesis as one of the Author's interior doubles (the lover betrayed), the second links the Author to his book, and the third pairs him with his poetic mistress.

By the conventions of medieval reading, each episode rises to sharp relief. Let us postpone for now the Fileno subplot, pausing here on the other two passages. Filocolo's dream vision, masked as the mating of a merlin and pheasant, has a certain logical connection with the oracle, since in the Middle Ages the *somnium,* too, was understood as a mode of prophecy.[19] The oracle predicts that Boccaccio will write the *Filocolo* (4.1); the *somnium* predicts that he will fall in love with Fiammetta (4.13). Populated with a whole host of birds that enact a bizarre sequence of events, this "strange vision," as Filocolo calls his dream, is a seductive moment. It interrupts the narrative and sidetracks us into a veiled story within the story, pricking our curiosity, asking us to linger and decode human activities disguised in an Aesop's puzzle of the Gothic era. The antecedent oracle, not nearly as complex in symbolic terms, owes its salience primarily to another factor, not exotic *amplificatio,* but placement within the text. Boccaccio reserved for its structural location one of the most important slots available in the body of his romance, the incipit of a new book.

---

19. Macrobius *Commentarium in somnium Scipionis* 1.3.8–10; *Commentary on the Dream of Scipio,* trans. William Harris Stahl, Records of Civilization, Sources and Studies, no. 48 (New York: Columbia University Press), 90. According to Macrobius, the three categories of dreams worthy of interpretation are "oraculum," "visio," and "somnium." He argues that the last in particular requires decoding: "tegit figuris et velat ambagibus non nisi interpretatione intellegandam significationem rei quae demonstratur" [it conceals with strange shapes and veils with ambiguity the true meaning of the information being offered].

For all of its massive length, spread across several hundred chapters, the *Filocolo* has surprisingly few major divisions, or books. From Gaetano Tizzone da Pofi's mangled 1527 *Philopono* to Ettore De Ferri's late Romantic entry in 1927, editors repeatedly printed the text divided into seven "libri." Antonio Enzo Quaglio has shown how far they strayed from the structure devised by the author, a constant in all the earliest codices.[20] Boccaccio shaped the romance in not seven but five books. They are divided in turn into chapters, 459 altogether in Quaglio's modern critical reconstruction. In the manuscripts, these many, relatively short chapters come and go on the folios without much ado, a fortiori in copies belonging to one of the manuscript families that has lost its title rubrics.[21] No matter how modest the codex, however, the longer principal divisions of the prose stand apart, signaled by larger incipit initials and sometimes by painted miniatures. The historiated initial at the incipit of book 3 in a copy now at Venice (Biblioteca Marciana, MS Ital. 10.31) features a melancholy adolescent Florio dressed in crimson and daydreaming alone in a garden. The most luxurious handmade *Filocolo,* produced in 1464 for Prince Lodovico VII Gonzaga of Mantua, has a cycle of five magnificent illustrations, one to head each book (Oxford, Bodleian Library, MS Canon Ital. 85; figs. 2–6). Although these splendid miniatures were as carefully planned as they were executed, the artist chose not to depict Jove's oracle in the first chapter of book 4 (fig. 5). His courtly scene renders the beginning of the love quest, actually the final episode of book 3. We, of course, can read Filocolo's departure as proleptic, a scene that anticipates his pause for pagan worship in the ghostly temple on the "cerruto colle" [oaken hilltop], heights predestined to give birth to the poet Giovanni (*Filoc.*4.1). Disregarding that vatic pronouncement in the woods, the miniaturist instead paints Florio, alias Filocolo, with his search party and their mounts in an urban piazza near the sea. Like other illuminators who occasionally decorated manuscripts of the Filocolo, this one prefers to focus on the fiction rather than on its maker. It is revealing that none of

---

20. Editions of the *Filocolo* through 1587 are described by Bacchi della Lega in *Opere di Giovanni Boccaccio,* 101–8. Its most recent editor, Antonio Enzo Quaglio, has documented the disastrous impact of Gaetano Tizzone da Pofi on its publishing history in "Prime correzioni al *Filocolo:* Dal testo di Tizzone verso quello del Boccaccio," *Studi sul Boccaccio* 1 (1963): 27–252.

21. Quaglio, in his edition, does not reproduce the rubrics, which do not occur in all families of the manuscript. I believe they were probably part of Boccaccio's text, as elsewhere (*Filostrato, Teseida, Decameron*) and should be restored.

the illustrators seized the opportunity waiting here to provide the book with an author portrait, a visual counterpart to the signature.[22]

Even if the signature seems to have passed unnoticed by the artists, Dante's young follower in the Tuscan family of poets certainly knew what he was about. Before the *Filocolo*, in his *Filostrato*, he had begun working with the poetic possibilities for his name in its masculine and feminine variants as well as its etymology. For this Trojan tale, spun from medieval Homeric material, Boccaccio systematically Hellenizes the names of the new principal characters he has molded, both "in" the story and "outside" it for the frame: Pandaro, the pander between Troiolo and Criseida; a narrator called Filostrato; and a lady for whom he writes, Filomena. Since it is a romance, the cognate names are rooted in the Greek word for "love," *philos*. Forms occur here for the first time that will carry through to the *Decameron* and serve as *brigata* names for trecento Florentines. But already in *Filostrato*, the narrator and his mistress are bearing pseudonyms. *Filomena* is a *senhal* that must veil a "Giovanna," since Filostrato speaks in his proem of "vostro nome di grazia pieno" [your name full of grace]. She mirrors Filostrato, who is in turn a specular image of Boccaccio.[23] But never once in this book does anyone called "Giovanni Boccaccio" ever put in an appearance.

By contrast, when the epithet "full of grace" returns in the *Filocolo*, coupled with defining topography, its referent is unquestionably the Certaldan himself. In their vitae, poets always belong to places. Boccaccio will write most passionately on this theme of poetic citizenship in his

---

22. For the *Filocolo*, unlike the *Decameron, De mulieribus claris*, and *De casibus virorum illustrium*, no programmatic cycle of illustrations evolved. None of the several illustrated manuscripts depicts the author at the incipit of book 4. As was often the case, the artists probably were not familiar with the text, and in any event, an author portrait in the middle would have violated visual protocol, which typically puts the author's picture at the beginning of the text (less frequently, at the end). See Victoria Kirkham, "Renaissance Portraits of Boccaccio: A Look into the Kaleidoscope," in "Boccaccio visualizzato II," *Studi sul Boccaccio* 16 (1987): 284–305, updated in "L'immagine del Boccaccio." I have benefited from a typescript with a list of the five illustrated *Filocolo* manuscripts, compiled some years ago by my colleague Paul F. Watson, whom I thank for generously sharing with me his unpublished research. See also Vittore Branca, "Un primo elenco di codici illustrati di opere del Boccaccio," in "Boccaccio visualizzato I," *Studi sul Boccaccio* 15 (1985–86): 121–48; and *Boccaccio visualizzato*, ed. Vittore Branca (Turin: Einaudi, 1999), 2:88–89, 114–17, 129–30, 199, 253–54, 285–87, 295–97, 297–301, 360–75. More on the Bodleian *Filocolo* appears in the catalogue by Otto Pächt and J. J. G. Alexander in *Illuminated Manuscripts in the Bodleian Library*, 4 vols. (Oxford: Clarendon Press, 1966), 2:40.

23. *Filost.*, proem 16. Thomas Stillinger suggests these mirror images in "The Form of Filostrato," *Stanford Italian Review* 9 (1990): 191–210; see now also his *The Song of Troilus: Lyric Authority in the Medieval Book* (Philadelphia: University of Pennsylvania Press, 1992), 118–31.

Trattatello in laude di Dante, when he excoriates Florence for having
expelled its own most famous son, Dante Alighieri.[24] Fully seven cities, as
the legend goes, claimed the honor of having given Homer to the world.
Virgil belonged as much to Mantua, his birthplace, as to Rome and
Naples. If writers in antiquity *gave* their names to cities, the moderns
more often *took* a surname *from* a town. In *Filocolo* 4.1 we are in Tuscany—but not the Lucca of Bonagiunta, the Arezzo of Guittone, or the
Pistoia of Cino. In the man from a "cerrato" we immediately recognize
the Certaldo of Giovanni di Boccaccio. But why does Boccaccio postpone
his "signature" until so far along in the *Filocolo*? And why does he veil it
by punning on its Hebrew origin? Why is he not open about it, as he will
be in the acrostic of the *Amorosa visione,* not to mention the learned Latin
works of his maturity?

These latter always announce their maker. *De casibus virorum illustrium,* drafted in 1360, declares its authorship in the initial rubric,
addressed to the book's recipient: "Generoso militi domino Maghinardo
de Cavalcantibus de Florentia preclaro regni Sycilie marescallo Johannes
Boccaccius de Certaldo" [To the noble knight Maghinardo Cavalcanti of
Florence, distinguished marshal of the kingdom of Sicily, from John Boccaccio of Certaldo]. *De mulieribus claris,* transcribed about 1361 and dedicated to the sister of Niccolò Acciauoli, does the same: "Iohannes Boccaccius de Certaldo mulieri clarissime Andree de Acciarolis de Florentia
Alteville comitisse" [John Boccaccio of Certaldo to the most distinguished
woman Andrea Acciaiuoli of Florence, countess of Altavilla]. Typically,
this kind of information about who is writing occurs more than once in the
course of a manuscript, usually in the rubric that heads the body of the text
as a whole (before a proem or first book), or it may appear in rubrics that
return at each major division of the text, and it regularly enters the
colophon. Thus in an autograph manuscript of his encyclopedia on
ancient myth, Boccaccio was careful to sign himself twice, top and bottom.
At the incipit stands the rubric "Genealogie deorum gentilium ad Ugonem
inclitum Ierusalem et Cypri regem secundum Iohannem Boccaccium de
Certaldo Liber Primus incipit feliciter" [Genealogies of the Gentile Gods
to Hugo the peerless king of Jerusalem and Cyprus according to John Boccaccio of Certaldo, the First Book happily begins]. An explicit repeats the
notice: "Genealogie deorum gentilium secundum Iohannem Boccaccium
de Certaldo ad illustrem principem Ugonem, Ierusalem et Cypri regem,

---

24. *Trattatello* 1.95–97.

liber XV[us] et ultimus explicit" [Genealogies of the Gentile Gods according to John Boccaccio of Certaldo to the illustrious Prince Hugo, king of Jerusalem and Cyprus, the fifteenth and last book ends]. In his learned, nonfictional works, early humanistic compilations, Boccaccio is not coy. Rather he presents himself most openly and straightforwardly, as he knows he must to respect the dictates of tradition. Not only the name of the book but that of its author and dedicatee form a cluster of bibliographical information constituting, in effect, a full and complete title.[25]

The youthful Latin epistles of 1339 also display signatures, albeit not so assertively. They are dimly preserved in one of Boccaccio's working notebooks, the *Zibaldone laurenziano* (Florence, Biblioteca Medicea-Laurenziana, MS 29.8), a document of paramount importance to our understanding of his creative evolution in the 1330s and 1340s. Unlike the finished Latin encyclopedias, carefully transcribed in autograph manuscripts that may well have been presentation copies, the items in this miscellany were for Boccaccio's private use. Practically speaking, he did not need to sign his letters here at all. Since he apparently never intended to send them, rather like a student in penmanship class practicing to find just the right style for setting down his name, he must have been trying out his signature, "Johannes de Certaldo." Yet over and again in the manuscript, curiously, these signatures have been scratched out, not just in the salutation and closing of the early practice letters, but at the heading of other missives meant to be sent and in the title of Boccaccio's eclogue, *Faunus*. Henri Hauvette, the first scholar to describe the notebook systematically as a Boccaccian autograph, noted the peculiar erasures without attempting to explain them. Today, by scholarly consensus, we assume Boccaccio himself at some point sat down with a penknife and scraped off his own name wherever it appeared in this *Zibaldone*. What could his motive have been for suppressing his signatures?[26]

---

25. Giovanni Boccaccio, *De casibus virorum illustrium,* ed. Pier Giorgio Ricci and Vittorio Zaccaria, in *Tutte le opere,* vol. 9 (Milan: Mondadori, 1981); *De mulieribus claris,* ed. Vittorio Zaccaria, in *Tutte le opere,* vol. 10 (Milan: Mondadori, 1967); *Genealogie,* ed. Romano. In the *Genealogie,* proem 9d, there is a dialogue between Donino of Parma, speaking on behalf of King Ugo of Cyprus, and "Giovanni." Donino calls his interlocutor "mi Iohannes."

26. These letters and the other contents of the *Zibaldone laurenziano* (Florence, Biblioteca Medicea-Laurenziana, MS 29.8) were described by Henri Hauvette in "Notes sur des manuscrits autographes de Boccace à la Bibliothèque Laurentienne," in *Etudes sur Boccace (1894–1916)* (Turin: Bottega d'Erasmo, 1968), 87–146 (first published in *Mélanges d'Archéologie* 14 [1894]: 87–146). The erasures (for which see especially 106–7, 136–38) appear methodically at the top of folios 46–58. These deletions affect not just the practice

Close in time to *Filocolo,* the oldest letters in the *Zibaldone laurenziano* give the impression of an epistler less anxious to announce himself than to earn his credentials as Virgil's apprentice. Emblazoned in the closing of the first of the four exercises, "Crepor celsitudinis Epyri principatus" [Fame of the heights of the principality of Epirus], to the duke of Durazzo, is a dateline at Virgil's tomb: "Written at the foot of Mount Falerno near the bust of Virgil Maro, April 3, 1339, Your humble, etc." The second, to a "Mavortis milex estrenue" [Valorous soldier of Mars] (presumably to Petrarch), ends, "Written at the foot of Mount Falerno, etc., Yours always, John, etc." The third, to an unknown destinatee, skips all fringe formalities and has only an abbreviated "Written, etc." at the end. The fourth, whose destinatee is also a mystery, opens, "To the beloved man strong with holy and angelic fame, greetings from John of Certaldo, enemy of Fortune, in the name of him who fills with good things the hungering," and it ends, "Written at the foot of Mount Falerno near the bust of Virgil Maro, the 28th of June." Boccaccio's decision at some later point to scratch out his name, "Johannes de Certaldo," could have been in keeping with the literary game that dictated the letters: to reinforce the fiction that they were drafts of "real" (but nonexistent) fair copies. How different in character they are from missives with later dates, real addresses and very practical requests to clearly designated recipients, is clear from the next item chronologically in the canon of the Certaldan's collected *Epistole,* preserved in an Italian translation in two other manuscripts. Boccaccio wrote it to Niccolò Acciaiuoli, who had just returned to Naples from a three-year expedition in Greece. The Certaldan flatters his old friend, risen politically to a position of prominence at the Angevin court, and hints that

letters but missives presumably mailed, from Boccaccio to Cecco da Mileto and from Cecco to Boccaccio. Signatures still discernible to Hauvette were in block capitals. The same erasures appear in the *Zibaldone laurenziano,* MS 33.31. Sebastiano Ciampi (*Monumenti d'un manoscritto autografo di messer Giovanni Boccacci* [Florence: G. Galletti, 1827]) was convinced that only Boccaccio could have erased his name; others have proposed that the scratch-outs were the work of a reader who believed these works were not by Boccaccio; others have asked why Boccaccio did not just destroy entire works, instead of simply removing his name, if they embarrassed him. Scholarly consensus now sides with Ciampi: Boccaccio must have been responsible for the erasures. See F. Di Benedetto, "Considerazioni sullo Zibaldone Laurenziano del Boccaccio e restauro testuale della prima redazione del *Faunus,*" *Italia Medioevale e Umanistica* 14 (1971): 91–129; and for a detailed description of where his signatures occur in the *Zibaldone laurenziano,* see Victoria Kirkham, "Iohannes de Certaldo: La firma dell'autore," in *Gli Zibaldoni di Boccaccio: Memoria, scrittura, riscrittura,* ed. Claude Cazalé-Bérard and Michelangelo Picone (Florence: Franco Cesati, 1998), 455–68. A recent summary of the extensive bibliography on Boccaccio's letters is provided by Auzzas for her edition of the *Epistole.*

he wishes Niccolò would invite him back to the southern capital, where he had been happier than he now is in Florence. It is a letter filled with rhetorical hyperbole, including Boccaccio's plaint that he really should be writing with tears, not ink. These are not just fantasies whimsically penned in the service of poetry but flourishes calculated to catch the ear of an influential courtier, whose meteoric career was to lift him to the exalted position of grand seneschal of Naples. In closing, Boccaccio reinforces his plea for patronage by bowing, as it were, to Niccolò and blaming his own current bad luck: "Written in Florence on the 28th day of August in the year of the Lord 1341, Your Giovanni di Boccaccio da Certaldo and enemy of Fortune, paying due reverence, commends himself to you." Now there is no doubt as to the name of the destinatee; we are no longer in a territory of the imagination hallowed by Virgil's tomb but in Florence plain and simple; the date is given not in classical terms of ides and calends but according to the Christian—and Florentine—formula of day, month, and year from the Incarnation. Like the rest of the information that surrounds this historical (not fictional) letter, the signature is full and straightforward, including a patronymic as well as the toponymic, just as it appears in his *Amorosa visione,* "Giovanni di Boccaccio da Certaldo."[27]

Boccaccio recorded his signature when young and old, in actual correspondence and in manuscripts of his encyclopedias, but the deciding factor seems to have been less the language he was using than the category of literature he was composing. The signed Latin pieces represent a different and more scientific kind of writing from the fiction, which was mainly in vernacular. Perhaps Boccaccio rubbed out his signatures in the *Zibaldone* when his aggressive autodidacticism led him to discover the rule of writing that for the sake of humility forbids an author from naming himself except in very narrowly defined circumstances of necessity. He could have found one important formulation of that caveat the first time Dante's *Convivio*

---

27. *Epistolae* 1.6: "Data sub monte Falerno apud busta Maronis Virgilii nonas aprilis III, anno vero Incarnationis Verbi divini MCCCXXXVIIII, vester humilis etc."; 2.14: "Data sub monte Falerno etc., Vester in omnibus Johannes etc."; 3.21: "Data etc."; 4, incipit: "Sacre famis et angelice viro dilecto forti, Iohannes de Certaldo inimicus Fortune, in Eo salutem qui bonis exurientes implevit"; 4.35: "Scripta sub monte Falerno apud busta Maronis Virgilii, iulii kalendas IIII; 5.8, to Niccolò (which survives only in its trecento Italian translation): "Data in Firenze adí XXVIII d'agosto anni Domini MCCCXLI, Il vostro Giovanni di Boccaccio da Certaldo ed inimico della Fortuna la debita reverenzia premessa, vi si raccomanda." See Boccaccio, *Epistole,* ed. Auzzas, for the commentary by Auzzas on Boccaccio's 1341 epistle 5 to Niccolò Acciaiuoli, with its statement "Dell'essere mio in Firenze contra piacere niente vi scrivo, però che piú tosto co' lagrime che con inchiostro sarebbe da dimostrare." Boccaccio had used the same formula in epistle 2.6.

came into his hands (1.2.2), but it had been stated as well by others. As his horizons widened, bringing him into contact with many other literary models both classical and vernacular, he would have understood that how an author signed a work varied depending on genre, style, and the material vehicle of its transmission. The possibilities run a gamut from full disclosure to deliberate anonymity. Boccaccio's signatures, as we might expect given his fondness for onomastic games, conform to the most sophisticated protocol.

Sometimes, of course, lack of a signature could reflect a loss due to accidents of manuscript transmission. After all, title pages and colophons, where we expect to find the author's name, are the book parts most easily damaged and lost. Surely, it would have pained him to think that after he sent them out into the world, they could be forgotten and orphaned. That fate befell his first fiction, *Diana's Hunt,* preserved in only six manuscripts. Of those six surviving copies, all begin and end somewhat differently, two are missing either the incipit or the explicit, and none bears a trace of the person who wrote it. Girolamo Claricio announced in the 1521 first edition of a sister piece, the *Amorosa visione,* that he would soon publish "the charming and delightful little *Caccia di Diana,*" but that Milanese humanist died before he could carry out his plan. Not until 1832 did the *Hunt* find its way into print, thanks to Ignazio Moutier's project of publishing Boccaccio's complete works in Florence, but even he confessed reservations about the attribution. Hesitations, not to mention flat denials, concerning Boccaccio's paternity persisted in the absence of a signature. The poem was not definitively given to Boccaccio until 1938, when Branca settled the question once and for all, arguing from stylistic evidence and archival data on the families whose women are catalogued in the poem.[28] For a slight medieval allegory (1,047 verses), the *Hunt* was quite lucky in the end. It could finally, after six hundred years, reclaim its father. But were it not from the quill of a

28. The manuscripts, briefly described by Cassell and Kirkham in *Diana's Hunt,* 152–53, are L (Florence, Biblioteca Medicea-Laurenziana, MS Plut. 90. sup. 93); F (Florence, Biblioteca Nazionale, MS II,IX,125); FR (Florence, Biblioteca Riccardiana, MS 1059); FR[1] (Florence, Biblioteca Riccardiana, MS 1060); FR[3] (Florence, Biblioteca Riccardiana, MS 1066); WE (Wellesley, Mass., Wellesley College Library, Plimpton Collection, MS 854). L begins "Incipit Venatio Diane" and ends "Explicit Venatio Dianae"; F begins "Incipit primus cantus Venacio Diane" and breaks off four cantos before the end; FR has no title or incipit; FR[1] begins "Incipit Venatio Diane" and ends "Explicit Venatio Diane"; FR[2] begins "Caccia di Diana" and ends "compiuto capitoli Diane"; WE is acephalous and ends "Qui finisce la caccia di Diana e sue compagne." Irrefutable arguments for the authorship are advanced by Vittore Branca in "Per l'attribuzione della Caccia di Diana," in *Traditione delle opere,* 1:121–43, especially 124–27.

classic and prolific writer whose canon we want complete, Boccaccio's first work would probably still be a waif in the world of books.

Diana's Hunt was deprived of its rightful inheritance in his corpus because in the transition from manuscripts to print, editors no longer understood medieval criteria for book compilation. Although, with only six surviving manuscripts, we cannot exclude the possibility that his signature disappeared from *Diana's Hunt* with outer folios, it is much more likely that the author deliberately kept his name out of it. His whole focus is on naming fifty-eight noble ladies of Naples, as virtue-nymphs in his fantasy in terza rima, to win favor with their families. He assertively refuses to identify the fifty-ninth, a Mystery Lady symbolic of Prudence, and that silence pays homage to Dante, who humbly closes the *Vita nuova* with an admission that he is not adequate to praise Beatrice as she deserves. Speaking in what Leo Spitzer calls a "poetic I" (as opposed to the "empirical or pragmatical I") borrowed from Dante, Boccaccio, in one of his typical reversals, alludes to the final paragraph of the earlier writer's *libello* in canto 1 of his allegorical *ternario*.

> . . . né nomo lei
> perché a suo nome laude più sovrana
> si converria, che qui dir non potrei.

[. . . nor do I name her, since praise more sovereign would suit her name than I could here set forth.] (*Hunt* 1.52–55)

Names—and the refusal to name—are, in effect, the very essence of the *Hunt*. It is all names, at once a pocket bestiary and a social register. Boccaccio would have called it a *sirventese*, a poem related by genre to Dante's *serventese* that listed names of the sixty most beautiful women of Florence.[29] Counting the goddess Diana, Boccaccio's little poem also assembles exactly sixty women.

---

29. In considerations of first-person medieval narrative, it is useful to recall Leo Spitzer's distinction between the fictional "Author" and the historical person in "Note on the Poetic and the Empirical 'I' in Medieval Authors," *Traditio* 4 (1946): 414–22. The *Caccia* is a list, a favorite medieval literary form. Medieval manuscript anthologies and compilations have received thoughtful attention in, e.g., Sylvia Huot, *From Song to Book: The Poetics of Writing in Old French Lyric and Lyrical Narrative Poetry* (Ithaca: Cornell University Press, 1987), and Stillinger, *The Song of Troilus*. See Cassell and Kirkham, *Diana's Hunt*, introd., 30–68, on the allegory; 18.52 and commentary, 194, on the Mystery Lady's symbolism as Wisdom; and 10–11, on repetitions and variations of the women's names: there are nine called Caterina, three called Vanella (a diminutive of *Giovanna*), and three called Zizzola (a diminuitive of *Costanza*), and three are Jacopas—Jacopa, Giacovella, and Covella.

Apart from his chivalrous bid for patrons, there was another reason why Giovanni could remain anonymous in the *Hunt*. The manuscript tradition preserves it in a trilogy of poems all by Boccaccio, all in terza rima, and all containing a *sirventese* in praise of women. It is an overwhelming likelihood, as Branca convincingly proposes, that Boccaccio himself compiled the anthology. It has come down to us in two textual families, each with the contents in a different order. The first, which has no title rubric with an author's name, gives the *Caccia*, the *ternario* "Contento quasi," and the *Amorosa visione*. The order in the second has *ternario, Amorosa visione, Caccia;* rubrication in this second family explicitly assigns the *Visione* to Boccaccio. To account for the fact that the *Hunt* is unsigned in all extant manuscripts, Branca suggests that the first group, reflecting the author's plan, at some point lost its front page (the title folio), while the disposition in the second, which he sees as a later development, rendered unnecessary a signature with the *Hunt*, since it immediately follows the *Amorosa visione*. Branca makes an important point when he recognizes the need for no more than one signature in the three-part anthology. Although Claricio must have been in possession of a codex with the whole trilogy (since he is thinking ahead to the *Caccia* while presenting to his readers the *Visione*), he clearly did not realize that by publishing the pieces separately, he was violating a unity. Once severed in transmission from its signed sister, the unsigned *Caccia* lapsed into anonymity and lost authority.

My guess is that the rubric naming the author of the *Amorosa visione* in the second manuscript family could well be a scribal interpolation. Rubric or no, "Giovanni di Boccaccio da Certaldo" appears twice as the author of the *Amorosa visione* in both manuscript groups, and both occurrences are inside the fabric of the work as the poet originally wove it—in its "foreword" sonnets and again in the acrostic at canto 15. For this reason I find it appealing to think that the second family preserves the trilogist's original arrangement. The two shorter works then frame with pleasing symmetry the most substantial, his mammoth acrostic in fifty cantos, with the little *ternario* before and the modest *Caccia* after. Boccaccio attaches his name—and does so conspicuously—only to one poem in terza rima, the most ambitious. A single signed piece suffices for all three. Significantly, that is both the midpoint and the artistic centerpiece of the trilogy. For a poet as self-conscious about name-dropping as Giovanni Boccaccio, manuscript accidents alone cannot explain why he for his part is sometimes nameless. He chooses when and whether to sign, depending on the language in which he indites and on his intended mode, fictional or not. As in all other aspects of his writing, he respects tradition.

The most striking instance of self-naming in Italian literature before
Boccaccio is surely Dante's. He postpones registering his name in the
Divine Comedy until a critical juncture in the journey toward Paradise.
The pilgrim has regained the Garden, at the top of Mount Purgatory,
there to be met by Beatrice once Virgil slips away. She rebukes him sharply
for loving her less after her death, when, of all times, he should have loved
her more, because by becoming a saint in glory, she had grown in beauty.
For the full impact of her reproach to be felt, Beatrice must call out to him
directly.

> **"Dante,** perché Virgilio se ne vada,
> non pianger anco, non piangere ancora;"
> . . . .
> . . . mi volsi al suon del nome mio,
> che di necessità qui si registra.

["**Dante,** because Virgil leaves you, do not weep yet, do not weep
yet!" . . . I turned at the sound of my name, which of necessity is registered here.] (*Purg.* 30.55–56, 62–63)

Behind her stern accusation moves the pen of the poet, who here, for the
first time, two-thirds of the way through the cantos of the epic, finally
reveals his identity. Not coincidentally, his self-naming follows a triple
naming of Virgil, repetition that expresses Dante's grief on realizing that
he has lost his "father."

> Ma Virgilio n'avea lasciati scemi
> di sé, Virgilio dolcissimo patre,
> Virgilio a cui per mia salute die'mi.

[But Virgil had left us bereft of himself, Virgil sweetest father, Virgil
to whom I gave myself for my salvation.] (*Purg.* 30.49–51)

Robert Hollander has noticed that by signing his *Divine Comedy* here—
the only place in all his opus where he did leave a signature—Dante imi-
tates Virgil's precedent in the *Georgics.* There, following a triple invocation of Eurydice, the Roman poet placed his sole poetic signature. In the
Italian verses, Virgil replaces Eurydice as the object of loss, and Dante

takes over for Virgil when he leaves an authorial signature. In the succession of poetic generations, Dante locates himself "after" Virgil. Not until the "father" has departed can his son, the vernacular poet, step forward.[30]

The modern critical edition establishes this verse in *Purgatory* as the only place in the *Comedy* where Dante's name occurs. In the fourteenth century, however, the text for *Paradise* 26 sprouted a variant that permitted the poet to be named again, not coincidentally by the world's most qualified expert in nomenclature. To Adam went the honor, he who had named the animals and all created things in Eden. In his *Expositions on the Comedy,* Boccaccio finds that it was as fitting for Dante to have been named by Adam as by Beatrice. He quotes Adam from dialogue between the father of the race and the pilgrim.

Dante, la voglia tua discerno meglio.

[Dante, I better discern your wish.]

The line in his version was corrupt at the beginning, and the passage should read,

. . . Sanz'essermi proferta
da te, la voglia tua discerno meglio.

[. . . Without its being told to me by you, I discern your wish better than you.] (*Par.* 26.103–104)

For Boccaccio, the name *Dante* means "divine gift" and "giver," since God gave Dante inspired wisdom, a gift he in turn shared with others through his poetry. Beatrice, whom Boccaccio believes personifies Theology, names him to signify that in their encounter and the words she enunciates, Dante has reached her acme of wisdom. As she calls out to him, perforce by name, she ratifies the "divine disposition" by which he had been christened. When Adam speaks his name (as he satisfies Dante's curiosity

---

30. Robert Hollander, *Il Virgilio dantesco* (Florence: Olschki, 1983), 133 n. 24, recalled by Rachel Jacoff in "Intertextualities in Arcadia: *Purgatorio* 30.49–51," in *The Poetry of Allusion: Virgil and Ovid in Dante's Commedia,* ed. Rachel Jacoff and Jeffrey T. Schnapp (Stanford: Stanford University Press, 1991), 131–44. The triple invocation of Eurydice appears in *Georgics* 4.525–27.

about the origins of language), he confirms the sacred, predestined nature of its etymology.[31] For Dante's early commentators, these namings corroborate nothing less than his vatic nature, a privileged identity as *poeta-theologus*. Charged with all the intensity that, from elemental religion to philosophical nominalism, can resonate in the act of calling of a thing by its name, Dante's autodesignation(s) are deeply meaningful moments.

If form and meaning collaborate with high purpose wherever *Dante* is written, other poets name themselves in a more entertaining spirit. Courtly to start with, the tradition of the inscribed signature travels the generations, and as it does so, it branches into types both didactic and comic. The first true signed piece in Italian, which glistens in a lighter vein, is a sonnet by the man cited as the inventor of that genre, Giacomo da Lentini's "Meravigliosamente" (ca. 1240). The poet, a notary at the Palermo court of Emperor Frederick II, sends his songlet on an errand as a billet-doux. To make sure there is no misunderstanding about whom the lady receiving the sonnet is to grace with her love, he gives a return address. The signature, in two halves, identifies him by his profession and his city of origin in Sicily.

> Canzonetta novella,
> va' canta nova cosa;
>   lévati da maitino
>   davanti a la più bella,
>   fiore d'ogni amorosa,
>   bionda più ch'auro fino:
>   "Lo vostro amor, ch'è caro,
>   donatelo al **Notaro,**
>   ch'è nato **da Lentino.**"

[New little songlet, go, and sing a new thing; arise in the morning, say before the fairest, flower of lovesome ladies, blonder than beaten gold: "Your love, which is dear, give it to **the Notary,** who was born in **Lentini.**"][32]

Giacomo's autodesignation would make him "the Notary" by antonomasia. When Bongaiunta of Lucca speaks to Dante from the shelf of gluttony

---

31. *Esposizioni sopra la Comedia, accessus* 37–41.
32. Gianfranco Contini, ed., *Poeti del Duecento,* 2 vols. (Milan: Ricciardi, 1960), 1:57. Giacomo da Lentini died between 1246 and 1250.

about the generations of Italian poetry, we hear the common noun as his name, heading the bygone thirteenth-century group.

"O frate, issa vegg' io," diss' elli, "il nodo
che 'l Notaro e Guittone e me ritenne
di qua dal dolce stil novo ch'i' odo!"

["O brother," he said, "now I see the knot which kept the Notary, and Guittone, and me, short of the sweet new style that I hear."]
(*Purg.* 24.55–57)

The Notary, leader of the Sicilian school now outmoded by a "dolce stil novo," naturally had acolytes who also sometimes tucked their names into their rhymes. Giacomino Pugliese, an "Apulian" and "little James" who lived in the first half of the twelfth century, refers to himself and his lady in the closing lines of his canzone "Isplendïente." The form, metrically unusual, juxtaposes five-syllable and six-syllable verses (*quinario, senario*) to make the last four verses of each stanza a hendecasyallable.

Che due amanti s'amâro di core
canta assai versi di **Giacomino,**
che si diparte di reo amore.

[How two lovers loved with all their hearts sing many a verse by **Giacomino,** who stays away from evil love.][33]

Not only lyric writing but also narrative could provide the proper occasion for a signature. Still in the Sicilian cultural orbit, a judge of Messina composed a Latin history of the fall of Troy, motivated by an urge to correct what he felt was "the failure of the great authors, Virgil, Ovid, and Homer." Unlike their "untruthful" epics and the abridgment by Cornelius Sallust, this will be an accurate and complete chronicle, he avows, drawn from eyewitness accounts. Since his claims to be an

---

33. For Giacomo Pugliese's canzone "Isplendiente," see Carlo Muscetta and Paolo Rivalta, eds., *Parnaso italiano,* vol. 1, *Poesia del Duecento e del Trecento* (Turin: Einaudi, 1956), 59. According to Contini, *Poeti del Duecento,* 1:145, Giacomino signs his name three times in the eight poems that survive by him, all preserved in the same Vatican *canzoniere* (MS 3793). Nothing at all is known about his life. The surname *Pugliese* is common and could be Sicilian.

authentic version, based on Dictys the Greek and Dares the Phrygian, the author of this *Historia destructionis Troiae* naturally enough calls attention to his own name in the prologue, referring to the book "transcribed by me, **Judge Guido delle Colonne of Messina.**" Again, at the end, after the epitaphs of Hector and Achilles, he returns to sign off: "I, **Guido delle Colonne,** have followed the aforesaid Dictys the Greek in all things." Being fearful of not finishing, given life's uncertainties, he has avoided rhetorical amplification and, with the help of the Holy Ghost, has pushed himself to complete it in just three months, from September to November of 1287.[34] Lacking firsthand knowledge of Homer, who was not restored to the Latin West until late in the fourteenth century (and thanks to Boccaccio's patience in dealing with Leontius Pilatus), Guido is typical of his culture, which venerated the spurious authority of Dares and Dictys when it came to the Trojan War. How thoroughly unclassical he was in his treatment of his epic subject matter is evident even in the conspicuous signatures he leaves. From Homer onward, epic was properly a genre unsigned. But that tradition, respected by Virgil, could not have been appreciated by the judge of Messina, who had no access to its Greek origin. His self-naming reflects a *contaminatio* of the ancient heroic form with the medieval practice of scribal rubrication.

These options for signing—deep inside a work, as Dante does in the *Comedy;* with a closing inscription, as do the Notary and Giacomino Pugliese; or at both beginning and end, as in a proper apparatus of incipit and explicit rubrics—had already been taken up by the Tuscans well before the turn of the trecento. An international scholar and poet of Florence, writing sometime after 1260, announces himself in the opening verses of his small thesaurus. It opens to a dedication, heavy with praise for a patron who surpasses the world's most famous men for their finest qualities.

---

34. Guido delle Colonne, *Historia destructionis Troiae,* trans. Mary Elizabeth Meek (Bloomington: Indiana University Press, 1974). The title rubric, heading book 1, reads, "Here begins the prologue of the History of the Destruction of Troy, composed by Judge Guido delle Colonne of Messina." See also the closing, 35.205–35. Proceeding from a suggestion by Carlo Dionisotti, Roberto Veruda applies structuralist methodology to argue that Boccaccio was influenced by Guido's Latin romance in the narrative articulation of the *Filocolo;* see *Il Filocolo e la Historia destructionis Troiae: Strutture e modelli della narratività boccacciana* (Florence: Atheneum, 1993). Homer's epics were unknown except indirectly and were consequently often judged pejoratively during the Middle Ages. In their place, the apocryphal accounts by "Dares" and "Dictys" were credited with eyewitness authority. See, e.g., R. K. Gordon, *The Story of Troilus* (1934; reprint, Toronto: University of Toronto Press, 1978), introd., xi–xv.

E posso dire insomma
che 'n voi, segnor, s'assomma
e compie ogne bontate,
e 'n voi solo asembiate
son sí compiutamente
che non falla neente,
se non com'auro fino:
io **Burnetto Latino,**
che vostro in ogne guisa
mi son sanza divisa,
a voi mi racomando.

[And I can say in short
that in you, lord, every good
is summed up and fulfilled;
and in you alone these goods
are assembled so fully
that nothing is lacking,
just like beaten gold:
I, **Brunetto Latini,**
who am yours in every way,
without any reservation,
commend myself to you.]

The peerless man of "high lineage" whom Ser Brunetto addresses in his *Tesoretto* has not been identified. Candidates proposed include the French king Louis IX; his brother, Charles I of Anjou (grandfather of King Robert of Naples); or alternatively, a wealthy Florentine Guelf who protected Brunetto while he was a political exile in France. It is possible, too, that Brunetto purposely left the name blank, as it were, until he had decided whom to target for patronage. In any event, this unknown dedicatee's virtues require a list of names of the illustrious men he surpasses: Solomon for sensible rule; Alexander for wealth and liberality; Achilles, Hector, Lancelot, and Tristan for valor; Cicero for oratory; Seneca and Cato for wisdom. Modesty does not stop Ser Brunetto from inserting his name next. By implication, he has a right to circulate with such august company, even more right than his unnamed patron.[35]

35. Brunetto Latini, *Il tesoretto,* ed. Gianfranco Contini, in Contini, *Poeti del Duecento,* 2:175–277. For the English, I consulted but have not strictly followed *Il Tesoretto (The Lit-*

Whereas Brunetto introduces himself at the outset of an allegorical trek in the *Tesoretto,* a Florentine contemporary who "made" another educational book will not release his name to the reader until after proving his qualifications as a bona fide Christian. In the middle of a dark night, Lady Philosophy arrives to doctor the suffering narrator, whom we know from the title rubric only as "il fattore dell'opera": "Here begins the book of the Vices and the Virtues and of their battles and admonishments. It starts with the lament of the maker of the work who gave birth to this book." Luckily for him, he will be healed from his misery by no less a lady than once before came to help Boethius, Lady Philosophy. The cure will require some moving about and an impressive diorama. First, traveling on horseback with her charge in tow, Filosofia heads to the Inn of Faith, where her dear friend Faith quizzes the narrator on his beliefs (with a notary present) and receives him into the Church. Then, after a grand-scale battle, in which crack troops led by Prudence conquer Pride and her allied hordes, he meets the victorious captain in her tent. To show he is ready to join the Virtues, he pulls from his pocket and flashes the card that he had been awarded by Faith. Now, finally in the last sentence of the book, the person who has kept calling himself only "the maker of the work" accedes to a full legal identity: "And as soon as they had blessed me and made the sign of the cross on me and received me as a believer, they wrote **BONO GIAMBONI** in their guild registry." Certain procedural formalities in the patient's rites de passage, such as the official witness to his oral examination by Faith, are humorous touches that betray Bono's professional activity as a jurist. Yet he was also a *litteratus* of note and talent. Not only did he recast the *Psychomachia* by Prudentius (ca. 500) in this lively Tuscan update that would influence Dante and Boccaccio, but he also translated from Latin into Italian Paulus Orosius's *History against the Pagans,* Vegetius's *Art of War,* and the hugely successful treatise by Lotario de' Segni, better known as Pope Innocent III, *On the Misery of the Human Condition.* We could guess that more than a legal technicality, then, requires Bono's signature at the close of his allegory. His *prosonomasia* and simultaneous admission into Christian fellowship recall the sacrament of baptism, when one is

tle Treasure), trans. Julia Bolton Holloway (New York: Garland, 1981), vv. 63–73. Contini's commentary suggests that the dedicatee was either Louis IX—whose rule (1226–70) embraced the years that Brunetto spent in exile in France, between the battles of Montaperti and Benevento, from 1260 to 1266—or Charles of Anjou, the brother of Louis. Peter Armour suggests that the *Tesoretto* was dedicated to a Florentine in France, in "The Love of Two Florentines: Brunetto Latini and Bondie Dietaiuti," *Lectura Dantis* 9 (1991): 11–28.

named, blessed with the sign of the cross, and (re)born to the spiritual community—an onomastic ceremony whose parts telescope in the English noun *christening*.

Dante's own examination in faith has features in common with Bono's. Before the later poet reaches that plateau in Paradise with Saint Peter, he must pass a hurdle raised by Beatrice at the moment of their encounter in *Purgatory* 30. It requires his self-naming. Perhaps Bono Giamboni's progression toward moral perfection impinged as well on the shape of that episode in Purgatory, which replays a sequence of events from Dante's— and Everyman's—infancy at the baptismal font. With the single *nominatio* "Dante," once again the pilgrim "becomes God's child," in renewed birth, baptism, and christening.[36]

A century later and in a very different vein, another Florentine compiles a comic catalogue, deservingly praised as a small masterpiece. He is Antonio Pucci, bell ringer, town crier, and a friend of Boccaccio's who crams into rhyming couplets a list of all the things that make up the wonderful "properties" of his city's Old Market—from delicatessens, doctors, and dicing to singers, prostitutes, and pederasts. This jocose versifier wraps up the 228 verses of the *ternario* known as *Proprietà di Mercato Vecchio* with a signature.

Di questo **Antonio Pucci** fu poeta.
Cristo vi guardi sempre in vita cheta.

[Of this **Antonio Pucci** was poet.
May Christ ever keep your life quiet.]

The poet names himself one other time, inside his colorful catalogue (v. 165). In that passing moment, it is as if he were daring fate not to let him down when it comes to women. After he has heaped together all sorts of goods assembled for sale (things like butchered meat, songbirds in cages, doves and rabbits for breeding, weasels, cats, and household utensils), he

---

36. Bono Giamboni, *Il libro de' vizi e delle virtudi,* ed. Cesare Segre (Turin: Einaudi, 1968), 3: "Incominciasi il libro de' Vizi e delle Virtudi e delle loro battaglie e ammonimenti. Ponsi in prima il lamento del fattore dell'opera onde questo libro nasce"; 120: "E dacché m'ebbero benedetto e segnato e ricevuto per fedele, scrissero BONO GIAMBONI nella matricola loro." Bono was a Florentine judge whose legal documents date from between 1264 and 1292. The naming at *Purg.* 30 signals a new beginning for the pilgrim, linked to the first pronouncing of his name at baptism, as Dino Cervigni argues in "Beatrice's Act of Naming," *Lectura Dantis* 8 (1991): 85–99.

mentions in the same breath the female who comes to market to catch serving wenches, and he interjects, "pognàm ch'el non bisogni a **Antonio Pucci**" [let's hope **Antonio Pucci** doesn't need her!]. Pucci, who was a great admirer of Dante, may here consciously parody the interior naming that constituted such a solemn moment for Dante in the *Divine Comedy*. Here is no divine necessity, just a lusty fellow who hopes that he can keep up his supply of girlfriends without having to resort to the services of a go-between. Whether he was thinking of Dante or not, he certainly pokes fun at poets of the high style in the refined lyric tradition inaugurated by Giacomo da Lentini.

Another rhymster, comically lowbrow in his iconoclastic mode, was Cecco Angiolieri of Siena, one of Dante's contemporaries and correspondents. Cecco booms out his name in the second tercet of his most famous sonnet, "S'i' fosse fuoco, ardereï 'l mondo" (If I were fire, I would burn up the world). Anaphora connects a fanfaronade of contrary-to-fact conditional and result clauses that bluster what havoc he would wreak if he were a destructive element (fire, flooding waters, etc.) until we come at the end to his signature, so factual it is banal, and a masculine wish like Pucci's for sexy female company.

S'i' fosse **Cecco,** com'i' sono e fui,
torrei le donne giovani e leggiadre:
le zoppe e vecchie lasserei altrui.

[If I were **Cecco,** as I am and was, I would snatch up the young and lovely ladies; the lame and the old ones I would leave for others.][37]

---

37. Antonio Pucci, "Proprietà di Mercato Vecchio," vv. 227–28, in Muscetta and Rivalta, *Parnaso italiano,* 1:794. Armando Balduino characterizes it as a "piccolo capolavoro," in *Boccaccio, Petrarca e altri poeti del Trecento* (Florence: Olschki, 1984), 31. In his *Profilo biografico,* Vittore Branca mentions several times Boccaccio's friendship with Pucci. Pucci's "legiadro sermintese pien d'amore" of 1335, a poem composed to honor the most beautiful ladies of Florence, is related to both Boccaccio's *Caccia di Diana* and his *ternario.* See Giovanni Boccaccio, *Rime,* ed. Vittore Branca (Padua: Liviana, 1958), 69n. Pucci also authored the romances *Brito di Brettagna* and *Madonna Lionessa,* and he addressed a sonnet to Boccaccio. See David Wallace, *Chaucer and the Early Writings of Boccaccio* (Woodbridge, Suffolk: D. S. Brewer, 1985), 147. Cf. also *Enciclopedia dantesca,* s.v. "Antonio Pucci," an article by Michele Messina that cites Sacchetti's assessment of this Dante cultist: "Piacevole fiorentino, dicitore di molte cose in rima." Pucci's *Centiloquia* was a rhymed compendium of Villani's *Cronica.* Cecco's poem appears in Contini, *Poeti del Duecento,* 2:377.

Mutatis mutandis, these poets express the same hope for amorous conquest as did Giacomo da Lentini.

Generalizing from these examples, both courtly and parodic, we could say that one family of signatures asserts not only poetic identity but also masculinity. Even Dante's name, spoken at the final and most painful turning point in his relationship with Beatrice, can be assimilated to this type. At their encounter on Mount Purgatory immediately after Beatrice speaks his name, she takes on male authority as if she were the "admiral" of a ship commanding "on poop and prow," and she names herself emphatically, "Ben son, ben son Beatrice" [indeed I am, indeed I am Beatrice!]. Stricken by her reproach, Dante's strength drains, and he crumples in tears like a child. In the next canto, we understand that the penitent has progressed in the crisis to the point of facing his guilt when she instructs him to "look up" at her by lifting his "beard": "alza la barba." *Barba,* a word that the poet stresses with equivocal rhyme and threefold repetition (31.62–74), is a synecdoche for his face, as the pilgrim realizes: "per la barba il viso chiese" [by the beard she asked for my face]. More than a rhetorical trope, the beard is a symbol of his manliness. Because he had wavered in his fidelity to Beatrice after her death, he nearly lost her; hence he was threatened with deprivation of his own manly vigor. Regaining her, he can raise his "beard." His masculinity returns to visibility.

Among the Sicilians, the first literary circle to compose in Italian vernacular, and then among their cultural successors on the peninsula, poets not infrequently registered their identity with an inscribed signature. Since they use the device selectively, there must be codes governing its application. What are the conventions and where do they originate? Although medievals are not altogether silent about these questions—addressed by Dante, for one, in an important policy statement—there is no handy body of theory surrounding authorial self-naming. Where and when to sign seems to be a game rather like numerology—everyone knows how to play it, but no one wants to explain the rules. For the most part, we must deduce policy from practice, or extrapolate from literary criticism in related areas, such as commentary introductions. Since these do not exist for the fragmentary genre of lyric (with the notable exceptions of Dante's *Vita nuova* and *Convivio*) and were not attached to vernacular romances, the *accessus ad auctorem* is of limited assistance in an effort to reconstruct young Boccaccio's assumptions. Nevertheless, that instrument is a useful starting point, since it serves to forearm readers with information about the author. Scholiasts naturally broached his name, whether in Aristotelian philosophical terms as an "efficient cause" or more poetically in response to the query "Who is the author?"[38]

On occasion, the commentator might actually share his thoughts about where and how a signature has been embedded, as did Boccaccio speaking of "Dante" in his *accessus* to the *Esposizioni sopra la Comedìa*. But such revealing insight is rare. More likely, the name triggers a brief *vita*. Standard procedure also dictates that the name be equipped with an etymology. The origin may encapsulate a famous attribute or signal a person's probity and talent. Commenting on the poets of Dante's Limbo, for instance, Boccaccio traces "Homer" to a triple compound from *o* + *mi* + *erò*, that is, "I / do not / see" (*Esposiz.* 4.1.95). His simple formula for the blind Greek bard contrasts with far weightier etymologies imaginatively attached to Ovid by other expositors. "Publius Ovidius Naso" was said to be of the "Publius family," so called because he enjoyed much public favor (or founded a school of public morality), *Ovid* meant "he who distinguished the parts of the egg" [ovum dividens], because the egg is a symbol of the world and hence alludes to the cosmology of the *Metamorphoses;* the cognomen *Naso* came from "the quantity of his nose," not so much a physical measurement as a figurative facial feature that enabled him to have good moral intuitions. What was good for the ancients was good for the moderns. Thus when Albertino Mussato received the laurel crown in Padua on Christmas Day, 1314, by one fanciful account of the event, he changed his name from *Musso* to *Mussato,* as if to signify "apt for the Muses" [Musis aptus]. In the following century, the Florentine civic humanist Matteo Palmieri would reduce Boccaccio's name to *bocca* (mouth) plus the pejorative suffix *-accio,* which amounts to "Badmouth," no more than the man deserved, complained Palmieri, for filling his *Decameron* with so many risqué novelle.[39] Boccaccio's own optimistic punning on the name *Giovanni* with the epithet "full of grace" surely was prompted by the medieval habit of glossing the names of poets like Ovid with complimentary etymologies in the *accessus*

---

38. Alastair J. Minnis, in *Medieval Theory of Authorship,* 2d ed. (Philadelphia: University of Pennsylvania Press, 1988), 28–33, discusses the Aristotelian prologue. See there also his remarks on the "human *auctor*" (94–103).

39. Ghisalberti, "Mediaeval Biographies of Ovid." Mussato was never known as "Musso." See Antonio Zardi, *Albertino Mussato: Studio storico e letterato* (Padua: Angelo Draghi, 1884), 155. Palmieri's unflattering remarks, made in his *De vita civile,* are recalled in Victoria Kirkham, "John Badmouth: Fortunes of the Poet's Image," in *Boccaccio 1990: The Poet and His Renaissance Reception,* ed. Kevin Brownlee and Victoria Kirkham, *Studi sul Boccaccio* 20 (1992): 355–76.

ad auctorem. Since there was no one of stature in Naples to do it for him, he remedied the deficiency and became his own promoter. The *Filocolo,* so far as it is by genre a romance, has no extrinsic apparatus, so he slips the derivation into the heart of fiction. It is, in fact, characteristic of the early Boccaccio to incorporate what he has learned from commentary into what he writes as poetry.

E. R. Curtius, who briefly looked into the matter of the authorial signature, found that the poets of antiquity "authorize both suppression and mention of the poet's name." Virgil does not sign the *Aeneid,* but he does put his name to the *Georgics.* Among medievals, the signature may or may not appear. Bernard Silvester (1080?–1167), author of the encyclopedia *De mundi universitate,* assumes a clever stance when he leaves it up to his dedicatee, Thierry of Chartres, to decide whether or not his book deserves to have its author's name published. The general rule in the twelfth century, Curtius found, was for poets to sign, as did the Sicilians. Perhaps, he speculates, their inclination toward signed pieces was a carryover from their workaday activities as jurists and witnesses to legal transactions. Whatever they dealt with professionally *had* to be signed.[40]

But sonnets and canzones by the sophisticated Sicilians depart most elegantly from court bureaucracy. Cast in quite another register, they caressingly echo the exquisite musicality of the troubadours, from whom their authors inherited the idea for self-allusions in song. Among those of the earlier generations was Marcabru (fl. 1129–50), an itinerant master of the *trobar clus* attached for a time to the court at Poitiers. He proudly signed himself in his verse with a wish for peace in the name of the Lord.

Pax in nomine Domini!
Fètz **Marcabruns** lo vers e'l son.
Aujatz qué di!

[Pax in nomine Domine! **Marcabru** composed the verse and music. Listen to what he says!][41]

Superlative among all singers of Provence—from the Italians' point of view—was another Occitan, active at the end of the twelfth century. He

---

40. Curtius, "The Author's Name in Medieval Literature."

41. Robert Lafont and Christian Anatole, eds., *Nouvelle Histoire de la littérature occitane,* 2 vols. (Paris: Presses Universitaires de France, 1970), 1:63. A sketch of this moralizing poet's life and themes appears in ibid., 1:57–63.

was Arnaut Daniel, awarded the honor of having invented the sestina, and the greatest of those who practiced the *trobar ric,* a poetics exotic in its lexicon and close to opaque in its meanings. In his daring, bizarre style, he, too, named himself.

> **Ieu sui Arnauts** qu'amàs l'aura
> e chaç la lèbre ab lo bòu
> e nadi contra subèrna . . .

> [**I am Arnaut** who collects the wind and hunts the rabbit with the ox and swims against the current . . .][42]

Arnaut's first-person signature was so striking that Dante accords him the privilege of speaking it again, in his native Provençal, when the two poets meet on the seventh terrace in Purgatory. Guido Guinizelli deferentially points him out as the man who was "miglior fabbro del parlar materno" [a better smithy of the mother tongue], and now, as Dante has him speak, he comes out from under his old hermetic cover.

> Tan m'abellis vostre cortes deman
> qu'ieu non me puesc ni voill a vos cobrire.
> **Ieu sui Arnaut,** que plor a vau cantan;

> [So does your courteous request please me that I neither can nor would conceal myself from you. **I am Arnaut,** who weep and sing as I go.] (*Purg.* 26.140–42)

The Sicilians have several good reasons, none legalistic, for occasionally interweaving their avocational verse with a signature: to emulate their most brilliant predecessors from the south of France, to elevate their poetry in artistic worth, and to declare their own sense of masculinity and creative pride.

Examples of this custom crossed the Alps not just from Provence but also from the Île-de-France. One twelfth-century northern signer of renown, the greatest of the French romancers, was Chrétien de Troyes. It is in fact his habit to sign. At the outset of *Erec et Enide,* he announces himself with a didactic admonition.

---

42. Ibid., 1:93. For a brief presentation on Arnaut, see ibid., 1:92–94.

Por ce dist **Crestïens de Troies**
que reisons est que totevoies
doit chascuns panser et antandre
a bien dire et a bien aprandre;
et tret d'un conte d'avanture
une molt bele conjointure.

[Therefore **Chrétien de Troyes** says that it is right for everyone always
to be mindful and careful to speak well and to learn well; and from a
tale of adventure he draws a most beautiful conjoining.]

His rule is to record his name speaking in the third person, not the first.
Thus we hear him launch into the narrative proper of his *Lancelot.*

Del *Chevalier de la charette*
comance **Crestïens** son livre.

[**Chrétien** begins his book about the knight of the cart.] (vv. 24–25)

At the start of *Cliges,* he identifies himself in a more oblique fashion, with
reference to what he has written. The inventory of his books, both poems
and translations, becomes an extended periphrasis, or *pronominatio*—in
place of the Author is all that he has authored.

Cil qui fist d'Erec et d'Enide,
Et les comandemanz d'Ovide
Et l'art d'amours an romans mist,
Et le mors de l'espaule fist,
Del roi Marc et d'Ysalt la blonde,
Et de la hupe et de l'aronde
Et del rossignol la muance,
Un nouvel conte rancomance.

[He who wrote of Erec and Enide, and who put Ovid's command-
ments and the art of love into romance, and who wrote of the shoulder bite, and of King Mark and Iseult the Blond, and of the hoopoe
and of the swallow and of the nightingale's metamorphosis, once
again begins a new tale.] (vv. 1–8)

In the final line of *Cligés,* still in the third person and sounding more like a scribal colophon than the signature of the author in person, he signs off: "Ci finist l'uevre Crestïen" [Here ends Chrétien's work]. Sylvia Huot comments on the result of his technique: "the narrative voice is available for appropriation by performers (or scribes) without any subsequent displacement of Chrétien as an authoritative presence in the text. The romance can be thought of as a script prepared by the poet for future presentation by others."[43]

Acrostic signatures, like Boccaccio's in the *Amorosa visione,* were practiced by the French, too. In its ancient origins, the acrostic had been a prophetic form of diction. Saint Augustine reports in the *City of God* that the Sibyl of Erithraea, the island where poetry was said to have been born, composed an acrostic prophesying "JESUS CHRIST THE SAVIOR." From antiquity, double-vectored script was to enjoy a long history, one that flourished in contexts sacred and profane. Plautus used it in the arguments to his comedies, to spell out the titles; Ennius used it to sign his name. Acrostics are also found in early Christian hymns and writers, such as Venantius Fortunatus. Italians of the duecento—among them Guittone d'Arezzo, Biondo Bonichi, and Dante da Maiano—wove the device into their verse.[44] Dante's *Comedy* has its acrostic moments, such as his condemnation of Christian rulers in the nine *terzine* in *Paradiso* 19 constructed on a triple anaphora whose initials spell *LVE* (*la lue,* "pestilence"). The same alphabetic technique ironically spells *VOM* (*uomo,* "man") on the terrace of Pride in *Purgatory* 12. At this nexus in his poem, following so close after his scathing—if ambivalent—comments about the vanity of writers and artists who waste their time chasing after fame, Dante may well have in mind the particular conceit of signing one's name acrostically. Humility, the virtue that will cure the prideful, should dictate not such artful and capital-lettered claims to ownership but rather quiet anonymity.

---

43. Chrétien de Troyes, *Erec et Enide,* ed. Mario Roques, vol. 1 of *Les Romans de Chrétien de Troyes* (Paris: Honoré Champion, 1966), vv. 9–12; *Cligés,* ed. Alexandre Micha, vol. 2 of *Les Romans de Chrétien de Troyes* (Paris: Honoré Champion, 1965); Huot, *From Song to Book,* 42.

44. For examples of the period, see Laurence de Looze, "'Mon nom trouveras': A New Look at the Anagrams of Guillaume de Machaut—the Enigmas, Responses, and Solutions," *Romanic Review* 79 (1988): 537–57; "Signing Off in the Middle Ages: Medieval Textuality and Strategies of Authorial Self-Naming," in *Vox Intertexta: Orality and Textuality in the Middle Ages,* ed. A. N. Doane and Carol Pasternak (Madison: University of Wisconsin Press, 1991), 162–78. Acrostic signatures were a favorite device of the French. For more on the history of this literary game, see Kirkham, *The Sign of Reason,* chap. 2; Jon D. Boshart, "Giovanni Boccaccio's *Amorosa Visione:* A New Appraisal" (Ph.D. diss., Johns Hopkins University, 1974).

Sources that best account for Boccaccio's self-naming in the *Amorosa visione* are French romances of the Gothic era, a genre with which Dante also was familiar. Boccaccio must have read all the latest when he was a young man at Naples, whose Angevin king was a native speaker of French from the city of Avignon. These clever texts employ the acrostic as a device in which to embed information about the authorship of a poem, usually at closure. Thus the late thirteenth-century *Romance of the Chatelaine de Coucy,* which Boccaccio may have used as a source for the *Filostrato,* is signed in an acrostic at the end, by a certain "JAKEMES." Writing in the second half of the same century, Adenet le Roi identifies himself with his works (as had Chrétien) in the prologue to his romance *Cléomadès:* "Je qui fis d'Ogier li Danois / et de Bertain qui fu ou bois" [I who wrote about Ogier the Dane and about Bertha who was in the forest] (vv. 5–6). He saves the acrostic to name at the end his two female patrons, "La Roïne de France Marie" and "Madame Blanche" (vv. 18,541–61, 18,563–75).[45] Boccaccio's *Filocolo,* in the episode of the vows on the peacock, takes material from a continuation of the *Roman d'Alexandre,* Jacques de Longuyon's *Voeux du Paon* (ca. 1320), which in turn spawned two of its own sequels, close both in time and in spirit to the *Amorosa visione.* The second, *Le Parfait du Paon* (The perfection of the peacock), is an aristocratic tale in 3,015 verses whose author, Jean de la Mote, works his signature and the date 1340 into an acrostic at the end.[46] Boccaccio far outdid everyone else in this mode. The longest acrostic in the world, his *Amorosa visione* restates and doubles the crosswords. Normally, they only appear once, inside the text where horizontal and vertical letters intersect, but he recopied the vertical message in an extrinsic verse prologue, the three sonnets that announce his project and his name, Giovanni di Boccaccio da Certaldo. Hence the authorial identity, embedded in earlier acrostics for an alert reader to pick out letter by letter, can emerge from hiding and march openly across the folio at the very head of the *Visione.*

From across the Channel, fourteenth-century England has bequeathed us other acrostics, favored by men of the church. Traces of such a signature appear in one version of *Piers the Plowman* by William Langland, a clergyman born around 1332. After the narrator of this dream vision has

---

45. Huot, *From Song to Book,* 40–43.

46. Jean de la Mote, *Le Parfait du paon,* ed. Richard J. Carey, University of North Carolina Studies in the Romance Languages and Literatures, no. 188 (Chapel Hill: University of North Carolina Press, 1972). Stillinger ("The Form of Filostrato") mentions "Jakemes." He quotes Muscetta as suggesting that Boccaccio used it for the *Filostrato.* Boccaccio cites the *Dama del Vergiù,* the Italian translation of the *Chatelaine de Coucy,* at the end of the Third Day in the *Decameron.*

long traversed a sprawling allegorical countryside inhabited by all sorts of
symbolic characters, he discloses his own identity. First he tells his baptismal name, William, and then he gives his full name in a cryptogram: "I
have lived all over the land, and men call me Long Will." In one branch of
the manuscript tradition, at the textual location of this line (15.145), an
acrostic can be read that spells "Long-land." Another Englishman who,
like "grace-filled" Giovanni Boccaccio, capitalized on his Christian name
was John Gower (ca. 1330–1408). In the Latin poem entitled *Vox claman-
tis*, he allegorizes the peasant uprising of 1381 and attacks corruption in
the Church of England. Signing in an acrostic, he identifies himself as a
namesake of John the Evangelist and his biblical precursor, John the Baptist, he who had been the original "voice crying" in the wilderness.[47]

But even though not all medieval poets craved anonymity, the cliché of
humility does often hold good. Dante, for instance, never names himself in
the *Vita nuova*. Twice he pointedly refuses to do so in *De vulgari eloquentia*. Among those who have "most sweetly and subtly" composed vernacular poetry in Italian, he names "Cynus Pistoriensis et amicus eius" [Cino
da Pistoia and his friend] (1.10.4). The grand themes of arms, love, and
rectitude have been subjects of the greatest Romance poets, to wit, Arnaut
Daniel, Guiraut de Borneil, and Cino di Pistoia and "his friend" (2.2.9).
Whether he names himself or not depends on a decorum that he enunciates
at the beginning of his *Convivio*. It is inappropriate, he states, for poets to
name themselves, unless there is a compelling reason: "Non si concede per
li retorici alcuno di sè medesimo sanza necessaria cagione parlare." This is
so because we cannot talk of anyone, including ourselves, without express-
ing either praise or blame. For a person to publicize his faults would be as
unacceptable as to vaunt his strengths. Exceptions can, however, be made
in two cases: first, when a writer must speak out to defend himself in the
face of calumny, as Boethius did in his *Consolation of Philosophy;* and second, when he has a lesson to teach that can benefit others, as did Augustine in the *Confessions.*[48]

We are fortunate to have such an explicit formulation of Dante's rationale for signing a piece or not. What Dante does not tell us, however, is

47. William Langland, *Piers the Plowman,* trans. J. F. Goodridge (Harmondsworth: Penguin, 1966), introd., 9. Minnis, in *Medieval Theory of Authorship,* 168–71, assembles other
examples of acrostic signatures in fourteenth-century commentators on theological texts and
writers of treatises on the art of preaching. Robert of Basevorn, for example, signs in an acrostic his *Forma praedicandi* (but names God and his friends as other efficient causes of his work).

48. *Convivio* 1.1.1.2 ("parlare alcuno di se medesimo pare non licito") and the discussion
following, 1.2.2–14.

where a poet should sign. There were, as we have discovered, various options: verse interweavings (the Notary from Lentini); incipit and explicit rubrics (Boccaccio's Latin encyclopedias, Guido delle Colonne); a name close to the beginning (Chrétien de Troyes, Brunetto Latini), at the conclusion of a narrative (Virgil, Bono Giamboni, Chrétien), or somewhere between those two limits (Dante, Pucci); acrostic onomastics with introductory or closing information (Giovanni di Boccaccio da Certaldo, Jakemes, Adenet le Roi, Jean de la Mote, Long-land, John Gower). Beginning, middle, and end—these are the most important moments in a medieval text.[49] Signatures are positioned in those zones. Paramount among the three locations is the center.

Centers, which medievals conceived in terms both philosophical and aesthetic, were places of tremendous power. Whoever occupies a center is by definition privileged. Inversely, the center bestows prominence on whatever or whomever it contains. In Chrétien's *Lancelot,* or *Le Chevalier de la charrete* (7,112 verses), the protagonist rides as a mystery knight until the crucial turning point in the narrative when he liberates Queen Guinevere by fighting with the evil Méléagant. His victory turns on a double revelation of names: the queen tells his to her serving maid (and to us as readers); the maid then calls him by name, to revivify his flagging masculine strength by telling him that the lady Guinevere for whom he fights is present as a witness to the combat. Guinevere pronounces Lancelot's name to magical effect at a moment meant to coincide with the center of the romance.

> Lanceloz del Lac a a non
> li chevaliers. . . .

> [The knight's name is Lancelot of the Lake. . . .] (vv. 3,660–61)

In the *Filocolo* love court, Boccaccio arranges for his double, Caleon, to debate with Fiammetta the seventh of thirteen questions, which is central both structurally and conceptually. At the center of the *Decameron,* on Day 5, Fiammetta again appears to rule as queen. He reveals Fiammetta's name in her central appearance in the *Amorosa visione.* If the *Amorosa visione* was set by Boccaccio at the center of his trilogy in terza rima, as I like to think, then he signed himself at the center of a manuscript compila-

---

49. William W. Ryding, *Structure in Medieval Narrative* (The Hague: Mouton, 1971), especially chap. 1, "The Question of Beginning, Middle, and End."

tion. Sylvia Huot has helped us appreciate how sophisticated the medieval manuscript can be as a *compilatio* and how sensitive readers were to signs of authorial identity. For example, an anthology of Old French romances at the Bibliothèque National (Ms. fr. 1450) frames works by Chrétien inside the *Brut* and puts at the center of the center the text of *Cligès,* where Chrétien catalogues his own oeuvre in an extended oblique signature. In its own narrative structure, the central verses of *Cligès* carry it through the crucial turn that will resolve the heroine's dilemma of being promised to one man while loving another.[50]

Dante respected the poetics of centering when he placed in the central cantos of the *Divine Comedy* (*Purg.* 17–18) his discourse on love and free will, framed by a pattern of number symbolism with 7 at the center, revealed to our eyes by Charles Singleton. Still sensitive to what François Rigolot calls this "structuration médiane" were Dante's Renaissance readers, among them Rabelais, who planned the central chapter of his *Pantagruel* (17) in intertextual dialogue with *Purgatory* 17. So, too, Dante's signature occupies a center in the *Comedy,* but on a different measuring scale. He makes us wait for Beatrice to speak his name until *Purgatory* 30. Although, counting by cantos, this occurs two-thirds of the way through the poem, in another sense the proper noun *Dante* could not be more central to his poetic cosmos. He is at the top of Mount Purgatory, at that midpoint where earth meets heaven, in the center of the hemisphere of water, directly opposite Jerusalem, the center of the hemisphere of land. Moreover, he is in Eden, that biblical "center" from which had flowed the four rivers of Paradise to water all the land. Satan, Hell's hideous king locked prisoner at its lowest point, in the center of the earth, caricatures grotesquely the triune Godhead, the Trinity that governs the whole universe from the ethereal center of the cosmos in the Empyrean. By analogy with the Triune Creator, Dante the poet "places himself" in a trinitarian canto (the thirtieth) at the center of his own creation. There is one God, at the center; there is one "Dante," at the center of his microcosm.[51]

Scholars have noticed a secondary center in the *Comedy* (apart from

---

50. Huot, *From Song to Book,* 28.

51. Charles S. Singleton, "The Poet's Number at the Center," *MLN* 80 (1965): 1–10; François Rigolot, "La 'Conjointure' du *Pantagruel:* Rabelais et la tradition médiévale," *Littérature* 41 (1981): 93–103. See also Victoria Kirkham, "*Purgatorio* XXVIII," in *Dante's Divine Comedy: Introductory Readings,* pt. 2, *Purgatorio,* supplement to *Lectura Dantis* 12 (1993): 411–32; and "Dante's Polysynchrony: A Perfectly Timed Entry into Eden," *Filologia e critica* 20, nos. 2–3 (1995): 329–52.

Purg. 17 and 18), midway through the *Paradiso.*[52] There again Dante is the focus, but he speaks of himself at several removes, through the generations of his ancestors, when he meets his great-great-grandfather Cacciaguida. Naming is an issue in their conversation, specifically, naming at the sacrament of baptism. Cacciaguida recalls that liminal event in his life, in the old San Giovanni baptistery.

> Maria mi diè, chiamata in alte grida;
> e ne l'antico vostro Batisteo
> insieme fui cristiano e Cacciaguida.

[Mary, called on with loud cries, gave me; and in your ancient Baptistery I became at once a Christian and Cacciaguida.] (*Par.* 15.133–35)

We cannot help thinking back to Bono Giamboni's entrance into Christian fellowship and, more immediately, Dante's "christening" in the *Comedy* at *Purgatorio* 30. In one sense, Cacciaguida's self-naming is an oblique reference to his descendant Dante, and not by accident, as Francesco Bruni has observed, this scene is set at the center of *Paradiso.*[53] Yet Cacciaguida, in all their long and affectionate dialogue, never once names his living representative, Dante. The silence is significant. In a correct version of the text, he could no more do so than could Adam. No matter how plausible to Boccaccio, Adam's vocative is apocryphal; for Dante, the central signature must be the unique signature.

If Dante was that "Ser Durante" who inscribed his name twice in *Il fiore,* a Tuscan version of the *Romance of the Rose,* he had not yet formulated his philosophy of naming. The ongoing debate about whether Durante is a Dante—and, if so, which one—reveals how even internal signatures, those not subject to loss with the outer folios of a manuscript, do not always assure the author's survival. Whoever this one was, he made his translation late in the duecento and chose to cast it in an unusual format, a sequence of 232 sonnets. The Italian sonneteer reveals his name in poem

---

52. J. L. Logan, "The Poet's Central Numbers," *MLN* 86 (1971): 95–98.

53. Francesco Bruni, *Boccaccio: L'invenzione della letteratura mezzana* (Bologna: Il Mulino, 1990), 179–80; and cf. "Il *Filocolo* e lo spazio della letteratura volgare," in *Miscellanea di studi in onore di Vittore Branca,* ed. Armando Balduino et al., vol. 2, *Boccaccio e dintorni* (Florence: Olschki, 1983), 1–21.

82, where Amor marshals his barons and announces that he must help "Durante." This passage corresponds to a moment in the *Rose* when Amor entreats his troops to comfort the author, "sorrowful William." Durante will again name himself in stanza 202 of *Il fiore,* which has no counterpart in the original. This time, humorously it seems, he takes the title *ser,* cognate with English *sir, sire.*

> Ma spesso falla ciò che 'l folle crede:
> Cosí avenne al buon di **ser Durante.**

[But what the fool believes is often fallacious, and thus it happened to good **Sire Durante**].

Neither of these signatures satisfies an aesthetics of centering. While fidelity to the source text accounts for the first, the second seems to have no logic. A mature Dante Alighieri would have frowned on it as superfluous and quite unjustifiable, going by standards spelled out in the *Convivio.* Is the lack of a coherent poetics for self-naming in *Il fiore* to be explained by the theory that assigns it to Dante's most youthful period?[54]

If we follow this theory, Dante missed some fundamental markers, and a lot was lost in translation, for the *Romance of the Rose* does in fact most wonderfully honor the medieval decorum of signing at centers. The name in the *Rose* that prompted *Il fiore*'s first "Durante," "douleureus Guillaumes," falls at verse 10,658, very near the midpoint of the poem, which has a total of 21,780 verses. After Amor has thus referred to Guillaume de Lorris, whose contribution breaks off at verse 4,058, he goes on to name Jean de Meun as the narrator who will complete the poem.

---

54. *Il fiore,* ed. Gianfranco Contini, in Dante Alighieri, *Opere minori,* ed. Domenico de Robertis and Gianfranco Contini vol. 1, pt. 1 (Milan: Ricciardi, 1984), 553–798. Contini considers *Il fiore* among the works that are "attributable" to Dante, partly on linguistic evidence, and partly because it is hard to imagine how some "Durante" or "Dante" we have never heard of could have had sufficient poetic stature to accomplish such a competent translation. The title *ser* does not mean "notary" but is simply a quaint form of "mister." A recent biography of Dante accepts the attribution. See Giuseppe Mazzotta, "Life of Dante," in *The Cambridge Companion to Dante,* ed. Rachel Jacoff (Cambridge: Cambridge University Press, 1993), 1–13. At an opposite pole, Lino Pertile reads "Ser Durante" as a jocose allusion to the phallus. The lively controversy continues in two recent volumes: the proceedings of a 1991 conference, *The Fiore in Context,* ed. Zygmunt G. Baránski and Patrick Boyde (Notre Dame: University of Notre Dame Press, 1997); and Zygmunt G. Baránski, Patrick Boyde, and Lino Pertile, *Lettura del "Fiore,"* vol. 22 of *Letture Classensi* (Ravenna: Longo, 1993). Pertile's provocative suggestion appears in the latter, in "Lettura dei sonetti CLXXXI–CCX (4 aprile 1992)," 131–53.

. . . quant **Guillaumes** cessera,
Jehans le continuera,
Emprès sa mort, que je ne mente,
Anz trespassez plus de quarante.

[. . . when Guillaume shall cease, more than forty years after his death—may I not lie—Jean will continue it.] (vv. 10,587–90)

Both namings are obviously the work of the second poet, who has been busily at work turning out rhymed lines to carry on the plot since verse 4,059, when his continuation begins. But he deliberately waits until this point to inscribe his predecessor's name and his own, in order to place the two author(s) side by side at the center.[55]

Can we really believe that Dante, even as the rawest beginner, could have been oblivious to the location of Guillaume and Jean's double naming? The device is all the more striking because it is "out of order" chronologically in the fiction of the *Rose:* Amor (speaking diegetically) prophesies the coming of Jean de Meun, who will write a continuation to Guillaume's dream-vision; but Jean de Meun's advent has already taken place, and he (writing historically) has been there making text for more than six thousand verses. If we are surprised that our Dante could have been insensitive to the centered namings in the *Rose,* we cannot turn for reassurance to external evidence. Dante's acolytes are silent on the subject. Boccaccio's *Trattatello* does not list *Il fiore* among Dante's works. It is hard to imagine that a composition of such substantial length would have escaped the biographer's notice. Why, anyway, would Dante sign himself "Durante," and why would he do so only in this one project, thereafter to become silent about his name until it springs to the center of his *Comedy*? Was he not most acutely sensitive to centers, symbolic as well as structural, from a youthful age? What about the drive toward centers in the *Vita*

---

55. Guillaume de Lorris and Jean de Meun [Jean Chopinel] , *Le roman de la Rose,* ed. Ernest Langlois, 5 vols. (Paris: Firmin Didot, 1914–24); *The Romance of the Rose,* trans. Charles Dahlberg (Princeton: Princeton University Press, 1971). See Kevin Brownlee, "Jean de Meun and the Limits of Romance: Genius as Rewriter of Guillaume de Lorris," in *Romance: Generic Transformations from Chrétien de Troyes to Cervantes,* ed. Kevin Brownlee and Marina Scordilis Brownlee, 114–34 (Hanover, N.H.: University Press of New England, 1985); Bruni, *Boccaccio: L'invenzione della letteratura mezzana,* 180. The signings in the *Romance of the Rose* deal with "the issue of authorial identity by setting the poem's only instance of the authors' names within a literary genealogy, a *translatio,*" as noted by Kevin Brownlee in "The Practice of Cultural Authority: Italian Responses to French Cultural Dominance in *Il Tesoretto, Il fiore,* and the *Commedia,*" *Forum for Modern Language Studies* 33, no. 3 (1997): 258–69.

nuova? Apart from Love's reproach of Dante for not being "central" (like Amore himself and like the center of a circle), the central event of the central verse of the central canzone of that "little booklet" is the death of Beatrice, as it indeed must be, since her analogue, Christ, had entered the world to die at the center of history.

Equally center-conscious, Boccaccio puts himself "in the middle" of the *Filocolo.* Certaldo, we have seen, three times enters the romance, always disguised as the *cerreto* that characters traipse into at key plot junctures. It first appears in connection with Fileno, the disappointed lover who melts into the oak trees as a tearful fountain (3.33). The sequence of chapters surrounding Fileno's metamorphosis closes as we reach 3.38, the midpoint of the third book, which has seventy-six chapters in all. Since the *Filocolo* has five books, the third is the central one. At the center of that center, Boccaccio chooses to locate the *cerreto,* ancient site and code name for the like-sounding Certaldo. Behind Fileno's tirade against love and women, we recognize the voice of the poet who took that place as his personal toponymic: in Latin, "Johannes de Certaldo"; in the vernacular, "Giovanni di Boccaccio da Certaldo." By metonymic association, the oak grove that receives Fileno alludes to Giovanni Boccaccio. Centering the *cerreto,* then, he situates himself at the center of the central book.

Jean de Meun, as Kevin Brownlee puts it, prophesies his advent as poet before he has been officially admitted into the plot. When, not long after the Fileno episode in the *Filocolo,* Boccaccio alludes to himself as the poet with a name "full of grace" from an "oak grove" (4.1), the speaker is a sixth-century oracle. It is a *pronominatio* and another prophecy, announcing what *will be written* in the fourteenth century. Significantly, although we are at the beginning of book 4 in a five-book romance, we are at the dead center of the *Filocolo* in terms of folio or word count. If one picks up the book and opens it to the middle, the pages should ideally fall open at a crucial upturn in the peripeteias, where Florio sets forth as Filocolo (end of book 3) and "the composer" comes forth as "John of Certaldo."

David Wallace has connected Boccaccio's central naming in the *Filocolo* with Jean de Meun's namings at the center of the *Rose.* It is an appealing suggestion. The centrality of Dante's self-naming in the *Purgatorio* would not have had the compelling impact for him that it does for us, since he thought the name *Dante* appeared twice in the *Comedy,* spoken once by Beatrice and once by Adam. Boccaccio could have found reinforcement for Jean's example in the learned poetry of another Frenchman, a Neoplatonist of Chartres active a century before. Alan de Lille's *Anticlaudianus,* an epic he knew from his early period, provides a model for the epiphany of the poet-as-prophet that would resonate again in Dante's *Paradiso*. Francesco Bruni has noticed how Alan ratchets up to a higher stage as writer just at the center of his allegory. There the *poeta* becomes *propheta*.

Hactenus insonuit tenui mea Musa susurro,
hactenus in fragili lusit mea pagina versu,
Phebea resonante cheli; sed parva resignans,
maiorem nunc tendo liram, totumque poetam
deponens, usurpo michi nova verba prophete.
Celesti Muse terrenus cedet Apollo,
Musa Iovi . . .

[Thus far my Muse has sung in a gentle whisper; thus far my page has sported in fragile verse to the accompaniment of Phoebus's lyre of tortoise shell. But abandoning things petty, I now pluck a mightier chord, and laying aside entirely the role of poet, I appropriate a new speaking part, that of the prophet. The earthly Apollo will yield to the heavenly Muse; the Muse will give place to Jupiter; . . .][56]

Similarly, Dante's final canticle opens with an invocation for redoubled inspiration: "Infino a qui l'un giogo di Parnaso / assai mi fu . . ." [Thus far one peak of Parnassus was enough for me . . .]. Writing on this loftier summit, he places the prophecy of his great poem in the mouth of his spokesman, Cacciaguida, who speaks at the center of *Paradiso*.

While Boccaccio alludes to himself in the *Filocolo* and does so at moments chosen to coincide with midpoints of his book, he does not really sign his name there as he will so prominently at the start of the *Amorosa visione*. In *Filocolo* the signature is partial and cryptic. In the *Amorosa visione* it is a full name that amounts to a legal signing. Clearly, context

---

56. Cited from Alan of Lille, *Anticlaudianus,* 146. Bruni, who cites the passage in Alan's *Anticlaudianus* (5.265–71) in *Boccaccio: L'invenzione della letteratura mezzana,* 57–58, speaks of it as a model for Boccaccio's central self-naming in the *Filocolo;* so does Wallace in *Chaucer and the Early Boccaccio,* 62; Velli, "Sull' *Elegia di Costanza,*" *Studi sul Boccaccio* 4 (1967): 241–54 (now also in *Petrarca e Boccaccio,* 118–32), refers to Boccaccio's knowledge of Alan of Lille from the early *Elegia di Costanza.* The two centers of the *Filocolo,* one based on a count of structural divisions and one based on total bulk, have an analogue in the *Teseida.* There as well we find two centers, a central rubric and a central verse. For discussion of this elaborately wrought structure, see Kirkham "'Chiuso parlare' in Boccaccio's *Teseida.*"

conditions the form of the signature. The *Amorosa visione* quite literally spells out the author's name in black and white. Acrostics seem to have authorized direct information, more characteristic of expository prose than of poetry's oblique figures and circumlocutions. In the French and English examples known to me, crossword signatures come toward the end, almost as if they were a kind of built-in colophon. Boccaccio reverses the tradition by incorporating information usually reserved for the closing of a poem into the preface of his acrostic. Everything about the author's identification in the *Filocolo,* by contrast, is "hidden." The name of the "new author" is not at the beginning of the book, where we might expect to find it in a conspicuous place. Nor does Boccaccio reveal that he alludes to himself at two midpoints; that is for us as readers to deduce. His toponymic, translated into the *cerreto* in the central chapters of book 3, and his embedded name as the "man full of grace" (4.1) are enigmatic. He constructs them as riddles that require decoding.

If the *Filocolo* had enjoyed its own private Glossator, as *Teseida* did, that bookish jotter would have noted approvingly the oracular signature at 4.1, for it rings with solemnity suitable to the anciently ordained, vatic mission of bards as Boccaccio understood their privileged company. Such a commentator, privy to the composer's thoughts, might also have written: "But why Jove? Wouldn't some other pagan deity have done has well? Indeed not!" Jove is more than a decorative presence in the mythological panoply devised by Boccaccio to decorate his *Filocolo.* Whatever the Olympians do in the narrative needs to be understood allegorically, and in the Christian key to meanings, the king of the pagan gods naturally translates to God himself. This is significant, because just as authors should not sign themselves without what Dante called a "necessary reason," so the rhetoricians instructed that they should never resort to self-commendation. Self-praise does not redound to a man's credit; approval should always come from others. So the Bible teaches, as Guido Faba reminded students in his *Summa dictamina,* an exhaustive treatise on epistolary art. A chapter entitled "On Avoiding Self-Praise" warns that in the salutation there should be no words praising the sender, only praise of the recipient, since we read in Scripture, "Let the mouth of another praise you, not your own" (Proverbs 27:2). Thomas Aquinas gives a more specific interpretation of the verse from Proverbs in his *Commentary on John,* when he affirms that the other is God; only God should praise a man, for only he has the perfect knowledge to do so. Authorized by Scripture and medieval rhetoric, Boccaccio arranges to have "Another" present his name, wrapped in a laudatory prophecy, in the *Filocolo*. The speaker of the prophecy, by poetic necessity, is no less than Jove, oraculating from a temple on the sacred ground that will give birth to Giovanni Boccaccio.[57]

All of Boccaccio's signatures, Tuscan as well as Latin, have in common the place-name Certaldo. While romantic license allows him to make his colorful and lusty interior doubles natives of Paris, the man as poet most consistently claims that Tuscan city of origin. Later biographers and scribes were to call him "Giovanni Boccaccio of Florence," and still today there is uncertainty about his birthplace, given as either Florence or Certaldo.[58] Yet Boccaccio's own authorial signature and testimony of those closest to him point unwaveringly to the latter. Manuscripts he personally transcribed, such as his Terence and his transcription of the *Commentary on the Nicomachean Ethics* by Thomas Aquinas, are consistent on the identity of their maker, as are his *Zibaldoni:* he is "Johannes de Certaldo." His beloved friend Petrarch, who bequeathed him fifty gold florins to purchase a cloak to keep warm in drafty rooms during scholarly vigils and lucubrations, specified in his will that the gift should go to "Domino Iohanni de Certaldo seu Boccaccii" [Lord John of Certaldo, that is, Boccaccio]. From his earliest poetic signatures to the Latin quatrain of his autoepitaph, this man is John, the son of Boccaccio, of the town of Certaldo.

---

57. Aquinas and Faba are both cited in the commentary on Dante's *Convivio*, ed. Busnelli and Vandelli, 1.2.2–3. See further Kirkham, "Iohannes de Certaldo: La firma dell'autore." Boccaccio's statements on poetry and the mission of poets are in his *Genealogie* 14–15 and *Trattatello* 1.125–62. Even though these are both from a much later period than the *Filocolo*, Boccaccio was already formulating his ideas on pagan literature and allegory from readings in his study of canon law, which offered guidelines concerning the education of priests—how both to protect them from the corrupting influence of ancient culture and yet preserve what was worthwhile in it. See below, chap. 3.

58. In the biographical tradition, Boccaccio's birthplace shifts from Certaldo to Florence as early as the late trecento and in the writing of a single historian, Filippo Villani. His first edition of *De origine civitatis Florentie et de eiusdem famosis civibus* (1381–82) states that Boccaccio "was born in the town of Certaldo" [natus est in Certaldi oppido]; the revised edition of his chronicle of Florence and its famous citizens (1395–97) appropriates the view of those who "cultivate" the poet's own writings and embraces the myth of a romantic birth in Paris, by an amorous father: "dum mercandi studio Parisius moraretur . . . ut cultores operum Johannis volunt . . . genitus est Johannes." This split gives rise to a double tradition, since both versions of Villani were transmitted. Domenico Bandini of Arezzo (ca. 1400) says Boccaccio was from Certaldo; Sicco da Polenton (1433) affirms that his *patria* was Florence; Giannozzo Manetti (after 1436) puts it back in Certaldo. Oscillation of opinion has continued to this day. See Massèra, "Le più antiche biografie del Boccaccio."

Hac sub mole iacent cineres ac ossa Iohannis:
Mens sedet ante Deum meritis ornata laborum
Mortalis vite. Genitor Bocchaccius illi,
patria Certaldum, studium fuit alma poesis.

[Under this stone lie the bones and ashes of John; his spirit stands in
the presence of God, adorned with the merits his mortal labors on
earth have earned him. Boccaccio sired him; his native Fatherland
was Certaldo; he cherished the nurturing Muses.][59]

59. The text of the epitaph appears in Giovanni Boccaccio, *Carmina,* ed. Giuseppe Velli,
in *Tutte le opere,* vol. 5, pt. 1, 454. I cite the translation by Thomas G. Bergin in *Boccaccio*
(New York: Viking, 1981), 64. Hauvette, "Notes sur des manuscrits autographes," described
Boccaccio's autograph manuscripts; they have been more recently catalogued by Auzzas, in
"I codici autografi." He signed the Terence, in red: "Explicit. liber. Terrentii. . . . Johannes de
Certaldo scripsit." The text of Petrarch's will was published by Theodore Mommsen in
Petrarch's Testament (Ithaca: Cornell University Press, 1957); for the bequest to Boccaccio,
see especially 82–83.

CHAPTER 3

The Reluctant Canonist

Boccaccio's fictional voices are many. As Author, Narrator, Scribe, Commentator, Dreamer, Lover, Scholar, Canonist—even as a Pine Tree, a Woman, and a Stag—he speaks from the folios of his vernacular inventions, a polyhymnic mime. Above all arches an identity that umbrellas all the others: Poet. The art of poetry, to delight and instruct with literary creations—that was his life calling. This destiny sprung not just from early manhood or youth but from so deep inside his being that he could say it had already been cast from the time he lay in his mother's womb.

> Whatever the vocation of others, mine, as experience from my mother's womb has shown, is clearly the study of poetry. For this, I believe, I was born. I well remember how my father even in my boyhood directed all my endeavors towards business. As a mere child, he put me in charge of a great business man for instruction in arithmetic. For six years I did nothing in his office but waste irrevocable time. Then, as there seemed to be some indication that I was more disposed to literary pursuits, this same father decided that I should study for holy orders, as a good way to get rich. My teacher was famous, but I wasted under him almost as much time as before. In both cases I so tired of the work that neither my teacher's admonition, nor my father's authority, who kept torturing me with ever renewed orders, nor the pleas and importunities of my friends, could make me yield, so great was my one passion for poetry.[1]

His determination to have it his own way, to resist his father's pressures, are memories the older Boccaccio records in the last pages of his

---

1. *Genealogie* 15.10; trans. Osgood, *Boccaccio on Poetry,* 131–32.

Genealogies of the Gentile Gods. The moment may be autobiographical, but language reminds us of another, fictional portrait. It had figured in the tale that opens the Fifth Day at the center of the *Decameron,* that of a Cypriot recalcitrant to his father's efforts to make him an educated man.

> . . . il cui vero nome era Galeso; ma, per ciò che mai né per fatica di maestro né per lusinga o battitura del padre o ingegno d'alcuno altro gli s'era potuto metter nel capo né lettera né costume alcuno, anzi con la voce grossa e deforme e con modi più convenienti a bestia che a uomo, quasi per ischerno da tutti era chiamato Cimone, il che nella lora lingua sonava quanto nella nostra 'bestione.'

> [. . . his true name was Galeso, but because neither by his teacher's toil nor his father's blandishment nor beating nor anyone else's cleverness had it ever been possible to put into his head any inkling of letters or good breeding, and because instead he had a coarse and uncouth voice and manners more befitting a beast than a man, he was by everyone scornfully called Cimone, which in their tongue signified as much as "brute beast" in ours.] (*Dec.* 5.1.4)

In both cases sons refuse what their fathers try to impose. Nothing avails, neither paternal pressure, nor a tutor's pleadings, nor friendly persuasion from other quarters. But whereas uncouth Cimone spurns learning that his father rightly wants to instill, Boccaccio rebels against a parent whose stubbornness forces him away from culture. Cimone's father is a gentleman; Boccaccio's—so he would have us believe—a Philistine. Boccaccino the businessman had his boy study the abacus; of reading and writing he let him learn only the rudiments. Eventually, grudgingly aware of the lad's literary bent, but still determined that he become a moneymaker, he put him in school at the University of Naples, enrolled for a curriculum of canon law.

Although denied a humanistic education, Boccaccio remembers in his *Genealogies* that he was already spontaneously writing poetry while still a child. We may be reminded of the hermit Filippo Balducci, who failed in his efforts to repress his seventeen-year-old son's urge for a "gosling" (*Dec.* 4.1, introd.). The boy knew what he wanted; that was Nature's way. And Nature will have out.

> I remember perfectly that before I reached my seventh year, or had ever seen a story, or heard a teacher speak, or scarce knew my letters,

a natural impulse to composition seized me. I produced some fictionlets [fictiunculas], slight as they may have been. Of course, at that
tender age genius was as yet too weak for so great a function. But I
had scarce reached my majority when my mind, by its own impulse,
seized and assimilated the little I had already learned of poetry, and
I pursued the art with the utmost zeal, and delighted myself above all
things in reading, studying, and trying with all my might to understand poetry. This took place without a word of advice or instruction
from anyone, while my father continually resisted and condemned
such a pursuit. (*Genealogie* 15.10)

Boccaccio recalls, bitterly it seems, dissension with his father, whom he
blames for causing him to waste precious years in uncongenial pursuits.
Beginning with Filippo Villani in the late trecento, biographers made
much of this generational struggle, good material for a romantic life
drama. And the facts undisputed are, after all, that Boccaccino was a mid-
dle-class banker who trained his son for practical careers, first in accounting and then in canon law, neither of which professions the poet admits to
practicing.

Tension between them must have been real, but it has been blown up to
legendary proportions. We know, for example, that Boccaccio cooperated
in his family business affairs. After his father had returned from Naples to
Florence, the son stayed behind to help renew a contractual arrangement
entered into by Boccaccino at the nearby city of Capua.[2] At the same time,
the presentation of Boccaccino as "the Philistine" just does not fit docu-
mentary evidence of him in his public life either at Naples, where he was
named "counsellor and chamberlain" to the king, or in Florence. When
the narrator of the Ameto, stepping away from his pastoral retreat, hints
at a misanthropic monster in ambush at home, that icy old character can
hardly be the same man who repeatedly served his Tuscan city of resi-
dence. During the Black Death of 1348, he helped as an official of the
"Abbondanza," the committee with the very sensitive responsibility for
overseeing distribution of food and maintaining public hygiene. Documents also confirm this wealthy civic leader as Counsel of the money
changers' guild, Official of Finance, Counsellor of the Office of Merchants, Prior of the guilds, and an ambassador.[3] Boccaccio himself is
responsible for the birth of the myth, which he shapes with hyperbole from

2. Branca, *Profilo biografico*, 54.
3. Ibid., 14, 71–72, 78–79.

his own pen in the long autobiographical passages from the *Genealogies*. Poetry was his destiny not merely from birth—and that alone is a strong statement—but from before birth, from the uterus. At the tender age of six, even though barely literate, he was already composing on impulse "fictionlets." Between father and son there was nothing but enmity; the elder man was relentless in his opposition, doing everything he could to thwart grimly a talent struggling to bloom.

   In the father's rigidity and the son's rebellion we can recognize an actual conflict reproportioned to the measure of a time-honored fictional motif. How much of a story could there have been in the *Filocolo* if the king of Spain had not been so determined to keep his son, the prince, from loving Biancifiore? What sad conflict could have developed in *Filostrato* if the priest Calcas had not wanted to reclaim his daughter? In the *Decameron,* where a younger generation over and again presses its natural demands, Cimone of Cyprus and Filippo Balducci are only two among many fathers and sons caught in family tugs-of-war. To deny Nature invites trouble, if not tragedy, as Prince Tancredi of Salerno bitterly learned when he refused his daughter Ghismonda's needs.

   Boccaccio writes of his struggle to become a poet at a borderline between literary models and heartfelt experience. In just the same kind of authorial space, hovering between fiction and truth, he takes up his quill in the 1340s to write a biographical sketch of a fellow sufferer, *De vita et moribus domini Francisci Petracchi.* Petrarch too, it seems, had trouble with his father, employed as a notary at the papal court of Avignon. Like Boccaccino the banker, Ser Petracco wanted to establish his son in a proper profession and so destined him for civil law. While away at university, however, Petrarch fell under the sway of Apollo and the Muses and so sneaked quite a lot of poetry instead of concentrating on his law books. Informed by several sources, the father summoned him home for stern reproach: "Studium quid inutile tentas? Meonides nullas ipse reliquit opes" [Why are you wasting your time on this useless study? Homer himself died a poor man"]. If we wonder how Boccaccio could have known exactly the words that erupted from Petrarch's frustrated father, especially before he had even met Petrarch, an answer lies in the memoir by another victim of paternal overbearing. That person was Ovid. Like Boccaccio, Ovid began to serve the Muses while still in boyhood. Try as he might to obey his father, who intended him to be a lawyer, he just could not manage expository writing; everything he put down came out spontaneously as verse—or so he reminisces during the sad later years of his exile. And what did his father often have to say about that? According to Ovid: "Saepe pater dixit 'studium quid inutile temptas? / Meonides nullas ipse reliquit opes'" ["Why do you try a profitless pursuit? Even the Maeonian (Homer) left no wealth."].[4]

The Roman love poet's same recollection returns in Boccaccio's *Expositions on the Comedy,* this time openly acknowledged. We can see how much in common the poet of Sulmona had with his sympathizer from Certaldo—at least as literary autobiographies go. Ovid's genius, which revealed itself in his boyhood, proved irrepressible.

. . . dalla sua fanciulleza maravigliosamente fu il suo ingegno inchinevole agli studi della scienza.

Per la qual cosa, sì come esso mostra nel preallegato libro [*Tristia*], il padre più volte si sforzò di farlo studiare in legge . . . ; ma traendolo la sua natura agli studi poetici, avveniva che, non che egli in legge potesse studiare, ma, sforzandosi talvolta di volere alcuna cosa scrivere in soluto stilo, quasi sanza avvedersene, gli venivano scritti versi; . . . della qual cosa il padre dice che più volte il riprese, dicendo:

"Sepe pater dixit: studium quid inutile temptas?
Meonides nulla ipse reliquit opes."

Per la qual cosa, eziandio contro al piacer del padre, si diede tutto alla poesia.

[. . . from his childhood his mind inclined marvelously to desire for knowledge.

For that reason, as he shows in the above-cited book [*Tristia*], his father many a time tried to make him study law . . . ; but, since his nature pulled him toward poetic studies, it happened that, not only could he not study the law, but when he sometimes made an effort to write something in prose, almost without his being aware of it, what came out were verses; . . . for this he says that his father often reproached him,

---

4. *De vita et moribus Domini Francisci Petracchi de Florentia secundum Iohannem Bochacii de Certaldo,* ed. Fabbri, 898. The date of composition, whether early or late in the 1340s, has been much disputed. See Fabbri's introd., 881–85. The lines from Ovid are *Tristia* 4.10.21. Hollander pointed to this parallel between Boccaccio and Ovid, in *Boccaccio's Two Venuses,* 115–16.

"Sepe pater dixit: studium quid inutile temptas?
Meonides nullas ipse reliquit opes."

For that reason, even contrary to his father's wishes, he gave himself
entirely to poetry.] (*Esposiz.* 4.1.116–18)

In their real histories, Ovid, Boccaccio, and Petrarch are not excep-
tional as poets who began as lawyers. We learn from the ancient life of Virgil by Suetonius-Donatus, that he too must have read the law, since he is
said to have argued one case at Cremona after taking the toga. Italy's early
vernacular lyricists, functionaries at the Palermo court of Emperor Frederick II, composed poetry as an avocation. Giacomo, the Sicilian poet who
signed his sonnet "Meravigliosamente" as "il Notaro da Lentini," would
have been professionally involved in drawing legal contracts. Pier della
Vigna, who studied law at Padua, became a judge on Frederick's supreme
court, encouraged legislative reforms, and is attributed a collection of the
laws of Sicily. Among the Tuscan lyricists, Cino da Pistoia was a sought-
after jurist. After studying law at Bologna under the famous Franciscus
Accursius, Cino taught jurisprudence at Siena, Florence, and Perugia. In
August, 1330, King Robert extended him a formal invitation to come and
teach in Naples, salaried directly by the citizens. Cino read civil law at that
southern *studium* during 1330–31 and probably the following academic
year as well. It is a period that coincides with Boccaccio's six years at the
University of Naples, from the time he was seventeen or eighteen in
1330–31 until he was about twenty-three or twenty-four in 1336–37. Since
there would have been close contacts between students and faculty in
canon and civil law at the university, Boccaccio probably met Cino, an
encounter that can explain his early familiarity with Tuscan literary texts,
to which he must have had access through the poet of Pistoia.[5]

For the Sicilian poets, there was not an incompatibility between their
jobs and their entertainments. Nor did his double life as lawyer and poet
apparently bother Messer Cino. Clear-cut enemies in the topos—obsessive

5. Wesley Trimpi's ample studies have shown connections between legal training in
rhetoric and literary activity; see, e.g., "The Quality of Fiction: The Rhetorical Transmission
of Literary Theory," *Traditio* 30 (1974): 1–118. For Virgil, see Colin Hardie, ed., *Vitae virgilianae antiquae* (Oxford: Clarendon Press, 1966). Brief biographical notice of the medieval
poets can be found in Contini, *Poeti del Duecento.* Boccaccio's encounter with Cino is discussed by Vittore Branca and Pier Giorgio Ricci, "Notizie e documenti per la biografia del
Boccaccio," pt. 4, "L'incontro napoletano con Cino da Pistoia," *Studi sul Boccaccio* 5 (1969):
1–12; cf. Branca's *Profilo biografico,* 30–32.

materialism and noble intellectualism—can go hand in hand in everyday life. What, then, was Boccaccio's attitude toward the canons? Romantic biographies would certainly have us believe that his resentment of them was every bit as fierce as his father's determination to track him for financial success. But might he not in retrospect, and to rhetorical effect, exaggerate that hatred in the *Genealogies,* even as he magnifies the signs of his inborn poetic identity?

A sprinkling of references to canon law appears elsewhere in Boccaccio's later writings. Not necessarily disdainful and sometimes positive, they are particles that may be charged with irony or ambivalence. One passage where he holds up this area of endeavor as a positive example occurs in the *Corbaccio.* To deprogram the Dreamer of his love for the widow, her husband's shade discourses on wisdom, first as people conventionally understand it and then as his disgusting ex-wife actively construes the term. One route to the former is the study of church law.

> Alcuni sono savi chiamati, per ciò che ottimamente la scrittura di Dio intendono e sannola altrui mostrare; altri, per ciò che intorno alle questioni civili et ecclesiastiche, sì come molto in legge e in decretali amaestrati, sanno ottimamente consigli donare; altri, per ciò che nel governo della republica sono pratichi . . . ; et alcuni sono savi tenuti, però che sanno bene guidare i fondachi, le loro mercatanzie e arti e' lor fatti di casa.

> [Some are called wise because they understand God's Scripture thoroughly and can teach others; others because they can give excellent counsel concerning civil and ecclesiastical questions, being very learned in laws and decretals; others because they are experienced in the government of the republic . . . ; some are considered wise because they can well manage their warehouses, their merchandise, their craft, and their household affairs.][6]

In other words, theologians possess wisdom, as do civil and canon lawyers (Decretalists) and political leaders; so, too, do provident merchants, mem-

---

6. Giovanni Boccaccio, *Corbaccio,* ed. Giorgio Padoan, in *Tutte le opere,* vol. 5, pt. 2 (Milan: Mondadori, 1994), par. 257; *The Corbaccio,* trans. Anthony K. Cassell (Urbana: University of Illinois, 1975), 48. I cite Cassell's translation throughout. A schematic breakdown of the divergent critical assessments accompanies Robert Hollander's essay on the text in *Boccaccio's Last Fiction: "Il Corbaccio"* (Philadelphia: University of Pennsylvania Press, 1988).

bers of the craft guilds, and householders. The widow, though, belongs to a sort of nymphomaniacal sorority, the Cianghella Club, that rates women wisest who are sexually most promiscuous. Earlier in the *Corbaccio,* the Dreamer, not yet disabused, had touted his expertise as a canonist. To defend himself before the widow's dead spouse, he argues that canon law entitled him to press his suit with the woman, since her husband's demise left her a free agent: "come tu dalla nostra vita ti dipartisti, secondo che le ecclesiastiche leggi ne mostrano, quella ch'era stata tua donna non fu più tua donna, ma divenne liberamente sua; per che in niuno atto potresti con ragione dire che io mi fossi ingegnato di dovere alcuna tua cosa occupare" [when you departed from our life, as canon law shows us, she who was your wife was yours no longer, but became free unto herself; for this reason by no act could you reasonably say that I contrived to take possession of anything of yours] (par. 82). Of course, like the scholar tricked by the widow Elena in *Decameron* 8.7, here is a character long on book learning but short on common sense. His legal argument at the bar of a husband who has seen it all smacks of prissiness and silliness. By rights he may be perfectly entitled to this preening female, but he is blind to the rottenness beneath her paint, ornaments, and borrowed feathers. Ironically, while the husband's reference to canon law recognizes it as a legitimate intellectual pursuit and a cornerstone of social order, the protagonist's "practice" of that discipline makes him out to be a fool. Humorous irony pierces the Author's pose in the *Corbaccio.* Fine in the abstract—or in their proper forum—canons cannot be much help when it comes to sexual pursuit.

Church law will again take its place as one of the major fields of human knowledge in Boccaccio's *Genealogies of the Gentile Gods.* He compares it to poetry twice in the last book of his encyclopedia. As we would expect, he contrasts the two. One opposition, quite neutral, occurs in a passage that does not put the law to invidious disadvantage. In fact, here poetry comes out the weaker.

> The great text of both civil and canon law has grown in bulk throughout generations of human failing, by editorial apparatus from many a doctor. The books of the philosophers also carry with them their commentaries compiled with great care and zeal. The books of medicine are filled with marginal notes from countless pens that resolve every doubt, and so with sacred writings, and their numerous expositors; so also with the liberal and the technical arts— each has its own commentary, from which anyone may select on

occasion according to his preference. Poetry alone is without such honor. (15.6)

By comparison to law, medicine, and philosophy, poetry suffers because it has not come down through the ages in unbroken chains of transmission. Preservation of those other books, through dark and violent ages of human history, could be assured by the glossarial apparatus that accumulated around them, a sort of bulwark encasing the texts. Literature, sad to say, survives only in a hit-and-miss manner, dispersed in pieces "like fragments of a mighty wreck strewn on some vast shore" (*Genealogie,* preface, 11).

As intellectual activity goes, some people might think specialties like law are more serious than poetry, but in another passage of the *Genealogies,* Boccaccio quickly undercuts them. "For example, there are the laws of the Caesars, and canon law, and medicine—subjects that many consider most sacred, because they have so often been the means of making greedy men rich" (15.10). Whether you are talking about the Justinian Code and its interpreters or the canons in Gratian's *Decretum* as debated by the Decretalists—it is all still law, and the cliché requires that we blame lawyers for undisguised rapaciousness. As for philosophy and theology, they rate a good deal more respect—the former because it teaches us the causes of things and differences between false and true, the latter because through the Bible we learn to despise worldly goods and discern the way to heaven. Boccaccio respects the established medieval hierarchy, ranking study of the sacred books as the most noble science. But all studies are necessary. We human beings, like strings of varying lengths on a harp, vibrate with different aptitudes—as theologian, philosopher, poet, judge, lawyer, king, priest, merchant, sailor, carpenter. To "sound" together in social harmony, people must pursue the careers for which Nature has best suited them. In that sense, all these sciences are ultimately respectable because their unison works for the preservation of the race. It is in this context that Boccaccio defends his own determination to hold out for a poetic career, the calling for which Mother Nature had destined him from the womb.

Our poet catapults his sharpest missiles against the lawyers in his Christian encyclopedia of universal biography, *De casibus virorum illustrium* (On the falls of famous men). The suicide of Appius Claudius in Rome, a power-mad decemvir and corrupt judge who caused the death of innocent Virginia, raises a platform from which the Author can launch into a diatribe on the entire legal profession (3.10). Serving as his foil is antiquity,

when, fortunately, it was rare to find lawyers like Appius, who is a far cry
from philosophers and paragons of virtue like Phoroneus (the founding
lawyer of Greece), Minos, Licurgus, Solon, and Cato the Censor. He
argues that nowadays, though, people rush around robbing the cradle—
literally, "snatching babes from the nipples of their wet nurses"—to stock
law schools, and they do it not to impress laws indelibly on such young
minds but just so that avarice can be mastered at an age more tender.
According to Boccaccio, those who ascend the bench all gussied up in their
ribbons and birettas toss out philosophical arguments, on which justice
and human reform depend, and "they say, with filthy, obscene language,
'Let's forget those; they're superfluous, and they do not instruct us in getting our bread.'" What's worse, these "asses," not content with disregarding what they do not know, try to besmirch what is left, pressing with all
their might to see if they can succeed in milking from the "simplicity and
the salubriousness of the laws" conflicts not meant to surface, "so that
they can drag out litigations eternally with cavils of the contenders." O
heavenly justice, Boccaccio protests, how long can you endure it? He sar-
castically concludes that the community of Italians should rejoice that
Caesar's laws are protected by such holy patrons, "with claw-hands,
shameless eyes, raging lust, hearts of stone, faked gravity, honeyed tongue,
teeth of iron, and, in a word, an insatiable appetite for gold."[7]

Rapacious beasts like these fit right into the human zoo whose members
stir Boccaccio to moralizing prose in *De casibus;* there are hundreds and
hundreds of them, from Adam to his own day. His tirade on the lawyers
answers an expository pattern in the structure of this late medieval encyclopedia: chapter after chapter, as the Author sits musing and writing in
his study, throngs of the fallen mighty press on his imagination, much as
in *Inferno* the damned file before Dante, whose curiosity prompts them to
speak of their lives and sins. Amid the babble that hums in Boccaccio's
mind, a few voices rise above the others, each with a sad story to tell. After
the visionary scribe has duly recorded individual examples of guilt in a
particular category, he proceeds to an invective against that evil more generally—pride, disobedience, avarice, women, and so forth. In other words,
even though Boccaccio may have penned this criticism with some special
personal relish, context makes it mostly rhetorical. Canonists are not
under the slinging machine here; his targets are civil lawyers, administra-
tors of "laws of the Caesars" as codified by the emperor Justinian. And

7. *De casibus* 3.9.

they in turn are a professional screen for the deeper problem Boccaccio attacks, the bane of human greed that his book tirelessly batters.

If the university path Boccaccino chose for his boy left him sizzling with endless hostility toward canon law, the poet's writings do not betray very much evidence of it. In real life, as Pier Giorgio Ricci has suggested, he may actually have practiced as a canonist. Although he did not receive a formal university degree, he took courses for six years, a period sufficient for him to be recognized as an authority in the subject. Professional accomplishment in that field must have earned him the designation *dominus,* a rare honorific reserved only for knights and judges, and the title by which Petrarch addresses Boccaccio in his will. Florentine tax registers from the year 1352 list only seventy citizens who held it in a population of several tens of thousands. Ricci speculates that he earned the right to the title *dominus* when called to serve in a judicial capacity on a military expedition led by Francesco Ordelaffi in 1348. Subsequent years saw him actively involved in Florentine foreign service. Sensitive diplomatic missions, several of them to the papacy in Avignon, were entrusted to him. He represented the Commune of Florence on an important diplomatic mission to Pope Innocent VI at Avignon in 1354. Again in 1365 and 1367 he successfully carried particularly delicate diplomatic embassies from the Florentine Signoria across the Alps to Urban V. Official correspondence from the latter assignments reports choosing "magistrum Johannem Bocchacij honorabilem civem florentinum, oratorem [Master John Boccaccio, honorable Florentine citizen, orator]. His compatriots considered him "a man circumspect," someone "worthy in those matters that he would represent with unquestioned trust." The confidence of the *comune,* whose messages he carried, reflects his capacity in oratory as well as his culture as a jurist.[8]

Church law, which evolved through a complex history, first came into a systematic Western compilation thanks to Gratian, a jurist and Camaldolese monk of the twelfth century at Bologna. He gathered and ordered under subject headings a vast body of authoritative statements on issues relating to the definition and jurisdiction of the church. First known as the *Concordantia discordantium canonum* (Concordance of the conflicting

---

8. Ricci documented Boccaccio's honorific title, in "Notizie e documenti per la biografia del Boccaccio, pt. 5." Notice of Boccaccio's ambassadorial activity appears in Corazzini, *Le lettere edite e inedite,* introd.; Vittore Branca, "Notizie e documenti per la biografia del Boccaccio," pt. 1, "Una nuova ambasceria (1359)," *Studi sul Boccaccio* 3 (1965): 7–16; Branca, *Profilo biografico,* 96–97; 148–50.

canons), his treatise was published around 1148. This book, which later came to be known simply as the *Decretum,* is comprised of three parts: (1) the sources of canon law and definitions of ecclesiastical persons and offices, contained in 101 distinctions (*distinctiones*) subdivided into canons (*canones*); (2) thirty-six cases (*causae*) proposed for solution, subdivided into the questions (*quaestiones*) arising in connection with the cases, with canons inserted under each question (this part includes as well a long section on penitence); (3) *On Consecration,* which in five distinctions deals with church ritual and the sacraments. Gratian's authorities range from Christ and the apostles, down through their inheritors the popes, to the early councils of the church, the fathers of the church, episcopal capitularies, and a work as recent as the *Glossa ordinaria* (Ordinary gloss), itself a patchwork of patristic commentary on the Bible. Of approximately 3,700 chapters in the *Decretum,* about one-third come from writings, both Greek and Latin, by the church fathers, such as John Chrysostom, Basil, Jerome, Augustine, and Gregory the Great. Later expanded with decretals that were codified through the effort of Pope Gregory IX in 1234 and with material assembled at the order of Pope Clement V in the early fourteenth century, the *Decretum* still stands as one of the greatest medieval encyclopedias, the summa of reference for its branch of learning. It was to remain at the core of ecclesiastical law and ramify widely through works of the scholastic theologians, notably Thomas Aquinas, whom Boccaccio read attentively.

Since biographers so long assumed that Boccaccio hated the law, his education as a canonist has still not been studied as a moving force in his literary activity. Yet just as much as it advanced his public life in Florence, canon law pervaded his meditations as a poet. It freely infiltrates not only his fiction (as we should expect, from the first, when he was still a student at Naples) but also writings (from his last years) with his richest thoughts on the theory of literature. Boccaccio's vigorous "Defense of Poetry" at the end of the *Genealogies,* embracing warmly works by pre-Christian poets, marches along a trench line of resistance dug by strict religious constructionists like Saint Jerome. Their views, collected in Gratian's distinctions and questions, give him ready arguments for focused rebuttal of poetry's "enemies." For example, distinction 37 asks: What place should classical culture have in Christian education? In training for the priesthood, should secular texts be taught alongside Scripture and its commentators? Boccaccio's arguments on behalf of poetry are one side of an issue that had found theological support at least from the time of Augustine. In his defense for preserving the myths of the gentile gods, he tropes the historical movement by which Christian culture appropriated classical pagan literature. Like Moses and David, who studied the Egyptians and despoiled them figuratively of their gold and silver (i.e., their wisdom and eloquence), the Certaldo poet preserves pagan treasure by converting it to Christian allegory.[9]

Polar opposites in his rhetoric, canons and poetry cooperate in his practice as a writer. In *Diana's Hunt,* features of the allegory find points of reference in the sacrament of baptism, with its liturgical ritual, as taught in Gratian's *Decretum.* In *Filocolo,* the parlor-game problems at Fiammetta's "court" recall artificial issues debated by civil-law students in rhetorical exercises set to develop their declamatory skills. Boccaccio elaborates the two-sided question, or debate *in utramque partem,* with a double back-and-forth. First, the question is presented as if it were a legal case: Should a man love a married woman, a virgin, or a widow? Should a lady choose for her lover a man who is physically strong, courteous, or wise? Second, speaking as judicial arbiter, the queen gives her decision. Third,

---

9. For the canon law text and tradition on these issues, I have consulted the following three sources. On canon law and Gratian's *Decretum,* see *Encyclopedia Britannica,* 11th ed., s.v. *Decretum.* For the Fathers and the canons, see Gratian, *Corpus juris canonici:* pt. 1, *Decretum Gratiani,* ed. Emil Ludwig Richter (Leipzig: Bernhard Tauchnitz, 1839) I, dist. xxxvi and xxxvii. For discussion of good examples of attitudes toward the ancient poets, see Charles Munier, "A Propos des textes patristiques du Décret de Gratien," in *Proceedings of the Third International Congress of Medieval Canon Law,* ed. Stephan Kuttner, Monumenta Iuris Canonici, ser. C: Subsidia, vol. 4 (Vatican City: Biblioteca Apostolica Vaticana, 1971), 43–50. According to Gratian's *Decretum,* an illiterate man is not apt for the priesthood, and priests should not read ancient comedies to the exclusion of sacred Scripture. On Exodus 3:22, Gratian writes that Moses and David studied the Egyptians and despoiled them figuratively of their gold and silver, that is, their wisdom and eloquence. He argues that the parable of the prodigal son (Luke 15:16) reveals how for the fundamentalists a tiny detail could loom as a mighty admonition against empty siren songs of pagan poets. He notes that the Bible tells how the prodigal, after squandering his inheritance in a foreign land, was reduced to living as a swineherd, "and he would have gladly fed on the pods that the swine ate." The *Glossa ordinaria* (*Patrologia latina*) elucidates: "The pods are the food of the devils, the songs of the poets and secular teachings resonant with sterile sweetness. For although they delight, in them there is nothing that pertains to life, but only sound and fury of words, no refreshment." Gratian further argues that among the plagues visited on Egypt (Exodus 8:18), the mosquitoes signify sophistic reasoning of philosophers, whose dialectic is just so much buzzing, while the frogs are "figments of the poets," puffed up to no purpose. On the opposing side, we have Augustine's more tolerant opinion, which manages to accommodate pagan and Christian learning. He contends that as in the Bible the Children of Israel despoiled the Egyptians, so we should loot the treasury of gentile writings for the gold of their wisdom and the silver of their eloquence. In fact, argues Augustine, the pagans can teach us to be better readers of sacred texts. Munier cites the example of the pods and commentary.

the questioner rebuts and presents an opposing view. Fourth, the queen reaffirms her original ruling. In their presentation and resolution of conflicting opinions, Boccaccio's *questioni d'amore* take a legalistic turn that also repeats the method of Gratian's *Decretum,* which had collected and reconciled discordant points of view.[10]

We need not, however, wait until the *sic et non* love debate in *Filocolo* 4 to hear its composer's voice as canonist. Unnamed to be sure, he is nonetheless present as a student of ecclesiastical law from the first chapter. In his hands the simple story of two lovers separated and rejoined swells to a Pentecostal epic with the Roman church as a central protagonist. Telling the story of how the Spanish prince Florio "journeyed" to conversion, baptism, and Santiago de Compostela during Justinian's reign, Boccaccio restages the history of all Western Europe coming to the church. Florio, alias Filocolo, will find Christ through a catechism in the Lateran taught by Friar Ilario, a Greek fountain of wisdom. As he preaches the Good News, Ilaro (literally, the "glad" or "joyous one," from Latin *hilarus*) recites the history of the church, its orthodox doctrine, its Credo—all, naturally, with special emphasis on baptism, the sacrament that crowns his successful effort. From this Ilario, every bit as much a fictional character as Florio and Biancifiore, the Author claims to have received his story. What better authority for a saga of Christianity triumphant than an informant who himself represents the church?

The young student of canon law at the University of Naples who wrote Italy's first "novel," an epic love story of nearly a quarter million words, counted on his academic status for some moral support from God. Excited and nervous about the project, this one assigned by his lady Maria to save the tale of Florio and Biancifiore from "fanciful parlance of the ignorant," he invoked grace from heaven.

> . . . o donatore di tutti i beni, ad impetrar quella quanto più posso divoto ricorro, supplicandoti, con quella umiltà che più può fare i miei prieghi accettevoli, che a me, il quale ora nelle sante leggi de' tuoi successori spendo il tempo mio, che tu sostenghi la mia non

---

10. On canon law and baptism, see Cassell and Kirkham, *Diana's Hunt,* 54, 56. The debate *in utramque partem,* like the Scholastic *sic et non* method, reflects a binary system based conceptually on antinomies characteristic of medieval thought. On such disputes and Boccaccio's love of debate, see Surdich, *La cornice di amore,* chap. 1, "Il *Filocolo:* Le *questioni d'amore* e la *quête* di Florio," 11–75.

forte mano alla presente opera, acciò che ella non trascorra per troppa volontà sanza alcun freno in cosa la quale fosse meno che degna essaltatrice del tuo onore, ma moderatamente in etterna laude del tuo nome la guida, o sommo Giove.

[O Giver of all good things, devoutly as I can I turn to you, and I ask with that humility that may make my prayers most acceptable, that for me, who now spend my time on the holy laws of your successors, you sustain my hand, not strong for the present task, so that it not rush overzealously, unchecked, into something that might be less than worthy exaltation of your honor; but guide it moderately in eternal praise of your name, O mighty Jove.] (*Filoc.* 1.1.30)

If we translate to a rhetoric not quite so formal, we apprehend that Boccaccio here prays for inspiration, discipline, and a style tempered by religious piety. Although he appeals to the ruler of Mount Olympus, the power he really calls on to steady his pen is a Christian counterpart to Jove, Christ. Christ's successors are the popes, they who have compiled the canon-law texts now pressing their claim on the poet.

Time put into his fiction as well as pleasure the effort brought him return in his parting words to a monumental creation, at last complete. As he bids his labor farewell, authorial modesty dictates that he dismiss it with a double diminutive: "O piccolo mio libretto, a me più anni stato graziosa fatica, il tuo legno sospinto da graziosi venti tocca i liti con affanno cercati" [O little booklet of mine, who have been gracious toil to me for several years, your bark pushed by gracious winds touches the shores you struggled to seek] (5.97). But authorial pride must also have a say, quite justifiably, for Boccaccio knew that the *Filocolo,* anything but a "piccolo libretto," was far and away the most ambitious prose yet written by anyone in the Italian vernacular. Pretending at closure to be a lowly latecomer—hardly on a par with Virgil, Lucan, Statius, Ovid, and Dante—Boccaccio boldly matches stride with his ancestral masters. His canon are artists of heroic fiction, those who poetized at encyclopedic length. With them he will contend, but in the new language, not in Latin; in prose, not in verse. He steps along with them as did Dante before him in Limbo, "sixth among so much wisdom (*Inf.* 4.102)."

Much as he later will in his *Decameron,* our author comes forward at three moments in the *Filocolo:* at the beginning, in the middle, and at the end. The unnamed "composer" of the prologue, smitten by Maria, studies the canons. At center, the "grace endowed" man of Certaldo stages his self-naming and prophesies his fame, but he is careful to do so decorously, in the voice of another, none other than Jove. At the *congedo,* he attaches himself to the canon of authors at the acme of accomplishment. Homer, who headed the list in Dante's Limbo, has disappeared from Boccaccio's lineup and yielded to Dante himself, whom Boccaccio consecrates as the founding poet of the Tuscan vernacular. "Giovanni" is his immediate successor. When he steers his little booklet into port, several years after embarking on the project, the Certaldan can remind us again of his name, while at the same time refusing to state it, with recurrence to his "grace-filled" epithet. The effort has been "graziosa fatica" favored by "graziosi venti"; his "graceful toil" has cut across seas deep with words, blown on its way by "graceful winds" (*Filoc.* 5.97).

Jove's prediction of Giovanni's fame did, of course, come true, but not on account of the *Filocolo.* Although popular in the Renaissance and never completely lacking apologists, the book went into rapid decline after the sixteenth century and reached a nadir with the rise of Romanticism. One judgment typical of the best in the earlier period comes from Girolamo Squarciafico, who enhanced the Venetian edition of 1472 by appending his inventive *Life of Boccaccio,* complete with all the "facts" on Fiammetta. He speaks again from the preface of the 1503 *Philocolo vulgare,* where the letter of dedication to his patron fairly glows with praise for the book.

> . . . per non fastidire el lectore è variato cum ornamento di molti exempli e amorosi advenimenti. Gli si legano cocenti suspiri, ansietate grande, miserie maggiore, amorose lachrime, dogliose lamentiatione, cum una sincera sempre e degna fede, ne mal [sic] per contrarietate di fortuna mutata . . . e non mancho oratore, historyco che poeta il [Boccaccio] iudicamo.

> [. . . so as not to irk the reader, it is varied with the adornment of many examples and amorous occurrences. Laced into it are searing sighs, great anxieties, greater miseries, amorous tears, sorrowful lamentations, with an ever true and worthy faith that never wavers against fortune's adversity . . . and we judge him no less an orator and historian than poet.]

Still, one cannot help but suspect that all those clever rhetorical variations and ornaments may not really have been enough to stave off boredom.

Squarciafico himself, after advertising the volume's exciting qualities, had to add a reservation on Boccaccio's style: "più volte oltra lo conveniente si abunda; per questo ha più bissogno di freno che di speroni. Meritamente possiamo dire di lui quello che di Ovidio dice Quintiliano, che troppo amatore fu del suo ingegno" [he often abounds beyond the suitable; for this reason, he has more need of a brake than spurs. We can rightly say of him what Quintilian says of Ovid, that he was overly in love with his own ingenuity].[11]

Too much of a good thing even in the age when most appreciated, it is not surprising that for a later public attuned more to the heart than to the mind, the *Filocolo* should have become little of anything good at all. By the nineteenth century, this brick of a book had turned into the cross that dutiful Boccaccisti had to bear. At least one maverick, John Addington Symonds, did manage to escape his peers' martyrdom. For him the *Filocolo* proclaimed no less than "the advent of Renaissance art." He esteemed its fusion of medieval and classical material as a felicitous modern hybrid, a "marriage of Faust and Helen."[12] But representative of the majority was Francesco De Sanctis, who squibbed in a wry aside on the audience of young lovers to whom, beyond Maria, the Author addresses his book: "Probabilmente i giovani vaghi e le donne innamorate avrebbero desiderato una storia d'amore più breve e meno dotta" [Probably the eager young men and enamored ladies would have wished for a shorter and less learned love story].[13] Length and erudition, hand in hand, were now only responsible for a "wearying and complicated desert of words."[14] So overwhelming was this "mass of verbiage" that as late as 1930, Boccaccio's biographer Thomas Chaldecott Chubb could still resentfully wonder whether Maria herself would have bothered to read it.[15] Deemed in particularly poor taste was the very hybridism that the Renaissance and its Victorian

---

11. *Philocolo vulgare,* ed. Hieronimo Squarzafico (Venice: Donino Pincio Mantuano, 1503).

12. Symonds, *Giovanni Boccaccio as Man and Author,* 29.

13. Francesco De Sanctis, *Storia della letteratura italiana* (1870; reprint, Florence: Sansoni, 1965), 267.

14. Thus it was described by Hutton in *Giovanni Boccaccio,* 68. Hutton's dismal image of the desert has continued to accompany withering opinions of the *Filocolo.* See, e.g., Antonio Enzo Quaglio, "Tra fonti e testo del *Filocolo,*" *Giornale Storico della Letteratura Italiana* 139, no. 427 (1962): 321–69, especially 323: "Dalle righe del romanzo si alza un panorama culturale di vario livello, stridente e provvisorio nel plastico, dove predominano gli abissi più che le vette, le zone brulle e desertiche più che il verde rigoglioso della vegetazione."

15. Thomas Chaldecott Chubb, *The Life of Giovanni Boccaccio* (New York: Albert and Charles Boni, 1930), 72: "Giovanni, to please his lady-love, piled up such an overwhelming mass of verbiage as to make one wish we knew what she really thought of it, if indeed she ever

connoisseur Symonds had admired. Thus Luigi Settembrini, late in the 1870s, merely echoed his European contemporaries as he complained, "we certainly feel disgust when we read in the Filocopo that the pope is the high priest of Juno, who urges him to avenge Dido wronged by Aeneas by persecuting to the death the last descendant of the Roman emperors, King Manfred."[16]

Better tolerated today, the *Filocolo* still troubles commentators on the same score.[17] After all, what peculiar artistic etiquette can permit Juno to drop in for a chat with the pope? Is it not a strange onomastic decorum that casts Lucifer as Pluto, his realms as Dis, Adam as Prometheus, the twelve apostles as the "new knights" of Jupiter? To appearances, at least, the poet's classicism and Christianity make a gauche ensemble. Their coupling forces us to sight-transpose the style from its endless rhetorical devices—amplifications, grand circumlocutions, mythological allusions— as we pick our way through a plot coded in pagan terms. All those gods and goddesses who keep dipping down to intervene in mortal events seem to overmotivate the "real" characters and undermine their autonomy.[18]

---

read it at all." Luigi Malagoli, in "Timbro della prosa e motivi dell'arte del Boccaccio nel *Filocolo*," *Studi mediolatini e volgari* 6–7 (1959): 97–111, writes that he finds "seeds" of Boccaccio's future art in the *Filocolo* but judges its language clumsy and pronounces its "artistic weave" nonexistent.

16. Luigi Settembrini, *Lezioni di letteratura italiana dettate nell'Università di Napoli*, vol. 1 (Naples: Antonio Morano, 1879), 182: "si sente certo disgusto quando si legge nel Filocopo che il Papa è il gran sacerdote di Giunone, la quale lo stimola a vendicare Didone offesa da Enea, perseguitando a morte l'ultimo discendente degl'imperatori romani, re Manfredi." The title of the *Filocolo* varied as different editors saw fit to "correct" it. The incunabula carried *Philocolo;* representing the possibilities thereafter are *Philocholo* (Milan, 1520), *Philopono* (Venice, 1527), *Philocopo* (Venice, 1538), *Filocolo* (Florence, 1594), and *Filocopo* (Venice, 1612). See the catalogue by Francesco Zambrini in *Le opere volgari a stampa dei secoli XIII e XIV*, 4th ed. (Bologna: Zanichelli, 1878); see also Ernest Hatch Wilkins, "The 1527 *Philopono*," in *The Invention of the Sonnet and Other Studies in Italian Literature* (Rome: Edizioni di Storia e Letteratura, 1959), 139–45.

17. The first English translation of the *Filocolo*, by Donald Cheney with Thomas G. Bergin (New York: Garland, 1985), is evidence of renewed interest in the Anglo-Saxon world. Recent Italian criticism is also returning to Boccaccio's first romance, with provocative results: see Surdich, *La cornice di amore*, especially chap. 1; Bruni, *Boccaccio: L'invenzione della letteratura mezzana*, 102ff., 174ff. Bruni, however, remains essentially negative, finding the prose "overabundant . . . for the multiplication of episodes and the prolixity of descriptions and speeches" (178).

18. Critics have universally objected to this heterodoxy. See, e.g., Nicolas J. Perella, "The World of Boccaccio's *Filocolo*," *PMLA* 76 (1961): 330–39; Perella finds the gods the most annoying feature for the modern reader. He argues that since Boccaccio's psychological realism is enough to explain character motivations and actions, they are "too often factitious and purely ornamental."

Then suddenly, after finale power displays for the marriage of Florio and Biancifiore in Alexandria, gone are the Olympians. Not ready to wrap up his story with everybody's conversion and Florio's ascent to the throne of Spain, as had Old French minstrels before, Boccaccio appends a continuation of nearly fifty thousand words. It meanders with purpose to San Giovanni in Laterano, where Florio and his friends hear a full catechism from the Greek friar Ilario. Enter the pope in person. No more "Juno's vicar," he is Vigilius, Christendom's high pontiff from 537–55, and he baptizes Florio and Biancifiore into the faith at the Lateran font. So much liturgy, prayer, and Roman pomp—and, on top of that, the protagonists' pilgrimage to Santiago de Compostela—seem an anticlimactic exercise in piety. What a strained distance we have come from that Jove on high whom the canon-law student invoked as he set sail under the flag *Filocolo*. Maybe he was right to fear that his hand might run away with the quill on the folio, overenthusiasm tugging the "booklet" beyond proper limits.

Why did Boccaccio believe he could pull it all together? From the opening scene, that passage so offensive to Settembrini, pagan myth and Christian history meet as the two forces at contention in his epic. Juno comes driving down to Rome from heaven in a vehicle pulled by peacocks (fig. 2), her mission to chide "the man who through her held the holy office." That person is the pope, whom she stirs to summon Charles of Anjou into southern Italy and establish a new dynasty by uprooting Manfredi, the last of the Swabian emperors planted there. For the picture to make full sense, we need to see that this Juno is not really just the queen of the pagan gods, riding around the sky in search of wrongs to avenge. Symbolically, she is the church. Her advent at the incipit of the *Filocolo* defines the book as an epic fiction and settles Boccaccio's story into a contemporary political matrix. Guelphs, the papal party, have eclipsed their Ghibelline rivals, those marshaled under the Fredericks and the old banner of empire. The new rulers, whose capital is Naples, are the French Angevins descended from Charles and allied with the papacy in Avignon. Most powerful was that conqueror's grandson and Boccaccio's sovereign, the pious Robert of Anjou.

When the new poet launches his *Filocolo* into waters whose currents carry Guelph flattery, it is to Robert he pays tribute, Robert whose crown in Naples Christ's vicar and Queen Juno had parleyed to secure. Juno's mission must have been just before 1266, when Charles of Anjou defeated Manfredi at Benevento. It sets in motion a chain of events that will permit Boccaccio, four generations later, to write the *Filocolo* for a woman he claims was Robert's daughter. Actually, as he puts it, she was a secret family member, because she had been born the monarch's love child. Did Robert of Anjou, close ally to the pope and author of some four hundred sermons, ever father such a girl? Surely he did not. But in Boccaccio's strategy, it is so much the better if she is an imaginary creature. There is no blot on the king's reputation here; poetic beauty and virtue can more neatly enhance the Angevin dynasty. Matched to her nature is her name, *Maria,* chosen by a wise parent, as Boccaccio pointedly tells us: "he named her with the name of the woman who contained in herself redemption for the miserable loss that befell for what the first mother dared to taste" (1.1.15).

Heedful of the political climate, Boccaccio sets a course that puts him in line with the great poets of Italic history, Virgil foremost. But the text against which his ambitious entry best has to stack up is its singular vernacular foil, the *Divine Comedy.* What Boccaccio writes must respond to what Dante had written, a close-towering antecedent. Boccaccio's practice was to follow Dante, not only by direct imitation, but also by moving in where he found openings or gaps. Whereas Dante's medium for his masterpiece was Tuscan verse, Boccaccio now prefers Latinate prose (although he had not long before debuted with terza rima in the slighter *Diana's Hunt*). Whereas the *Comedy* taught how man comes to Christ in the mind, the *Filocolo* will narrate how the world came to Christ in history. This is the greater story that enfolds the romance of Florio and Biancifiore—children born on the same day and raised together at court in pagan Spain, true lovers forced apart by fate but at last reunited happily ever after as Christian man and wife.

The canonist chooses a frame tale suited to his intellectual concerns. It is Pentecostal. Its theme is the establishment of the universal Church. He will tell how Christianity, after spreading from Jerusalem to Rome, reached the world's westernmost point, the Spanish Peninsula and its spiritual capital, Santiago de Compostela. This Pentecostal epic is the vehicle that carries Florio and Biancifiore through their adventures, and that romance in turn encloses multiple shorter tales spun around secondary characters, spaced throughout the book. Still another story encircles the whole. This outermost ring is the Author's tale. It begins with his *coup de foudre* for Maria, Holy Saturday morning in the Neapolitan church of San Lorenzo. How it will end we do not yet know; he hopes his book will win him her love. While emulating literary ancestors in the European heroic genre, Boccaccio builds his book like nested Chinese boxes, strung in sequences like Ovid's *Metamorphoses*. For the *Filocolo* he merges epic with romance and develops the structure that will make him most famous, the frame tale.[19]

Universal in scope, both temporally and spatially, it carries an encyclopedia of classical and Christian culture. The "desert" Edward Hutton saw in these pages is neither a trackless nor an arid place. Its landscape rolls across the pages, well plotted and wonderfully planted. To begin with, Boccaccio sectored the surface into five books, successive phases of the story. Each book opens into many subdivisions, which I shall call "chapters." Of varying length, they usually contain one episode and correspond roughly to what a dramatist might construct as a single scene in a play.

Across this grid of books and chapters stretch plotlines and subplots, their points of entry and closure staggered. Plots are keyed to characters, mortals as well as immortals. The longest line follows Florio and Biancifiore. From the sacred heights of Mount Olympus, actors with parts most extensive are Juno, Diana, Venus, and Mars. Like the book itself, these character-focused plotlines fall into articulated parts. Important events, usually narrative turning points, may apportion the parts, or sometimes an entire line is balanced on either side of a significant center.

In all, for the *Filocolo* Boccaccio assembled some sixty characters. By comparison with his known source tales, none of which named more than a dozen, the cast is huge. Its members count pagan divinities, from Iris, the rainbow goddess who heralds Juno's descent in the epic, to Mars, companion of Venus and Florio's protector in the perils of his love—right up to the couple's cliff-hanger escape from death at the stake. Personifications, too, take turns at performing, as when Sleep orchestrates a premonitory dream or when Jealousy plants a wrong impression. Every so often, to vary the gallery, we come upon a metamorphosis victim, some hapless soul like Idalogos, whom Venus turned into a pine tree, or the gur-

---

19. See below, chap. 4, for further discussion of narrative organization in the *Filocolo*. Its logic has attracted structuralists and semioticians, who have attempted to describe the patterns in their own technical languages and geometric schemes. Boccaccio's *roman fleuve* obeys the most elementary rules of universal narrative. See Claude Cazalé-Bérard, "Les Structures narratives dans le premier livre du *Filocolo* de Giovanni Boccaccio," *Revue des Études Italiennes,* n.s., 17 (1971): 111–32; Ada Testaferri, "Modello narrativo e semiotico nel *Filocolo,*" *Quaderni d'Italianistica* 8, no. 2 (1987): 139–48. See also Surdich, *La cornice di amore,* chap. 1. In both the *Filostrato* and the *Teseida,* he fused the genres of epic and romance. Winthrop Wetherbee offers insights on the latter work in his graceful essay "History and Romance in Boccaccio's *Teseida,*" in *Boccaccio 1990: The Poet and His Renaissance Reception,* ed. Kevin Brownlee and Victoria Kirkham, *Studi sul Boccaccio* 20 (1991–92): 173–84.

gling Fileno, melted into a fountain by his tears of grief. There are black villains, the most horrid being Massamutino, King Felice's murderous seneschal. And there are white villains, best of all the Admiral of Alexandria, who locks Biancifiore in a harem tower but forgives Florio for gaining her chamber when a family ring reveals the boy to be his nephew. Souls passed on to glory may come back for a say and assist the sainted on this earth—Christ with the promise of martyrs' crowns, the apostle James in answer to a prayer, a pilgrim long gone with a message for his daughter. To teach the doctrines of the church and convert the infidels, there comes from Greece a "member of the order of the knights of God," Friar Ilario. Many more high personages animate the pages, from God to Lucifer and mostly fictional. These include Biancifiore's parents, the Roman nobles Quinto Lelio Africano (descended from Scipio Africanus) and Giulia Topazia (descended from Julius Caesar), as well as Florio's father, King Felice of Spain (a grandson of Atlas). For the climactic episode in Rome, when the couple convert to Christianity, Emperor Justinian's son, Bellisano, and Pope Vigilius put in ceremonial appearances.

To pace the peripeteias, Boccaccio invokes two kinds of calendars. One is astrological; one is liturgical. Thus Florio and Biancifiore, so much alike they could almost be twins, have as their natal sign the constellation Gemini. But what marks the actual day of their birth is the feast of Pentecost. A variant chronology defines the Author's tale—the story of his bedazzlement by Maria in San Lorenzo, her subsequent request at the convent of Sant'Arcangelo a Baiano that he write the book on Florio and Biancifiore, his fervent hope that it will sway her to answer favorably his love. For him, the significant season is Easter, since Amore became his master during services on Holy Saturday.

Even though the *Filocolo* seems, so to speak, all over the map, geography helps coordinate scenes, as they shift from one setting to another. These settings include Naples, where Robert rules and Maria dwells; Certaldo, albeit in its primeval state as an oak grove; Marmorina, the pagan court city of Florio and Biancifiore's childhood (it is Verona, known in the Middle Ages as "city of marble");[20] Alexandria of Egypt, the Admiral's bailiwick and the site of the Arab's Tower (Torre dell'Arabo); Santiago de Compostela, the sepulchre of Saint James and a Christian pilgrimage site;

---

20. Virginio Bertolini, "Dalla 'Marmorina' del Boccaccio all'appellativo di 'Città marmorea' dato a Verona nel medio evo," in *Atti e memorie della Accademia di Agricultura, Scienze e Lettere di Verona* 18 (1966–67): 321–32.

Seville and Cordova, capitals of the old Spanish kingdom; and Rome, the seat of the popes. Most important is Rome, a magnet. In that powerful urban center, main roads through the book begin and end. Thence Biancifiore's parents set out for Santiago de Compostela on the journey that will lead to their deaths; thither the grown children find their way to restore family ties and to receive baptism in the mother church of Christendom.

The *Filocolo* moves toward a double conclusion. One narrative line guides Florio and Biancifiore safely through an obstacle course that culminates with their marriage. A second line of events carries them forward to their Christian destiny, baptism. As romance, the epic moves toward resolution in matrimony; as history, it attains fulfillment when Spain accepts the church. Florio and Biancifiore's rebirth in the faith is a synecdoche for all Iberia, whose masses follow suit in response to Ilario's itinerant preaching. With Spain's conversion to Christianity, the Word has completed its sweep from East to West. James the Apostle had first brought its message to Hesperian shores. His shrine at Santiago, an initial and final goal of Boccaccio's fictional characters, rises to signal the book's cultic center, just as Rome, revered urban mistress, stands at its spiritual hub. Since Justinian ruled from 527 to 566 and Vigilius sat in the chair of Saint Peter's from 537 to 555, Boccaccio's chronology puts us sometime in the latter span, at the middle of the sixth century.[21]

Symbolic forces create fields of mutual attraction for romance and history, fiction and doctrine. Marriage and Pentecost, concepts at poles quite separate, can merge emblematically in the number 5. For that reason, Boccaccio privileges the pentad. It informs his most important structures, starting with the layout of the *Filocolo,* a volume in five books.[22]

---

21. See below, chap. 6 and chap. 6 n. 24 for a more precise chronological accounting.

22. Its most recent editor, Antonio Enzo Quaglio, has collated all known manuscripts to demonstrate how Boccaccio's original five-book structure degenerated in Renaissance editions to seven books. Corruptions ran deep in Gaetano Tizzone da Pofi's influential 1527 edition, which had seven books with arbitrary chapter divisions. Cf. its French translation, *Le Philocope de messire Jean Boccace florentin, contenant l'histoire de Fleury et Blanchefleur, Divisé en sept livres traduitz d'italien en français par Adrien Sevin, gentilhomme de la Maison de Giè* (1542). Although Ignazio Moutier restored the format of five books (Florence, 1829), a century later Ettore De Ferri reverted to seven for his two-volume text (Turin: UTET, 1927). Salvatore Battaglia again corrected the structure, giving five books for the text (Bari: Laterza, 1938). See Quaglio, "Prime correzioni al *Filocolo.*"

Book 1 = 45 chapters
Book 2 = 76 chapters
Book 3 = 76 chapters
Book 4 = 165 chapters
Book 5 = 97 chapters

After four chapters to take care of preambles—Juno's descent to prod
the pope, the Angevin conquest, the Author's lightning-like love attack,
Maria's wish for the book (1.1); his dedication of the book to young lovers
everywhere (1.2); a microhistory of the world from Creation to the
Crucifixion, the journey of the apostle James to Galicia, the spreading of
his cult to the four corners of the world (1.3); the strength of the cult in
Rome (1.4)—the fifth chapter of book 1 brings us around to the plot that
will unwind from the capitol of Christendom. In 1.5 we make the acquaintance of Quinto Lelio Africano, a noble young man whose "fame
redounds throughout Rome." He has taken as his "legitimate wife" Giulia
Topazia, "in accordance with the new law of the Son of God." Five times
since their marriage, Phoebus has returned to the House of Virgo, but still
there is no sign of a child. Lelio prays for one in church before a statue of
Saint James, who that very night personally answers his supplicant with a
visionary promise. In thanks, the couple vow a pilgrimage to Santiago de
Compostela.

Boccaccio plays a medieval game when he embeds in the background to
Biancifiore's birth the same figure that regulates the number of books in
his *Filocolo*. Biancifiore's father-to-be, Lelio, could have had just as much
Roman cachet with a surname like *Sextus* or *Septimius,* but instead he
bears the name *Quintus,* "the fifth." It is a point underlined when Lelio's
pilgrimage party falls ambush to Spanish "Arabs" en route to Santiago.
The battle of their martyrdom brings to the fore his right-hand man, captain of the first rank of Christians and a hero named Sesto Fulvio (1.26).
Again, this Quinto Lelio Africano, descended from Scipio Africanus,
could just as well make his initial appearance in the fourth chapter or the
sixth, but instead Boccaccio calls him to the scene in the fifth, at *Filocolo*
1.5. Whereas earlier versions of the romance put Blanchefleur's conception
in the fourth year of her parents' marriage, Boccaccio's astrology makes
them wait for exactly *five* years.

E già era con lei, poi che Imineo coronato delle frondi di Pallade fu
prima nelle sue case e le sante tede arse nella sua camera, dimorato

tanto, che Febo cinque volte era nella casa della celestiale Vergine
rientrato, e ancora di lei niuno figliuolo avea potuto avere, de' quali
egli sopra tutte le cose era disideroso.

[And by now he had lived with her for so long since Hymen, crowned
with the garlands of Pallas, had entered his house and the holy
torches had burned in his chamber that Phoebus had returned five
times to the house of the heavenly Virgin, and he had still not been
able to have a child by her, something that he desired more than anything else.] (1.5.3–4)

The fact that Quinto Lelio and Giulia Topazia conceive a child soon
after their fifth anniversary gives us a clue for decoding this cluster of 5s at
Filocolo 1.5. The whole passage is heavily tagged with references to marriage. We hear first that Quinto Lelio married Giulia according to the
"new law," that is, in a Christian ceremony. But Hymen, pagan god of
nuptials, played a part in blessing the rites. The bridal chamber blazed
with his torches—Boccaccio calls them "tede," a learned term from the
Latin *taeda,* "nuptial torch"—and Hymen must have stood protecting
that matrimonial sanctum as an olive-garlanded image to augur chaste fertility. Auspicious, too, for marital fidelity is the house of the Zodiac that
Phoebus Apollo enters for the fifth time, that of the "heavenly Virgin"
Virgo, whose sign marks the couple's anniversaries.

Like all of Boccaccio's other vocabularies here—Christian, mythic,
astrological, Latinate—the language of arithmetic contributes to a semantic sense of "marriage." In Pythagorean numerology, 5 is the marriage
number. Its meaning derives from the fact that the Pythagoreans gendered
numbers. Uneven numbers, being indivisible and hence strong (primes, as
we would say), are superior to even numbers, which can split into warring
parts. Hence the Pythagoreans considered odd numbers, the better kind,
masculine, and they considered inferior, even numbers feminine. All
things, they believed, are contained in the decad, which proceeds from the
monad, primal unity. In the sequence from 1 to 10, since 1 stands apart as
the origin of numbers, the first "real" number is 2, and the second "real"
number is 3. Summing 2 and 3, the first male number and the first female
number, the Pythagoreans saw "marriage." Boccaccio learned this Greek
philosophy of numbers through late antique communicating links, Neoplatonists like Martianus Capella and Macrobius. He would later put the
marriage number secretly to work in his *Teseida* and allow it more open

play in the *Decameron,* where on Day 5 stories programmatically marry off their protagonists.[23]

The number 5, defining "marriage" in *Filocolo* 1.5, has a second meaning in the romance on its Christian register. For example, Pluto's resentment at being cheated of lordship over so many new Christians spurred pagan King Felice to attack the pilgrims en route to Santiago precisely in the fifth month of their pilgrimage (1.15). On the blood-soaked field, Quinto Lelio, Sesto Fulvio, and all their other men perish. Giulia Topazia, rescued and sheltered at the Spanish court, then lives just long enough to bear a daughter. By a remarkable coincidence, on the same day that Giulia's child is born and Guilia dies, the queen of Spain gives birth to a son.

> . . . nel giocondo giorno eletto per festa de' cavalieri, essendo Febo nelle braccia di Castore e di Polluce insieme, non essendo ancora la tenebrosa notte partita, sentirono in una medesima ora quelle doglie che partorendo per l'altre femine si sogliono sentire.

> [. . . on the joyful day designated as the Knights' Holiday, when Phoebus was in the arms of Castor and Pollux together, before shadowy night had yet passed, they felt at the same time those pains that other women birthing are wont to feel.] (1.39.1)

What date corresponds to this chivalric holiday, the "festa de' cavalieri"? In Old French, the tradition brought Fleur and Blanchefleur into the world on Palm Sunday, *Pâques fleuris.* Because they had their birthday on "Floweried Easter," it was natural that they be christened as "Flower" and "White Flower." Those onomastics carried into most other language versions of the story, even accounts like Boccaccio's, where their date of birth has drifted to another day. Boccaccio Italianized the names but departed from his models when it came to chronology. Gemini is the children's birth sign, a point on which he is most explicit. Since the sun is in Gemini between May 21 and June 21, that sign cannot coincide with Palm Sunday, which is necessarily earlier on the lunar calendar. It can, however, accommodate another major religious holiday, *Pasqua rosata* (literally, "Rosied Easter" or "Easter of the Roses"). That is the liturgical feast more properly known as Whitsunday, or Pentecost.

---

23. See Kirkham, *The Sign of Reason,* 42–43, for the pentad as the Pythagorean, Neoplatonic marriage number. Further references are listed in the index of that work, s.v. "number."

The "Knights' Holiday" can only be Pentecost. This we deduce for two reasons. First, Biancifiore's gestation had to come to term. Since Giulia Topazia conceived just as she and Quinto Lelio were entering their sixth year of marriage, while the sun must have still been in Virgo, that moment could plausibly have been sometime during the first three weeks of September. Palm Sunday would be much too soon for the corresponding birth date, a time that cannot come until late May or June, as the sun passes through Gemini.[24] Second, number symbolism corroborates Pentecost as the date in question. With a name rooted in a Greek base cognate with *pentad, Pente*cost is crucial to Boccaccio's plan for 5 in the *Filocolo*. Whereas some 5s are defined by context as marriage numbers, the pilgrimage cut short after five months seems to imply something else. In fact, its field of meaning orbits around a different pole, one that is a gravitational center for whatever concerns the Christianization of Spain, the western outpost where the Word completes its trajectory in history. To accompany the church in its reach to Galicia, symbols will naturally be Pentecostal.

Pentecost derives from the Greek for "fiftieth" and refers to the "fiftieth day." In Jewish tradition, the Pentecost celebration fell fifty days, or a week of weeks (7 x 7 days + 1), after Passover. The Christian feast commemorates that New Testament Pentecost when, in keeping with his promise, the newly risen Lord sent down the Holy Ghost as tongues of fire onto the apostles' heads and inspired them to speak in tongues (Acts 2:1–47).

And when the days of Pentecost were drawing to a close, they were all together in one place. And suddenly there came a sound from heaven, as of a violent wind blowing, and it filled the whole house where they were sitting. And there appeared to them parted tongues, as of fire, which settled upon each of them. And they were all filled with the Holy Spirit and began to speak in foreign tongues, even as the Holy Spirit prompted them to speak.

To the multitude (people gathered in Jerusalem from every nation), Peter preached, explaining that the miracle fulfilled God's declaration as prophesied by Joel.

---

24. This inconsistency between the children's names and birth date in Boccaccio's account still bothers a bit his most recent editor. See Quaglio's commentary in his edition, n. 1 at 1.44. But the calendar requires Pentecost, as Quaglio and others recognize. See Smarr, *Boccaccio and Fiammetta,* 46–47.

I will pour forth of my Spirit upon all flesh; and your sons and your daughters shall prophesy, and your young men shall see visions, and your old men shall dream dreams. . . . And I will show wonders in the heaven above and signs on the earth beneath, blood and fire and vapor of smoke.

Peter admonishes all assembled to repent and be baptized. The company of Christ's followers, which before had been about 120, grew by 3,000:

Now they who received his word were baptized, and there were added that day about three thousand souls. And they continued steadfastly in the teaching of the apostles and in the communion of the breaking of the bread and in the prayers.

This event, at which the apostles miraculously spoke in every language and converted the multitudes from all corners of the earth, marks the foundation of the community of the faithful. In the liturgical calendar, Pentecost is part of Eastertide. It is the great feast that concludes the paschal cycle, which begins with Lent forty days before Easter, continues after Easter for another forty days until Christ's Ascension, and then continues for ten more days until the descent of the Spirit. A symmetry shapes the spring liturgical season. To the penitential weeks of Lent (in Latin, *Quadragesima*) corresponds Pentecost (in Latin, *Quinquagesima*), a time for rejoicing to celebrate the new law, the new people of God, and the gift of the Spirit.[25] On the day of Pentecost was founded the Pentecostal, or universal, Church. And so, for the *Filocolo,* Florio and Biancifiore's birth date shifts forward from Palm Sunday to Pentecost, a feast in Gemini nine months after Virgo, and a day related by etymology to the number 5. As *romancier,* Boccaccio keeps his calendar on a realistic schedule; as canonist, he paces it symbolically.

The original Pentecost, recorded in the Acts of the Apostles, prepares the Twelve for their mission of disseminating the gospel to the four corners of the earth. In that biblical account originates the movement leading to the Christianization of Spain by James, whose legendary voyage, militant

---

25. John XXII added Trinity Sunday, the first after Pentecost, to the church calendar in 1334. But Pentecost was to remain the great culminating feast in the paschal cycle; from it subsequent Sundays were reckoned up to the end of the liturgical year. The Jewish Pentecost had celebrated the Sinai covenant and formation of the chosen people. On the meaning of Pentecost, see the *New Catholic Encyclopedia.*

zeal, and sainthood at Santiago de Compostela helps Boccaccio set the
stage for his love saga.

> . . . e mandato a' prencipi de' suoi cavalieri lo 'mpromesso dono del
> santo ardore, volendo che l'ultimo ponente sentisse le sante oper-
> azioni, elesse uno de' suddetti prencipi, quello che più forte gli parve
> a potere resistere alle infinite insidie che ricevere dovea, e sopra
> l'onde di Speria trasportare il fece a un notante marmo. Il quale, per-
> venuto nella strana regione, con la forza della somma deità, comin-
> ciate contro quelli, i quali resistenti trovò, aspre battaglie, acquistò
> molte vittorie, e molti delle celestiali armi novelle vi rivestì. . . . I cui
> seguaci, dopo la sua passione, prese le martirizzate reliquie, in nota-
> bile luogo reverentemente le sepelliro non sanza molte lagrime. E ad
> etterna memoria di così fatto prencipe, poco lontano all'ultime onde
> d'occidente, sopra il suo venerabile corpo edificarono un grandis-
> simo tempio, il quale del suo nome intitolarono

> [. . . and when the Son of God had sent the princes of his new knights
> the promised gift of holy fire, since he wanted the remotest west to feel
> his holy operations, he elected one of the aforementioned princes, the
> one who seemed to him strongest for resisting the traps that would be
> set for him, and he caused him to be transported over the waves of
> Hesperia on floating marble. When he reached the strange region,
> with strength from the highest deity he began to wage harsh battles
> against them, whom he found resistant, and gaining many victories, he
> reclothed many people in the new celestial arms. . . . His followers,
> after his passion, having gathered his martyred relics, in a noteworthy
> place reverently buried them, not without many tears. And in eternal
> memory of so great a prince, not far from the remotest waves of the
> Occident, over his venerable body they constructed a very grand tem-
> ple, to which they gave his name.] (1.3.10–13)

The "princes," or leaders, of Christ's "new knights," or Christian soldiers,
are the apostles. To James was assigned the world's western corner, but
there he encountered fierce resistence. It was so strong, according to the
legend of his life by Jacopo da Varagine, that he only managed to make
one convert before being forced back to the Holy Land, a more hospitable
setting in which he won great victories for Christ by crushing the magician
Hermogenes. When he died, his disciples sealed the saint's corpse in a sar-

cophagus, which they shipped out to sea on a vessel without a helmsman—
the miraculous "floating marble" of Boccaccio's account. Guidance came
from the Angel of the Lord, who delivered the sloop to the shores of Galicia.[26] Once he had passed on to sainthood, James, assisted by his mission-
aries in the Lord's service, performed many knightly feats, successfully
winning Spaniards and arming them with faith.

Florio, heir to the Spanish throne, will grow up to convert his parents
and the whole kingdom, following in the footsteps of James, who himself
had followed Christ. In a predestined chain of transmission, Quinto Lelio
fathers the daughter whose family religion will pull Florio and Biancifiore
back to Rome and eventually bring all Iberia into the fold. What better
day for the children to come into the world than the "festa de' cavalieri,"
the "Knights' Holiday"? Their birthday prophesies their future in a new
order of Christian chivalry.

Pentecost figures in the *Filocolo* as a nexus between Florio and
Biancifiore's love story and their spiritual mission in the conversion of
Spain. Boccaccio never actually calls the day by its proper name in the
entire book. But he refers to it, first in the hagiographic capsule on James,
then when providence has guided his young pagan hero into the Lateran
for lessons from the priest Ilario. Before a monumental crucifix, the effigy
of a man whose wounded hands, feet, and rib cage fascinate Filocolo (fig.
9), he listens as Ilario reviews the Old Testament and the first five ages of
the world (5.53). The Greek priest gives a much fuller account to the sixth,
present age, which he says is "filled with grace" (5.54). From the Annunciation to Christ's miracles, death, and resuscitation, we hear Father Ilario
on the gospel. His history culminates with the Resurrection, the Ascension, and Pentecost.

Poi al terzo dì ritornando al vero corpo, con quello veramente risus-
citò. . . . E dopo il quarantesimo giorno, vedendolo tutti i discepoli
suoi e la sua madre, se ne salì al cielo, faccendo loro nunziare che
ancora a giudicare i vivi e i morti ritornare dovea. E dopo il decimo
giorno tutti del Santo Spirito gl'infiammò, per lo quale ogni scienza

---

26. Differing from Jacopo, Boccaccio emphasizes James's success in the West, despite
fierce opposition. His source for the nautical miracle that transports the corpse to its final
resting place, as Quaglio suggests in his edition, may have been the *Compendium* by Paolino
Minorita. Cf. Jacopo da Varagine, *Leggenda aurea,* trans. Cecilia Lisi (Florence: Libreria
Editrice Fiorentina, 1984), 1:410–21. A useful compendium of information on the medieval
cult of Saint James has been assembled in William Melczer, trans., *The Pilgrim's Guide to
Santiago de Compostela* (New York: Italica Press, 1993).

e ogni locuzione di qualunque gente fu loro manifesta: e predicando la santa legge, tutti per diverse parti del mondo andarono.

[Then on the third day returning to his true body, with that he truly resuscitated. . . . And after the fortieth day, seeing all his disciples and his mother, he rose to heaven, making announcement to them that he must return again to judge the living and the dead. And after the tenth day, he inflamed them all with the Holy Spirit, through which all wisdom and every language of whatsoever people was manifest to them; and preaching the holy law, they all went out through diverse parts of the world.] (5.54.38)

From this platform, Ilario will exhort Filocolo and his friends to abandon their "false and abominable laws," to "chase away" the inimical trickster of our souls, and to come "new" before God the Creator ("nuovi davanti a Dio vostro Creatore vi presentate"). Catechism sessions follow; Ilario recites a well-annotated Credo (5.56); he calls Filocolo to the holy laver: "Correte al santo fonte del vero lavacro" (5.57). Kindled with the flame (5.58), Filocolo offers to reward his companions for their steadfastness with the gift of this faith (5.59), and they readily answer as one: "I vani iddii e fallaci periscano, e l'onnipotente, vero e infallibile Creatore di tutte le cose, sia amato, onorato, adorato e creduto da noi. Venga il vivo fonte" [Perish the vain and fallacious gods, and let us love, honor, adore, and believe in the omnipotent, true, and infallible Creator of all things. Let come the living font] (5.60).

Step-by-step from his felicitous arrival in Rome at 5.50, a chapter juncture that flashes the Pentecostal sign, Filocolo progresses on a moral path toward the Lateran baptistery. There Pope Vigilius will perform the ceremony in which the couple's marriage, their romantic fulfillment, finds its Christian analogue. It is a "gracious," or "grace-full," day ("grazioso giorno"), as all Rome congregates to watch Filocolo, his family, and his familiars receive the waters from the pontiff. In the font, he leaves behind his temporary name ("suo appositivo nome"), Filocolo, for rechristening is proper to baptismal immersion; where the old man dies, the new man is born.[27]

---

27. On the liturgy and symbolism of baptism, see Cassell and Kirkham, *Diana's Hunt,* introd., chap. 3. Another example of a new name for the new man can be found in *Decameron* 1.2, where the Parisian Jew Abraam converts and takes the baptismal name *Giovanni* by antonomasia.

For this climactic event in Florio and Biancifiore's spiritual itinerary, Boccaccio reserves chapter 71 of the final book. Its numbers perfectly describe the hero's passage from an old dispensation to the era of grace, from error to redemption. Since 7 defines the world, created by God in seven days, the first number beyond it stands for the beginning of a new cycle, a week outside secular time, where humankind enters eternal life. The number 8, sum of 7 + 1, signifies salvation. For that reason it became a symbol of baptism, which is why baptisteries and fonts—including the greatest in Christendom, at the Lateran—were typically octagonal structures. Boccaccio schedules the baptism in his fiction at a most proper textual octagon, 5.71, the chapter number in the fifth and final book whose digits total the Pentecostal transition into new life.[28]

Obdurate Felice, on the verge of disinheriting his son for endless and stubborn disappointments, must also finally hear the Word. It comes to him as a formidable nocturnal vision, recalling one part of Acts 2:17, the prophecy of Joel realized at the miracle of Pentecost at Jerusalem: "and your young men shall see visions, and your old men shall dream dreams." In a lightning-like bolt of splendor, the God of justice threatens to visit upon Felice ironic infelicity, with a curse of miserable last days.

> Io sono colui che tutto posso, e a cui niuno pari si truova, e in cui il tuo figliuolo con la sua sposa e co' suoi compagni credono novellamente, a' cui piaceri se tu benignamente non acconsenti, . . . vituperevolemente morrai, e abominevole a tutto il mondo.

> [I am he who is all-able, and to whom none is found equal, and in whom your young son with his bride and with his companions newly believe, and should you not consent benevolently to his wishes, . . . you will die in vituperation, an abomination to all the world.] (5.80.3–5)

Subdued by this voice of malediction, Felice soon after is happy to go to the holy laver, along with his queen and all the citizens. Then Florio sends legates throughout the kingdom to "scatter the holy seed," and

---

28. Vincent Foster Hopper, in *Medieval Number Symbolism* (1938; reprint, New York: Cooper Square, 1969), 77–78, refers to the transition from 7 to 8. Octagonal baptistries and the accompanying symbolism of number are elucidated in Richard Krautheimer, "Introduction to an 'Iconography of Medieval Architecture,'" *Journal of the Warburg and Cortauld Institutes* 5 (1942): 1–33, and Paul A. Underwood, "The Fountain of Life in Manuscripts of the Gospels," *Dunbarton Oaks Papers* 5 (1950): 41–138. See further below, chap. 5.

mandò commandando che chi la sua grazia disiderasse, prendesse il battesimo, e abbattessero i fallaci idoli a reverenza fatti de' falsi iddii: e de' templi fatti a loro facessero templi al vero Iddio dedicati, e lui adorassero e temessero e amassero.

[he sent orders everywhere that whoever wished to remain in his good graces should take baptism, and that they should strike down the fallacious idols made in reverence to false gods, and that they should make the temples built to them into temples dedicated to the true God and adore and fear and love him.] (5.82.4)

With this command, the evangelical vector of the *Filocolo* pushes to its final target. Christianity has triumphed over heresy and polytheism, even in remotest Spain, the land farthest to the west from the gospel cradle, Jerusalem. Of course, a few loose ends are left to tie up. To bring the romance full circle, Florio and Biancifiore make their own Santiago pilgrimage and collect the bones of her father for interment in Rome. Felice passes away, but not without leaving a deathbed testament to Florio on the virtues and vices. Pomp and circumstance at Cordova crown the fairytale prince, who sends his barons home with rich gifts and rides back with Biancifiore to Marmorina, where they live happily ever after.

Symbolic trackings crisscross Boccaccio's romance. We find them in chapter markers, which follow the rules of numerical composition; that is, Boccaccio positions subject matter so that it falls in aptly numbered chapters. Or, put another way, a template of symbolic numbers orders content throughout the *Filocolo*. For example, the lovers receive baptism at the Lateran in 5.71, a textual location that signals movement from mortality in time to salvation in eternity ($7 + 1 = 8$). When the octave comes openly as a round number, in 5.80, God himself thunders to Felice in a dream; it is an appropriate slot in the *Filocolo* for the Deity's sole apparition. By similar logic, Quinto Lelio, to whose marriage the olive-wreathed statue of Hymen had raised a torch five years before, enters the romance in 1.5. At 5.155, after Venus and Mars save them from death by fire, the newlyweds visit every Alexandria temple in thanks to the gods for their consummated nuptials.[29] Along the Pentecostal line of events, we are pleased to see Flo-

---

29. It may be significant that Florio and Biancifiore consummate their own marriage in the Arab's Tower assisted by Hymen—again crowned with olive, but this time in person— Venus, and Diana in 4.122 ($1 + 2 + 2 = 5$).

rio reach Rome, where Ilario soon will convert him, at 5.50. Through a happy coincidence, that chapter lets Florio, his wife, and their company find hospitality in the city as palace guests of Biancifiore's fraternal uncles. One brother is Mennilio; the second bears a name that Boccaccio more coyly drops, for in him, Quintilio, the long-dead pilgrim Quinto Lelio makes a kind of ghostly return.

Book and chapter numbers combine to produce a third variable, namely, the ordinal number of a chapter in the romance as a whole; that is, chapter numbers seem to be significant not just book by book but also by running count through the entire volume, as cumulative sums. For example, since book 1 has forty-five chapters, 2.1 becomes the forty-sixth in the *Filocolo*, 2.2 the forty-seventh, and so on. In books 1 and 2 the chapters are 45 + 76, respectively, for a total of 121. Then 3.1 becomes chapter number 122 and so on. In the *Filocolo*'s five books, there are 459 chapters all told: 45 + 76 + 76 + 165 + 97 = 459. I shall express these cumulative chapter sums formulaically with the qualifier F for *Filocolo*: 2.1 = 46F, 2.2 = 47F, 3.1 = 122F, and so forth.

On this level of the grid we can turn for orientation to the goddess of love and her energetic little boy. For example, Cupid, disguised as Felice, sparks Florio and Biancifiore to mutual desire at 2.2. But the six year olds do not profess their love and begin to kiss until 2.4, the forty-ninth chapter of the *Filocolo*. By that chapter's close, Venus has supplanted her chaste, sylvan rival: "già il venereo fuoco gli avea si accesi, che tardi la fredezza di Diana li avrebbe potuti rattiepidare" [the Venerean fire had already so kindled them that Diana's coldness would have been tardy in making them tepid] (2.4). Chapter 49F aptly registers love fires that have caught in Florio and Biancifiore. Summing the digits 4 + 9 gives 13, and 13 is a symbolic variant on the base number for Venus, always 3 in Boccaccio's numerology.

Venus is 3, quite simply, because as a planet she dwells in the third heaven. No doubt Dante's poetry reinforced the astrological connections Boccaccio knew among love, Venus, and the third planetary orbit in the cosmos. The earlier Tuscan's canzone to the moving intelligences of the third heaven in his *Convivio* and his apostrophe to Venus, on entering the third sphere with Beatrice in the *Comedy,* echo behind an exclamation by Dario, a gentleman of Alexandria who hosts Florio. When Dario hears how the king of Spain's son has crossed half the world in his quest for "the slave girl" Biancifiore, he cries out, "O più che altro potente pianeto, per la cui luce il terzo cielo si mostra bello, quanta è la tua forza negli umani cuori efficace!" [O planet more powerful than any other, through whose light the third heaven shows its beauty, how efficacious your force in human hearts!] (4.83).[30]

The star in ascendence at the couple's birth, Venus will begin her operations from Mount Cytherea as they enter their seventh year (2.1). At her instructions, Cupid drops his arrow-making chores, flies to Marmorina, and, disguised as Felice, embraces the couple with love puffs (2.2). Next, right on schedule with Boccaccio's arithmetic timetable, Venus makes her first personal descent to a character in the *Filocolo*. In the third chapter of book 2, she comes to her antagonist, King Felice, and conjures for the old man a dream prophetic of events to follow—from the children's birth to their baptism. Whereas Venus, who orbits the third heaven, herself intervenes in 2.3, she is present symbolically much later in the story, five months after shipwreck has grounded Florio at Naples. Disguised as Love's pilgrim Filocolo, he passes a pleasant afternoon in a garden with the king's daughter, Maria, and her entourage, during a love debate (fig. 10). Queen of the game is Princess Maria, known more familiarly as Fiammetta, the authority who rules on each case. Halfway through her love court, as a "little spirit" from the third heaven hovers around her head and haloes it with a "flamelet," she brings the discussion to its philosophical center, defining in good Aristotelian fashion the three kinds of love: utilitarian ("amore per utilità"), pleasurable ("amore per diletto"), and virtuous ("amore onesto").[31] All told, she settles thirteen queries, hypothetical problems posed by the thirteen members of her circle. As much as the "spiritlet" from the third heaven, this total of thirteen queries signals Venus in symbolic attendance at a debate on amorous matters whose central dialogue distinguishes love of three kinds.

When Cupid warms the hearts of Florio and Biancifiore at 2.4, on the surface of things there are no numeric signs of Venus. But once we switch to a kind of ultraviolet reading and bring out the cumulative chapter sum (49F), what comes to light is an allusion to love: 4 + 9 = 13. It is a planned

---

30. Cf. *Convivio* 2, canzone v. 1: "Voi che 'ntendono il terzo ciel movete"; *Par.* 8.2–3: "la bella Ciprigna . . . volta nel terzo epiciclo . . ." Connections between Venus and 3 are typical of Boccaccio's vernacular fiction. See Kirkham, *The Sign of Reason,* 277, for numerous other examples.

31. The triplicity derives from Aristotle, who defines three kinds of "friendship" (*Nich. Ethics* 1563). Thomas Aquinas explains in his *Commentary on the Nicomachean Ethics* (Chicago: Henry Regnery, 1964), 8.50.3: "He says that there are three kinds of lovable objects . . . namely, the good as such, the pleasurable, and the useful." Cf. Dante's *De vulg. eloq.* 2.2.8.

chapter location that repeats the number of thirteen questions in the love debate. Her proteges' enamorment opens a chain of miraculous appearances by Venus that stretch through the three central books of the romance. The last one occurs at 4.149, when she dissipates the smoke that had screened Florio and Biancifiore from death at the stake in Alexandria—the punishment assigned to them by the Admiral for their lovemaking in the Arab's Tower. Between these two widely separated moments—49F and 4.149—we meet Venus in action eleven other times.

(1) 2.1. Venus sends Cupid off on his love-cuddle mission, fully accomplished at 2.4.

(2) 2.3. Venus leads Felice to bed in his chamber and shows the slumbering king an "amazing vision." Animals mime future events in the story of a lion cub (Florio) and a doe (Biancifiore) who will turn into a young man and woman after they have jumped in a fountain (their baptism in the Lateran baptistery).[32]

(3) 2.42. In her first oneiric appearance, Venus warns Florio that Felice and his seneschal are plotting to murder Biancifiore and hands him a sword from her lover, Mars, to kill Massamutino.

(4) 2.48. Appearing for a second time in a dream, Venus brings nocturnal comfort to Biancifiore in her dungeon. "Your pleas," she informs her maidenly charge, "have reached our ears up here in our heaven." (Biancifiore's lament was so penetrating that it had carried as far as the third sphere.)

(5) 2.75. From her Montoro temple, Venus responds to Florio's prayer of thanks for sparing Biancifiore and places on his brow her crown of laurel.

(6) 3.18–19. Venus causes sleep to descend on Florio and reveals to him an "amazing vision." He sees Cupid royally crowned, holding his bow and a silver and a golden arrow, seated on two huge eagles, his feet resting on twin lions. As Florio nearly sinks on a ship in stormy waters, Biancifiore appears holding an olive branch to buoy him up with a message of her fidelity.

(7) 3.52–53. Venus receives a visit from Diana, who has decided to stop persecuting the couple. Henceforth Venus and Diana will

---

32. Animals also turn into men after they jump in a river in *Caccia di Diana*. There, too, the metamorphosis to human form signifies allegorically baptism. See Cassell and Kirkham, *Diana's Hunt*, introd., 33–38.

cooperate. Venus, now teamed with Diana, encourages Biancifiore in a dream, her third such appearance in the *Filocolo.*

(8) 4.89. Venus brings to Florio a fleeting vision of Biancifiore, whom she holds in her arms.

(9) 4.109. With "an invisible hand," Venus insures Florio's concealment in the basket of roses that hoists him up into the harem tower's window.

(10) 4.122. Venus rejoices at Florio and Biancifiore's secret wedding, together with Hymen and Diana.

(11) 4.126. Venus saves the lives of Florio and Biancifiore by receiving the Admiral's furious sword blow.

(12) 4.134. Venus shields both lovers from injury at the stake, hiding them inside a cloud of smoke.

(13) 4.149. Once the danger has passed, Venus dissipates the smoke. People are astonished to see the burning embers fall away from the couple, who come out "as fresh as a dewy rose picked at dawn."

From the pair's first shy kisses in their seventh year (49F)—engulfed in "Venerean fire" too strong for quenching by Diana—to their Alexandrian deliverance as man and wife from public "burning" (4.149), Venus determines Florio and Biancifiore's amorous destiny. This is as it should be, because the children's nativity was in Gemini, with her star at the height of its epicycle, ascendent near the sun in Taurus. As a result, love overpowered even the cold, hostile planet of Saturn and showered earth: "il saturnino cielo, non che gli altri, pioveva amore il giorno che elli nacquero" [The Saturnine heaven, not to mention the others, was raining love the day they were born] (2.9).[33]

Between 49F and 4.149, boundaries that signal her triadic identity (4 +

---

33. Boccaccio's authorities on astrology and planetary influence in the *Filocolo* are discussed in detail by Quaglio in *Scienza e mito nel Boccaccio;* for Venus, whom Boccaccio takes pains to privilege, see especially 101–6. Needless to say, my reconstruction of Boccaccio's numerology in his chaptering relies on the assumption that Quaglio's textual reconstruction in his edition of 1967, based on philological evidence, reflects the original authorial design, which doubtless served mnemonic as well as symbolic purposes. The *Teseida,* also divided into chapters in the poet's autograph copy, offers a close parallel to the *Filocolo* in its structural subdivisions. Were the rubrics restored to the *Filocolo,* a study of their content with regard to the symmetries and numerology of the text could confirm (or, as I think less likely, rule out) that Boccaccio himself composed them.

9 = 13), Venus has a total of thirteen epiphanies in the *Filocolo*. Three
times, starting at 2.3, she arranges for a character to have a vision (2.3,
3.18, 4.89). Three times she herself appears in dreams (2.42, 2.48, 3.53).
Boccaccio asserts her sway as a goddess from the beginning of book 2,
which transports us to Cyprus for a wonderful view of Venus stopping in
on Cupid, busy at Mount Cytherea replenishing his stock of arrows (fig.
3). It is a classic scene, openly reminiscent of another colloquy between the
two in Virgil's *Aeneid,* when Cupid made Dido fall in love by sitting in her
lap disguised as the boy Ascanius. Boccaccio, who quotes his source, will
indulge in a reversal, having his Cupid take on the "senile aspect" of King
Felice and breath love into a pair of children.[34] By the end of book 4, when
Florio and Biancifiore have been married for the second time, a formal
ceremony to ratify their secret tower nuptials, Venus has achieved her
aims. The poet laid her main plotline to coincide with the central three
books of his five-book composition, the core of his love story

   Book 5 brings back the Christian motifs dominant in book 1, as the
newly converted Florio and Biancifiore complete the pilgrimage to Santiago that her parents had undertaken from Rome so many years before.
But prior to their Lateran baptism (5.71), old gods still linger in several
episodes. Most remarkable is their sway over the narrator's double, Idalogos, a poet who has been turned into a pine tree, and over the four blas-
phemous ladies that troop along in his narrative train. His transformation
puts an amusing twist on what happened to Daphne, the nymph who preserved her chastity by freezing into a laurel. The very masculine Idalogos,
a "voice of the glade" who has taken some traits from Virgil's Polydorus
and Dante's Pier della Vigna,[35] burned so with passion that his alteration
was brought about by Venus, who made him become the seedy conifer
sacred to her.

---

34. Venus asks Cupid to take the rest of the day off to run an errand for her (*Filoc.* 2.1):
"E come già nella non compiuta Cartagine prendesti forma del giovane Ascanio, così ora ti
vesti del senile aspetto del vecchio re, padre di Florio" [And as you once took the form of
young Ascanius in unfinished Carthage, so now dress yourself in the senile appearance of the
old king, father of Florio].

35. On the meaning of Boccaccio's Greek name *Idalogos,* see Quaglio's commentary, n.
17, 916–17. Boccaccio cites Virgil but keeps silent on Dante (*Inf.* 13) in the comparison that
tells how Idalogos speaks: "non altrimenti che quando il pio Enea del non conosciuto Poli-
doro, sopra l'arenoso lito, levò un ramo" [no differently than when pious Aeneas, on the
sandy shore, lifted a branch from Polydorus] (*Filoc.* 5.6). Later in his *Esposizioni* in *Inf.* 13, he
would comment at length on the talking tree in Dante's forest of the suicides.

. . . Venere, di me pietosa, . . . I piedi, già stati presti, in radici, e 'l
corpo in pedale, e le braccia in rami, e i capelli in frondi di questo
albero trasmutò. . . . così come questo legno meglio arde ch'alcuno
altro, così io, prima stato ad amare duro, poi più che alcun amante
arsi, e per ogni piccolo sguardo sì mi raccendo come mai acceso fossi.

[Venus, taking pity on me, . . . transformed my feet, once quick, into
the roots, my body into the trunk, my arms into the branches, and
my hair into the greenery of this tree. . . . and as this wood burns better than any other, so I, first resistent to love, then burned more than
any other lover, and even the slightest glance rekindles me as if I had
never been kindled before.] (5.8.42–44)

Idalogos has heard that the hard-hearted woman who undid him was herself punished with imprisonment in a marble fountain, and he asks Florio
and Biancifiore to pay his stone lady a call. They oblige, an errand that
opens scenes of strange metamorphoses on anagrammatic girls. In
vengeance for hubris, Venus changes Alleiram (Mariella) to a cold piece of
aquatic statuary;[36] Phoebus strikes from Airam (Maria) a pomegranate;
the Moon makes a thornbush of Asenga (Agnese); Diana shrinks Annavoi
(Giovanna) to a fragile yellow flower (5.14–28).

So Venus is still present early in book 5, with magical powers that can
transmute two lovers into a flammable tree (5.8) and a petrous fountain
(5.24). Again, and for a third time in the fifth book, she hovers over events
as Florio and Biancifiore rectify a wrong for which they were unwittingly
to blame. This situation takes us into the subplot that revolves around
Fileno, Florio's rival in love. His hopes of winning Biancifiore dashed, he
had been melted into a fountain by a compassionate panoply of gods. On
the site of the oak grove where Fileno burbles in grief and Certaldo shortly
will rise, Florio offers a solemn prayer to the gentile gods most helpful to
him in his labors of love: Jupiter, Juno, Hymen, Venus, and Mars (5.34).
He and his party then witness the miracle of tearful Fileno's resurgence to
human form as Biancifiore's eternal admirer.

---

36. This "marble lady" obviously alludes to the topos on which Dante had capitalized for
his own rhymes to a "Petra." Robert M. Durling and Ronald Martinez have collaborated for
a brilliant and encyclopedic treatment of the tradition in *Time and the Crystal: Studies in
Dante's Rime Petrose* (Berkeley: University of California, 1990).

... i circunstanti videro le chiare acque coagularsi nel mezzo e dirizzarsi in altra forma abandonando il loro erboso letto, né seppero vedere come subitamente la testa, le braccia e 'l corpo, le gambe e l'altre parti d'uno uomo, di quelle si formassero, se non che, riguardando con maraviglia, co' capelli e con la barba e co' vestimenti bagnati tutti trassero Fileno del cavato luogo. . . . contento tacitamente si dispose al vecchio amore, credendo sanza quello niuna cosa valere.

[. . . those present saw the clear waters coagulate in the middle and rise straight up into another form, abandoning their grassy bed, and they could not possibly see how the head, the arms, the body, the legs, and the other parts of a man could be formed out of them, but, while staring with amazement, they drew Fileno from that hollowed space, his hair and beard and clothes soaking wet . . . content, he tacitly disposed himself to his old love, believing that without it he was worthless.] (5.37.5–7)[37]

Boccaccio must have smiled as he penned this amusing resurrection, which replays backward the Narcissus myth, a final Ovidian metamorphosis in the *Filocolo*. Pagan cultism, soon to be displaced by Christian devotion, has here its swan song. Florio's ultimate tribute to the "gods," foreshadowing their eclipse, and Fileno's return to human form—drenched and bedraggled, but ever and always a lover—end the role of Venus as a viable force in the romance.

How, then, has Boccaccio patterned her appearances? Thirteen times in the three books of the central love story (books 2, 3, and 4) Venus interacts with the protagonists. Afterward she figures in three peripheral episodes across thirty chapters between 5.8 and 5.37. The first and last of these chapter locations hint at her number. The first, 5.8, suggests the trinitarian sum 13 (5 + 8). The last, 5.37, corresponds to 399F, quite the right place for the goddess of the third heaven to enjoy her final moment of power and make a triadic exit.[38]

---

37. The cleanup operation that Filocolo and his friends perform on Fileno recalls Ameto as he emerges from his "bath" in *Comedia delle ninfe fiorentine* 44.

38. The Idalogos episode at 5.8, so heavily Venerean in its content and symbolism (the pine tree is sacred to Venus), reiterates the regular verse totals per canto in *Diana's Hunt* and in *Amorosa visione* (58 = 5 + 8 = 13); see Kirkham, *The Sign of Reason*, 109. Elsewhere Boccaccio associates 9 as the square of 3 with Venus. For example, in the long gloss on the dwelling of Venus (*Tes.* 7.50), he tells exactly nine myths about her to illustrate her powers and conquests.

                                  center
1.1————————————————————4.2————————————————5.37
                                  (199F)   (399F)
              Florio finds Fileno as a spring   Fileno recovers
                                                                   human form

Looking back from 399F, when Fileno recovers his manly form, we find
a parallel at 199F (4.2), the antecedent scene where Filocolo first stumbled
upon that talking spring. If we count from the beginning of the *Filocolo* to
399F (i.e., from 1.1 to 5.37), we find that 199F is exactly the halfway point.
In 199F Filocolo stoops to fill a goblet at the spring, which gurgles a
protest at this "molestation." (In much the same way, Idalogos later will
cry out with pain when Filocolo, hunting a stag, accidentally knocks a
piece of bark off his trunk with an arrow shot from his bow.) Then, in
200F (5.3), the waters recite their lachrymose history. Boccaccio's retrospective on Fileno at 5.3 implies a "centrality" in that character, whose
very name bonds him to Venus. Since Fileno seems to mean "Lover"
generically, fittingly he reveals his fate in the third chapter of the final
book. He had joined the *Filocolo* cast back in book 3, when Biancifiore
reluctantly gave him her veil to carry as a token in the joust of an upcom-
ing courtly feast of Mars (3.16 = 137F). But interest focuses on him most
intensely in the third decade of the third book, chapters 30–37. At 3.30
Diana brings him a dream to warn him of Florio's jealousy; by 3.33 he has
embarked on a bitter path of exile. At the end of 3.33 he wanders into that
oak grove of destiny, there to inveigh against love (3.34), to vituperate the
universal female sex (3.35). At 3.37 Fileno's plaint has risen to a pathetic
pitch; clutching his beloved Biancifiore's tear-drenched veil, in despair he
cries out for death. There Boccaccio abruptly abandons him, just as we
have come to the midpoint of book 3 (chapter 38 of its total of 76 chapters). Whisking us away to another strand of his story, the narrator will
not allow us a sequel until Filocolo ruffles the waters with his silver camp
goblet at 4.2 (199F).
        Lovesick Fileno attracts not only the number 3 (and its multiple 9) in
his intermittent scenes. Significant repetitions also attach to him 3 in
combination with 7. He comes into the *Filocolo* at 137F. Boccaccio
leaves him suspended in terminal misery at 3.37. Fileno regains his
humanity at 5.37, in a "demetamorphosis" both amusing and serious:
pagan Fileno rising up out of the waters "prefigures the general conversion and baptism of the company which occurs at the end of the

book."[39] Why was 3 (and 3 squared) not enough for Fileno? Why does Boccaccio make 7 part of the pattern, too? As we shall soon see, 7 is the number that attaches Fileno to Diana. For now, from Fileno's comings and goings in the story, we can deduce an aspect of Boccaccio's compositional strategy more basic than numerals. Both the abrupt break and shift at 3.37—the halfway point of book 3—and Fileno's autobiography as a spring at 199/200F—the halfway point in the *Filocolo* to his recovery at 5.37 (399F)—signal a poetics of centering.

Embracing architectures universal to literature and especially beloved by the Middle Ages,[40] Boccaccio from the start structured his narratives in symmetrical diptychs and balanced them around significant centers. The former technique divides the eighteen cantos of *Diana's Hunt*, his earliest fiction; it begins to repeat itself in the ninth canto with variations on motifs from the first part of the poem. Such interior replication, a simple division of the text into two parts with a second half cut to the same design as the first, appears most obviously in the master plan for the *Decameron*, where the ten days of storytelling occupy two weeks that each run from a Wednesday to a Tuesday. The *Decameron*, with a calendar that divides into a diptych, displays as well bilateral or concentric symmetry in the specular arrangement of content day by day around its median, Fiammetta's rule on the Fifth Day. Striking as an example of narration organized around a center before the *Decameron* is Boccaccio's verse epic, *Teseida delle nozze d'Emilia*, which actually has two hidden centers, textual homes for didactic high points where the Glossator allegorizes Mars and Venus.[41] In his prose epic, he was already practicing the same techniques. Centering of several kinds is clearest in the disposition of the thirteen *questioni d'amore* (*Filoc.* 4.14–70). But other chapter strings of greater length and for different plots also have their centers. So it falls out for the character Fileno.

---

39. David Wallace used the term *demetamorphosis* in *Chaucer and the Early Writings of Boccaccio*, 47. The perceptive observation concerning Fileno's recovery of human form as a prefiguration of the protagonist's baptism (and the more general baptism of all Spain) comes from Steven Grossvogel, *Ambiguity and Allusion in Boccaccio's Filocolo* (Florence: Olschki, 1992), 149.

40. R. G. Peterson, "Critical Calculations: Measure and Symmetry in Literature," *PMLA* 91 (1976): 367–75.

41. See Cassell and Kirkham, *Diana's Hunt*, introd., 23–27. See also Kirkham, "'Chiuso parlare' in Boccaccio's *Teseida*"; Hollander, "The Validity of Boccaccio's Self-Exegesis"; Janet Levarie Smarr, "Symmetry and Balance in the *Decameron*," *Medievalia* 2 (1976): 159–87. Smarr returns to the argument in *Boccaccio and Fiammetta*, 176–84.

As to Venus, by far the most powerful Olympian in the *Filocolo,* there can be no doubt that Boccaccio was thinking of her workings in terms of centers. Although her influence closes Fileno's story at 5.37, the last time she actually comes down to deal with a mortal is 5.24, when Alleiram meets her marbled *contrappasso.* Reckoning from 2.1, as Venus enters the epic for a little business with Cupid, to Alleiram's demise in *petra mortis* at 5.24, we obtain a total of 341 chapters. The halfway figure in this line is 171F, or 4.14. There Filocolo and his companions find and enter the garden where, at Fiammetta's courteous insistence, they stay on for an afternoon love debate. The questions, as we know, are thirteen, and it is in the decision she hands down on the central query (the seventh) that Fiammetta, aureoled by a "spiritello" from the third heaven, defines three kinds of love. It is significant that the *questioni d'amore,* poised on a philosophical fulcrum, form an interlude beginning at the center of the chapter sequence (2.1–5.24) containing all appearances of Venus in the romance.

Yet the Venus in book 5 remains eccentric to the Venus in books 2–4, where she makes thirteen major appearances on behalf of her protegés, Florio and Biancifiore. That line extends from 2.1 only as far as 4.149, when she clears the smoke from the Admiral's bonfire. The arc from 2.1 to 4.149 spans 301 chapters. An excellent Venerean sum, 301 repeats the figures (3 and 1) that designate the love debate (thirteen questions) and Venus herself in her thirteen benevolent operations for the young lovers. The midpoint of these 301 chapters is also significant. Halving 301 gives 151, and the 151st chapter after 2.1 is 3.75. The next-to-last chapter in book 3, it launches "Filocolo" on his quest incognito. His parents having admitted they sold Biancifiore to merchants headed for Alexandria, Florio now informs his friends that for purposes of their search party, he will assume an alias. The pseudonym he has elected, which puts to good use grammar from his school days, resonates naturally on a wavelength with Venus.

> . . . il nome il quale io ho a me eletto è questo: Filocolo. E certo tal nome assai meglio che alcuno altro mi si confa, e la ragione per che, io la vi dirò. Filocolo è da due greci nomi composto, da "philos" e da "colon"; e "philos" in greco tanto viene a dire in nostra lingua quanto "amore" e "colon" in greco similmente tanto in nostra lingua risulta quanto "fatica": onde congiunti insieme, si può dire, trasponendo le parti, *fatica d'amore.*

[. . . the name that I have chosen for myself is this, *Filocolo*. And surely such a name suits me better than any other, and I shall tell you the reason why. *Filocolo* is composed of two Greek names, from *philos* and from *colon;* and *philos* in Greek means in our language "love," and *colon* in Greek likewise in our language turns out to be "labor"; wherefore, joining these together, one can say, transposing the parts, "labor of love."] (3.75.4–5)[42]

Central to the median portion of the romance through which Venus maintains her ascendence (2.1–4.149), Filocolo's resolve triggers an upturn in the lovers' romantic history. So far Florio and Biancifiore have suffered progressively more assertive parental steps to separate them, but from now on, the tide of events will gradually bear them closer together. This center at 3.75 is particularly strong, since it is here that Boccaccio discloses the Greek etymology for the title of his learned rewrite of the popular old European tale, always before named after its two young lovers.

	center	
2.1———————	——3.75———	————4.149
First descent of	Florio > Filocolo	Thirteenth descent
Venus in *Filoc.*		of Venus in *Filoc.*

How long will Florio keep his *nom de voyage*? He remains Filocolo until his baptism, which occurs at 5.71. From 3.75 to 5.71, there are 237 chapters. That sequence also has a calculated center: $237 \div 2 = 119$; $3.75 + 119 = 4.118$. And where are we at that center? Or more to the purpose, where is Florio? He has bribed Sadoc, the castellan, to smuggle him into the Arab's Tower in a basket of roses, flowers picked for the "festa de' cavalieri," or "Knights' Holiday." Better yet, he has passed through the checkpoint of Biancifiore's nurse, Glorizia. He stands at the canopied bed in the maiden's chamber and begins to touch and kiss her, his hands eventually finding their way erotically down her body to "that place where all sweetness is enclosed." It is a sensual, nocturnal surprise, the classic male fan-

---

42. Sasso, in "*L'interpretatio nominis,*" characterizes *Filocolo* as "a talking name" [un nome parlante] because it alludes to the bearer's condition, and he notes that protagonists of romance had begun assuming such pseudonyms with Chrétien de Troyes. The French writer's example may have influenced Boccaccio, since the hero does not change his name in other, prior versions of the Floire and Blanchefleur legend.

tasy scene that Boccaccio will attach to his own "autobiography"—and exploit to comic effect often in the *Decameron.* Repetition through anaphora articulates the lover's refrain.

O bella donna, destati, acciò che tu conosca chi tu hai nelle tue brac- cia. Veramente tu n'hai ciò che tu in sogno alla santa dea [Venere] domandavi. Destati, o vita mia, acciò che tu più allegra ch'altra fem- ina col più lieto uomo del mondo ti ritruovi, e prendi la 'impromessa della santa dea. Destati, o sola speranza mia, acciò che tu vegga quello che agl'iddii è piaciuto: tu tieni nelle tue braccia quello che tu disideri, e nol sai.

[O fair lady, awake, so that you can know whom you have in your arms. Truly you have there what you asked for from the holy goddess [Venus] while dreaming. Awake, life of mine, so that you can find yourself more joyful than any other woman with the happiest man in the world, and take the promise of the holy goddess. Awake, o my only hope, so that you may see what has pleased the gods: you hold in your arms what you desire, and you do not know it.] (4.118.3–4)

Florio's travels as Filocolo culminate at their sequential halfway point in the romance. It is the blissful moment when at last, after long separation and searching—after countless "labors of love"—Filocolo can embrace his Biancifiore.

center

3.75————————————————————4.118————————————————————5.71
Florio > Filocolo   Filocolo reaches Biancifiore's bed   Filocolo > Florio

Among the pagan deities, Diana also makes her appearances according to a master plan. Although she plays a part more restricted than Venus, her operations cut deep into the plot at clearly assigned intervals. We first hear of her in passing, at the tail end of book 2. Biancifiore, it seems, acci- dentally forgot Diana on her round of thanks to all the gods' altars after Florio killed the seneschal (2.76). Not until 3.24 will Diana's harbored resentment explode, as she charges down to the Apennines to enlist help from the hag Jealousy. Diana's name, the opening word in the chapter, emphasizes her delayed arrival: "Diana, alla quale niuno sacrificio era

stato porto come agli altri iddii fu . . . discesa degli alti regni, cercò le case
della fredda Gelosia" [Diana, to whom no sacrifice had been borne as to
the other gods when Biancifiore had been saved from the grave danger,
had up to now kept in her holy breast her smoldering anger . . .] (3.24). As
the first step in her vindictive operation, Diana commands Jealousy to poison Florio with suspicions that Biancifiore has given not just her veil but
her heart to the knight Fileno. Fretting then that Florio might harm an
innocent victim, she descends a second time to Sleep, so that a dream can
alert Fileno to Florio's anger. Finally, as if this mischief were not enough
to thwart the lovers, she appears for the third time in her sylvan persona
and shatters the huntsman Felice with certain belief that Biancifiore will
yet be the ruination of Florio.

Boccaccio assists us by himself counting these descents. After the third,
we must continue numbering on our own. In toto, Diana puts down seven
times in the *Filocolo*.

(1) 3.24 = 121F. Diana enters as the chapter opens. Prodded by
    Diana, Jealousy commences to torment Florio with regard to
    Fileno.
(2) 3.28 = 125F. Diana asks herself what Fileno did to deserve an
    outrageous death at Florio's hands and concludes he did noth-
    ing. This said, "la seconda volta discese del cielo e cercò le case
    del Sonno riposatore" [the second time she descended from
    heaven and sought the home of restful Sleep] (3.28). She has
    Sleep warn Fileno by sending him a warning in the figments of a
    dream.
(3) 3.38 = 135F. Not content with the havoc she has so far wrought,
    Diana vents her spite in a frightening oracle to Felice, who sells
    Biancifiore as a slave to the merchant Antonio: "La santa dea,
    che due volte era discesa de' suoi regni per impedire il ferventis-
    simo amore tra Florio e Biancifiore . . . , propose del tutto di vol-
    ere la sua imaginazione compiere. E discesa del cielo la terza
    volta, sopra un'alta montagna in forma di cacciatrice si pose ad
    aspettare il re Felice" [The holy goddess, who had descended
    twice from her realms to obstruct the most fervent love between
    Florio and Biancifiore . . . determined wholly to achieve her
    wish. And having descended from heaven a third time, upon a
    high mountain in the form of a huntress she set herself to await
    King Felice] (3.38). Biancifiore anxiously protests to Felice that

she has vowed her chastity to Diana, the avenging goddess (3.46). Alone, she prays to Venus and Diana to let her save her virginity for Florio (3.51).

(4) 3.52. Diana leaves her seat in heaven and goes to pay a call on Venus in hers. Diana allows that her ire has passed; the two make a pact to cooperate henceforth.

(5) 3.53. Diana and Venus comfort Biancifiore, who is now woeful cargo on the high seas; each goddess speaks a reassurance to her as she sleeps.

(6) 4.122. Diana celebrates the couple's secret tower wedding with Hymen and Venus.

(7) 5.27. Diana punishes Alleiram's hard-hearted friend Annavoi (Giovanna) by turning her into a five-petaled flower.

Boccaccio's numerology, which assigns 3 to Venus, designates 7 as the number for Diana. The rationale in both cases comes from simple astrology. As the planetary hierarchy goes, Venus holds the third place if we count upward from earth. Counting down from Saturn, Diana circles in the seventh sphere as Luna. Both perspectives are equally valid, as Boccaccio's sky-conscious neighbors, Dante and Chaucer, could readily corroborate.[43]

7 Saturn 1
6 Jupiter 2
5 Mars 3
4 Sun 4
3 Venus 5
2 Mercury 6
1 Moon 7

For Diana's likeness to 7, Boccaccio had excellent authority, since the heptad had from antiquity been a symbol of both chastity and the moon. The Pythagorean school first honored 7 as "virgin," a prime number neither begotten nor begetting within the decad. The Neoplatonists Martianus Cappella and Macrobius transmitted that symbolism, along with numeric analogies between 7 and the lunar cycle. Already before the *Filocolo*, Boc-

---

43. Dante counted the spheres both ways in *Convivio* 2.13.20. See further Kirkham, "'Chiuso parlare' in Boccaccio's *Teseida*."

caccio had constructed *Diana's Hunt* in patterns of 3 and 7 allusive to Venus and Diana. From that earliest fiction onward in his oeuvre, at least through the *Decameron,* connections continue between these goddesses and their numbers.[44]

In the *Filocolo,* Diana enjoys a numerology less visible than the networks radiating from Venus, but nonetheless pervasive. Boccaccio's count of her earlier descents clearly invites us to keep counting after he stops, to see where the series goes. As it happens, she makes just four more appearances, bringing the total to seven. This seven-part sequence has its center in her fourth appearance, at 3.52. Arithmetic signals her number there (5 + 2 = 7), but there is much more at stake than a happy coincidence of digital sums. Here is the crucial scene when Diana makes her peace with Venus. It is the mythic turning point in the *Filocolo.* From this moment on, Diana and Venus can work as allies.

Diana's last appearance is in 5.27, seventy chapters before the end of the *Filocolo.* From her first descent at 3.24 to her final vindictive pass at 5.27, there are 244 chapters, a sequence whose central chapter is 4.70. At 4.70 the love debate ends. The center of Diana's activity in the *Filocolo* (halfway between 3.24 and 5.27, which is 4.70) complements a Venerean center, which is where the love debate begins (halfway between 2.1 and 5.24, which is 4.14).


```
                                    center
3.24————————————————————4.70————————————————————5.27
Diana's first descent       love debate ends        Diana's last descent
```


Perhaps now we can see why a character like Fileno, whom Diana protects in his suffering for love, should move through the romance marked by 3 and 7 together. He turns up for the tournament of Mars at 3.16, which is 137F. Later (3.37), Boccaccio leaves us dangling at the critical moment just before his metamorphosis, which will reverse itself as the Fileno plot-

---

44. On the logic of 7 as the virgin number, as well as its lunar associations, see Victoria Kirkham, "Numerology and Allegory in Boccaccio's *Caccia di Diana," Traditio* 34 (1978): 303–29; Kirkham, "'Chiuso parlare' in Boccaccio's *Teseida"*; Cassell and Kirkham, *Diana's Hunt,* 23–26. Although pagan myth seems quite absent from the *Decameron,* even there it resonates in the book's calendar. For example, Day 3 in the *Decameron* has a hidden Venerean agenda (see Kirkham, "Love's Labor's Rewarded and Paradise Lost (*Decameron* III,10)," in *The Sign of Reason,* 199–214 . Day 7 in the *Decameron* is set in a chaste female *locus amoenus,* the "Valley of the Ladies," where the women narrators bathe like nymphs of Diana.

line comes to resolution at 5.37. In all these episodes, Venus and Diana couple to keep silent numerical track of him—Venus because he is the lover, Diana to queer her rival's doings and sustain Fileno in celibacy.

Numbers conjoin Diana and Venus in larger patterns. The three central books of the *Filocolo* have 317 chapters.

book 2 = 76 chapters
book 3 = 76 chapters
book 4 = 165 chapters

books 2–4 = 317 chapters

As 13 is a variant on the triad of Venus, so 17 is a decimal variant of Diana's heptad. Venus and Diana preside over this central fictional space.

Their teamwork does not begin in earnest until Diana's conciliatory chat with Venus up in the latter's celestial parlor at 3.52 (fig. 8). Diana has left Luna, her own home, and pays her visit to the Venus of the third heaven. This planetary conjunction finds apt expression in the chapter number at which Chastity calls a truce with Love: $3.52 = 3 + (5 + 2) = 3 + 7$. Their pact, we saw, presents Diana in her central appearance of seven in the *Filocolo*. By a neat symmetry, Venus here puts in her seventh appearance, the center among her thirteen epiphanies in the three central books.

At 3.52 resonates a highly charged chiasmus. Before it Diana had made three descents, as Boccaccio tallies them, the third one at the center of book 3 (3.38). After those three descents, Diana goes to Venus in the third heaven, a *Filocolo* crossover that Venus embraces as she receives her visitor in her own seventh and central appearance. Later, in the *Teseida*, Boccaccio will set up another such epic conjunction; there it "marries" the gods Venus and Mars.[45] Here, however we look at 3.52, with a chapter sum at 173F, we see a textual address controlled by the Venus-Diana partnership.

In their new alliance, it is no surprise to find Boccaccio making them take turns at setting boundaries for the love debate. Venus has the upper hand, as thirteen noble folk sitting in a circle take turns, one by one, pos-

---

45. In the *Teseida,* Boccaccio gives the gods his usual numbers: 3 for Venus, 5 for Mars, 7 for Diana. Arcita's prayer wings to the House of Mars at 7.30, and Palemone's prayer to Venus reaches her dwelling on Cyprus at 7.50 (the reverse would have been predictable—Mars at 7.50 and Venus at 7.30). Later, to complete the sequence, Emilia prays to Diana at 7.70.

ing thirteen questions. But Diana, tutelar of chaste love, surfaces at the center in the seventh question. Caleon asks it, in his spot halfway around the circle, after he has improvised a madrigal to praise Fiammetta, his hoped-for lady, marvelously aflame as a "spiritlet" from the third heaven flits about her hair. Just at this moment, when Venerean fires begin to crackle, Diana exerts counterinfluences. We have come to the seventh question, located at 4.43 (4 + 3 = 7). The madrigal's placement precisely here, adding to the sense of "center," is quite deliberate, since its position duplicates numerically that of an earlier poem in the *Filocolo,* the epitaph in a single stanza of ottava rima carved on Giulia Topazia's tomb. Boccaccio recorded those verses, his very first literary octave and the only other poetry in the *Filocolo,*[46] at 1.43. The epitaph at 1.43 corroborates 4.43 as a correct symbolic niche for Caleon's madrigal. But when Fiammetta answers, she disappoints her suitor, for she is, after all, Maria, not Eve; not a conflagration, but a "flamelet." Thus had Caleon introduced to her Filocolo, the shipwrecked lover newly come to their garden in "Parthenope," a place whose name means "virgin."[47]

Il suo nome è da noi qui chiamato Fiammetta, posto che la più parte delle genti il nome di Colei la chiamino, per cui quella piaga, che il prevaricamento della prima madre aperse, richiuse.

[Among us she is known as Fiammetta, although most people call her by the name of the woman through whom that wound that the first mother's prevarication opened was closed.] (4.16.4)

Purity keeps her fire small; she is a flame in diminuitive because of her tempering chastity. There are three kinds of love, Fiammetta adjudicates, but only one is good and right. We must reject utilitarian love as self-serving materialism. As for pleasurable love, wisdom teaches us to flee that "because it is a depriver of honor, bearer of troubles, awakener of vices, copious giver of vain worries, unworthy conqueror of people's freedom, a thing to cherish above all else" (4.44). Only "honest love" is right, that which binds together the world in Boethian terms and assures continuation of the race through marital union.

As Diana goes to Venus at a juncture that is for both goddesses their

---

46. Ernest Hatch Wilkins, "Boccaccio's First Octave," *Italica* 33, no. 1 (1956): 19.

47. Boccaccio typically calls Naples "Parthenope" in his early fiction. See Cassell and Kirkham, *Diana's Hunt,* introd., 7; and see ibid., 155–56 for commentary on 1.12.

central *Filocolo* appearance (3.52), so the two goddesses again team at the center of the love debate. On its outer borders, too, they work in tandem, since the debate begins (4.14) midway through the Venerean plotline and ends midway through Diana's line of activity (4.70). By another reckoning, if we count the questions more narrowly, without preambles and just as replies and rebuttals, the debate begins at 4.19 and ends at 4.70, a total of fifty-two chapters. That sum repeats the digits in the chapter where Diana had her *pentimento* (3.52). The numbers 3 and 7 structure the *questioni d'amore* as numbers that underline the passage's ethical thrust: love for the sake of pleasure is fine in an aristocratic parlor game, but in the more serious domain of real life, we should practice virtue by pursuing the better kind of "honest" love that chastity tempers.

CHAPTER 4

Reckoning with Boccaccio's
Questioni d'amore

The best-known episode in Boccaccio's *Filocolo* is an extended digression containing thirteen *questioni d'amore*. Although this appears to be a confessional, lyrical interlude with no essential bearing on the tale of Florio and Biancifiore, it is actually a carefully structured narrative unit that duplicates the poetic plan of the romance as a whole.

The digression occurs in the fourth book of the *Filocolo* and thus belongs to the portion of the tale that relates the protagonist's "labors of love," that is, the long and adventurous journey undertaken by Florio, alias Filocolo, in search of his lady, Biancifiore. After setting out from Marmorina (Verona), Filocolo and his companions travel to Pisa and there embark for Sicily, but they are driven off course by a violent storm, which eventually delivers their battered ship to the port of old Parthenope. As a result of this seemingly adverse fortune, they are forced to spend an entire winter in Naples, and so it happens that one day the following spring, during a leisurely morning walk, they chance upon a beautiful garden where Fiammetta and a merry entourage have gathered. The travelers are invited to enter, and as midday is approaching, at the lady's suggestion, they retreat with a group of others to a shady corner of the garden to while away the warm afternoon. There, seated in a circle around a fountain, each in turn proposes a question concerning love, on which Fiammetta, who has been unanimously elected queen of the debate, passes judgment. At day's end, the guests depart and soon afterward resume their long-interrupted journey.

Critics have traditionally agreed that this episode is important, but what they could not understand was why Boccaccio had put it in the *Filocolo*. While Fiammetta's love debate made good sense as a chapter in the author's romantic autobiography and marked a significant poetic step in the direction of the *Decameron,* there just did not seem to be any way of relating it to the story of Florio and Biancifiore. A shipwreck was the fictional pretext for Filocolo's Neapolitan sojourn. But does that explain how the protagonist, a contemporary of Emperor Justinian, should suddenly come to spend a day with a lady named Maria and nicknamed Fiammetta, who duplicates the Author's fictional patron?[1] The *questioni d'amore* constitute a digression substantial by any standards—nearly thirty thousand words—and Boccaccio emphasizes their discontinuity from the immediate fictional setting by isolating them within a self-containing frame pattern. As far as most scholars in the nineteenth and early twentieth century were concerned, the obvious conclusion was that the *questioni* simply did not "belong" in the *Filocolo.*

There was a good deal of other material in the *Filocolo* that did not seem to "belong" there either. Boccaccio had, for instance, added several allegedly superfluous new characters to his version of the story. These included Fileno, Florio's disillusioned rival in love, who was transformed into a spring so that he could weep eternally; the tragic Idalogos, a poet turned pine tree who had also loved and lost; and Caleon, the lover who finally managed to sublimate the frustrations of yet another unrequited passion by helping to found the town of Certaldo. Each of them could be blamed for at least one more bizarre, distracting digression. Then, too, there was the entire fifth book of the *Filocolo,* where Boccaccio had expanded the tale by nearly fifty thousand words beyond its traditional conclusion[2] in order to introduce the learned Greek priest Ilario and relate

---

1. Janet Smarr, in *Boccaccio and Fiammetta,* especially 49–53, resolves the chronological inconsistency by distinguishing two Fiammetta's in the *Filocolo.* One is the lady whose eyes send a fiery arrow into the fourteenth-century Author's heart during mass in San Lorenzo at Naples on Holy Saturday. The other, queen of a love debate in Parthenope, later betrays Boccaccio's interior double Caleon, whom Filocolo will cure by giving him charge of Certaldo. The women, both daughters of the local king and both named after the lady who redeemed the world from Eve's sin, exemplify what she calls "the doubleness of the text," seen most obviously in the two loves it describes, pagan and Christian.

2. Cf. Crescini, *Il cantare di Fiorio e Biancifiore,* where the events subsequent to the protagonists' marriage are summed up in one final stanza: "E Fiorio ritornò di qua da mare, / ed arivò nella dolcie Toscana, / e andò in Ispangnia e fecie bategiare / lo re Felicie e la madre pagana, / e tutta la lor gente fe' tornare / a la fede catolica e cristiana; / poi di Roma fu eletto inperadore / più di ciento anni isté con Biancifiore" [And Fiorio came back to this side of the sea, and he arrived in sweet Tuscany, and he went to Spain and he had King Felice and his pagan mother baptized, and he brought all their people back to the Catholic and Christian faith; then he was elected emperor of Rome; for more than a hundred years he lived with Biancifiore].

the circumstances surrounding Florio's conversion to Christianity. But all of this extraneous material had to be accounted for somehow, because the fact remained that it had been invented by Boccaccio, who had written the *Decameron,* which everyone accepts as a masterpiece. The answer was simple: the *Decameron* was the product of a mature writer, whereas the *Filocolo* was a product of youth and inexperience. Boccaccio had decided to write this romance to rescue the tale of Florio and Biancifiore from the "fanciful parlance of the ignorant," but in an excess of pedantic enthusiasm, he had bungled the job. Expressed and best intentions to the contrary, he had taken a perfectly good love story and ruined it.

Nevertheless, to dismiss the entire *Filocolo,* except perhaps for the *questioni d'amore,* as the clumsy creation of a misguided young author is to ignore two important facts. First, we know from the record of manuscripts, printed editions, and editorial commentaries dating from the Renaissance, that although never a best-seller, the *Filocolo* did enjoy a respectable measure of popularity and was judged to be an edifying, entertaining tale during the fifteenth and sixteenth centuries. In the visual arts, too, the tale of Florio and Biancifiore could serve as an example for real-life brides and grooms, as attested by a panel from a marriage chest, or *cassone,* at the Elvehjem Museum of Art in Madison, Wisconsin. Painted around 1425 in Florence by Giovanni di Francesco Toscani, it illustrates the first question in the love debate, posed by Filocolo (*Filoc.* 4.19–22): a lady is asked to indicate by some sign which of two men she loves; she designates her preference by removing her garland and placing it on his head (fig. 10).[3] Second, if Boccaccio had any doubts concerning his book's liter-

---

3. For a description of the manuscripts, fifty-two in all including several partial texts, see Branca, *Tradizione delle opere,* vols. 1 and 2. The editions, listed by Francesco Zambrini in *Le opere volgari a stampa,* total thirty-four for the period between 1472 and 1594; during the next three hundred years the *Filocolo* was only reprinted three times. Our own century has seen three editions, those of Ettore De Ferri (Turin: UTET, 1927), Salvatore Battaglia (Bari: Laterza, 1938), and Antonio Enzo Quaglio (Milan: Mondadori, 1967). In the 1503 edition, Girolamo Squarciafico praises the *"Philocolo"* because it shows how Boccaccio finally came to love one woman; Squarciafico argues that since it is morally superior to love one woman than to love many, the tale offers a valuable lesson. He goes on to say that whereas the story of Florio and Biancifiore was still circulating "in un librazolo de triste & mal composte rime che meglio starebbe a li scombri & a l'uso de le latrine che d'esser lecto," Boccaccio had turned it into a "degno & elegante libro"; that is, according to Squarciafico, Boccaccio had rendered "worthy and elegant" his source, "a rag of a book in low and malcomposed rhymes that would better suit outhouses and latrines than being read." One particularly enthusiastic description came from Gaetano Tizzone da Pofi in his 1527 *Philopono,* for which see Ernest Hatch Wilkins, "Variations on the Name *Philocolo,*" in *The Invention of the Sonnet and Other Studies* (Rome: Edizioni di Storia e Letteratura, 1959), 139–45. The literary source for the

ary merits, there is no evidence to prove so. On the contrary, three passages in the text of the romance make it clear that he himself had at the time a high opinion of the work.

The first such passage is the Author's introduction, where we are given to understand that his immediate purpose in writing the Filocolo was to take a popular old love story and develop poetically its potential, something that no true artist had ever done before. To avoid self-praise, Boccaccio speaks obliquely, through his Flame Lady, who argues the need in his prologue chapter.

Certo grande ingiuria riceve la memoria degli amorosi giovani, pensando alla grande costanza de' loro animi, i quali in uno volere per l'amorosa forza sempre furono fermi servandosi debita fede, a non essere con debita ricordanza la loro fama essaltata da' versi d'alcun poeta, ma lasciata solamente ne' fabulosi parlari degli ignoranti.

[Certainly it does injury to the memory of the amorous young people, considering their great constancy of spirit, they who by love's power were always firm in keeping due faith with each other, not to have their fame exalted with due remembrance by the verses of any poet but to be left only in the fanciful parlance of the ignorant.] (*Filoc.* 1.1.25).

A further piece of evidence comes at the beginning of the fourth book, just halfway through the romance, when Jove's oracle addresses Filocolo in the oak grove and prophesies what John of Certaldo will write to "manifest your fortunes to the ignorant." With its reference to the "ignorant," this passage expressly recalls the Author's purpose as announced by the princess Maria; now Boccaccio anticipates the recognition to which his "memorable verses" will entitle him. Finally, at the end of the *Filocolo,* in his farewell to the book, the Author modestly states that this humble little book is unworthy of comparison to the works of Virgil, Lucan, Statius, Ovid, and Dante, thereby employing a conventional disclaimer to suggest that these are the writers to whom he was most indebted and, more impor-

---

cassone panel was identified in Paul F. Watson, "In a Court of Love: Giovanni Toscani and Giovanni Boccaccio at the Elvehjm," *Elvehjem Museum of Art. University of Wisconsin-Madison, Bulletin/Annual Report,* 1985–86, 4–16. See now also Branca, *Boccaccio visualizzato,* 2:199. Boccaccio's love debate belonged to a popular European genre tracked by Margaret Felberg-Levitt, *Les Demandes d'amour* (Montreal: Ceres, 1995).

tantly, the ones among whom he eventually hopes to be ranked as a great poet.

When great poets digress—and Boccaccio was certainly aspiring to greatness when he wrote the *Filocolo*—they do so for legitimate poetic reasons. Why, then, did Boccaccio introduce so many new and digressional episodes in his adaptation of a relatively simple popular romance? Specifically, what reasons could he have had for guiding the reader through a fictional excursion into a sixth-century garden of Parthenope, from Filocolo's quest to Fiammetta's *questioni*?

The detour can, of course, be justified on general grounds as an abstract, theoretical inquiry into the subject of love, which on a concrete level animates the plot of the tale. This was Salvatore Battaglia's line of reasoning,[4] and it makes sense, because if the *Filocolo* is a love story, it is also a book of stories about love. To begin with, it tells of the love between Florio and Biancifiore, a bond that was created by Cupid and then nurtured by Venus, whose constant tutelary guidance eventually enabled the lovers to marry. Within this broad fictional outline (the love story with a happy ending) is a series of secondary tales, revolving around the characters Fileno, Caleon, and Idalogos, each one providing a contrapuntal variation (love stories with unhappy endings) on the major theme. Finally, the entire romance is itself framed by still another love story (ending not yet known), that of the Author for Maria-Fiammetta, the lady who supposedly invited Boccaccio to compose the *Filocolo* in the first place and to whom the work is dedicated.

While Battaglia's analysis can account for the relevance of the *questioni d'amore* in a work that deals with love generically, however, it fails to explain why Boccaccio should have thought that this digression would so enhance the *Filocolo* in particular. After all, we can hardly say that the *Filocolo* is unique among Boccaccio's Italian works, at least as far as themes and subject are concerned. Can the immediate appropriateness of this narrative interlude be argued more persuasively?

Excluding the queen, nine men and four women participate in the debate. They are distributed in a systematic alternating arrangement around the fountain that stands at the center of their circle: the order is Filocolo, Longanio, Cara, Menedon, Clonico, Unnamed Lady, Caleon, Pola, Ferramonte, Ascalion, Giovanna, Parmenione, and Messaalino.

---

4. Salvatore Battaglia, "Schemi lirici nell'arte del Boccaccio," in *La coscienza letteraria del Medioevo* (Naples: Liguori, 1965), 625–44 (first published in *Archivium Romanicum* 19, no. 1 [1935]: 61–78).

Reducing the names of men and women to numbers we get: 2–1–2–1–1–1–2–1–2, in other words, a perfectly balanced numerical sequence pointing to the presence of a center-oriented pattern. The complete circle and order of questioning would appear in the chart.

Fiammetta

1. Filocolo	Messaalino 13.
2. Longanio	Parmenione 12.
3. Cara	Giovanna 11.
4. Menedon	Ascalion 10.
5. Clonico	Ferramonte 9.
6. Lady	Pola 8.
7. Caleon	

Interestingly enough, the circle, too, was envisioned as a symmetrical structure with men opposite men and women opposite women. But there is one pair of notable exceptions, Fiammetta and Caleon. This is certainly no coincidence, for the exchange between Caleon and Fiammetta deviates from the established order in more ways than one. When it comes his turn to ask a question, Caleon remains silent, gazing on the queen in rapt admiration. At length, after some prompting on her part, he replies that he had been temporarily struck dumb by a miraculous vision of her beauty, and then he recites a madrigal in the manner of the *stilnovisti* to describe the irresistible flame of love she inspires in the hearts of all who behold her. Finally, he asks his question: "Graziosa reina, io desidero di sapere se a ciascuno uomo, a bene essere di se medesimo, si dee innamorare o no" [Gracious queen, I desire to know if every man, for his own good, should fall in love or not] (4.43). Pronouncing a harsh judgment for the hopeful lover, Fiammetta reluctantly replies in the negative. There are, she explains, three kinds of love: honest love, love for the sake of pleasure, and love for the sake of utility. Caleon's question, along with those of the others in the group, concerns the second kind, love for the sake of pleasure, but it, like the third, must be eschewed in favor of the first. No one who wishes to lead a virtuous life should submit to love for the sake of pleasure, according to Fiammetta, because "egli è d'onore privatore, adducitore d'affanni, destatore di vizii, copioso donatore di vane sollecitudini, indegno occupatore dell'altrui libertà, più ch'altra cosa da tenere cara" [it is a depriver of honor, bearer of troubles, awakener of vices, copious giver of vain worries, unworthy conqueror of people's freedom, a thing to cherish above all else] (4.44).

This ruling comes as something of surprise in a debate that otherwise derives its whole raison d'être from the supposition that love for the sake of pleasure is, in fact, a perfectly legitimate pursuit. The assumption actually becomes explicit in the question proposed by Pola, who follows Caleon in the circle. She prefaces it by saying to Fiammetta:

> O nobile reina, voi avete al presente determinato che alcuna persona questo nostro amore seguire non dee, e io 'l consento; ma impossibile mi pare che la giovane età degli uomini e delle donne, sanza questo amore sentire, trapassare possa. Però al presente lasciando con vostro piacere la vostra sentenza, terrò che licito sia l'innamorarsi, prendendo il mal fare per debito adoperare. E questo seguendo voglio da voi sapere . . .

> [O noble queen, you have for the moment determined that no one should embrace this love of ours, and I grant it. But it seems impossible to me that the youthful age of men and women can pass without feeling this love. Therefore, putting aside by your leave for the moment your sentence, I shall hold that to fall in love is licit, taking wrongdoing for right behavior. And pursuing this I want to know from you . . .] (4.47)

We could say that the exchange between Caleon and Fiammetta is unique because it is a personal one. Since he is obviously in love with her, he wants to know if he should pursue his love, and she says that he should not. But on another level, Fiammetta is rejecting more than Caleon; she is really condemning all those who worship Cupid and along with them the entire concept of "courtly love," which is ultimately what she means by "love for the sake of pleasure." Caleon's question left her with no choice, for while it is possible to argue ad infinitum, for example, the relative merits of an affair with a virgin, a married woman, or a widow,[5] when the issue centers on the preferability of adulterous passion to lawful matrimony, there can only be one acceptable alternative. If, to use the terminology of C. S. Lewis, courtly love was a kind of game (a characterization that seems particularly appropriate to the *questioni d'amore* since Cara-Giovanna lit-

---

5. This is the problem debated in the ninth question.

erally invokes "the power of our game" in requesting the queen's opinion on her question), then Fiammetta's seemingly abrupt departure from the rules of play must be understood as the requisite retraction. It so happens that this retraction falls exactly at the center of the debate. Six questions precede Caleon's and six follow it. Moreover, since Christian morality is nowhere an issue except in the seventh judgment, the line of questioning appears to be based on a numerical sequence with numerological significance. If the number 6 is taken as symbolic of humanity's earthly existence, the number 7 comes to represent Christian salvation.[6] Subdividing the total of 13 according to another scheme, $6 + 1 + 6 = 13$, we arrive at the same dual pattern of the worldly as contrasted with the divine, for just as God is unity and hence perfection, so Caleon asks the "one" question on which Fiammetta cannot pass judgment within a purely worldly— hence incomplete—frame of reference.

The *questioni d'amore* thus appear to be structured around a double perspective involving, on the one hand, the relative, or peripheral, supremacy of Cupid and, on the other, the absolute and central supremacy of God.[7] If they are poetically relevant to the *Filocolo,* then the presence of this twofold pattern may provide a clue that would allow us to reintegrate the well-known text of the digression into its less popular but proper context. Since it was traditionally believed that Boccaccio's love debate could be read as an autonomous unit, the episodes immediately preceding and following it have been virtually ignored. However, within the double perspective of courtly and Christian love, they are not only relevant but integral to the digression, since they function, in fact, as its frame passages.

On the morning of the day that he is to meet Fiammetta, Filocolo

---

6. The most obvious model for this pattern would have been the six days of Creation followed by the Sabbath, God's day. Thus Dante dedicated the sixth canto of each canticle in the *Comedy* to political or "worldly" issues and used the number 7 as a symbol of conversion at the center of the poem. See Charles S. Singleton, "The Poet's Number at the Center," *MLN* 80 (1965): 1–10. Patristic commentators derived two symbolic formulas from the week in Genesis, one culminating in 7 (6 + 1), the other in 8 (7 + 1). See above, chap. 3, n. 28; below, chap. 5.

7. This dualism, an aspect of the "doubleness" Smarr has described in the *Filocolo, (Boccaccio and Fiammetta,* 35–36) finds a counterpart in Hollander's Robertsonian meditations on Boccaccio's Venus, a goddess both of lust and chastity; see Hollander, *Boccaccio's Two Venuses,* especially 31–40 for the *Filocolo.* Surdich, in *La cornice di amore,* 23–55, reproduces my circular diagram of the debaters and also discusses this central question, in which he sees Boccaccio's assertion of a new bourgeois ethics of marriage at the Angevin court. In this sense, as Surdich asserts (*La cornice di Amore,* 55), the love debate dovetails with the protagonist Florio's "progressive ascent to superior forms of humanity, morality, civil and social fulfillment."

awakes from a terrible nightmare. He dreamed he saw a merlin fly south-ward from the "cerreto" where he and his companions had found the mis-erable fountain Fileno and where Boccaccio's future greatness had been prophesied. Near Ovid's birthplace, the merlin espied a beautiful pheas-ant, whom he eventually managed to capture in a Neapolitan garden. Sud-denly, a host of other birds began attacking the pheasant and the merlin; then a fierce mastiff appeared and devoured the pheasant. The hapless merlin, who had meanwhile been transformed into a turtledove, was finally abandoned to the ravages of an apocalyptic storm.

Several days after the love debate, Filocolo, who had found his way into yet another Neapolitan garden, has another vision: he sees himself on a boat in a tranquil sea with seven beautiful ladies, but only four of them are immediately discernible. In a burst of light, there appears another lovely woman, who washes him with precious water, thus enabling him to behold the remaining three ladies, dressed respectively in red, green, and white. Suddenly, these three ladies sweep him upward, into the skies, where it seems that the mysteries of the heavenly bodies are revealed to him, and he sees the glory emanating from the face of Jove.

Filocolo's dream is an allegorical account of Boccaccio's ill-fated affair with Maria: a merlin from Certaldo seizes a pheasant from Aquino, but his claim is threatened by a host of pretenders (the other birds), and he is finally displaced by an overpowering rival (the mastiff). In its immediate context, however, this allegorical excursus serves as a prelude to Fiammetta's actual appearance and the approaching debate. To begin with, although the ornithological symbolism of the dream certainly points to a much later episode in the *Filocolo*,[8] the juxtaposition of a gathering of birds and thirteen *questioni d'amore* is suggestive because there did exist literary precedent for linking birds with disputes and judgments concern-ing love, in several French poems dating from the twelfth and thirteenth centuries.[9] Furthermore, Filocolo had dreamed that the merlin caught the pheasant in "un bellissimo prato . . . rivestito d'erbe e di fiori dilettevoli

---

8. In *Filoc.* 5.8.29–40, Idalogos uses birds as symbols to tell the same sad love story. Boc-caccio had a particular fondness for masking men as animals, a strategy he adopted begin-ning in his first work, *Diana's Hunt*. For discussion of the device there and elsewhere in his writings, see Cassell and Kirkham, *Diana's Hunt,* introd., 33–38.

9. For instance, Florence and Blanchefleur, who could not agree whether it was better to love a knight or a cleric, took their question to the god of love for a ruling. He convened his court, consisting entirely of birds, and the dispute was finally settled by a duel between the nightingale and the thrush. See Charles Oulmont, *Les Débats du Clerc et du Chevalier dans la littérature du Moyen Age* (Paris: Honoré Champion, 1911).

assai a riguardare" [a most beautiful meadow . . . clothed with grasses and with flowers very delightful to see] (4.13); similarly, the love debate, in which Caleon functions as the merlin's double, takes place in a "prato, bellissimo molto d'erbe e di fiori, e pieno di dolce soavità d'odori" [meadow . . . most beautiful with grasses and with flowers and filled with a soft sweetness of scents] (4.17). In the dream the pheasant's identity rests on a geographical allusion to the birthplace of "our poet Naso," the authority par excellence on love; this pheasant then resurfaces as Fiammetta, another indisputable expert on questions of love, so far as she is a lady to whom "the hidden ways of love are all open" (4.18).

The allegory of Filocolo's vision is, by contrast, entirely Christian. There can be no doubt that the seven ladies, divided into two groups (4 + 3), represent the cardinal and theological virtues, respectively. Since Filocolo is a pagan, he cannot "see" Charity, Hope, and Faith until he has been baptized by Grace personified, whose divine intervention then enables him to discover God and the Christian order of the universe. This miraculous, comforting vision prefigures Filocolo's actual conversion to Christianity, which does not occur until the fifth book of the romance, some sixty-five thousand words later. However, the vision falls within the immediate spatial orbit surrounding the *questioni d'amore,* structurally and thematically complementing the nightmarish fantasy that precedes the mock love court. Moreover, Filocolo's prophetic conversion, accomplished in the presence of the seven virtues, adds another dimension to the seventh question and judgment in the debate. The number 7 comes to be a symbol of totality,[10] for just as Filocolo's understanding was incomplete until he could see the second group of three ladies as clearly as the first group of four, so Fiammetta can say that Caleon is blind in his mind's eye if he believes that love for the sake of pleasure is admissible within the universal, all-embracing context of Christian morality.

It can hardly be a coincidence that the dream leading into the digression is pagan and courtly while the vision that follows is Christian and moralistic, because the same double perspective is also present in the love debate. If the dream and the vision are understood as frame passages marking the outer limits of the digression, the allegory of conversion would read as a palinode, the traditional return to sobriety after a playful discussion of pagan love. Taking the dream-debate-vision sequence as a

---

10. Hopper discusses 7 as the number of universality, in *Medieval Number Symbolism,* 79, 95, and passim.

single narrative unit, we can say that the theme of retraction emerges at two structurally significant points, the center and the end.

In a brief note appended to the 1938 edition of the *Filocolo,* Salvatore Battaglia wrote, "If you want to consider the *Filocolo* in its structure as a romance, you do not see the unity: it is dispersive, too episodic, discordant in tones and proportions."[11] Battaglia continued, however, by conceding that Boccaccio's source tale had also been characterized by an episodic structure and that the *Filocolo* was dictated primarily by considerations of human, lyrical unity, not narrative unity.

Nevertheless, we know that Boccaccio was very much concerned with problems of structure and narrative unity, and the *questioni d'amore* and their corresponding framing episodes provide clear evidence of his interest in these problems at a relatively early date. The entire digressional unit is built around a series of concentric spatial centers (the fountain at the center of a circle of young people sitting in a meadow inside a garden in Naples); it has a sequential center (6 + 1 + 6) and a poetic center (embodied fictionally by Caleon and Fiammetta, marked by the embedded madrigal) and a thematic center (pagan vs. Christian love), which is in turn duplicated by the dream and the vision of the outer frame passages.

Given the carefully structured pattern of this original narrative sequence, would it not be reasonable to suppose that the other major innovative passages in the *Filocolo* were added to the rough material of the source tale in accordance with a similar narrative scheme? Since Boccaccio was working with a rambling, episodic popular romance, would he not have attempted to invest his new and improved version of the story with greater structural balance and thematic unity? The first and most obvious evidence for a desire to achieve structural balance can be observed in the fivefold division of the *Filocolo.* Book 1, which may be regarded as the prologue, describes the tragic pilgrimage of Biancifiore's parents to Saint James and ends with the birth of Florio and Biancifiore. Books 2, 3, and 4 tell how the children grew up together, fell in love, were then treacherously driven apart, and were finally safely reunited. Book 5, an epilogue, relates the pious deeds of the couple after their marriage.

This final book is the longest of all, and although anticlimactic for the modern reader, it deserves special attention because it is entirely new and literally represents Boccaccio's "finishing touches" to the story. After their

---

11. Battaglia, *Giovanni Boccaccio e la riforma della narrativa,* 155–67: "A voler considerare il *Filocolo* nella sua struttura romanzesca, non se ne vede l'unità: è dispersivo, troppo episodico, discordante di toni e di proporzioni."

marriage, Florio and Biancifiore decide to visit Biancifiore's relatives in Rome. While in that city, Florio meets the venerable priest Ilario, whose learned discourses on biblical history and Christian catechism persuade the pagan prince to embrace the Catholic faith. He is then baptized in San Giovanni in Laterano by none other than the pope himself. Eventually, moved by a sense of filial obligation, Florio takes his wife and the infant son she has meanwhile borne him back to Marmorina, where his parents live as the king and queen of Spain. A happy reconciliation follows, and Florio converts all the inhabitants of Marmorina to Christianity. Florio and Biancifiore then undertake a pilgrimage to Saint James, during the course of which they participate in a miracle. Next they return to Rome, where the mortal remains of Biancifiore's parents are at last given honorable Christian burial. Finally, word of Felice's impending death summons the young couple to Cordova, and after the dying king has preached a sermon on the seven vices and virtues, their peregrinations come to an end with the celebration of Florio's coronation.

It should be obvious from this brief summary that the fifth book of the *Filocolo* is no mere otiose appendage to the body of the love story. Not only does it bring us full circle with the pilgrimage motif, but it also carries us into a qualitatively different fictional arena, replacing pagan Marmorina with Christian Rome, the adoration of Cupid with the worship of God, and the labors of love with the duties of marital life. Book 5 represents, in short, the fulfillment of that vision that had come to Filocolo shortly after his departure from Fiammetta. It is the final palinode.

That the *Filocolo* is divided into five books (1 + 3 + 1) and is itself framed by the love story of Boccaccio-Author and Maria-Fiammetta would tend to suggest the presence of a center within the three central books. Turning to the middle of the third book, we find, not unsurprisingly, another episode of Boccaccio's own invention. Like the *questioni d'amore*, it is a digression. It revolves around Fileno, the young man who had aspired to Biancifiore's hand only to be rewarded by humiliation and exile. After wandering throughout Italy, he reaches an ancient oak grove near the confluence of the Elsa and the Agliena. There he determines to spend the rest of his days nurturing his terrible grief, which explodes forthwith in an extended tirade against love and women. Addressing Cupid, he fulminates: "tu, giovanissimo fanciullo, con piacevole dolcezza pigli gli stolti animi degli ignoranti. . . . Ahi, quanto è cieca la mente di coloro che ti credono e che del loro folle disio ti fanno e chiamano iddio, con ciò sia cosa che niuna tua operazione si vegga con discrezione fatta!" [you, most childish boy, snatch the foolish souls of the ignorant with pleasurable sweetness. . . . Ah, how blind the minds of those who believe you and who make and call you god of their mad desire, seeing as how you never operate with discretion!] (3.34). This condemnation of love is a poetic replication of the ruling that will later be prompted by Caleon's question. Fileno's vocabulary of rejection naturally differs somewhat from Fiammetta's because he is not a Christian, but in each case the theme of retraction is clearly present. Love is an evil, and Cupid is a false idol.

A pattern now begins to emerge. Just as the worship of Cupid is condemned at the center of the *questioni d'amore,* so it is rejected at the center of the *Filocolo.* Similarly, conversion to the worship of God as a positive alternative for what has thus been negated follows allegorically at the end of the love debate and then "in reality" at the end of the romance. In other words, the thematic and structural organization of the *questioni d'amore* suggests the presence of an analogous arrangement governing the composition of the *Filocolo* as a whole—retraction at the center and again at the end.

But there is more. The original major digressions in the *Filocolo* all achieve their resolution through a variation on the theme of recantation and conversion. Fileno condemns love and women and then, when he has been restored to his human form, eventually embraces the true faith: "I vani iddii e fallaci periscano, e l'onnipotente, vero e infallibile Creatore di tutte le cose, sia amato, onorato, adorato e creduto da noi" [Perish the vain and fallacious gods, and let us love, honor, adore, and believe in the omnipotent, true, and infallible Creator of all things] (5.60). Idalogos concludes his sad story by saying, "Potete adunque per le mie parole e per me comprendere quanta poca fede le mondane cose servino agli speranti, e massimamente le femine, nelle quali niuno bene, niuna fermezza, né niuna ragione si truova" [You can thus comprehend from my words and from me how little trustworthiness worldly things reserve for those who put their hope in them, least of all women, in whom is found no well being, no constancy, and no reason] (5.8). Caleon is cured of his love for Fiammetta by Filocolo, who entrusts him with the edification and governorship of Certaldo: "così come già ti fu caro l'essere suggetto ad amore, così ora carissimo partirti del tutto da lui ti saria: alla qual cosa fare, ottimo oficio t'ho trovato, quando e' ti piaccia" [thus as once it was dear to you to be love's subject, now it should be most dear to you wholly to depart from him, and toward that end I have found you an excellent task, if it please you] (5.47). The romantic vicissitudes of these secondary characters correspond poetically to the ideal trajectory within which Boccaccio, as "nuovo autore" (1.2), chose to recast the adventures of Florio and Biancifiore. The labors of love inevitably lead to the remedies of love. Whether these remedies take the form of marriage (which spells death for love in the courtly sense), conversion (Ovidian metamorphosis as well as Christian baptism), or simply moral healing, in each case we can observe the familiar pattern of retraction.

If we read the *Filocolo* as a substantially new version of the source tale, altered and expanded to accommodate the added dimension of Christian ethics, it does indeed display a design of narrative unity. By our standards the design may seem a failure because it seems so alien to the story at hand and thus generates material that appears irrelevant or anticlimactic. Nevertheless, the convention of retraction as applied to the *Filocolo* represents Boccaccio's attempt to dignify a popular love story by framing it within a coherent poetic structure. Viewed in this light the *questioni d'amore* become a logical interpolation, for they assume the function of poetic echo, reproducing on a diminished scale the governing narrative scheme of the *Filocolo* itself.

CHAPTER 5

The Poisoned Peacock

The Bodleian Library's princely *Filocolo* opens to a magnificent hitch of peacocks pulling Juno's gem-encrusted wagon along a rainbow track in the sky, hung over Rome like a hammock (fig. 2). Below and to the right, clustered at a palace portal with a cardinal and bishop, the pope, in his tiara, looks up round-eyed, arms extended from a crimson mantle as if to gesture both amazement and welcome, while opposite, in the marble-faced courtyard, two fashionably dressed youths pose witness. What we see is the opening scene of the romance, Juno's descent from heaven to Clement IV, whom she urges to send for Charles of Anjou. Her peacocks, a passing detail in the text, are in the artist's scene giant creatures, powerfully muscled locomotors all the more impressive for the stark contrast formed by the deep cadmium of their undersides with the ethereal blue in which they glide. Did the illuminator allow a fondness for ornament to get the better of his sense of fairness to the story? Or might his patron have asked for a vignette in which visual interest converges on the lady riding a rainbow and reigning those amazing birds? Empty at the center and passive in the left corner, the picture pushes our glance over to the pontiff and his brightly clad retinue, then refracts it upward, to follow his gaze and focus on the celestial apparition, a goddess-queen driving birds as big as pterodactyls, her wheel rims rolling in imaginary grooves scored by stripes of color on an inverted rainbow looping beyond sight across the sky.[1]

---

1. This sumptuous humanistic manuscript was made for Prince Lodovico VII Gonzaga at Mantua in 1464. See, for its description, Pächt and Alexander, *Illuminated Manuscripts in the Bodleian,* 2:40; Branca, *Boccaccio visualizzato,* 2:297–301. Cf. the first picture in an early edition of the *Filocolo* (Naples, 1478), illustrated with forty-one woodcuts by a northern artist. Its title page shows the Author writing his book for a crowned Fiammetta, seated demurely on a bench. That first cut is indicative of the whole run, which emphasizes Boccaccio's romantic plot and action scenes involving the gods (figs. 7–8). Christianity recedes into the background.

Exquisitely realistic in details of costume and background, the miniature captures Boccaccio's prologue scene, not in its amorous moments with Madama Fiammetta, but in its historical and political setting, shaped by an alliance—between the papacy and Angevin monarchs—that would have appealed to the patron from another princely dynasty for whom this manuscript was made, Lodovico VII Gonzaga. Beyond pictorial realism, the image has implied content that subtends later plot developments and resonates symbolically in harmony with the text. Juno will continue to participate in the *Filocolo,* visiting earth or listening from heaven, to steer events toward the marriage of Florio and Biancifiore. As for the peacocks, a key episode will bring one of their kind back, roasted and replumed on a platter as banquet fare for seven knights, who use it to honor a chivalrous ritual and each swear a vow on the bird. And as for the pope, his sixth-century predecessor, Vigilius, will reenter to pontificate over the climactic ceremony of Boccaccio's *Filocolo,* the young couple's baptism at San Giovanni in Laterano.

The meeting Boccaccio arranges between Juno and the pope, fiction at its most improbable and imaginative, also veils an allegorical truth. Literally, Juno comes as her old self, in one of her usual vindictive moods. What distresses her this time is seeing that a "branchlet" of empire still clings at the tip of the "Ausonian horn."[2]

E posti i risplendenti carri agli occhiuti uccelli, davanti a sé mandata la figliuola di Taumante a significare la sua venuta, discese della somma altezza nel cospetto di colui che per lei tenea il santo uficio; e così disse:—O tu, il quale alla somma degnità se' indegno pervenuto, qual negligenza t'ha mosso in non calere della prosperità dei nostri avversarii?

[And when she had hitched her carriage to the oculated birds and sent ahead the daughter of Thaumas to signify her coming, she descended from the supreme height to the presence of him who through her held the holy office, and she spoke thusly: "Oh, you who have unworthily reached the supreme dignity, what negligence has made you not care about the prosperity of our adversaries?" (1.1.3–4)

---

2. For the ancient poets, Ausonia was southern Italy. Cf., e.g., Ovid *Met.* 14.7, 15.647; Virgil *Aen.* 10.54. Boccaccio owes his adjectival phrase "Ausonian horn" most directly to Dante *Par.* 8.61: "quel corno d'Ausonia" [that horn of Ausonia].

In allegory, Juno personifies a newer "woman," the church, the body through whom popes hold their right to highest "holy office." That being so, her birds and her rainbow must have supporting roles in a corresponding mode of symbolism. Whoever commissioned the manuscript picture seems to have recognized such deeper possibilities of meaning in Juno's herald, the rainbow goddess, Iris (otherwise known as the daughter of Thaumas); in Juno's birds, the long-tailed peafowl; and in Juno herself, whose role as prime mover of the *Filocolo* his visualization so effectively conveys. The scene is, in fact, a telescopic gloss that reaches through the text as a three-dimensional construct, both across its surface and down into a submerged layer of symbols and allegory.

In this honeycomb of iconography, the liveliest juncture for Juno's bird is, ironically, its passive performance as an entrée laced with poison. The episode in which it serves as centerpiece, Boccaccio's vows on the peacock, is a textual site that invites excavation. A probe performed with tools of literary archaeology opens the *Filocolo*'s richly furnished three-dimensional space and reconnects us as readers with the marvels of a medieval cultural world. Living and dead, the peacocks in the *Filocolo* are composite inventions molded by the poet's fantasy working on his astonishingly varied sources of information, a body of pseudoscience and symbolism extending from pagan antiquity to the fourteenth century—from natural history to mythography, from Ovid's *Metamorphoses* to Old French romance, from Galenic medicine to Roman cuisine, from the Bible and *Glossa ordinaria* to the bestiaries, from Augustine to the Victorines.

The old love story of Florio and Biancifiore, which survives in many European languages, branched into three main families of texts, all with archetypes dating from the twelfth century. Although Boccaccio has his Author claim for the *Filocolo* a Greek source, transmitted to him by its "truthful witness" Ilario (5.97), that attribution must be artful pretense. Ilario, with all the appearance of a fictional character, serves a topos—the book supposedly based on eyewitness account. Here it authenticates Boccaccio's original Hellenic title while lending his romance the exoticism and solemnity of a source in Byzantium.[3] Topoi aside, as Patricia Grieve has discovered, Boccaccio definitely had access to an account of Spanish origin. He

---

3. Boccaccio uses the same ploy in the introduction to the *Decameron,* where "a person worthy of trust" supposedly witnessed and recorded the *brigata* from its first gathering in Santa Maria Novella: "addivenne, sì come io poi da persona degna di fede sentii . . ." (introd. 1.49).

may also have been familiar with the tale through an Old French model and in an oral Italian version.[4]

---

4. The story may have had ancient, remote origins in the East, as did many other narrative motifs that would later enter the *Decameron,* along a route from India or Persia to Greece and then into Europe via the Arabs. Until recently, it was generally believed that the medieval romance originated in France during the first half of the twelfth century, but it now seems that Spain was its European source—a logical enough conclusion in light of the story's geography and cultic focus on Santiago de Compostela. Contact between the Spanish and the Arabs could also explain exotic "oriental" elements of the tale (e.g., the sultan's harem tower in Alexandria), features that need not argue so much a traceable literary source as broad realms in the Western imagination from which spring "the idea of the East for romance," as Jocely Price has put it: "The confrontation with the East is not an escape from, but part of Western experience"; see Price, *"Floire et Blancheflor:* The Magic and Mechanics of Love," *Reading Medieval Studies* 8 (1982): 12–33. For a broader discussion of this issue, see María Rosa Menocal, *The Arabic Role in Medieval Literary History* (Philadelphia: University of Pennsylvania Press, 1987). The story was transmitted in three families, or strains: Hispano-Italic, French "aristocratic," and French "popular." The Old French accounts were transcribed in verse toward the end of the thirteenth century, but they must date from the late twelfth. The Middle High German *Flore und Blanscheflur* by Konrad Fleck, the Dutch adaptation *Floris ende Blancefloer,* and the oldest English manuscript of *Floris and Blauncheflur* belong as well to the thirteenth century. In addition to a fourteenth-century Icelandic saga, there was a Norwegian *Saga af Flores ok Blankiflur,* translated by a Swedish poet before 1311 as *Flores och Blanzeflor,* which served in turn as model for the Danish prose *Eventyret om Flores og Blantzeflores.* The Greek tale of Phlorios and Platia Phlore dates from the fifteenth century, and a Bohemian account dates from the sixteenth. A prose romance, *Historia de los dos enamorados Flores y Blancaflor,* was published several times in Spain in the sixteenth century. Two Yiddish versions are also reported. An anonymous Italian *Cantare di Fiorio e Biancifiore* is more or less contemporary with the *Filocolo* (1330s), and Boccaccio's romance itself inspired several sixteenth-century Italian and German versions. One of the most interesting is the play written by a Florentine nun for performance in her convent theater; see Beatrice del Sera, *Amor di Virtù: Commedia in cinque atti, 1548,* ed. Elissa Weaver (Ravenna: Longo, 1990).

Texts and discussion can be found in du Méril, *Floire et Blancheflor;* Hans Herzog, "Die beiden Sagenkreise von Flore und Blanscheflur," *Germania,* n.s., 17 (1884): 137–228; Emil Hausknecht, ed., *Floris and Blauncheflur: Mittelenglisches Gedicht aus dem 13. Jahrhundert* (Berlin: Weidmann, 1885); Crescini, *Il Cantare di Fiorio e Biancifiore;* Joachim Reinhold, *Floire et Blancheflor: Etude de littérature comparée* (1906; reprint, Geneva: Slatkine Reprints, 1970); D. C. Hessling, ed., *Le Roman de Phlorios et Platia Phlore* (Amsterdam: Johannes Müller, 1917); A. B. Taylor, ed., *Floris and Blancheflour: A Middle-English Romance Edited from the Trentham and Auchinleck Manuscripts* (Oxford: Clarendon Press, 1927). The Old French "aristocratic" version has been translated by Merton Jerome Hubert as *The Romance of Floire and Blanchefleur: A French Idyllic Poem of the Twelfth Century* (Chapel Hill: University of North Carolina, 1966). It continues to circulate in a modern French prose edition designed for a general reading public, *Le conte de Floire et Blanchefleur: Roman pré-courtois du milieu du XIIᵉ siècle,* trans. Jean-Luc Leclanche (Paris: Honoré Champion, 1986). For a survey of the European tradition of the tale, see Victoria Kirkham, "The *Filocolo* of Giovanni Boccaccio with an English Translation of the Thirteen *Questioni d'amore*" (Ph.D. diss., Johns Hopkins University, 1972), chap. 1. A more recent essential tool is Marvin J. Ward, *"Floire et Blancheflor:* A Bibliography," *Bulletin of Bibliography* 40, no. 1 (1983): 45–64. The

Until John of Certaldo put his quill to this story, Juno's bird had never entered the plot, either alive or dead. To mark his departures from the tradition known in Italy and to jog our memory of Florio and Biancifiore, whose fame has dimmed since the Middle Ages, the *Cantare di Fiorio e Biancifiore* makes a convenient text of reference. Roughly contemporary to the *Filocolo,* it is a much simpler composition, written in the rhyming octaves of the *cantastorie,* or minstrel singer.[5] In the following paraphrase, italics indicate Boccaccio's additions; underlined italics show where he interpolated the vows on the peacock.

At Juno's instigation, the pope calls Charles of Anjou to Italy. The Author falls in love with Charles's great-granddaughter, who asks him to write the book which begins with a history of the world from the Creation to the cult of Saint James. After five years of marriage, two early Christian nobles of Rome, *Quinto Lelio Africano and Giulia Topazia* (in the *Cantare,* Jacopo and Topacia) conceive a child, vowing in thanks a pilgrimage to Santiago de Compostela. Ambushed by the king of Spain, Lelio perishes, but his widow finds refuge in the royal household. There, at the time of the "Knights' Holiday," the Spanish queen gives birth to a son; Giulia bears a daughter and dies. The children grow up together and fall in love. King Felice, disapproving, sends Florio away to school and conspires with his seneschal to trick Biancifiore into serving a poisoned dish at his birthday banquet. *The food is a peacock. Before tasting it, King Felice and each of the six barons seated at his table make a vow to the bird.* When the taster's

most comprehensive and up-to-date list of all the versions of the story appears in the well-informed reassessment by Patricia Grieve in *Floire and Blancheflor and the European Romance* (Cambridge: Cambridge University Press, 1997): 210–15. Grieve "charts . . . nuances that rejuvenate the story as it passes from country to country and century to century," anchoring her study to the discovery in the 1960s of a Spanish archetype, the *Crónica de Flores y Blancaflor,* datable to the late thirteenth century. As she demonstrates, this Spanish form accounts for Christian material that Boccaccio uses in book 5 of the *Filocolo* as well as for other details of the Italian text that do not appear in the Old French tradition. Boccaccio, she concludes, may have known some French strain of the romance, but he also had access to a version of the Iberian archetype. A reassessment of the *Filocolo* in light of Grieve's important publication is in order.

5. Florio and Biancifore were already famous by the time the author of *La gran conquista de Ultramar* (ca. 1300) honors them for their memorable devotion, "los muchos enamorados de que ya oystes hablar" (cited by Grieve in *Floire and Blancheflor,* 29). The relationship, if any, between Boccaccio's *Filocolo* and the *Cantare* is disputed. Crescini (*Il cantare di Fiorio e Biancifiore,* 1:75–80, 488–92) dated the latter to about 1330 and considered it independent of the *Filocolo.* Angelo Monteverdi believes it postdates and was influenced by Boccaccio's romance; see "Un libro d'Ovidio e un passo del *Filocolo,*" in *Autori diversi: Studia Philologica et letteraria in honorem L. Spitzer,* ed. Anna Granville Hatcher and Karl Ludwig Selig (Bern: Francke, 1958), 335–40.

ghastly death has revealed its bane, Felice accuses Biancifiore of attempted murder, and his minions throw her into a death-row dungeon. *Venus and Mars help as* Florio liberates Biancifiore and inculpates the seneschal. The Spanish sovereigns sell Biancifiore to merchants bound for Alexandria. Florio, *alias Filocolo,* finds her there and secretly slips into the tower where she is held captive. *Before consummating their love, the couple step out of bed to exchange wedding vows beneath an image of Cupid, who must substitute for Hyman as officiating deity at this private ceremony. Venus and Diana also attend the nuptials.* Discovered and sentenced to death at the stake, the lovers are saved by Florio's companions *with assistance from Mars and Venus.* The Admiral, *illumined by this prodigy,* recognizes in Florio his nephew and decrees a magnificent public wedding, at which, *after invocations to Hymen and Juno,* the pair remarry. *They journey to Rome and receive baptism from the pope in the Lateran;* after their conversion, they convert the whole kingdom, and Florio ascends the throne.

The vows on the peacock (*Filoc.* 2.35), unique in Boccaccio's version, occur as part of a larger episode that does figure in accounts before his. It describes Biancifiore's first pitfall, a trap laid by the king and queen of Spain to assure her disappearance. Their agent in crime is the seneschal, a stock villain suitably blackened in Boccaccio's handling by his Arabic-sounding name, Massamutino. Felice instructs this scoundrel to prepare "a peacock, fine and fat, and full of poisonous juices" (2.29). They will cajole Biancifiore into serving it, and to allay her suspicions, she will be invited to pause with the bird before everyone at the table, "domandando le ragioni del paone" [asking them to pay the peacock its due]. Later, on the day of the dinner and in Biancifiore's presence, Massamutino informs Felice's wife:

Madonna, oggi si celebra, sì come voi sapete, la gran festa della natività del nostro re, per la qual cosa volendo noi la nostra festa fare maggiore e più bella, provedemmo di fare apparecchiare un paone, il quale noi vogliamo far davanti al re presentare e a' suoi baroni, acciò che ciascuno, faccendo quello che a tale uccello si richiede, si vanti di far cosa per la quale la festa divenga maggiore e più bella.

[My lady, as you know, today we celebrate the great feast of our king's birthday, and since we want to make our feast grander and finer, we made provision to have a peacock prepared, which we wish to have presented to the king and his barons, so that everyone, doing

what is requisite for such a bird, may vaunt that he will do something
to make the celebration grander and finer.] (2.33.4)

The complicitous queen sends Biancifiore to serve the bird. Felice and his
barons each make a vaunt over it, then some bits of its meat are thrown to
one of the king's pet dogs. Suddenly, the little animal swells, its eyes bulge
red, and it explodes and drops dead—"proof" of Biancifiore's guilt, and
grounds for her death sentence.

Precedent for the conspiracy to blame her for a lethal dish at the king's
table survives in one of the Old French archetypes. In that *Roman de Floire
et Blancheflor,* the king asks his nefarious seneschal Maydien to contrive a
scheme for eliminating the maiden. It develops as follows:

> Li seneschax se part du roi
> Por Blancheflor mestre en effroi:
> Jusqu'à dó jors s'est porchaciez.
> Oiez que fist li desvoiez.
> Un lardez prist, si le toucha
> Et en venin l'envelopa;
> Puis apela un sien serjant:
> "Pinel," fait il, "ge te commant;
> Cest mes porteras mon seignor:
> Si li diras que Blancheflor
> Li a cest present envoiez;
> Ge cuit qu'il en sera molt liez."

[The seneschal takes leave of the king; for two whole days he plotted
to affright Blancheflor. Hear what the deviant did. He took a larded
roast, rubbed it, and wrapped it in poison. Then he called a servant
of his: "Pinel," he says, "I command you, carry this dish to my lord.
You tell him that Blancheflor has sent him this present. I believe he
will be delighted by it."]

The king, upon receiving the dish, gives a piece to one of his squires, who
obligingly accepts, to his detriment.

> Or oiez qu'il i gaaigna.
> Quant il en ot un mors gouté,
> Endui li hueil li sont volé,

Et chiet toz morz entre la gent,
Toz estanduz el pavement.

[Now hear what it earned him. When he had tasted a bite of it, both of his eyes popped out and he fell flat dead among the people, stretched flat out on the floor.]⁶

Despite broad similarities, Boccaccio's story differs on certain points from that of the Old French poet. In the latter, poisoned food is the seneschal's idea, not the king's; a servant, instead of Blancheflor, brings it to the table (Blancheflor is blamed more indirectly, for having ordered the dish sent); a squire, rather than a dog, is the taster; and the plate itself is described as a "lardez," a descriptor that derives from the custom of preparing roasts, usually venison, by lacing them with lard and that designates not fowl but meat.⁷

To this same family of texts belongs the anonymous Italian *Cantare di Fiorio e Biancifiore,* representative of an orally transmitted form that may underlie Maria's disparaging allusion in the *Filocolo* to the "fanciful parlance of the ignorant" (1.1). Convinced that the "lying harlot" Biancifiore has bewitched his son, Felice swears vengeance and commands his seneschal (unnamed):

quando saremo a tavola a mangiare,
comandoti per questo sacramento
'na galina mi mandi avelenata,
che Biancifiore ne sia incolpata.

[When we are at table eating, I command you by this oath to send me a poisoned hen, so that Biancifiore gets the blame for it.]

The canonically evil seneschal, "a miscreant dog," obeys, with deadly consequences.

---

6. *Floire et Blancheflor,* vv. 393–428, ed. du Méril in *Floire et Blancheflor.* Of the two Old French archetypes, which du Méril labels an "aristocratic" and a "popular" version, this episode occurs only in the former. See Grieve, *Floire and Blancheflor,* 57–60, for a summary of the European versions in which it is present and a *mise-au-point* of the original features in Boccaccio's episode.

7. See Adolf Tobler and Erhard Lommatzsch, *Altfranzösisches Wörterbuch* (Weisbaden: F. Steiner, 1963), s.v. "lardé" ("gespicktes oder zum Spicken geeignetes Lendenstück"), with reference to *Floire et Blancheflor,* vv. 1461–64: "De bon mangier ont a fuison, / Et volailles et venison, / Lardes de cerf et de sengler / Ont a mangier sans refuser."

E 'l re co' suo' baroni andò a mangiare,
e la galina fue apresentata,
e quel dongelio chella andò a portare
dicie: Biancifiore l'a mandata.
e uno dongello la prese a tagliare;
la cossa ad uno braco l'a gitata:
lo cane cade morto incontanente
davanti a re, che 'l vidde la sua gente.

[And the king with his barons went to eat, and the hen was presented, and the squire that had fetched it said, "Biancifiore has sent
it." And a squire took it to carve; he tossed a drumstick to a hound;
the dog dropped dead right away before the king, who saw it with his
people.][8]

As in the Gallic prototype, Biancifiore does not personally serve the dish,
but the cismontane *cantastorie,* like Boccaccio, tests the poison on a dog.
Similarly, the plate named in the minstrel's ottava rima is fowl—a hen to
be precise—rather than meat.[9] Summing up, we see Boccaccio diverging
from the roman and *cantare* in three matters: Biancifiore herself presents
the dish; it is a peacock; and before the tasting, all the king's barons pro-
nounce vows on the bird.

There are seven vows. To start, Felice dissimulates his true intentions
by swearing, "for love of the present peacock," to give Biancifiore, within
the year, one of his highest barons as a husband. Next, Parmenione
promises the peacock that on the day when Biancifiore rides in procession
to her bridegroom's home, he and other young nobles, richly garbed and
adorned with gold, will escort her on foot, leading her mount. Valorous
Ascalion vows that although his arm now trembles with age, on the day of
her wedding he will duel with whosoever challenges him, shedding not a
drop of blood. Messaalino follows, giving his word over the peacock that
at Biancifiore's nuptial banquet he will offer her ten date palms laden with
golden coins of Byzantium. As Biancifiore passes with the platter to Duke
Ferramonte's place, he pledges that on the same future occasion and for as
long as celebrations shall last after, he will be her cupbearer. Sixth to

---

8. Crescini, *Il cantare di Fiorio e Biancifiore,* vol. 2, octaves 29–31.

9. It is also a hen in the fifteenth-century Spanish edition of the tale, and chicken comes to
the table in the Renaissance Greek account. See du Méril, *Floire et Blanceflor,* lxxxii n. 1.

speak, the baron Sara promises to give Biancifiore, on the day she is joined in marriage, a gold crown richly set with precious stones. Finally, Menedon vows on the peacock that throughout her wedding festivities, he and his friends, dressed in silk, will ride carrying colorful banners and perform ceremonial jousting.

Why does Boccaccio, in a departure from precedent, specify peacock as the pièce de résistance, underlining his switch on the menu by making it the object of seven oaths? The answer rests in part on his familiarity with one of the finer points in the chivalric code of honor, a ritual that involved voicing one's solemn oath over a noble bird, usually delectably roasted. The earliest example seems to have been an assembly at Westminster on May 22, 1306, when two swans encased in goldwork were borne into the hall on a large tray by a seneschal. Edward I and the Prince of Wales, who had just been knighted, vowed on these swans to march into Scotland against the Bruce. The latest instance is alleged to have taken place at a banquet held on February 17, 1454, at the court of Philippe le Bon, duke of Burgundy. On that occasion, the duke swore over a pheasant to undertake a crusade against the Turks and personally challenge the sultan, a vow never fulfilled.[10]

Between these two instances, spanning a century and a half, we find the custom in reports with a less factual ring. One is a short fourteenth-century French narrative of 440 verses, *The Vows on the Heron,* which relates an incident purported to have taken place in September, 1336. King Edward III of England, answering an accusation of cowardice brought by Robert of Artois, swears on a heron at his table to invade France. His attending nobles also pledge—one to keep an eye closed for the war's duration; others to engage an enemy prince in singular combat; and another still to plunder, rape, and kill the French in indiscriminate violence. The ladies participate as well. The earl of Darby's daughter swears not to give herself to her lover until he has accomplished his vow, and the queen affirms that she will kill herself and the child she is expecting if it sees the light before the invasion announced by Edward. Although real personages and grim truths from the Hundred Years' War provide a background for *The Vows on the Heron,* it was apparently the creation of a

---

10. R. L. Graeme Ritchie cites these events in a still valuable survey, his introduction to *The Buik of Alexander,* by John Barbour, 4 vols., Scottish Text Society, n.s., vols. 12, 17, 21, 25 (Edinburgh and London, 1921–29), 2:xxxix ff. Philippe's pheasant vow is also mentioned in B. J. Whiting, "The Vows on the Heron," *Speculum* 20 (July, 1945): 161–78.

dovish author who wanted to counterattack English aggression by mocking the custom of battle vaunts.[11] His poem can be ascribed to the same pseudohistorical circle as a somewhat earlier piece, comparably short, *The Vows on the Sparrow Hawk.*[12] This account embellishes an expeditionary sojourn made by the emperor Henry VII to Milan beginning late in 1311. During that visit, so the poet will have it, his brother's sparrow hawk escaped and by chance flew straight to the table where the emperor was dining. Henry capitalized on the occasion by inviting the gathered guests to make vows over the bird.

Wherever their truth-value may lie, *The Vows on the Heron* and *The Vows on the Sparrow Hawk* enter a larger tradition rooted less in the workings of royal history than in a wide-reaching work of Old French fiction, *The Vows on the Peacock,* penned by Jacques de Longuyon, who in 1312 dedicated the eight thousand verses he had spun to Thibaut de Bar, bishop of Liège (1310–16). They form a sequel to the *Roman d'Alexandre,* a gigantic twelfth-century monument to medieval fascination with the life and legends of the Macedonian conqueror. Longuyon's poem takes its title from a banquet, prompted when Alexander's prisoner Porrus one day kills a peacock.[13] Twelve ladies and gentlemen gather, the latter both partisans and captive opponents of Alexander in his ongoing military campaign. All vow on the roasted bird in alternating order as it is carried around the table by a damsel of high degree, the fair maid of Elyot. Cassamus initiates the ritual, swearing that if Clarus becomes unhorsed during the forthcoming battle, he will set him back on the saddle. Aristé vows to fight until Fesonas has been avenged; Perdicas to dismount in the fray; Porrus to seize Emenidius's steed, the Baudrain, to capture Alexander's sword; Caulus to tear off the Baudrain's helmet; Lyoné to duel with Clarus's first son; Floridas to deliver the Baudrain a prisoner to Alexander; and Gadifer to smite

---

11. B. J. Whiting describes *Les Voeux du hairon* in his "The Vows on the Heron." At least one pot-boiling pseudochronicler of English history today still remembers this kingly banquet of Edward's: see Jean Plaidy, *The Vow on the Heron* (1980; reprint, New York: Putnam, 1982).

12. *Voeux de l'epervier,* ed. G. Wolfram and F. Bonnardot, *Jahrbuch der Gesellschaft für Lothringische Geschgichte und Altertumskunde* 6 (1894): 177–280 (also published separately at Metz in 1895). Its author may have been Simon de Marville (Marville was a town near Longuyon), treasurer of the cathedral chapter at Metz and dead before 1326. Ritchie (*The Buik of Alexander,* 1:xxxvii) believes the work refers to events that the poet knew had taken place. He was clearly an author who also knew *Les Voeux du paon.* See below, n. 24.

13. On dating and authorship of *Les Voeux du paon,* see Urban Tigner Holmes, *A History of Old French Literature from the Origins to 1300* (New York: Russell and Russell, 1962), 326–27. Ritchie summarizes the episode, in *The Buik of Alexander,* 3:ciii–civ.

down Clarus's battle standard. Whereas the men aggressively pledge chivalric military feats, the ladies' vows are more gentle. Fesonas will wed only the man Alexander chooses, Ydorus will be true to her lover, and Edeas will restore the peacock in a commemorative golden image after the war.

The Vows on the Peacock left influential tracks in both literature and the visual arts.[14] In France the poem impinged on the heron and sparrow-hawk poems, both from the first half of the fourteenth century. Jacques de Longuyon can also be held accountable for a set of twelve vows made by twelve knights in the roughly contemporary Perceforest, a sprawling prose compilation written to join the Alexander legend with the cycle of tales that had grown up around the heroes of the Holy Grail.[15] Peacock likewise crops up in Hugues Capet, a chanson de geste dated to between 1312 and 1340. When presented with this bird at a banquet, its protagonist recalls the oaths taken of yore by Porrus and Cassamus. Thus inspired, Hugues vows to make a foray from Paris into the besieging enemy encampment and seek out its leaders for dueling unto death.[16]

So successful was The Vows on the Peacock that it was singled out for scarification by Philippe de Mezières. That pious bishop of Paris in 1389 attacked it as one of those "novels that are full of fibs and that often entice the reader to the impossible, to folly, to vanity and sin."[17] But his battle

---

14. Les Voeux du paon, sometimes called the Roman de Cassamus, survives in at least thirty-four manuscripts. Ritchie describes thirty-one of them, in The Buik of Alexander, 2:xx–xlviii. One manuscript now in the Vatican, bearing the arms of Pope Gregory VI, has been identified as the same book that was in an inventory of volumes bequeathed by Pietro Bembo to Fulvio Orsini. Another copy, now lost, is known to have been in collection of the Gonzaga duke Francesco I. The most popular French poem of the fourteenth century, Les Voeux du paon introduced the Nine Worthies (three pagans, three Jews, three Christians), a group that enjoyed a famous afterlife in both literature and the arts. For the happy fortunes of Les Voeux, see George Cary, The Medieval Alexander (Cambridge; Cambridge University Press, 1956), 32. The Alexander manuscripts, often illustrated, depict peacocks in proximity with the hero.

15. Holmes, A History of Old French Literature, 326–27.

16. Hugues Capet: Chanson de geste, ed. Adélaïde Edouard Le Lièvre de la Grange (1864; reprint, Nendeln, Liechtenstein: Kraus Reprint, 1966), vv. 1167–76: "Mais au noble paon iert de moy fait ung veus, / Et s'aquievez n'estoit, j'en saroie honteus, / Car je veu au paon si comme aventureus / Que demain au matin voray estre soingneus / De partir de Paris, et m'en iray tous sceuls / Tout droit au pavillon véoir noà hayneus. / Là me conbateray à ung prinche ou à .ii. / Auquelz sera par moy donné ly cos morteuls, / Et puis m'en revenray se j'en suis éureus, / et se jou y muir, Deiu soit à m'ame piteus."

17. Ritchie (The Buik of Alexander, 1:xliv–xlv) cites the bishop's condemnation of this book as one of those "romans qui sont remplis de bourdes, et qui attraient le lisant souvent a impossibilitè, a folie, a vanité et pechié."

was a lost cause, for this dangerous French reading had already crossed the Channel some twenty years earlier to serve a Scot—and a clergyman at that—as model for the *Buik of Alexander,* the earliest extant work of Scottish literature.[18] Traveling abroad on the Continent, too, *The Vows on the Peacock* enjoyed translation into the Dutch *Roman van Cassamus* and furnished matter for a medieval Spanish version, *Los votos del pavon.*[19] The vaunts were so well known by the latter years of the fourteenth century that Chaucer could puckishly parody them in the *Canterbury Tales,* as he lets Sir Thopas swear in his own style on "ale and bread" to vanquish Fairyland's evil Sir Olifaunt.[20]

Back at home, meanwhile, *The Vows on the Peacock* engendered two sequels. First is *The Restoration of the Peacock,* a romance of 2,660 alexandrines that takes as it point of departure Edeas's unfulfilled promise to replace the peacock with a gold copy.[21] Jean Brisebarre, who wrote the romance sometime before 1338, begins by noting the "omission" of this episode in the earlier account and sets about to remedy the situation. For

---

18. Ibid., 1:xiv–xvi.

19. The Middle Dutch *Roman van Cassamus,* ed. Eelco Verwijs (Gronigen: J. B. Wolters, 1869), survives only in fragmentary form according to Ritchie (*The Buik of Alexander,* 1:xi–xii). The lost *Los votos del pavon* are known only through secondary reference. See A. D. Deyermond, *The Middle Ages: A Literary History of Spain* (New York: Barnes and Noble, 1971), 67; Marqués de Santillana, *Paginas Escogidas,* ed. Fernando Gutierrez (Barcelona: Luis Miracle, 1939), 242; Grieve, *Floire and Blanchefleur,* 60.

20. Geoffrey Chaucer, *The Canterbury Tales,* ed. F. N. Robinson (Boston: Houghton Mifflin, 1961), 7.872–74: "And there he swoor on ale and breed / How that the geauant shall be deed, / Bityde!" The peacock vows were well known in England. John Lydgate refers to them. Via an Old French adaptation of *Les Voeux du paon* (*Histoire des trois nobles fils de Rois*), they figure prominently in later fiction (ca. 1500); see *The Three Kings' Sons,* ed. F. J. Furnivall, Early English Text Society, no. 67 (London: K. Paul, Trench, Trübner and Co., 1895), 136. In this less than stirring narrative, gentlewomen enter a great hall and present a "Poo" to King Alfour of Sicily, whose enemy is the Turk. The text reads, "And the kynge made to the Poo his advowe first / and promised to diffende his reaume to his power." Then the sultan's son Orcays, a captive who loves the king's daughter, swears to make peace, and all the other Turkish prisoners echo his vow. But Ferant, the king's general, retorts, swearing "that, for the grete crueltees that he had seen without nombre in the Turkes persone, wold he neuir yelde him unto him / and if the Turke came in his daunger, he wolde neuir put him to raunsom." The text continues, "The Halle was fulle of noble folkes, and the Poo was brought bifore them / and euery man helde vp his hande, & sware with lowde voice the same promesse that fferaunt had made." Vows on a peacock are also important in the Scottish *Clariodus* (ca. 1550), which came from the French *Roman de Cleriadus et de Méliadice, fille au roy d'Angleterre.* As late as 1835, in the Royal Academy Exhibition at London, there was a picture called *Vow on the Peacock,* by Daniel Maclise, who decorated Saint Stephens and the House of Lords. See Ritchie, *The Buik of Alexander,* 1:xlii–xlvi.

21. Jean le Court dit Brisebarre, *Le Restor du paon,* ed. Richard J. Carey (Geneva: Droz, 1966). It follows the *Voeux du paon* in sixteen of the thirty surviving manuscripts.

the final banquet in a fifteen-day marriage celebration Alexander has
sponsored, Edeas brings out her magnificent, gem-encrusted bird. Its
unveiling reminds Alexander of the real peacock for which this one will
stand as a lasting substitute, and he proposes that the group debate the relative merits of promises they made on that former occasion. A lively
exchange in the manner of a "jeu-partit," or court of love, follows; they
settle the question of whose vow was most worthy with a drawing, the win-
ner being the dead warrior Cassamus. The second sequel of *The Vows on
the Peacock* is *The Perfection of the Peacock,* whose author, Jean de la
Mote, weaves his name and the date 1340 into an acrostic at the end of his
3,015 verses.[22] The setting for this account that "perfects," or completes,
the cycle is the chateau of Mclidus, where Alexander and his peers join the
lord and his family in an "amorous chamber" decorated with scenes of
Dido and Aeneas, Paris and Helen, Venus and Mars, Cupid and Diana,
and Jupiter with Saturn. There they debate questions of love and compose
ballads. Later, Edeas's "restored" peacock is brought for a banquet.
Alexander begins the banquet by vowing war on Melidus, who retorts by
swearing to defeat Alexander. Festion promises to kill one of six men in
present company; Betis to aid Porrus; Philoté to bear the king's banner;
Marcien to cut down Alexander's tent; Porrus to fight fiercely; Buchiforas
to seek out Alexander in combat; and Antigonus to cut off Buchiforas's
arm and shoulder. The daughters of Melidus vow, too: Clareté will watch
over the three Greek prisoners; Préamuse will let herself be killed by the
first comer on the field if she finds her father and brother dead; Dermo-
madaire will take her life by sword and fire if Melidus comes to harm; Sai-
gremor will eat only bread and water until the fighting has ended.

So the fertile cycle that had taken shape around the middle of the
twelfth century in the *Roman d'Alexandre* came to spawn in the fourteenth
an imaginative series of peacock-centered postscripts. The earliest,
Jacques de Longuyon's *Les Voeux du paon,* has two sequels, *Le Restor du
paon* and *Le Parfait du paon.*[23] Also depending on it is a collateral line of
other bird-vaunt literature no longer bound to Alexander's life and exem-
plified by the antiwar *Voeux de l'hairon* and Emperor Henry's *Voeux de*

---

22. Jean de la Mote, *Le Parfait du paon,* ed. Richard J. Carey, University of North Carolina Studies in the Romance Languages and Literatures, no. 118 (Chapel Hill: University of
North Carolina Press, 1972).
23. A good literary analysis of this minicycle is Renate Blumenfeld-Kosinski, "The Poetics of Continuation in the Old French *Paon* Cycle," *Romance Philology* 39, no. 4 (1986):
437–47.

l'epervier. Some member of the former family, the peacock cycle attached to Alexander, had journeyed as far south as Naples by the 1330s, where in a climate influenced by the French connections of its court, Boccaccio composed the *Filocolo.*

For Boccaccio, there were two very different Alexanders. One was the conqueror he came to know as a humanist through Latin histories and whom he portrays in his *De casibus virorum illustrium,* a cruel tyrant who horribly mutilates his critic Callisthenes. But to the youthful author, Alexander was a still paragon whose adventures and generosity had been the stuff of fanciful vernacular poetry. This fabled hero steps into Boccaccio's mind as he helps us envision the great hall for Felice's birthday banquet. Marble reliefs carved on the walls, a visual catalogue of the Western epic tradition, display the most memorable moments of antiquity with scenes from the battles of Thebes, Troy, and Pharsalus and "the great victories of the great Alexander." While Biancifiore passes with the bird around the table, Boccaccio identifies in turn each of the barons who speak. The first, seated in the place of honor at Felice's right, is called Parmenione. His name recalls Parmenio, a character in the branch of Alexander histories by Quintus Curtius Rufus. Last is Menedon, whose name seems to be an altered form of *Menedemos,* the name of another of the Greek leader's high military commanders. Finally, to round out the literary setting for Felice's dinner, we should remember that Alexander himself was a victim of poisoning at table. By discreet allusion, the peacock vows linked with Alexander's exploits in Old French literature return to Boccaccio's continuation of the tradition, in the motif of poisoning, in the proper names, and in the dining-room decor.[24]

---

24. The battle scenes on the wall are the first mention of Alexander in the *Filocolo* (2.32). Grieve (*Floire and Blancheflur,* 113) rightly observes how they link the setting for the vows on the peacock with the French *paon* cycle. Subsequently in the *Filocolo* Alexander is remembered for his generosity (4.28, 1) and as a descendant of Saturn and Jupiter who, in the Fifth Age of the World, conquered the Medes and Persians (5.53). The *Ameto* also mentions his "liberality" ("le liberalità d'Alessandro," 1.3), but the *Amorosa visione* (7.76–78) refers to his subjection of the world in a less flattering light. By the period of *De casibus virorum illustrium* (after 1360), Alexander has become an irascible maniac demanding deification. Reproved for it by Callisthenes, he cut off the philosopher's hands and feet, blinded and disfigured him, and cast the still living trunk into a cave filled with bloodthirsty hounds. Boccaccio's *Esposizioni sopra la Comedia di Dante,* his last work, includes, in his commentary on *Inferno* 12, a brief life history of the vicious Alexander, "crudelissimo ucciditore" [most cruel killer]. Quaglio's commentary in his edition of the *Filocolo* (777 nn. 19 and 24) glosses the overlap between names of Felice's barons and Alexander's men. Parmenione is twice mentioned in

Assuming that Boccaccio wrote the *Filocolo* between 1336 and 1338, his source could not have been Jean de la Mote's *Le Parfait du paon,* signed and dated 1340. Its immediate predecessor, *Le Restor du paon,* written before 1338 and surviving in a relatively large number of manuscripts, might have reached him by then. Most likely, though, it was the older and better-established poem by Jacques de Longuyon, *Les Voeux du paon* itself, that gave Boccaccio his primary model.

Jacques de Longuyon set a style that permitted emperors, kings, and knights, often joined by ladies at court, to make promises over any aristocratically worthy fowl, preferably peacock, although a heron, sparrow hawk, or pheasant would do.[25] Striking about the ritual is that while the birds may vary, the substance of the vows they elicit remains remarkably constant. Women swear wifely or amorous loyalty to their menfolk. Men invariably make soldierly pledges, or they had, until Boccaccio put a twist on custom. Banned from the boasts at his banquet table, masculine militarism retreats to mute testimonial in the dining hall's mural carvings. Replacing it center stage on the birthday board are vaunts on the bird for a maiden's wedding.

Why has martial prowess yielded to matrimony? Earlier poets had welcomed to their trenchers peacock as "la viande as preux," fare most suited

---

anecdotes about Alexander by Valerius Maximus, at *Factorum et dictorum memorabilium* 3.8 ext. 6 and 6.4 ext. 3. Beyond Alexander and the vows on the peacock, there may be another point of contact between *Les Voeux du paon* and the *Filocolo.* Boccaccio's *questioni d'amore* are an interpolation that could have been suggested by the love debate in *Les Voeux.* The debate there includes whether Betis would rather look on Ydorus face-to-face or with the mind's eye, in solitude. The answer is the latter, because when with her, he is tongue-tied. Also debated is which two things in love are sweetest, which are determined to be hope and remembrance, and which two are most grievous, which are determined to be longing and fear. The debate is cited by Ritchie in *The Buik of Alexander,* 2:cxiii.

25. The extent to which this custom may have been historical reality is uncertain. Ritchie (*The Buik of Alexander,* 1:xxxix–xl) believed it originated in the Lorraine and that its chief promoter was Bishop Thibaut de Bar. Since Thibaut was a relative of King Edward I, whose court was French speaking, he could have promoted the Westminster swan vows. As he certainly suggested the subject for Jacques de Longuyon's poem, thereby, according to Ritchie, bringing "the knights of Alexander into line with the most recent practice of chivalry (89, l.1)." He apparently also inspired *Les Voeux de l'épervier,* a poem that borrows numerous lines from *Les Voeux du paon.* Such vaunts resemble the chivalric vow undertaken by knights errant. See Martin de Riquer, *Caballeros andantes españoles* (Madrid: Espasa-Calpe, 1967), 9–21. Grieve (*Floire and Blanchefleur,* 59–60) believes that in the *Filocolo,* "the banquet during which the peacock is served represents a faithful recreation of such a feast in Boccaccio's time." She further argues (112–13) that Boccaccio introduces this scene to attack politically the enemy of King Robert of Anjou, Henry VII of France, whom evil Felice is supposed to resemble.

to stalwart knights.[26] But if the French knew peacock as "the meat of the brave," Boccaccio sees it otherwise. He has invested the bird with a dignity transcending the manorial roundtable and reaching back to an older, higher society, an elite who dwelt on Mount Olympus. Biancifiore reveals its restored classical identity in her presentation address to King Felice.

> Poi che gl'iddii si mostrano verso me graziosi e benigni, avendomi conceduto che io a questo onore, più tosto che alcuna altra giovane, eletta fossi a portare davanti alla vostra real presenza il santo uccello di Giunone, il quale per quella dea, al cui servigio già fu disposto, merita che qualunque alla sua mensa il dimanda si doni alcun vanto; il quale poi ad onore di lei con sollecitudine adempia: onde io per questo prendo ardire a dimandarlovi, e caramente vi priego che voi né i vostri compagni a ciò rendere mi siate ingrati, ma con benigni aspetti continuiate la valorosa usanza.

[Since the gods are revealing their grace and benevolence to me by granting me that I, rather than any other girl, should be chosen to carry before your royal presence Juno's holy bird, which, for the sake of that goddess to whose service it was long ago disposed, deserves that whosoever demands it at his board should commit himself to some vow and take care to fulfill it in her honor, therefore I make bold to ask this of you, and I dearly beg that neither you nor your companions begrudge rendering me what I ask, but that with benign countenance you reaffirm your valorous custom.] (2.34)

Acceding, Felice agrees that "Juno's holy bird" merits indeed most generous vows and commences the round. Parmenione speaks next, with a vow that elicits delight from their ceremonial hostess. He and his companions, dressed in robes shining with gold, will lead her horse in the wedding procession to the groom's door.[27] "Well then," said Biancifiore, "Più che

---

26. Cassamus, for example, who intitates the oaths in *Les Voeux du paon,* cries out, on seeing the bird, "C'est la viande as preux, a ceux qui ont amie!" [It is the meat for the brave, for those who love!]. His praise served to fix the fowl's feudal epithet in a formula later recollected by Hugues Capet, who proclaimed it "la viande au preus" (v. 1164).

27. This was, in fact, the custom in Boccaccio's time. See Christiane Klapisch-Zuber, "Zacharie, ou le père évincé: Les rites nuptiaux toscans entre Giotto et le Concile de Trente," *Annales Economie, Sociétés, Civilisations* 6 (1979): 1216–43; reprinted as "Zacharias, or the Ousted Father: Nuptial Rites in Tuscany between Giotto and the Council of Trent," in *Women, Family, and Ritual in Renaissance Italy,* trans. Lydia G. Cochrane (Chicago: University of Chicago Press, 1985), 178–212.

Giunone mi potrò io di conducitori gloriare" [I can be prouder of my escorts than Juno]. Juno's "conductors," of course, are none other than the brilliantly colored peacocks who pull her airborne chariot. Equipped thus, she made her entrance into the *Filocolo,* a *dea ex curru* headed for Rome on the rainbow road.

Goddesses are often called on to travel, and being ladies strong of personality, each has her preferred means. Venus favored a coach hitched to swans; Diana's flights were powered by stags.[28] So, too, Juno travels in a skycraft drawn by the creatures most aptly her own. Boccaccio knows them from Ovid, who pictures Juno in her peacock-pulled wagon when she sails off to settle the score on the latest count of her husband's infidelities. This time the other woman is Callisto, a nymph whom Jove plucked to safety by promoting her and her bastard son, Arcas, to a place in the celestial vault. Outraged, the queen of the gods visits Oceanus, demanding as vengeance that those stars never dip beneath his waves. The passage concludes, "The gods of the sea granted her prayer, and Saturnia, mounting her swift chariot, was borne back through the yielding air by her gaily decked peacocks, peacocks but lately decked with the slain Argus' eyes."[29]

---

28. Boccaccio explains why Venus has a chariot pulled by swans, in his *Genealogie* 3.22: "Quod a cignis eius trahatur currus, duplex potest esse ratio, aut quia per albidinem significant lautitiam muliebrem, aut quia dulcissime canant, et maxime morti propinqui, ut demonstretur amantum animos cantu trahi, et quod cantu amantes fere desiderio nimio morientes passiones explicent suas" [As for why her cart is pulled by swans, the reason can be twofold, either because they signify in their whiteness womanly elegance, or because they sing most sweetly, and especially when they are near death, in order to show how the spirits of lovers are attracted by song, and because through song lovers almost dying from too much desire reveal their passions]. On Diana's vehicle he writes (5.2): "Currus autem ideo illi additur, non solum ut ex hoc celi circuitio assummatur quam etiam velocius ceteris planetis peragit, quin imo ut et montium atque nemorum circuitiones venantium designentur. Qui a cervis ideo trahi dicitur, eo quod a silvestribus animalibus venantium desiderium trahi vedeatur" [A cart is thus assigned to her, not only so that it can be taken as the circuit in the heaven, which she circles even more swiftly than other planets, but further to designate the hunters' circuits in mountains and groves. They say stags pull the cart because it seems that a hunter's desire is drawn by sylvan animals].

29. Ovid *Met.* 2.531–33: "Di maris adnuerant: habili Saturnia curru / ingreditur liquidum pavonibus aethera pictis, tam nuper pictis / caeso pavonibus Argo." Inspired by Ovid, artists of Italy painted Juno riding the skies with her peacocks. See Paolo Schiavo's *Myth of Callisto,* a marriage panel of the early quattrocento (Museum of Fine Arts, Springfield), reproduced in Paul F. Watson, *The Garden of Love in Tuscan Art of the Early Renaissance* (Philadelphia: Art Alliance Press, 1979), pl. 10. The tradition holds familiar through the Renaissance, as witnessed by Sebastiano del Piombo's *Juno,* a mural at the Farnesina in Rome, painted for Agostino Chigi (ca. 1512–14), in which a pole hitches Juno's chariot to two flapping peacocks. Sometimes her team served other travelers, such as the goddess Nature, whom Alan of Lille, back in the thirteenth century, had imagined riding in a glass

In an earlier episode of his *Metamorphoses,* Ovid had disclosed how this bird Juno drives came to have ocular decorations. He tells the sad fate of Argus, Arestor's son with one hundred eyes, whom Juno assigned to guard Io from Jupiter's advances. Her supervisory measures failed, though, because Mercury, sent as Jupiter's agent, freed the cow-maiden by lulling all of Argus's eyes to sleep and then lopping of his head. So the poet laments: "Argus, thou liest low; the light which thou hadst within thy many fires is all put out; and one darkness fills thy hundred eyes. Saturnia took these eyes and set them on the feathers of her bird, filling his tail with starlike jewels."[30]

Argus-of-one-hundred-eyes found his afterlife in the peacock's oculiferous tail. The myth of how he met his demise and of Juno salvaging his most famous parts, a pathetic tale remembered by Ovid in connection with Callisto, underlies Boccaccio's image of Juno at the *Filocolo* incipit, as well as her bird's return for the vows on the peacock.[31] Since Juno rides into the *Filocolo* on a peacock cart, what could be more natural than for her to be remembered again when, later in the book, a peacock comes back? Under

chariot pulled by "Juno's birds." Although Alan's English translator calls them doves, they must be peacocks. See Alan of Lille, *Plaint of Nature,* trans. James J. Sheridan (Toronto: Pontifical Institute of Medieval Studies, 1980), 108.

30. Ovid *Met.* 1.720–23: "Arge, iaces, quodque in tot lumina lumen habebas, / exstinctum est, centumque oculos nox occupat una. / Excipit hos volucrisque suae Saturnia pennis / collocat et gemmis caudam stellantibus inplet."

31. Io's seduction was one of Boccaccio's favorite myths, recalled not just in the *Filocolo* but over and over throughout his writings. Twice he finds occasion to retell the whole of her tale: when the warriors process in the *Teseida,* Mercury's son Evander carries a historiated shield that triggers an ekphrasis about the cow-maid (see *Teseida* 7.38 and gloss); and in the *Amorosa visione* (37.1–42), the daughter of Inachus returns for a longish visit in Love's triumph, among worldly pleasures painted inside the castle that are attractive to the narrator errant. The tale of Io is also recalled when, notwithstanding his rustic background, Ameto realizes that when he hears Emilia's song, it sounds dulcet in his ears, as Mercury's had to Argus (*Ameto* 35.1). When Madonna Fiammetta argues in the *Elegia* (chap. 1) how far superior are her sufferings to those experienced by women of yore, Io heads the grim rundown of such ancient miserables as Myrrha, Dido, and Phaedra. *De mulieribus claris* (7) also nods to Argus in the biography of Io (Isis), although there Boccaccio suppresses the watchman's afterlife as a peacock, since his aim is to write learned histories, not myth and fable. Finally, the chapter on Juno in his *Genealogies of the Gentile Gods* explains in passing why the peacock is her bird (9.1): "Avem etiam pavonem in tutelam eius dixere, caude cuius, eam, Argi pastoris sui, occisi a Mercurio, oculos apposuisse dicit Ovidius" [They also said the bird in her tutelage is the peacock; on its tail Ovid says she put the eyes of her shepherd Argus after he had been killed by Mercury]. At this late date, however, Boccaccio edits out what must have seemed an unacceptable poetic lie. Her peacock "conductors" have now vanished, and she soars through the skies in the grander style of another antiquity newly reborn, the horse-drawn chariot of Homer's *Iliad.*

altered circumstances, to be sure, the bird in its second appearance still would not have looked like the image that might come to our mind's eye in the twentieth century—pullet plumped supine on its serving plate, stripped to the indignity of bare breast and drumsticks. Instead, the peacock presented by Biancifiore would have been close to life in its culinary death, wired to sit tall with head high, and artfully reclothed in its brilliant plumage.[32]

Stable as Juno's attribute ever since Ovid, peafowl feathers could ruffle to display different symbolic hues. Their changeant reflects Juno, whom scholars from late antiquity, including Boccaccio, had invested with several mythographic personalities: the element air (or earth and water), a patron of marriage and childbirth, a goddess who fosters riches and power.[33] To these facets of hers our canonist added yet another, one he himself seems to have invented, when he brought her down to the *Filocolo* as a personification of the Catholic Church. For Felice's banquet, however, he returns to poetic tradition, invoking Juno as tutelar of marriage.

In that role, as Ovid told, she was notable for her absence at the ill-omened wedding of Tereus and Procne, and she could not attend disconsolate Ianthe's scheduled unisex ceremony until Isis had magically provided the groom.[34] To this same Juno Dido and Anna pay special devotions at their local temple, "for the ties of marriage lie in her care." Soon afterward, Juno schemes to scotch the continuation of Aeneas's journey with a stormy matrimonial ambush.[35] Boccaccio, who quotes Virgil's verses in his *Genealogies,* there connects Juno with marriage in various ways, citing Plautus, Terrence, Albericus, Fulgentius, and Macrobius. For example, in a lunar aspect, either she is Juno Domiduca, because her

---

32. According to the culinary historian Barbara Ketcham Wheaton ("How to Cook a Peacock," *Harvard Magazine,* Nov.–Dec., 1979, 63–65), peacock was "the ultimate medieval display dish." Recipes for their preparation are plentiful. Her reconstruction of the bird encloses its cooked parts within the carcass, preserved as an armature over which to resew the skin with its feathers. She recommends as finishing touches gilding the beak and inserting glass eyes. Photographs show the final product, a remarkably lifelike bird complete with crest and full tail feathers. Peacock began to decline as fare in Europe in the sixteenth century, when turkeys imported from Mexico were discovered to be meatier and better flavored. Flemish genre painting of the seventeenth century still preserves examples of replumed peacocks on dinner platters; see, e.g., Willem Buytewech, *Merry Company in the Open Air,* in *Masters of Seventeenth-Century Dutch Genre Painting,* ed. Peter C. Sutton et al. (Philadelphia: University of Pennsylvania Press, 1984), pl. 5.

33. See *Genealogie* 9.1 for Boccaccio's entry on Juno and all her attributes.

34. Ovid *Met.* 6.428–29, 9.762–63.

35. Virgil *Aen.* 4.59, 125.

light helps "lead home" new brides discreetly in the night (that is, it accompanies them to the groom's house for defloration), or she is Lucina, invoked in childbirth. Initially, though, she is the goddess of marriage because she fosters wealth and therefore makes possible the dowry, financial backing essential if a woman were to enter into matrimony.[36]

The gifts promised Juno's peacock in the *Filocolo,* among them date palms blossoming with golden bezants, will dower the orphan Biancifiore. Juno personally keeps watch over the maiden, especially in direst straits, and the last time Florio invokes her, he addresses her as "Giunone, la quale con felice legame congiungni e servi longevi i santi matrimonii" [Juno, you who with happy tie join and preserve holy marriages long-lastingly] (5.34). Throughout the *Filocolo,* in fact, Juno in her secular identity is Juno Pronuba, the goddess of marriage. That is why marriage becomes the subject of the vows on her peacock. Around that episode remain traces of a debt to the Old French legends of Alexander the Great, but Boccaccio classicizes Jacques de Longuyon with his erudition as a mythographer. For military feats and courtesies, deeds all endued with medieval chivalry, he finds a substitution from ancient culture and brings to Juno's "holy bird" vows for a bride-to-be.

The banquet dish that in earlier versions of the tale of Florio and Biancifiore had been simply a prop, the medium needed for a false accusation of murder, gains with Boccaccio full symbolic force. Before, whether the seneschal cooked up larded venison or a hen or just plain generic roast really did not matter. The point was that it be soaked in poison, as a taster at the credenza would prove. In the *Filocolo* that culinary detail is an item most calculated; nothing will do but peafowl. While seeding Boccaccio's narrative for Biancifiore's wedding, it glides about the table on her tray as the hopeful sign of Juno Pronuba. This platter, over which one knight promises an escort of "conductors" as splendid as Juno's, must remind us of the goddess we saw at the beginning of the *Filocolo.* Traveling by air with a mighty team of peacocks, she was Juno Ecclesia. At the same time,

---

36. *Genealogie* 9.1 (p. 438): "Coniugiorum autem deam volunt, eo quod ut plurimum dote media eatur in coniugium, que dos iuris Junonis est." Boccaccio credits an impressive range of authorities in his chapter on Juno, among them Martianus Capella, for whose marriage of Mercury and Philology Juno plays an important part. The derivation of her name also associates her with brides and childbirth, as Isidore had declared (*Etym.* 8.11.69): "Junonem dicunt quasi ianonem, id est, ianuam, pro purgationibus feminarum, eo quod quasi portas matrum natorum pandat, et nubentum maritis" [they say *Juno,* almost *Jano,* that is, *janua,* or "portals," for the purgations of women because, as it were, she opens the doors of mothers for giving birth and to brides for their husbands].

Boccaccio's lethal bird anticipates later sequences in the romance when the barons fulfill their vaunts, remembering and repeating what once they swore. In its twin thrust, both retrospective and prospective, the part of the tale containing the vows on the peacock is an episode through which pass connecting lines that harness, so to speak, all the far-flung peacock references in the *Filocolo*. Taken together, they can readily accommodate in the same mythic persona both Juno Pronuba and Juno Ecclesia. To see the connections, we must sort the strands. These wind from peacocks in the flesh to peacocks in the spirit, from pagan myth to Christian allegory.

Quite another peacock, neither dray foul nor toxic fare, appears in a work Boccaccio composed at midcareer, his *Little Treatise in Praise of Dante* (1351–55). In this first full-length biography ever written of Dante Alighieri, the bird again manifests itself to symbolic purposes. Luckily, Boccaccio himself explains what this peacock means. From his allegoresis we can extract clues that make it possible to identify the scientific and theological traditions from which he had culled his information. It is lore that will lead through a medieval labyrinth of ideas around the bird. As we emerge on the other side, we can revisit "Juno's bird" in the *Filocolo* armed with the resources to interpret its Christian resonance.

   True to form for the life of a poet, this vita opens with a miraculous sign of future greatness, revealed to Dante's mother in a dream shortly before his birth. The expectant woman seemed to see herself beneath a laurel in a meadow beside a fountain, where she bore a son who took nourishment from the tree's berries and fountain waters. He became a shepherd and tried to pluck leaves from the tree. In the effort he fell, but then he rose again, transformed from a man into a peacock. No one at the time could guess what such a prodigy might foretell. Now, with the advantage of hindsight, Boccaccio relieves our curiosity at the close of his *Trattatello*. The laurel is poetry, to which Dante was destined from birth by heavenly disposition; its fruits are the books and doctrines of poets, and the wellspring is philosophy. That the child became a shepherd signifies that his writings provide guidance for our soul and intellect. His reach for the tree's leaves means he wished for the laurel crown; and his fall, the one that must come to us all, is death. By the metamorphosis from shepherd to peacock we are to understand Dante's "posterità"—what came after him, the *Comedy* that rose following his death to preserve his name among future generations.

   Pressing the comparison, Boccaccio finds four points of likeness between Dante's poem and the peacock.

Il paone, secondo che comprendere si può, ha queste proprietà: che la sua carne è odorifera e incorruttibile; la sua penna è angelica, e in quella ha cento occhi; li suoi piedi son sozzi, e tacita l'andatura; e, oltre a ciò, ha sonora e orribile voce: le quali cose con la *Comedia* del nostro poeta ottimamente si convengono.

[The peacock, as we can understand, has these properties: its flesh is odoriferous and incorruptible; its plumage is angelic and in it are one hundred eyes; its feet are filthy and its gait quiet, and beyond that, it has a piercing horrible voice, which things optimally suit the *Comedy* of our poet.] (*Trattatello* 2.151)[37]

At its allegorical level, where lies hidden what Boccaccio calls the moral or theological "sense," the *Divine Comedy* holds "immutable truth," which, like peacock flesh, is a substance of "incorruptible sweetness," immune to decay. On its surface, at the literal level, the poem has beauty comparable to the peafowl's feathers, a covering of plumage deemed "angelic." The story told in the *Comedy,* as rare and beautiful as ever conceived, occupies one hundred cantos, exactly the same as the number of eyes that peacocks are said to have in their tails. Corresponding to the bird's "ugly feet" and "quiet gait" are the poet's verses, or metrical "feet," composed in plain vernacular with a "lowly" style, the level suited to comedy. Finally, the peacock voice, a frightful screech that lent the bird its Latin name (said to be from *pavor,* "fear"), finds a moral counterpart in Dante's harsh judgments, delivered as terrifying invective against faults of living and dead. "For which thing and for the others demonstrated above," Boccaccio concludes, "it is most obvious that he who, while living, was a shepherd, after death became a peacock, as we can believe was shown by divine inspiration to his dear mother."

Boccaccio's allegoresis collects a wealth of lore, secular as well as sacred, and all from sources unacknowledged. One vein we recognize from Ovid, whose Argus accounts for the parallel between the number of "eyes" on peacock tails and cantos in the *Commedia.* But for the bird's other attributes—incorruptible flesh, foul feet and silent step, angelic feathers, a frightfully screeching voice—matters are more complex. A good place to start is Boccaccio's mature portrait of Juno in the *Genealogies of the Gentile Gods.* For the ancients, he says, she was "above all goddess of king-

---

37. For a longer exposition on Dante's mother's dream, see the more compendious first version of the *Trattatello,* ed. Ricci, 1.208–27.

doms and riches." To back that up, he cites the fifth-century mythographer Fulgentius, who explained her patronage of these things in his allegorical glosses on the Judgment of Paris. Fulgentius writes that Minerva and Venus, with their offerings of wisdom and love, stand for the contemplative and voluptuary lives in that fable, while Juno is "in charge of the active life, for Juno is named for getting ahead (a iuuando)." He continues:

> She is said to rule over dominions, because this kind of life is so much concerned with riches; she is also depicted with a scepter, because riches and dominions are close kin. They say that Juno has her head veiled, because all riches are always hidden; they choose her as the goddess of birth, because riches are always productive and sometimes abortive. They also place the peacock under her patronage, because the whole acquisitive life of power is always looking to adorn its appearance; and as the peacock adorns its front by spreading out in a curve the star-spangled sweep of its tail, and thereby shamelessly exposes its rear, so the striving for riches and renown is alluring for the moment but eventually exposes itself.[38]

Thanks to Fulgentius, Juno's peacock took on a pejorative meaning, which stuck through the later Middle Ages. Among those who transmitted the word on its deceptively fine plumes was the Third Vatican Mythographer, known to Boccaccio as Albericus. "Albericus" follows Fulgentius closely.

> They also assert that Juno is the mistress of riches. . . . She has the peacock in her tutelage because the life of wealth is always hungry for adornment. And as the peacock adorns its anterior parts by concavely spreading the starred curve of its tail and thereby foully denudes its posterior ones; so riches and worldly glory are adornments for a moment but in the end leave naked those whom they had adorned.[39]

Finally, the mythographers' peacock, its reputation splotched by association with the Juno of riches, migrates back full circle to its Ovidian hatch-

---

38. Fabius Planciades Fulgentius, *Fulgentius the Mythographer,* trans. Leslie George Whitbread (Columbus: Ohio State University Press, 1971), 65–66.
39. G. H. Bode, ed., *Scriptores rerum mythicarum latini tres* (1834; reprint, Hildesheim: Georg Olms, 1968), Mythographus 3.4.5.

ing grounds. Once salvaged from the lifeless body of Io's pastoral chaper-
one and placed so benevolently by Juno on her bird, the eyes of Argus
carry for the anonymous fourteenth-century versifier of *Ovide moralisé* all
the parlous appeal of the money with which the queen of heaven had
hoped to entice Paris. After relating the tale of Io and her guard, Ovid's
moralizer gets on to the really important matter.

> . . . Or veon
> Que ceste fable senefie.
> De richesce et de seignorie
> Est Juno deese et roïne,
> Et tous li mondes li encline,
> Quar tous li mondes s'estudie
> d'aquerre avoir et seignorie:
> C'est or li propos plus eslis.
> Les iues sont les mondains delis,
> Dont li paons se glorefie.
> Li paons home senefie,
> Plains d'orgueil et d'outrecuidance.

[. . . Now let's see what this fable signifies. Of riches and lordship is
Juno goddess and queen. And everybody inclines toward them,
because everybody tries to acquire possessions and power. Nowadays it is the most favored goal. The eyes are worldly delights,
wherein the peacock glories. The peacock signifies man, full of pride
and foolishness.]

The commentator explains that when Juno's bird "makes a wheel of his
tail," then he is most typical of men who want to be called "Mister" and
"Lord" as they mindlessly pursue food, clothes, beds, riches, and honor.
As he displays this gaudy train, a peacock forgets all about his ugly feet,
which are "his end" [sa fin]. At death, as a consequence, like the body part
under his tail, the peacock's soul will be shamefully ugly and naked.
Imparting an obvious lesson, the commentator concludes:

> . . . Pas ne deüst
> Avoir tant sa coë eslevee
> Quil en eüst s'ame afolee:
> Folz est qui pour l'avancement
> Dou cors met s'ame a dampnement.

[He never should have raised so high his tail that he trampled his soul. Mad is the man who for advancement of the body puts to damnation his soul.][40]

The vanity and pride that have here come to roost with riches and power predictably cloud Boccaccio's account of the peacock's bright fan in his *Genealogies*.

They assign the peacock to Juno's tutelage, so as to signify characteristics of rich men. For the peacock is a clamorous bird, in which they understand the clamors, elevated voices, boasting, and bellowing of rich men. The peacock also inhabits rooftops and always ascends to the higher reaches of buildings, as it seems that rich men crave all preeminences and seize whatever is not given them. It glitters all over with colored plumage and is delighted by praises, and to show itself off it goes so far as to raise its oculated tail in a circle and leaves its posterior parts nude and filthy. These things obviously designate the purple of rich men, and golden clothing, and vainglory, and futile pomp, ears open to adulations, things into which as many times as they heedlessly stumble, it happens that mayhaps the sordid part could be hidden, but it is exposed and there appears under that splendor a miserable heart exasperated with anxious cares; worthlessness, fatuousness, folly of habits, the smut of vices, and often bodies rotting with foul corruption.[41]

---

40. *Ovide moralisé*, ed. C. de Boer, *Verhandelingen der Koninklijke Akademie van Wetenschappen*, Afdeeling Letterkunde, n.s. 15 (1915): 1.4099–4150.

41. *Genealogie* 9.1 (pp. 439–40): "Pavonem vero illi [Junoni] in tutelam tribuunt, ut qualitates ostendantur divitum. Est enim clamosa avis pavo, in quo clamores, elatas voces, iactantiam, boatusque intelligunt divitum. Incolit et pavo tecta et edificiorum semper celsiora conscendit, ut appareat divites preminentias omnes appetere, atque si non dentur arripere. Picta insuper penna nitet undique, et laudibus delectatur, et ad ostentationem sui adeo trahitur, ut erecta in girum oculata cauda, nuda atque turpia posteriora relinquat. Per que purpura divitum, et vestis aurea, et inanis gloria, et futilis pompa, aures adulationibus patule designantur, in quas quotiens minus advertentes incurrunt, evenit ut, quod forsan sordidum latere poterat, detegatur, et appareat splendore sub illo cor miserum, curis anxiis lacessitum, ignavia, stultia, morum ineptia, viciorum spurcities, et non nunquam cadavera turpi marcentia tabo." Predictably, the peacock as an invidious term of comparison for female vanity makes appearances in Boccaccio's unflattering portraits of the widow in the *Corbaccio* and of amorous Fiammetta in the *Elegia di madonna Fiammetta*. Recall, from the latter, this statement (1.4): "E mentre che tutta mi mirava, non altramente che il pavone le sue penne . . . non so come, uno fiore della mia corona . . . cadde in terra" [And while I was admiring myself all over, no differently than the peacock does its feathers . . . I know not how, a flower from my crown . . . fell to earth] (my trans.). Fiammetta is too foolish to realize that this omen betokens pride before a fall.

Contrary to what evolutionary biology now can confirm—that peacocks display and shiver their trains to preserve their species, and that those with the most elaborate tails, hence the most eyespots, are males that peahens find most attractive for mating[42]—to Boccaccio and his colleagues in mythography, conspicuous feathers portend death of the worst kind.

Whereas Ovid's moralizers branded Juno's bird with worldly vanity, another tradition from pagan times was to pass into the Christian era and privilege the peacock with a very different value. In its Christian glory, the bird-of-the-long-tail acquired meaning as an emblem of eternal afterlife. Clearly, Dante's metamorphosis is a "resurrection" with such positive connotations. How that iconography evolved from antiquity into the Common Era has not yet been fully traced, but one authority often cited (wrongly) as its source is Saint Augustine, whose curious testimonial from the *City of God* was surely known to Boccaccio. Wrestling with the paradox of eternal damnation in all-consuming hellfire, Augustine asks why bodies of the damned do not perish but survive whole to suffer their punishment. This apparent impossibility finds contradiction in the salamander, who lives in flames, and in Mount Etna, which can burn yet remain intact. Likewise, asks Augustine, "who if not God, the creator of all things, has granted to the flesh of the dead peacock immunity from decay?" Augustine personally verified this wondrous natural phenomenon when once at Carthage he was served a roast peacock. He sampled some of it, then more again twice within the next month, and amazingly he was still able to eat from the same bird a full year later. Although drier and shrunken a bit, the flesh had not yet spoiled.[43]

Did Augustine's peacock really last a year? Or did he embroider the story, taking cues from ancient books on animal science, to drive home more effectively his belief in endless hellfires? Whatever his motives for inserting this marvel into the great apology for monotheistic Christianity,

---

42. Marion Petrie, Tim Halliday, and Carolyn Sanders, "Peahens Prefer Peacocks with Elaborate Trains," in *Animal Behavior* 41 (1991): 323–31. Peacocks gather to form leks on mating sites, where they purposely raise their train into a fan to expose their genitalia—that "foul posterior" of which the mythographers speak. A female approaches a male from the rear, then walks around in front of him, after which he makes a "hoot-dash" toward her. The variable that determines whether she accepts him for copulation or not, as this British research group has documented, is train morphology. In ten out of eleven mating sequences observed, the female chose among the several males she had visited the one with the highest eyespot number. I thank Tim Halliday for telling me of this research when we met at the Rockefeller Center, Bellagio.

43. Augustine, *De civitate Dei contra paganos,* trans. William M. Green, 7 vols., Loeb Classical Library (Cambridge: Harvard University Press, 1972), 26.4: "Quis enim nisi Deus creator omnium dedit carni pavonis mortui ne putesceret?"

he probably had indeed dined on peacock. The wealthy ate it in the Latin West, more for fashionable exoticism than for the gustatory qualities of its flesh, which is actually quite tough. Livy relates that the first person to serve it in Rome was the orator Hortensius at the inaugural banquet of his priesthood in the first century B.C. The fattening of peacocks, he further reports, was instituted by one Marcus Aufidias Lurco, who made a profit of sixty thousand sesterces in the trade.[44] Even before the period that producer is said to have ventured into the business (ca. 67 B.C.), Cicero was happily "disposing" of these birds at a rate he jocularly claimed surpassed normal rhythms of "squablet" consumption, and the same orator, who tells of turning, in forced retirement, to gastronomic refinement, can boast that he had even ventured successfully to serve a dinner for finical gourmets without including a peacock.[45] Varro, recalling when people began to raise the birds for market, reiterates Livy's note on their pioneering breeder and encourages others to follow his lead, since "no bird is so profitable as the peacock." Still, he appends a disapproving note on Quintus Hortensius's lavish banquet, "an extravagance which was at that time commended only by the luxurious, not by men of virtue and prudence."[46] So fashionable did it become to serve this food that Horace could satirize the custom as conspicuous consumption, and the trend-setting Hortensius would be disparagingly remembered by Macrobius in later antiquity as a fop so notoriously extravagant that he irrigated his plane trees with wine.[47]

Regardless of its social appeal, though, peafowl was neither tender nor

---

44. Livy, *Ab urbe condita* 10.23.45.

45. Cicero, *Epistolae ad familiares* 9.18 and 9.20, in *Epistolae,* vol. 1, ed. L. C. Purser (1901; reprint, Oxford: Clarendon Press, 1979); trans. W. Glynn Williams, Loeb Classical Library (Cambridge: Harvard University Press, 1959).

46. Marcus Terentius Varro, *Varro on Farming,* trans. Lloyd Storr-Best (London: G. Bell and Sons, 1912), 3.6. Varro recommends feeding them barley—a peck every month, with more in the breeding season. The yield should be three chicks per hen. Columella (8.11.3) tells how to house them, in raised structures that prevent serpents from entering. They should have a clean outdoor walking space. Their droppings can be used for fertilizer and chicken litter.

47. Horace, *Satires* 2.2, in *Satires and Epistles of Horace,* trans. Smith Palmer Bovie (Chicago: University of Chicago Press, 1959), "But once you've been offered a peacock, I'll never root out / Your urge to brush your palate with this, and not chicken. / You are taken in by appearance, the conspicuous expense / Of a rare bird who puts on a show with his colorful tail." Macrobius, *The Saturnalia,* trans. Percival Vaughan Davies (New York and London: Columbia University Press, 1969), 3:13. Peacock eggs were also prize fare; see Helmut Lother, *Der Pfau in der altchristlichen Kunst* (Leipzig: Dieterich, 1929), 47. More on peacocks in Roman cuisine can be found in Maria Luisa Incontri Lotteringhi della Stufa, *Desinari e cene: Dai tempi remoti alla cucina toscana del XV secolo* (Florence: Editoriale Olimpia, 1965), 19–30. She mentions a dish said by Suetonius to have been ordered by Vitellius consisting of pheasant and peacock brains.

succulent. Hence Galen could warn about difficulty in digesting this hard, fibrous meat, and ancient cookbooks reflect the problem when they suggest preparing it as mincemeat or encased in a crust to keep it moist. Although we do not have the recipe for peacock by Apicius, we do know how he rated the bird: "Entrees of peacock occupy the first rank, provided they be dressed in such manner that the hard and tough parts be tender." Had his instructions for cooking it survived, one can speculate that they might have gravitated toward the rubric "Treatment of strong smelling birds of every description," that is, those whose "goatish smell" will be masked by a mulch of spices "and the fat preserved, if you envelop them in a dough of flour and oil before baking them in the oven."[48]

From antiquity until well into the Renaissance, thanks to other manuals on food and health, such as the *Tacuinum sanitatis,* the practice of breeding and eating peacock persisted. Only with the discovery of the New World would peacocks go out of fashion, supplanted by an import more tender and succulent, the "turkey." Baldassare Pisanelli, a medical doctor from Bologna, synthesizes the scientific tradition in his manual on food and drink of 1611.

> Peacock is difficult to digest, and so its meat can be preserved for a long time, and Saint Augustine reports having eaten of the meat of the peacock and that it had lasted a year. Its meat is harder than that of other birds, and so they must be taken for eating when they are very young and tenderish, in the winter, after their bodies have been aired for many days. And the peacock is of mean complexion and vile feeding habits, and it increases melancholy amazingly and induces sadness in the spirit. One must drink excellent wine with it. In its third year the peacock becomes pregnant, and it lives twenty-five years. So envious is the bird that it eats its dung to keep people from using it to advantage. Alexander the Great set a very stiff

---

48. Galen was the first to report in the literature (second century) that peacock flesh is particularly hard and fibrous, hence harder to digest than the meat of other birds (*De alimentorum facultatibus* 3.18). This notice, however, seems not to have widely circulated (see Lother, *Der Pfau in der altchristlichen Kunst,* 27, 47). The next-best entrees, Apicius lists as follows: "the second place in the estimation of the gourmets have dishes made of rabbit, third spiny lobster, fourth comes chicken, and fifth young pig"; see Apicius, *Cookery and Dining in Imperial Rome,* ed. and trans. Joseph Dommers Vehling (New York: Dover, 1977), 66, 147. A twentieth-century chef verifies that the lean bird produces but scanty juices, and she describes its roast meat as "dry, chewy, and rather dull" (Wheaton, "How to Cook a Peacock").

penalty for whoever killed a peacock. The first person who served peacock at table as food was Quintus Hortensius the Roman orator, a man most addicted to gluttony.[49]

Hyperbolic though it may sound, what Augustine said about the unusual durability of his roasted bird may have had some basis in fact.

---

49. Composed in the eleventh century by Ibn Butlan el Bagdadi and translated into Latin in the thirteenth at the court of King Manfred of Sicily, the *Tacuinum sanitatis,* or *Guide to Good Health,* was a kind of illustrated encyclopedia for practical living, with information on the properties and uses of plants, animals, and minerals. Under each entry were typically five categories: the nature of the thing, the thing at its best, its benefits, its contraindications, and how to render it as innocuous as possible. Concerning peacocks, it pronounces: "Of nature hot and moist in the second degree. They are best when young. They are good for hot stomachs. They are harmful for people with digestive problems. They can be rendered less harmful if they are suspended by the neck with some heavy object tied to their feet and left that way for one day." See *Tacuinum sanitatis, Codex 2396 der Österreichischen Nationalbibliothek, Wien, Enchiridon virtutum vegetabilium, animalium, mineralium rerumque omnium explicans naturam iuvamentum nocumentum remotionemque nocumentorum eorum, Autore anonymo* (Graz: Akademische Druck und Verlagsanstalt, 1985), s.v. "Pavones," 48. See also Brucia Witthoft, "The *Tacuinum sanitatis:* Studies in Secular Manuscript Illumination in Late Fourteenth-Century Lombardy" (Ph.D. diss., Harvard University, 1973). See further Baldassare Pisanelli, *Trattato della natura de' cibi et del bere* (Venice: Domenico Imberti, 1611), 93–94: "Il Pauone è difficil digestione, e però lungamente la sua carne si conserua, e S. Agostino riferisce hauer mangiato della carne del Pauone, e c'haueua durato vn'anno: e la sua carne più dura, che quella de gli altri augelli, e però si deueno prendere per mangiare, che siano molto giouani, e tenerelli; e che sia d'inuerno, e che siano stati morti all'aria per molti giorni. E il Pauone di cattiua complessione, e di tristo nutrimento, et accresce mirabilmente la melanconia, et induce tristezza all'animo. Beuasi apparesso di quello vino ottimo. Il Pauone all'anno terzo s'ingrauida, e viue venticinque anni. Mangia il suo sterco, perche l'huomo non ne caui vtile, tant'è inuidioso. Alessandro Magno pose grandissima pena a chi ammazzaua vn Pauone. Il primo che ponesse il Pauone nelle tauole per cibo fu Quinto Hortensio Oratore Romano, huomo deditissimo alla gola." Dr. Pisanelli cites information that goes back as far as Pliny and was transmitted into such medieval encyclopedias as Bartholomaeus Anglicus's *De proprietatibus rerum* (18). See, e.g., Bartholomaeus Anglicus, *Natural History,* trans. H. Rackham, Loeb Classical Library (Cambridge: Harvard University Press, 1967), 10.22: Most beautiful of all birds, the peacock delights in admiring its tail, but "when it moults its tail feathers every year with the fall of the leaves, it seeks in shame and sorrow for a place of concealment until others are born again with the spring flowers." Pliny characterizes the bird as both ostentatious and spiteful. That nastiness can explain why, in Pisanelli's profile, the bird plays dog-in-the-manger and eats its own dung. That strange characteristic, which explains why peacock droppings are never to be found, had not passed unnoticed among earlier compendiasts. The Franciscan Marcus of Orvieto authored a *Liber de moralitatibus* (ca. 1290) that most disapprovingly relates the peacock's dung eating to human selfishness; see John Block Friedman, "Peacocks and Preachers: Analytic Technique in Marcus of Orvieto's *Liber de moralitatibus,* Vatican lat. MS 5935," in *Beasts and Birds of the Middle Ages,* ed. Willene B. Clark and Meradith T. McMunn (Philadelphia: University of Pennsylvania Press, 1989), 179–96.

Thanks in part to his account, to lore transmitted as natural philosophy, and to the continuing custom of eating the bird, in the Middle Ages knowledge of its resilience was a commonplace that turned up in scholarly compendiums practically wherever peacocks did. So, in the seventh century, Isidore of Seville knows their immunity to putrefaction, which makes them tough to cook, and he derives *pavo* (peacock) from *pavor* (fear), because the bird's voice is frighteningly shrill: "The peacock has its name from the sound of its voice; its flesh is so hard that it scarcely suffers spoilage, and it is not easily cooked. Concerning it a certain person says (Martial 13.[72]): 'Dost thou admire it, oft as it spreads its spangled wings, and hast the heart, unfeeling man, to deliver this bird to a cruel cook?'"[50]

Some two hundred years afterward, Rabanus Maurus passes on the same information in his encyclopedia, but he expands his purview to the peafowl with many-colored tails fetched from afar by Solomon. They figure in parallel passages of the Bible, catalogued among precious objects collected by the king's fleet to adorn his holy temple in Jerusalem.

Once every three years the fleet of ships of Tarshish used to come bringing gold, silver, ivory, apes, and peacocks. (1 Kings 10:22)

For the king's ships went to Tarshish with the servants of Huram; once every three years the ships of Tarshish used to come bringing gold, silver, ivory, apes, and peacocks. (2 Chronicles 9:21)

Rabanus, allegorizing his Old Testament, opines that the peacock "signifies the gentile people coming from distant parts of the earth to Christ, who also by his grace are resplendent with the ornament of many virtues."[51]

Solomon's peacocks prompt a related analysis in Walafrid Strabo's *Glossa ordinaria* on the Bible, a medieval compendium of reference that

---

50. Isidore *Etym.* 12.7.48: "Pavo nomen de sono vocis habet; suius caro tam dura est ut putredinem vix sentiat, nec facile coquatur. De quo quidam sic ait (Mart. 13.70): Miraris, quotiens gemmantes explicat alas, / si potes hunc saevo tradere, dure, coco." Cf. Martial, *Epigrams,* trans. Walter C. A. Ker, Loeb Classical Library, 2 vols. (Cambridge: Harvard University Press, 1947–50).

51. Rabanus Maurus, "De bestiis," in *De universo libri XXII, Patrologia latina* 111:247–48: "Pavo nomen de sono vocis habet. Cujus caro tam dura est, ut putredinem vix sentiat, nec facile coquatur. De quo quidam sic ait. . . ."; on the bird in allegory: "significat populum gentilem de longinquis partibus terrae ad Christem venientem, qui etiam ejus gratia multarum virtutum ornatu risplendet."

had assumed its "standard" form by the mid-twelfth century. Those treasures, still as resistant to decay as Augustine remembered, retain for the exegetes their status as an item for cooking, but now to moral rather than palatal perfection. Scholars continue to report that the peacock's flesh remains unputrifiable if dried, and they can associate the pulchritude of the feathers in which it is clothed with the beauty of virtuous behavior, albeit with some ambivalence about the adornment. Commentary on 2 Chronicles finds a positive meaning in the peacock's display of caudal plumes, whose colors in this context do not imply the greed and vainglory that made the mythographers so leery of its splendor. Still, to strut one's feathers—no matter how many good deeds they may imply—is less than ideal Christian comportment for those who take the longer view: "The peacock who shows off his admired feathers signifies those who for the praises of men display the beauty of various virtues, but the preachers learned in doctrine teach that we should benefit from the knowledge of God alone and desire the delights of the eternal kingdom."[52]

Mythography, natural science, and scriptural exegesis all flow together into the most compendious medieval sources on peafowl, the bestiaries, collections of moralized animal lore that clearly fascinated Boccaccio from the time he composed his first fiction, *Diana's Hunt.* One example from the twelfth century, a member of the *Physiologus* family once attributed to Hugh of Saint-Victor, finds much hopeful potential in the bird's feathers, claiming that they announce virtuous fortitude and foresight pertaining to life beyond death. Acknowledging Isidore, this authority derives *pavo* from *pavor,* because the fowl's vocal stridency strikes sudden fear into all who hear it. Concerning the peacock's other characteristics, our anonymous text continues:

It has tough meat, resistant to putrefaction, which can scarcely be cooked by a chef in fire or by hepatic heat in the stomach. Such are the minds of the strong doctors, which neither the flame of cupidity burns nor the heat of sexual desire kindles. The peacock has a terrible voice, a simple step, a serpentine head, and a sapphire breast; it also has on its wings some reddish feathers; it has a long tail, such that, as I might say, it seems to be full of eyes. The peacock has, I say,

---

52. *Glossa ordinaria* (*Patrologia latina* 113:680) (on 2 Paralip. 9:21): "Pavo qui laudatas ostendit pennas eos significat qui propter laudes hominum variarum virtutum species ostantant, sed praedicatores doctrina instructi, discuntur benefacere intuitu solius Dei, et aptantur aeterni regis deliciis."

a terrible voice, as when the preacher warns sinners about the inextinguishable fire of Gehenna. It walks simply, as often as in its deeds
it does not exceed humility. . . . The sapphire color on its breast designates heavenly desire in the human mind. The red color signifies
love of contemplation. . . . The length of its tail points to the length
of future life. The fact that it seems to have eyes in its tail pertains to
what every doctor foresees, the danger that is imminent to individu-
als in the end.[53]

Throughout Europe, bestiaries echo the theology in this zoology. Early
in the thirteenth century, Peter of Beauvais can liken the bird's colorful
feathers to diverse virtues, its sapphire craw to humanity's desire for
heaven, and its long tail to life without end. The tail's eyes may be either
the doctor of the church who foresees the danger menacing the last days of
us all, as it had been for Pseudo Hugh of Saint Victor, or the preacher who
threatens sinners with fire and brimstone. When opened, the fan resembles
prelates who puff themselves up in vainglory; they should rather keep their
feathers down and dedicate themselves to honorable deeds.[54]

  Not surprisingly, the single feature of the peacock most fraught with
significance among its commentators is the tail, with its eerie and wonderful eyes. Those natural markers, magnetic in the bird's mating dance, had

---

53. For extensive discussion of Boccaccio's debt to the bestiaries, see Cassell and
Kirkham, *Diana's Hunt,* introd. and commentary passim. Pseudo-Hugh of Saint Victor, *De
bestiis et aliis rebus, Patrologia latina* 177:52–53: "Duras habet carnes, et putredini
resistentes, quae vix a coque coquuntur igni, vel a calore hepatis coqui possunt in stomacho.
Tales sunt fortium doctorum mentes, quas nec flamma cupiditatis exurit, nec calor libidinis
accendit. Habet pavo vocem terribilem, incessum simplicem, caput serpentinum, pectus sap-
pirinum, habet etiam in alis plumas aliquantulum ruffas, habet caudam longam, et ut, ita
dicam, quasi oculis plenam. Habet, inquam, pavo vocem terribilem, quando praedicator pec-
catoribus comminatur inextinguibilem gehennae ignem. Simpliciter incedit, quoties in
operibus suis humilitatem non excedit. . . . Color vero sapphirinus in pectore, coeleste
desiderium designat in humana mente. Color ruffus amorem significat contemplationis. . . .
Longitudi caudae longitudinem innuit futurae vitae. Quod autem quasi oculos in cauda
habet, ad hoc pertinet quod unusquisque doctor praevidet, quod periculum in fine singulis
imminet." Florence McCullough places this bestiary in the *Physiologus* family of texts, in
Medieval Latin and French Bestiaries (Chapel Hill: University of North Carolina Press,
1960), 25–30. Her volume remains a basic reference tool on bestiaries in the Middle Ages.
Useful as a manual on the same general subject, with selected texts translated into modern
French, is Gabriel Bianciotto, ed., *Bestiaires du Moyen Age* (Paris: Stock, 1980). Cf. also the
collected essays in Willene B. Clark and Meradith T. McMunn, eds., *Beasts and Birds of the
Middle Ages* (Philadelphia: University of Pennsylvania Press, 1989).

54. *Bestiaire roman,* trans. E. de Solms (Paris: Zodiaque, 1977), s.v. "Paon."

from antiquity given the bird a literary epithet, "oculatus." Martianus Capella, for example, pressed this epithet into service as he described the assembled council of gods at the marriage of Mercury and Philology. Beside Juno his queen, "a strong defender and supporter of marriage," Jove presides, sitting on a folded robe woven with "oculate" peacock feathers.[55] Precisely the same adjective comes into play as Boccaccio describes Juno's descent in the opening words of the *Filocolo,* driving a chariot drawn by her "oculated birds" [gli occhiuti uccelli].

A clever, merely descriptive modifier for the mannerist Martianus, "oculate" became for medievals a property charged with morality. Pseudo-Hugh of Saint Victor had related the tail eyes "to what every learned man foresees"—the danger of damnation ahead for vainglorious man. Many an authority was to follow him. Whether those eyes could be sufficiently farsighted would depend on how the bird positioned the tail. Lifted in display, it betrays vanity, as Brunetto Latini typically notes, adding a mantissa on its meat: "whenever he sees men admiring his beauty, he raises his tail in a fan to have men's praise, and he uncovers his ugly rear part, which he mean-spiritedly shows them. He much despises the ugliness of his feet. And his flesh is fiercely hard and has a high odor."[56] Lowered, though, the tail bespeaks humility and implies the wisdom of "providence," or foresight, as other writers explain. Around the mid–thirteenth century, for example, Richard of Fournival taught in his *Bestiaires d'amour* how properly to read the oculate feathers.

> Fair, sweet God, how one must respect the man or woman who knows how to provide against obvious misfortune and, even more, against misfortune in the dim and distant future! This is clearly signified for us in the peacock's tail, as I heard previously. For it is true that a tail, insofar as it is to come (that is to say, is behind), signifies the obvious fact that those who travel along their way are not completely secure from evil men. And the person who wants to

---

55. Martianus Capella, *The Marriage of Mercury and Philology,* trans. William Harris Stahl, 2 vols. (New York: Columbia University Press, 1971), 1.66 (2:25).

56. Brunetto Latini, *Li Livres dou Tresor,* ed. Francis J. Carmody, University of California Publications in Modern Philology, no. 22 (Berkeley: University of California Press, 1948), book 1, 169: "la ou il voit les hommes ki remirent sa beauté, il drece sa coue contremont pour avoir les los des homes, et descuevre le laide part deriere, k'il lor moustre vilanement. Molt deprise le laidece de ses piés. Et sa char est dure fierement et de grant odour."

guard against them should not travel alone, but should travel with every provision to avoid surprise. The provident person is not quickly deceived. Oh God, what is this providence? In God's name, that peacock's tail, which has so many eyes that it is bound to look ahead in more than one way demonstrates providence well to me, the more sorts of eyes are signified and shown us on the tail. For it seems to me that if one wishes to provide for oneself, it is necessary to see above, below, beside, and across.[57]

With this lesson in mind, we can better appreciate why Ovid's French moralizer so shook his head over the outcome of Io's shepherd, Argus. In the contrast between peacock feathers and the body beneath, he saw a grim fate for whoever might fail to look beyond the plumage. His warning sets him squarely in the didactic mainstream. A Tuscan bestiary, also from the fourteenth century, apprises us of the problem.

The peacock is a beautiful bird with a large tail, the whole of it made resembling eyes, and its nature is such that it raises this beautiful tail above its head and makes of it a wheel and sets its mind on it and has great vainglory, and after it has thus vaingloried, it looks at its feet, which are very ugly, and right away it lowers its tail and shrinks back to nothing, because they are so ugly.[58]

---

57. Richard of Fournival, *Master Richard's Bestiary of Love and Response,* trans. Jeanette Beer (Berkeley: University of California Press , 1986), 48; *Li Bestiaires d'amours di Maistre Richart de Fornival e li Response du bestiaire,* ed. Cesare Segre (Milan: Ricciardi, 1957), 49–50: "le keuwe del paon signefie porveance, por chu ke keuwe, de tant comme ele est derirre, senefie che ki est a avenir, et chu ke elle est plaine d'els senefie le prendre garde de chu ki est a avenir. . . . Dont senefie keue perveance, et nomeement keue de paon, por les ieux ki i sont. Et por chu di jou ke ausi laide cose com che est de paon san keue, ausi grant poverte est ce d'omne sans porveance." Cf. Roberto Crespo, ed., *Una versione pisana inedita del Bestiaire d'amours* (Leiden: Universitaire Pers, 1972), 93–103: "ché la choda de lo paone significha provedensa perciò che choda, di tanto chome li è dirieto, significha quelle cose che sono a venire, perciò ch'è di penna, significha di prendere guardia de quelle cose che sono a venire" [for the tail of the peacock signifies foresight beause the tail, insofar as it is behind, signifies those things that are to come; because it is feathered, it signifies being watchful over those things that are to come].

58. M. S. Gower and K. McKenzie, "Il bestiario toscano secondo la lezione dei codici di Parigi e di Londra," *Studi Romanzi* 8 (1912): 1–100: "Lo paone si e uno bello uccello con grande coda e è tuta facta a simigliança d'occhi, e ave in se cotale natura ch'elli si driça questa bella coda sopra capo e fanne rota e ponsell'a mente e ave grande vanagloria; et da che ave vanagloriato così, elli si mira li piedi che sono molto laidi, inmantenenti abassa la coda e torna nyente veggiendo li piedi tanto sono laidi"; cf. K. McKenzie, "Unpublished Manuscripts of Italian Bestiaries," *PMLA* 20 (1905): 380–433.

This means, paradoxically, that man must have "foresight of past deeds in this life" [provedença de tutte le cose passate] to reconcile them with hopes for salvation in the next. Embarrassment suffered by the bird due to its ugly feet also shows in the Catalan *Bestiaris,* and so does the lesson imparted by the tail, which should make man examine his life to see if he has pleased God and warn him, vile creature that he is, not to take pride in worldly things.[59] Similarly, a Waldensian bestiary teaches how delight in its fine plumage prompts this bird to want to fly, but such impulses are quickly squelched by a glance at its hideous feet. They signify "the vileness of the flesh," as opposed to the tail eyes, which are the foresight ("prevesença") we must have in all we do.[60]

Whether moralized *in bono* or *in malo,* as virtue or as vanity, peacock plumes point in the Christian tradition to the state of our soul after death. Actually, associations between peafowl and an afterlife are far older than Augustine, and they substantially predate the Common Era. In Greece, peacocks had been popular from the time of Alexander the Great, who brought them from India in the fourth century, and from the late second century they appear stamped on coins with the goddess Hera. Romans continued to honor them with Hera's counterpart, Juno, in Pompeian wall paintings and on consecration coins for the empress. That bird symbolized her apotheosis, the same role played by the eagle for the emperor. In other words, it was a sign of her continuing life after death. A parallel tradition was transmitted by the Pythagoreans, who believed in metempsychosis and claimed that their founder himself had been reincarnated as a peacock. Legend had it that Homer's soul, like that of Pythagoras, had migrated into the same beautiful creature—at least, so we have it from Rome's first epic poet, Ennius (d. 169 B.C.). At the beginning of his *Annals,* he imagines that Homer appeared to him in a dream and revealed that he had lived in the body of a peacock.[61] Many centuries later, thanks to Boc-

---

59. *Bestiaris,* ed. Saverio Panaunzio (Barcelona: Barcino, 1963), 95–97. In the bestiary published by G. Mazzatinti in *Un bestiario moralizzato tratto da un manoscritto eugubino del secolo XIV* (Rome: Accademia dei Lincei, 1889), no. 46, the deflating sight of this bird's feet teaches that "Chi male fonda, mura en perdimento" [He who lays badly foundations builds walls to his loss].

60. Luciana Borghi Cedrini, *Appunti per la letttura di un Bestiario medievale: Il bestiario valdese* (Turin: G. Giappicelli, 1976), 17.

61. Nathanial Hawthorne still could muse on the peacock "once thought to have held the soul of Pythagoras" when he wrote the tale "A Virtuoso's Collection" in *Mosses from an Old Manse.* But an early Christian father like Tertullian excoriated such myths of metempsychosis, heaping special ridicule on the absurd idea of Homer's reincarnation, which he had read in the *Annals* by Ennius. He contended that he would not want to listen to poets even when awake, and he asked whether it is not, anyway, odd for one of them to claim he turned

caccio and another oneiric event, Dante Alighieri took his place as Italy's founding poet in the tradition of Homer and Ennius, finding life after death as a hundred-eyed "peacock" in the enduring art of his *Commedia.* Perennial favorites of poets for beauty and allegory, peacocks, from their oriental and pre-Christian origins, would survive with longevity in Western visual arts as well. To the end of the Renaissance, in forms monumental and miniature, they flourish doubly advantaged, being subjects both decorative and instructive. Given their early cultic associations with the afterlife, it was logical that they should find ground most receptive in funerary art. Present in Jewish grave sites from around the time of Christ, peafowl enter Christian catacombs at the end of the first century in abbreviated scenes that came to adumbrate Paradise. Favored subjects on paleo-Christian sarcophagi, they make their most colorful displays from the fifth century onward in Byzantine mosaics, of which numerous examples survive in the Italian sphere from Aquileia and Ravenna to North Africa. Boccaccio could have seen peacocks in church art at Rome, and he surely noticed them in the paleo-Christian baptistery at Naples; a keen reader of bestiaries, he would have readily understood their connotations of life eternal.[62]

---

into a bird with such a raucous voice. No matter how lovely the peacock, he argues, Homer's fame is more pleasing than any such feathers. Of course, he adds, if they like, poets can go right ahead and migrate into peacocks or swans. See *On the Soul,* chap. 33, in Tertullian, *The Apologetic Works,* trans. Rudolph Arbesmann et al. (New York: Fathers of the Church, 1950); Otto Skutsch, "Notes on Metempsychosis," in *Studia Enniana* (London: University of London, Athlone Press, 1968): 151–56. For the peacock in pagan religion and its appearance on coins, see Lother, *Der Pfau in der altchristlichen Kunst,* 27–28, 46; *Paulys Realencyklopädie classischen Altertumswissenschaft,* ed. Georg Wissowa, Wilhelm Kroll, and Karl Mittelhaus, vol. 19, pt. 2 (Stuttgart: J. B. Metzlerscher, 1894–1972), s.v. "Pfau."

62. In the beginning, the birds are fenced in a schematic garden with flowers, following Roman patrician fashion. Later they join various other scenes, hovering over a virgin in the Catacomb of Priscilla or above the Twelve Apostles in the Hypogeum of the Aurelii. See also the Catacomb of Panfilo. It is not clear exactly when these peacocks took on full meaning as symbols of the Resurrection and eternal life. The earliest examples, from the first and second centuries, may still be mostly decorative, but from the period of Diocletian (284–305), their gardenlike enclosures could represent Paradise (see Lother, *Der Pfau in der altchristlichen Kunst,* 57–70). Peacocks are prominent, for example, in the mosaics of Santa Maria Maggiore and San Clemente in Rome, on which see Joseph Wilpert and Walter N. Schumacher, *Die römischen Mosaiken der kirchlichen Bauten vom IV–XIII. Jahrhundert* (Freiburg: Herder, 1976); Heinrich Karpp, *Die Mosaiken in Santa Maria Maggiore zu Rom* (Baden-Baden: Bruno Grimm, 1966). The Museo Paleocristiano at Aquileia preserves mosaics with peacocks from the Chiesa della Beligna (fifth century). They are plentiful in the Byzantine art of Ravenna, appearing, for example, in mosaics at San Vitale (sixth century), where they appear both in profile and frontal with raised tail fan, and in the Archbishop's Chapel, where two of the birds, in sidelong view, confront the monogram of the bishop. At Venice, in the

Although the earlier Middle Ages authorized poses of the bird either frontal, with plumes triumphantly raised full circle, or in profile, with a characteristic crest and lowered, sweeping train, in time the former position lost out to the latter, doubtless because the mythographers had decreed that display of the circular tail fan was a telltale sign of pride and vanity. Both poses, characteristic of the bird in nature, are depicted in the chapter on "Peacocks" in a trecento manuscript of the widely reproduced *Tacuinum sanitatis,* or *Guide to Good Health,* composed in the eleventh century by Ibn Butlan el Bagdadi and translated in the thirteenth from Arabic to Latin at the court of King Manfred of Sicily. Scientific context authorized illustrations of the male bird in its two characteristic postures, as well as a representation of the peahen, very plainly feathered by comparison. In religious settings, however, by the twelfth century the long, low train prevailed. So we see it on two huge peacocks in profile that occupy the Earthly Paradise at the base of the great apse mosaic in the Roman church of San Clemente. With their crested heads and imposing tails reaching back in horizontal extension, they manage to stand even taller and longer than the two quadrupeds they flank at the foot of the Cross Triumphant, a pair of stags drinking from the Four Rivers of Eden.[63]

Eventually, by the Renaissance, the birds tend by preference to perch on elevated spots that allow their tail feathers not only to stretch long but

---

Basilica of Saint Mark, they are found both on an internal mosaic floor (thirteenth century) and in a detail of the atrium mosaic that represents Noah putting peacocks on the ark. More somberly, but always as signs of promise, they stand carved in Christian sarcophogi and altar screens. On the sarcophagus of Saint Ecclesius (Ravenna, San Vitale, mid–sixth century), stags flank a central cross, while behind them, in striking disproportion, two enormous peacocks convey their symbolic message. On the sarcophagus of the Archbishop Theodore (d. 691) at Sant'Apollinare in Classe, peacocks confront a disk containing the Chi-Rho emblem of the cross. Framed by a tracery of foilage, they embody hope for eternal life on the Lombard sarcophagus of Theodota (ca. 720), where they confront the Fountain of Life with a cross at its summit (Pavia, Museo Civico). The choir screen at Santa Maria Trastevere in Rome has a panel with peacocks at the font, and an eighth-century relief panel from San Salvatore at Atrani shows two peacocks frontal with tails raised in circular fans. See Arthur Haseloff, *Pre-Romanesque Sculpture in Italy,* trans. Ronald Boothroyd (New York: Hacker Art Books, 1971); Theodor Klauser, *Früchristliche Sarkophage in Bild und Wort* (Olten, Switzerland: Urs Graf-Verlag, 1966), 85–86. Peacocks often inhabit gospel book incipits and preside ornamentally over columns of illuminated canon tables or among foliate and zoomorphic forms in the margins. See Engelbert Kirschbaum, *Lexikon der Christlichen Ikonografie* (Rome: Herder, 1972), s.v. "Pfau"; George Galavaris, *The Illustrations of the Prefaces in Byzantine Gospels* (Vienna: Österreichischen Akademie dere Wissenschaften, 1979).

63. For a reproduction of the whole apse mosaic at San Clemente and brief discussion, see Cassell and Kirkham, *Diana's Hunt,* 44.

to hang low and point. Two similar Florentine renderings of the Last Supper frescoed by Domenico Ghirlandaio—one at the convent of San Marco, one in Ognissanti—take place in a room decorated, at far right, with a vase of roses on the molding and, just above, balanced on the window ledge, a large peacock. The bird looks away, out the arched opening at the rear, where other Edenic fowl, such as pheasant and partridge, fly among vegetation emblematic of Paradise, fruit-bearing orange trees, a date palm, and the long-lived cypress. As the bird turns away from the viewer, we see in sharp contrast to the whitewashed wall the colorful texture of his graceful hanging tail, which angles over to the treetops, as if to indicate eternal life. Carlo Crivelli poises the bird over the Virgin in his *Annunciation* of 1486 at the London National Gallery, its train flowing downward to magnificent length. Again we are reminded of what the bestiarists believed: "The length of its tail points to the length of future life." That gift will come through Mary and soon after Christ's last breaking of bread with his apostles. For both Ghirlandaio and Crivelli, we must suppose, the tail's thrust, feathers discretely gathered, implies the opposite of vanity, which mythographers saw in oculate plumes fanned up in a circle. A tail kept low would properly signal humility, for representations both of the Annunciation and of the Last Supper.[64]

Scripture as framed by Rabanus Maurus and the *Glossa ordinaria* was to be a hermeneutic brooding ground for peacocks painted in Florentine epiphanies, where the bird keeps watch over processions of gentiles winding their way toward the newborn Babe. With reference to these texts, still widely read throughout the Renaissance in printed editions, we appreciate why its angelic plumage—folded down in humility—hangs from stable rafters in such panels as the *Adoration of the Magi* of ca. 1445 by Fra Angelico and Filippo Lippi at the National Gallery in Washington. Their tondo's endlessly looping parade of "gentiles" promises multitudinous converts. Similarly, Sandro Botticelli's late-fifteenth-century *Adoration of*

---

64. Ghirlandaio lived from 1449 to 1494. The Venetian Carlo Crivelli was active from 1468 to 1493. Although not commonly in attendance at Annunciations, the peacock does appear in other examples. See, e.g., an Italian tapestry *Annunciation* (1506–19) at the Art Institute of Chicago: replacing the usual vase of lilies, the peacock occupies the center of the composition, standing profiled between the angel and Mary. Its tail, exaggeratedly long, points toward the Virgin, who kneels devoutly at her prie-dieu. Herbert Friedmann, in *A Bestiary for Saint Jerome: Animal Symbolism in European Religious Art* (Washington, D.C.: Smithsonian Institution Press, 1980), 284–85, notes that a peacock in the foreground of Antonello da Messina's *Saint Jerome in His Study* has its fan painted shut. The painter, then, stresses not pride and vainglory but immortality.

the Magi in the Uffizi harbors a peacock atop stone ruins of the nativity shelter. We perceive him looming in a dark, elongated profile, not through his colors, which are subdued to complement the falling tail. Sometimes, signs of the tail alone suffice for the bird in a visual metonymy, as when Gentile da Fabriano dresses one of the gentiles coming to Christ in the crowded procession curling through his *Adoration of the Magi* with a magnificent hat of peacock feathers.[65]

Centered on a peacock with a hundred-eyed tail, Dante's mother's dream in Boccaccio's *Little Treatise* plumbs a mine of iconography with a honeycomb of chambers reaching from the medieval world into remote classical and Christian antiquity. While telling us something of what he knows about the bird to demonstrate its affinity with the *Divine Comedy,* Boccaccio nevertheless keeps to a reticent mode of commentary. He suppresses much more than he discloses. A scholar and canonist at home as much with Ovid, Fulgentius, and "Albericus" as he is with Augustine, Isidore, Rabanus, and the *Glossa ordinaria,*[66] he does admit to knowing that the bird has one hundred eyes in its tail (the one hundred cantos in the *Comedy*);[67] that its flesh is incorruptible (the poem's enduring moral value); that it has humbling pedal appendages (verse in the vernacular and the "low" register of comedy); that its name derives from the Latin word for "fear" and signifies, some say, the church authorities who preach Gehenna's inextinguishable fire (Dante's frightening invectives against the sins of quick and dead).

---

65. Gentile da Fabriano's *Adoration,* signed and dated to 1423, hangs in the Uffizi. The heavily symbolic atmosphere of his panel, which holds such objects as pomegranate, dove, skull, and lizard, invites us to notice that the man at the far right, with the last face fully in view in the procession of gentiles winding toward the Madonna and child, wears a magnificent hat of peacock feathers. Beyond beauty, the peacock's promise for eternal afterlife must similarly inspire the oculated feathers on certain angel's wings, such as those attached to the celestial harbinger who kneels just to the right of the Babe in the *Adoration of the Shepherds* by Hugo Van der Goes (ca. 1440–82), also at the Uffizi. The bird's feathers, as Boccaccio had noted in his *Trattatello,* are "angelic."

66. Isidore is one of Boccaccio's stock authors; Rabanus, widely known and respected, is cited repeatedly in Boccaccio's *Genealogie*. The peacock's status as the bird of apotheosis would probably have been known to Boccaccio from Tertullian's *De anima* 33 (see above, n. 61).

67. If we look to leks rather than literature, we can surmise that for a very young peacock, one hundred eyes could be possible, but the mythical number is certainly more emblematic than realistic. Petrie, Halliday, and Sanders report variations in eyespot numbers on adult peacocks, from about 140 to 160 (see above, n. 42). The older the peacock is, the more eyespots it is likely to have. Presumably, males with fewer eyespots than their direct competitors will be unsuccessful in obtaining a mate.

But this much is only the beginning. Bird of apotheosis for epic singers, as Ennius certified—what form of afterlife could be more appropriate to the father of poetry in Italy? Christianity reinforces the symbolism, making the peacock an even more appropriate emblem for Dante, whose poem brings us in spirit to Christian salvation. For Rabanus, the peacock had represented "the gentiles coming to Christ." Likewise, the *Comedy* traces a journey that reveals, beyond the letter, "our redemption through Christ," and it signifies to us, in the moral sense, "the conversion of our soul from the sorrow and misery of sin to the state of grace" and, in the anagogical sense, "the departure of the sanctified soul from bondage to the corruption of this world into the freedom of eternal glory."[68] The poem with one hundred cantos helps us acquire spiritual "providence," reminding us through the law of *contrappasso* that what we are in this life determines what we shall be and where in the next. The *Comedy*, like the peacock, is pregnant with instruction concerning our viability in the afterworld. Both poem and bird are eschatalogical texts.

The animal of Dante's apotheosis and Juno's poisoned peacock may seem at first to have little in common. Yet they are, after all, birds of a feather. One points to resurrection and long life after death; the other, that deadly dish concocted by Felice's recreant seneschal, comes to table as Juno Pronuba's silent partner. As if under her spell, all the king's men swear by the bird to perform courteous deeds for a maiden's marriage. Afterward, however, their vows lie submerged through more than four hundred pages of text as the young lovers are swept along an obstacle course from Verona to North Africa, from crisis to crisis. So many adventures and delays intervene between the king's birthday dinner and the lovers' nuptial union that even though this happy outcome cannot be in doubt (it is reassuringly forecast in a dream), we must wonder whether Boccaccio will ever pick up an almost forgotten thread and weave it back into his plot. He does remember, of course, and it is just one more confirmation of the precocious authorial control that connects the epic spaces of his romance. By the time the vows are acted on, when Biancifiore marries her knight in

---

68. Thus the author of "The Letter to Can Grande" explains the meaning of the *Commedia* by analogy to the "Psalm of Exodus" (Psalm 114 in the King James Bible). For a translation of the text of the epistle, see Robert S. Haller, trans. and ed., *Literary Criticism of Dante Alighieri* (Lincoln: University of Nebraska Press, 1973), 95–111. The question of the letter's authenticity is addressed by Robert Hollander (who sides with the critics that believe it is by Dante) in *Dante's Epistle to Cangrande.*

shining red armor, we are passing out of the children's polytheistic world into a new epoch, the Spain of their adulthood, its spiritual climate warmed by winds of Christianity. The perfection of the vows on the peacock occurs against a background of "gentiles coming to Christ," religious conversions we could have guessed all along from Juno's descent to Rome with her peacocks on a rainbow.

At Felice's party, seven oaths had been sworn over the peacock, one each by seven men: the king himself, Parmenione, Ascalion, Messaalino, Duke Ferramonte, Sara, and Menedon, but as the story develops, circumstances nullify two of the vows. Ascalion, the senior knight in Felice's court and Florio's lifelong mentor, dies of old age. Felice's announcement that he will find a baron as husband for Biancifiore, a pretense to begin with, becomes in the end superfluous since she and her prince have already secretly married. Thus the promises kept come down to five. Although we might think this reduction from seven merely a consequence of fictional accidents, the remainder of five surely reflects some calculation on Boccaccio's part.

That just five of the vows to the peacock should be accomplished is most apt because in the Pythagorean tradition, as Boccaccio well knew, 5 is the nuptial number. Most evident in the *Teseida delle nozze d'Emilia* and present for the *Decameron* as well, 5 as a symbol of marriage first occurs programmatically in the *Filocolo*. The descents of Juno, goddess of marriage, seem to hint at the pentad. All told, twenty-three chapters mention her ($2 + 3 = 5$), and the vows on the peacock (2.35) coincide with the fifth.[69] In those schedules Boccaccio set up for the Olympians to visit his "little booklet," she was not left out, although he coupled Diana and Venus into a much more rigid timetable. Juno's fifth appearance in the five-book *Filocolo* relates, we now see, to other, less subtle arithmetic: *Quinto* Lelio Africano, in chapter *five*, conceives Biancifiore after *five* years of marriage; she and Florio are born on *Pente*cost, and on *Pente*cost they are finally reunited for a secret marriage in the Arab's Tower, where, beneath a statue of Cupid-Hymen, they exchange nuptial vows at 5.122 ($1 + 2 + 2 = 5$).[70]

---

69. Juno appears in the *Filocolo* at 1.1, 13; 2.19, 34, 35, 47, 53; 3.11, 34, 46, 76; 4.11, 13, 85, 120, 121, 128, 155, 160; 5.8, 20, 21, 35.

70. See above, chap. 3, on the programmatic and intersecting appearances of Venus and Diana, thirteen and seven, respectively. Along with Juno, Mars and Venus pitch in to help the couple, as when Venus gives Florio her lover's sword so he can quash the seneschal or when they save the two from death at the stake, Venus screening them from the flames while Mars stirs Florio's men in a clash of arms with the Admiral's wild crew. Although it will not

Only three of the five vows eventually accomplished are acted on when we should expect them to be, during celebrations for the public marriage of Florio and Biancifiore. At that time Ferramonte becomes Biancifiore's cupbearer; Parmenione "conducts" her in a procession to the Admiral's palace, and Menedon honors her with heraldic jousting. For the remaining two vaunts, we must wait until near the end of the book, when after their baptism in Rome, Florio and Biancifiore return to Marmorina with Ilario, who preaches the gospel to the populace. Righteous iconoclasm will be the general response. In this the residents of Marmorina reenact idol smashing first instituted by Gregory the Great, an authority whom Boccaccio as canonist would have especially admired. The images they are to destroy are "fallacious," following Isidore of Seville's etymology for the English word *idol* from the Greek *dolus* (fraud).[71]

E fatto in una gran piazza ragunare la molta gente della città, tacitamente la predicazione di Ilario ascoltarono, dopo la quale il re prima e la reina appresso e tutta l'altra gente, uomini e femine, piccoli e grandi, presero da Ilario il santo lavacro. La qual cosa fatta, Florio per tutto il regno mandò legati a seminare la santa semenza, e per tutto mandò comandando che chi la sua grazia disiderasse, prendesse il battesimo, e abatessero i fallaci idoli a reverenza fatti dei falsi iddi: e de' templi fatti a loro facessero templi al vero Iddio dedicati, e lui adorassero e temessero e amassero.

[And when the many people of the city had been gathered together in the great piazza, silently they listened to Ilario's preaching, after which, first the king and next the queen, and then all the other people, men and women, small and large, took holy laver from Ilario. And when that was done, he sent orders everywhere that whoever wished to remain in his good graces should take baptism, that they should strike down the fallacious idols made in reverence to false gods, and that they should make the temples built to them into temples dedicated to the true God and adore and fear and love him.] (*Filoc.* 5.82)

---

become definite until the *Teseida delle nozze d'Emilia,* Mars and Venus are probably already in the *Filocolo* a couple symbolic of marriage. See Kirkham, "'Chiuso parlare' in Boccaccio's *Teseida,*" 17–53.

71. Michael Camille, *The Gothic Idol: Ideology and Image-Making in Medieval Art* (Cambridge: Cambridge University Press, 1989), 18, 50.

In the midst of this happy reconstruction, Barons Sara and Messaalino arrive, belatedly and with no apologies offered. They come in a sequel to the Alexandrian celebration, this one marking a nation's conversion. Each bears the gifts he had promised the peacock, a priceless crown and date palms hung with coins of gold. The celebratory mood at the close of the romance begins in Alexandria for nuptials and continues in Marmorina for collective baptism and temple remodeling: "E in questa maniera la festa grande e notabile, rincominciata per lo preso lavacro, dura lungamente" [And in this manner the great and memorable festivity, renewed because they had taken the laver, long endures]. Boccaccio elides the two locations to double the intensity of his happy ending.

At the same time, he splits his narrative postscripts on the peacock vows into two distinct phases. One attends on marriage, the other on destruction of idols and salvation through Christ. The peacock is a "holy bird" in the *Filocolo* not just because it belongs to Juno Pronuba, a goddess who joins forces above the scenes with her pagan peers Venus, Mars, Diana, and Cupid-Hymen to assure the romantic ending for Florio and Biancifiore's love story. Their twin weddings mark only one terminus in the book's twofold thematic trajectory. The second pertains to their acceptance of Christ, which opens the door to Christianity's triumph over the old gods at the western ends of the world. Like the romance as a whole, Juno's bird is two-sided, in part nuptial, but also salvational. Clues scattered in chapter numbers hint at the peacock's hidden Christian import.

The vows on the peacock fall in the *Filocolo* at 2.35, when Juno's name recurs for the fifth time—with an allusion to the peacocks who pull her chariot. Biancifiore answers Parmenione, who has promised to escort her in an elegant procession on her wedding day: "più che Giunone mi potrò io di conducitori gloriare" [I can be prouder of my escorts than Juno]. The sum of that chapter's digits $(3 + 5 = 8)$ reiterates symbolically its ordinal position, since 2.35 is the eightieth chapter of the romance (80F). Fulfillment of the first three vaunts, after the public wedding of Florio and Biancifiore, takes place in a three-chapter sequence, 4.162–64. Its center lies exactly 280 chapters after the eightieth (2.35). In this configuration, 8 is the recurrent number—and not by accident. Thus the eightieth chapter in the romance (80F), distanced by 280 chapters from the vows' fulfillment, conforms to a larger pattern of 8s. At 5.44 $(4 + 4 = 8)$, after the couple's long peregrinations as pagans in not yet Christianized territories, Biancifiore will hear the call of Rome, a city that had not figured in the romance since 1.8, when her parents left the seat of Christendom on the pilgrimage of their martyrdom. When Florio and Biancifiore have reached Rome, they ride among a group of exactly eight people in a solemnly trumpeted cavalcade to the Lateran for baptism from Pope Vigilius at 5.71 (7 + 1 = 8). Better than any other addends, 7 and 1 express baptism as the transition from temporal to eternal well-being.[72] Soon a shift of scene transports us away from Rome to Marmorina, the stony city of still obdurate King Felice. While dreaming (5.80), he hears a thunderous voice (accompanied by a flash of light) that warns him of dreadful retribution should he refuse to accept his son's new religion. This prepares him for Florio's return in the company of Ilario, who at 5.82 (444R) will preach the word of Christ and convert Florio's parents along with all their subjects.

But there is other, less subterranean evidence that permits us to see more than matrimonial value in Juno and her peacock emblems. It stands at the high rhetorical incipit of the *Filocolo,* where the two collaborate as prime movers in machinery that will propel the epic from a pagan world into Christianized times. Preceded with pomp by her messenger, the rainbow goddess, Iris, Juno sweeps down from the skies in a resplendent chariot drawn by her "oculated birds." Still mindful of Aeneas's offense against Dido, and ever the enemy of imperial Rome, she heads straight for her "vicar," the pope, commanding that he summon Charles of Anjou to wipe out the last corrupt traces of empire in Swabian Sicily. She next journeys to the netherworld and enlists Alecto to foment rebellion in depraved Manfred's realm. The Fury obeys, but all hell laments Juno's orders, for they will "deprive it of prey."

Juno, as we have seen, "comes" to the book not as Juno Pronuba but rather as the Church. Wife of Jove, the mythological code name for Christ in the *Filocolo,* she doubles by analogy as bride of the Lord for the romance on its Christian register. So she enlists the pope, "he who through her held holy office," to demand that he vanquish Emperor Manfredi, son

---

72. Heptameral literature by the church fathers equates the seven-day week of Genesis with our life in this world; although the Bible speaks of no continuation, that week presupposes an ideal eighth day marking the passage from earthly to eternal time. Signifying Christian rebirth, the octave regulates octagonal baptisteries, structures like San Giovanni in Fonte at Naples and San Giovanni at Florence, whose interiors peacocks decorate as signs of life in Paradise after death. On 8 as the number of baptism, see the classic essay by Richard Krautheimer, "Introduction to an 'Iconography of Medieval Architecture'"; Hopper, *Medieval Number Symbolism,* 77, 114; Heinz Meyer, *Die Zahlenallegorese im Mittelalter: Methode und Gebrauch* (Munich: Wilhelm Fink, 1975), 140–41. Cf. also Kirkham, *The Sign of Reason,* 133, 247.

of Frederick II and last of the imperial progeny in Italy. Juno's twofold role as Jupiter's Olympian queen and ecclesiastical consort to Christ carries into the rainbow and peacocks that precede her.

Iris, whom Boccaccio names "the daughter of Thaumas," herald's Juno's descent. Iris is the pagan messenger best remembered as Juno's own and for her merciful errands of mediation between this world and the next.[73] Ovid had nodded to her early in the *Metamorphoses:* when Jove, to punish mankind, loosens the South Wind, who floods the earth, "Iris, the messenger of Juno, clad in robes of many hues, draws up water and feeds it to the clouds."[74] Later, when Juno reentered heaven from an errand of vengeance to Tisiphone on the slimy Stygian shores, "Iris, the daughter of Thaumus, sprinkled her o'er with purifying water"; again, Iris, cloaked in a many-colored cape "trailing across the sky in a rainbow curve," obliges her mistress, by asking that Sleep reveal to Alcyone the true story of her husband's fate.[75] Iris makes a momentary and spectacular showing in the *Aeneid,* too, descending at Juno's request to release Dido's soul: "Iris, all dewy on saffron wings, flits down through the sky, trailing athwart the sun a thousand shifting tints."[76]

Juno's harbinger who sweeps the sky with a thousand colors has counterparts in rainbows that shine in the Bible. They appear in the first and last books, and exegetes related them typologically. In the Old Testament (Genesis 9:13–17), the rainbow appears after the Flood, as a sign of God's covenant with Noah that he would never again destroy the world by water: "I set my bow in the cloud, and it shall be a sign of the covenant between me and the earth. When I bring clouds over the earth and the bow is seen in the clouds, I will remember my covenant which is between me and you and every living creature of all flesh; and the waters shall never again become a flood to destroy all flesh." Rainbows return to Scripture in John's Apocalypse. One frames the visionary throne of Christ in Revelation 4:2–3: "lo, a throne stood in heaven, with one seated on the throne!

---

73. Perhaps Iris plays such a mediating role because the rainbow touches both earth and sky. See *Oxford Classical Dictionary,* 2d ed., s.v. "Iris."

74. Ovid *Met.* 1.270–71: "nuntia Iunonis varios induta colores / concipit Iris aquas alimentaque nubibus adfert."

75. Ibid., 4.479–80: "laeta redit Iuno, quam caelum intrare parantem / roratis lustravit aquis Thaumantias Iris"; 11.585–91: "'Iri, meae,' dixit, 'fidissima nuntia vocis.' . . . dixerta: induitur velamina mille colorum / Iris et arcuato caelum curvamine signans / tecta petit iussi sub nube latentia regis." Cf. also 14.85, 829–51.

76. Virgil *Aen.* 4.700–701: "ergo Iris croceis per caelum roscida pinnis, / mille trahens varios adverso sole colores."

And he who sat there appeared like jasper and carnelian, and round the throne was a rainbow that looked like an emerald." Another crowns an angel in 10:1: "Then I saw another mighty angel coming down from heaven, wrapped in a cloud, with a rainbow over his head, and his face was like the sun, and his legs like pillars of fire."[77]

Boccaccio's "daughter of Thaumas" enters the *Filocolo* through conflated references, via the *Divine Comedy*. Dante had touched on the rainbow with exactly the same epithet, as "figlia di Taumante," which occurs when his Statius explains the meteorology of Purgatory (21.50). But Dante's Iris has her most stunning moment in *Paradiso* 12, as part of an extended simile comparing the theologians, whose souls levitate in two concentric circles, with a double rainbow, reminder of God's pact with Noah.

> Come si volgon per tenera nube
> due archi paralelli e concolori,
> quando Iunone a sua ancella iube,
>   nascendo di quel d'entro quel di fori,
> . . . .
>
>   e fanno qui la gente esser presaga,
> per lo patto che Dio con Noè puose,
> del mondo che già mai più non s'allaga:
>   così di quelle sempiterne rose
> volgiensi circa noi le due ghirlande,
> e sì l'estrema a l'intima respuose.

[As two bows, parallel and like in color, bend across a thin cloud when Juno gives the order to her handmaid—the one without born of the one within, . . . and make the people here presage, by reason of the covenant that God made with Noah, that the world shall never again be flooded, so the two garlands of those sempiternal roses circled round us, and so did the outer correspond to the inner. (*Par.* 12.10–21)

---

77. Genesis 9:13–17: "arcum meum ponam in nubibus, et erit signum foederis inter me et inter terram. Cumque obduxero nubibus caelum, apparebit arcus meus in nubibus; et recordabor foederis mei vobiscum et cum omni anima vivente quae carnem vegetat"; Rev. 4:2–3: "et ecce sedes posita erat in caelo, et supra sedem sedens. Et qui sedebat, similis erat adspectui lapidis iaspidis et sardinis; et iris erat in circuitu sedis similis visioni smaragdinae"; Rev. 10:1: "Et vidi alium angelum fortem descendentem de caelo, amictum nube, et iris in capite eius, et facies eius erat ut sol, et pedes eius tanquam columnae ignis."

Who was Iris *moraliter* for the scholars of Boccaccio's intellectual milieu? Mythographers on the whole made far less of Iris than of the peacock, but those who did comment on the rainbow sometimes associated it with Juno in her aspect as air. (She is air when Jupiter is fire, but Jupiter himself can be fire and air together, in which event she stands for earth and water.) Benvenuto da Imola calls on this tradition for his commentary on Dante: "*iris* is caused by the reverberation of the sun on an opposite cloud. . . . as Homer, Virgil, and other poets pretend, Iris is the messenger of Juno, which they pretend because Juno is the element air, of whom Iris is said to be the messenger, because it is indicative of the quality of air."[78] Boccaccio himself, in his *Genealogies,* mentions Iris as the most famous of Juno's fourteen attending nymphs, but he values her very negatively: "They attribute her to Juno, goddess of wealth, in order to designate the ornaments of rich men by her curvature painted with various colors." These colors flash wondrously into view for a moment, he explains, but even as the rainbow rises, it is already falling, like the splendors of riches, which "in a moment dissipate to nothing." People say, he adds, that the name *Iris* comes from *erim,* meaning "strife" (*certamen*), because that is the consequence of wealth.[79]

---

78. Benvenuto da Imola, *Comentum super Dantis,* 5:72: "iris causatur ex reverberatione solis in nubem oppositam . . . . sicut fingunt Homerus, Virgilius, caeterique poetae, Iris est nuntia Junonis, quod ideo fingunt quia Juno est elementum aeris, cuius Iris dicitur esse nuntia, quia indicat de qualitate aeris etc." The tradition that identifies Juno with air seems to originate with Servius, who from the beginning of his commentary on the *Aeneid* (1.47ff.) equates Jupiter with ether and fire, Juno with air; see Servius, *Servii grammatici qui feruntur in Vergilii carmina commentarii,* ed. Georg Thilo and Hermann Hagan, 2 vols. (Leipzig: Teubner, 1881), vol. 1. The anonymous author of *Ovide moralisè* accepts that line in his allegorization of the fable of Juno's descent to Tisiphone in the underworld (4.3766ff.): there Juno is "l'air bas" (low air)—presumably as opposed to higher "airs," like ether—whence comes to the world plenty as well as famine and sterility because of the diverse temperatures of the air. The author writes of Juno, "Cele est dou / mont dame et roïne, / Cele est deese de richesce / Et d'orgueil et de gentillece" [She is dame and queen of the world; she is goddess of riches and of pride and of nobility]. From the air, in this view, falls that which produces an abundance of temporal goods and corporal delights. Esoteric to us, this notion was still understood as late as the mid–sixteenth century. Bartolomeo Ammannati's fountain for Duke Cosimo I of Florence, commissioned in 1555, represents Juno as air, flanked by peacocks, standing above Ceres (earth), the river god Arno, and a female personification of Parnassus. The art historian who has reconstructed this composition plausibly gives its source for Juno as Boccaccio's *Genealogie;* see Elizabeth Macdougal, ed., *Fons Sapientiae: Renaissance Garden Fountains,* Dunbarton Oaks Colloquium of the History of Landscape Architecture, no. 5 (Washington, D.C.: Dunbarton Oaks, 1978), fig. 1, opposite p. 126.

79. *Genealogie* 9.1 (p. 439): "Hanc enim Junoni diviatiarum dea ideo attribuunt, ut per eius picturatam variis coloribus curvaturam opum ornamenta designent . . . sic et divitum splendores in momento resolvuntur in nichilum." For the Greek etymology, his source was probably the Third Vatican Mythographer, whom he thought of as "Albericus." Boccaccio also mentions Iris, "daughter of Thaumas," in *Ameto* 40.7.

Neither the "neutral" naturalistic approach to Iris that Benvenuto takes, inherited from authorities like Servius and Macrobius, nor Boccaccio's moralizing *in malo* as mythographer fits Juno's messenger in the *Filocolo*. She who quite literally paves the skyway for the goddess, as the Bodleian illustrator projects it, must signify *in bono*. She must have an allegorical aura close to that of Juno, who comes to her pope as the church. To find it, we must shift our soundings into the kind of books the canonist would have known (and that Dante had in mind when he alluded to the rainbow in his description of the theologians), commentaries on the Bible.

The rainbow that appeared in the sky after the Flood occasions this note in the *Glossa ordinaria* on Genesis 9: "God gave the rainbow as a sign of surety, lest men in terror fear being destroyed by another flood, often seeing inundations of rains. It was set in the sky so that it could be seen by all and so that we might take away the eyes of our hearts from whatsoever tribulation to him, who dwells in the sky." This sign of "propitiation" after a judgment by water in the earth's early history, which corresponds typologically to judgment by fire at the end of the world, had long buttressed patristic exegesis on the rainbows in John's Apocalypse. Bede, for instance, explained the "rainbow round the throne" of Revelation 4:3 as the faithful, through whom the church takes its strength: "Iris, which makes clouds when the sun shines, and which was made after the Flood, in the first judgment of propitiation, illustrates through the intercession of the saints those whom the lord designates as the church to be fortified." For Saint Anselm, the rainbow encircling Christ enthroned is "peace or the propitiation of God," a definition Richard of Saint-Victor transfers to the rainbow-crowned angel of Revelation 10:1, whom he calls "*iris,* that is, propitiation of the divinity and reconciliation with human kind, because God was reconciling the world to himself in Christ." Pseudo-Saint Augustine has a similar understanding of the two passages in Revelation. For him, the "rainbow round the throne" is the "reconciliation with the world . . . through the dispensation made by the incarnate Word," and the apocalyptic angel is "the Lord dressed in the church."[80]

Theology teaches, then, how beauteous is the promise of an arching

80. *Glossa ordinaria, Patrologia latina* 113:111 (on Genesis 9:13–17): "Arcum dedit Deus in signum securitatis, ne homines formidolosi timerent altero diluvio deleri, pluviarum inundationes saepe cernentes. Hic in caelo positus est, ut ab omnibus videri possit, et pro quacunque tribulatione ad eum attollamus oculos cordis, qui habitat in coelis." This rainbow is said to be two-colored so as to signify the two judgments: one that has come, by water; and one that will come, by fire at the end of the world. See, e.g., *Glossa ordinaria, Patrologia latina* 114:729, on the two judgments: "unum aeque quod praeteriit; aliud ignis, quod venturum creditur in fine saeculi." According to Anselm, *Enarrationes in Apocalypsin, Patrologia latina,*

rainbow, the symbol, under the old dispensation, of God's pact with mankind and, under the new, of his reconciliation with the world through Christ. "Iris," moreover, is close to the Church. For one exegete, she is even "the Lord dressed in the church." Among these readings, the line of analysis that seems most suited to Boccaccio's "daughter of Thaumas" is Bede's. To him she is not the church itself but rather the faithful, they who make it strong.

With all these Christian associations, Boccaccio's Iris is well qualified to announce the advent of his Juno Ecclesia, a *dea ex machina* who sets the *Filocolo* in motion with a journey from ethereal regions powered by birds pointing to salvation. Clearly, we are to remember this dramatic flight by peacock when her "holy bird" returns some two hundred pages later, roasted and poisoned on a platter. Parmenione's vaunt of a colorful escort on Biancifiore's wedding day makes her—and us—think of "Juno's conductors," iridescent creatures who will pale by comparison to the brilliant hues of the clothing displayed in that lavish procession. Later, to reinforce the parallelism between these two episodes, Biancifiore pleads from prison for justice from the goddess whose peacock has been so shamefully defiled.

O santa Giunone, nel cui uccello tanta falsità fu nascosa per conducermi a questo fine, vendica la tua onta, fa che questa cosa non rimanga inulta, ma sia letta ancora tra l'altre vendette da te fatte.

[O holy Juno, in whose bird such treachery was hidden to bring me to this end, avenge your shame, see that this not remain unpunished, but let it, too, be read among the other vendettas you have had.] (*Filoc.* 2.53.13)

In other words, Juno is to set this matter straight in the same avenging spirit that had propelled her to go to the pope in a coach drawn by her oculated peacocks.

162:1517, the two-colored rainbow of Genesis has its correspondents in the stones of jasper and carnelian, colors of the man seated in the throne at Rev. 4:3: the jasper, taken to be green, signifies the first judgment by water, hence baptism; the red carnelian is the future judgment by fire, hence the gift of the Holy Ghost. Bede, *Explanatio Apocalypsis, Patrologia latina,* 93: 143: "Iris, qui fit sole nubes irradiante, et post diluvium primo propitiationis iudicio factus est, intercessu sanctorum quos dominus illustrat Ecclesiam muniri designat"; Richard of Saint Victor, *In Apocalypsim Joannis, Patrologia latina,* 196:788: "*iris,* id est propitiatio divinitatis et reconciliatio humani generis, quia Deus erat in Christo mundum reconcilians sibi"; Pseudo-Augustine, *Expositio in Apocalypsim B. Joannis, Patrologia latina* 35:2419 and 2430: "reconciliatio mundi . . . per incarnati Verbi dispensationem facta."

Textual undercurrents bear Juno's skyworthy bird into iconographic proximity with Boccaccio's "resurrected" Dante. Juno in her secular role as patron of marriage seems to eclipse Juno Ecclesia for the vows on the peacock and all the peripeteias in the romantic saga of Florio and Biancifiore. Yet the goddess so well connected at Rome is always there in the background as the *Filocolo* gradually works its way back to Rome, for a baptism in the Lateran ministered by Pope Vigilius and, afterward, the Spanish nation's conversion, when the last peacock vows are fulfilled and the romance attains its Christian climax. Had Boccaccio glossed the *Filocolo,* as he later would his epic in verse, the *Teseida,* the proemial scene with Juno's "oculated birds" might have led him simply to indulge in retelling Ovid's story of hundred-eyed Argus. But like any good medieval symbolist developing a work of creative fiction, he would have been holding out on us. He also knew peacocks perfectly well under their sacred aspect, as signs of Christian resurrection and eternal life. So the dream vouchsafed Dante's mother in his *Little Treatise in Praise of Dante* discloses how her son, after an inescapable fall, arose in the form of his hundred-canto *Comedy*—"his posterity"—as a peacock. That was the bird whose flesh Augustine, Isidore, Rabanus, the *Glossa ordinaria,* and the bestiarists all considered immune to putrefaction. Its plumes, so menacing for the mythographers, including Boccaccio, brighten morally thanks to biblical commentators on the peacocks for Solomon's Temple, explained as adornments of virtue that teach us to wish for "the delights of the eternal kingdom." For an encyclopedist of the Victorine school and for many related bestiaries, the bird's long tail, when gathered low, is a sign of humility that points to "the length of future life." Finally, Boccaccio surely remembers his Rabanus, who saw in the peacocks shipped from Tarsus to Jerusalem a figure of the "gentiles coming to Christ." The image is fitting for the *Filocolo*'s Pentecostal trajectory from pagan idols to the one true God, a movement whose festive end coincides with fulfillment of the vows on a poisoned peacock.

CHAPTER 6

A Pentecostal Epic

Boccaccio constructed the *Filocolo* on an epic scale, its every register universal in sweep. Chronologically, the romance envisions history from Genesis to the Judgment; geographically, it marches from the centers of Christendom in Jerusalem and Rome to the western edge of the known world; evangelically, it progresses in triumph from the old gods to the coming of the Word; and spatially, it embraces the vastest plan, from celestial realms shared by the Olympians with God and his saints to the very center of the earth, that black abyss where Satan and his devils swarm ceaselessly to plot their evil. These militant enemies of man's salvation make their first appearance early in the romance (1.9), when, deep in his hell hole, "the miserable king whose realm Acheron surrounds" summons a council of ministers to machinate against the pilgrims en route to Santiago. By assigning nefarious agents of the underworld to the ninth chapter of the romance, Boccaccio equates the number 9 with infernal regions, and in so doing he recalls Dante's *Inferno* as a place ringed by the Acheron and defined by 9, since its space spirals down through nine circles.[1] The Devil's confabulations in the abyss follow immediately on the beginning of Quinto Lelio Africano's journey as a pilgrim (1.8). Boccaccio's back-to-back episodes, which cut with abrupt contrast from Rome to Hell, confront two great opposing forces: the followers of Christ and their arch enemies. In this way he stages the grand moral design of the *Filocolo* as a

---

1. Dante adopts 9 for his *Inferno* both as an anti-Trinitarian number (3 x 3 = 9) and as a symbol of sin, since it is defective and falls short with respect to the perfect number 10. It is possible that Boccaccio used 9 with similar negative implications when he structured the *Filostrato* in nine parts, the *Elegia di madonna Fiammetta* in nine books, and *De casibus virorum illustrium* in nine books. Satan here sponsors the Spaniards, who are (anachronistically) worshipers of Muhammad. Even later, in the *Decameron,* Boccaccio still links the "infernal" 9 with an Arabic world; see Victoria Kirkham and María Rosa Menocal, "Reflections on the 'Arabic' World: Boccaccio's Ninth Stories," *Stanford Italian Review* 7 (1987): 95–110.

cosmic battle between God and Lucifer, saints and sinners, good and evil. Christian allegory, not exactly what we should expect in a popular romance, was for an epic quite the right thing in Boccaccio's day.[2] Virgil, Statius, Ovid, and Dante, whom Boccaccio acknowledges in the *congedo* as his chief epic models, were all read as allegories in the trecento. Boccaccio could hardly imitate them and the heroic genre in so many of its conventions—universal "history" dotted with "fables" from myth and cast in rhetoric of the highest register—without conceiving his invention in allegorical terms, that is, as truth concealed beneath a veil of fiction.[3] In its veiled meanings, much of what happens in the *Filocolo* hinges on the doings of the gods. Thus we read a political allegory in Juno's descent as the church who stirs her pope to suppress lingering partisans of empire in Italy. Psychological allegory accounts for the invisible presence of Mars at Florio's side in mortal combat with Massamutino, the seneschal who ensnared Biancifiore in the business of the poisoned peacock. The mighty war god is there to signify that Florio drew strength and courage from hidden reserves of manly vigor.

As for Venus and Diana, rivalry notwithstanding, they actually cooperate all along to sponsor a passion chaste until marriage, proper in young protégés moving toward religious conversion. Long before Diana "goes" openly to Venus for a heavenly handshake (3.52), at the moment when Florio and Biancifiore first read Ovid's "holy book," by which time "the lady of their ascendent had wheeled around them in her circling six times," the two Olympian ladies had already secretly bonded. Venus is the influential planet here, but her annual orbits put the children at an age consonant with Diana, for they are just entering their seventh year. Consequently, a chaste impulse will check them as they learn from the Gallehault "how the holy fires of Venus should be carefully kindled in cold hearts" (1.45). The children's bond as pure young lovers prefigures their more perfect union as neophytes in Christ.[4] It correlates in a secular sense with the Christian

---

2. Dante, for example, believed that every epic concealed an allegory. See Giorgio Padoan, "Il mito di Teseo e il cristianesimo di Stazio," *Lettere Italiane* 11, no. 4 (1959): 432–57.

3. Boccaccio defines these terms in *Genealogie* 14.7 and 9.

4. As Smarr has noted, Venus and Diana are together from the prologue scene (1.1), where they symbolically accompany the narrator's lady. The cooperation between goddesses carries through to Florio and Biancifiore's first marriage, in the Admiral's Tower, where Venus and Diana are among attending deities. Smarr shows how Boccaccio contrasts the children to the adulterers Paris and Helen, characterizing the childrens' love as a chaste love leading to their conversion. See Smarr, *Boccaccio and Fiammetta*, 43–53.

charity toward which they incline by celestial destiny. Their wanderings through the plot on its literal level, which transports them finally to Rome, have spiritual meaning as an itinerary toward baptism. They come to Rome; they come to Christ. Florio and Biancifiore are travelers who stand for whole populations—she for Christianized Rome, he for Christianized Spain. Pilgrims in the end to Santiago de Compostela, they have followed the footsteps of the apostle who proselytized the Iberian Peninsula. Allegorically, they march in step with the history of the church, which completed its Pentecostal journey from East to West as the Word took hold on Hesperian shores.

From 3 and 7 as numbers of Venus and Diana, we can widen our scope and multiply associations that resonate in the sphere of Christian allegory. What, aside from the seven planets, comes in quantities of 7 in the *Filocolo*? Boccaccio uses the number in an unusual coinage when he refers to one of the marvels of Rome as "Settensolio, made for the study of the liberal arts" (5.44). Biancifiore's nurse, Glorizia, names this Settensolio among other wonders in the city, whose sweet breezes are calling her back now, so many years after she set out with Quinto Lelio and Giulia Topazia. From his information in *The Marvels of Rome,* a widely read medieval travel book, Boccaccio knew this place as a temple of the Sun where all the liberal arts were studied, whence comes its etymology: "its derivation is from the seven arts, that is, all the seven sciences."[5]

Rome, associated with universal learning, is the gateway in metaphor to another sevenfold series, the virtues. They rise to visibility just after the love debate, soon before Filocolo presses onward with his quest. Still in Parthenope and filled with melancholy, he shuts himself into a garden, where he is visited by a vision of 4 + 3 beauties. The closed garden, symbol of the church, is a setting that presages his baptism, as do the seven ladies, whom we recognize by their iconographic attributes as the cardinal and theological virtues (Prudence, Fortitude, Justice, Temperance; Charity, Hope,

---

5. According to the *Mirabilia urbis Romae,* which Boccaccio knew in one of its many versions (see Quaglio's commentary in his edition of the *Filocolo,* 939 n. 6), "derivatio sua est septem artium scilicet septem omnium scientiarum." The place is the Septizonium, a temple with "seven floors" (the literal meaning of *Settensolio*), probably near the Palatine. See *The Marvels of Rome. Mirabilia Urbis Romae,* ed. and trans. Francis Morgan Nichols, rev. Eileen Gardiner (New York: Italica Press, 1986), at 3.11: "the Septizonium was the Temple of the Sun and the Moon." The ancient tradition of the seven liberal arts is still alive in twentieth-century fiction, accounting for a character named "Settembrini" in *The Magic Mountain,* where Hans Castorp spends seven years, dines in a room that seats seventy at table, etc. See Oskar Seidlin, "The Lofty Game of Numbers: The Mynheer Peeperkorn Episode in Thomas Mann's *Der Zauberberg,*" *PMLA* 86 (1971): 924–39.

Faith). The prince, with a more limited perspective, can at first only make out the four standing nearer him, those known to the pagan world. But then the sky opens to cloak him in a cascade of light, a blessed lady washes his whole person from a special ampoule, and suddenly the water opens his eyes to their three companions, visible in wondrous particulars (4.74).

The seven virtues return to the romance (after a corresponding series of vices have been rejected to clear the way) when Felice imparts to Florio his dying words of wisdom (5.92).[6] For a man on his deathbed, he manages to deliver a very full set piece. Perhaps, though, verisimilitude can withstand the strain, since we are by now into the closing chapters of the *Filocolo* and events are rapidly unwinding to resolution. Rhythms of art at finales are not those of life in daily passing. Here, Boccaccio reviews at such length all the vices and then all the virtues because he wants to leave his audience of readers with matter for pious meditation. In the fiction, Felice preaches to Florio; but the king's didactic voice is pitched toward a public beyond. Its ideal receiver would have been another royal personage, King Robert of Naples, the monarch who had a hobby of composing sermons.

Since 7 implies Diana—and then, by numerical analogy, both wisdom and virtue—3 can shift from Venus, its claimant by astrological right, to Trinity in a Christian reading. As we could expect, the equation of 3 and Trinity finds a place in the sacred history laid out by Friar Ilario. When the providential march of time brings him to the Lord's birth, an event for which his account slows to admit much legendary detail, he retails the miracles marking that event around the globe, especially in Rome. On the day of Christ's nativity, the temple of Peace collapsed, the statue of King Romulus fell and smashed apart, images personifying the provinces rendering homage to Rome toppled, and not a single idol survived intact anywhere in the world.[7] Portents defied the laws of nature, causing night to shine as bright as day, oil to stream forth from a freshwater spring.

---

6. For Boccaccio the virtues and the vices held great appeal as personified concepts. He composed his *Comedia delle ninfe fiorentine* as an allegory of the seven virtues, and they return allusively as the seven female narrators in the frame tale of the *Decameron.* See Kirkham, *The Sign of Reason,* 278 (on the number 7), 162–64 (for discussion of the seven virtues in Florio's garden vision).

7. Quaglio, in his commentary in his edition of the *Filocolo,* 949 n. 20, cites Boccaccio's source, *The Golden Legend,* appropriated literally: "In ipsa die tres soles in oriente apparuerunt, qui paulatim in unum coprus solare redactae minebat." Boccaccio the canon-law student may also have been remembering the exemplary iconoclasm of Pope Gregory the Great in early Christian Rome. As Camille has shown, destruction of idols was an important part of cults of the saints from early in the Middle Ages. See Camille, *The Gothic Idol,* 18, 115–28.

E quel giorno medesimo, avvegna che alcuni dicano che prima apparissero, apparvero in oriente tre soli, i quali, poi che veduti furono, in un corpo tutti e tre ritornarono, per li quali assai aperto l'essenza della Trinità si manifestò.

[And on that very day, although some say they appeared before, three suns appeared in the Orient, and after they had been seen, all three returned to a single body, and they manifested most openly the essence of the Trinity.] (5.54.14)

This notice of the suns that were three-in-one, which Boccaccio took from Jacopo da Varagine's *Golden Legend*, is a passing reference to the Trinity in the *Filocolo.* Another, referring to the very heart of Catholic doctrine, comes soon after, as Ilario recites the Credo.

Noi prima fedelmente crediamo, e semplicemente confessiamo uno solo Iddio etterno e incommutabile e vero, in cui ogni potenza dimora. Crediamo lui incomprensibile e ineffabile Padre, Figliuolo e Santo Spirito, tre persone in una essenzia, in una sustanzia, ovvero natura semplice omnino.

[First, we faithfully believe and simply confess one God alone, eternal and unchanging and true, in whom all power dwells. We believe him to be an incomprehensible and ineffable Father, Son, and Holy Ghost, three persons in one essence, in one substance, that is, all in one nature.] (5.56.2)

In the cosmos of Christian signs, 3 always signifies, above all, the triple Godhead. The analogy is so powerful for the Middle Ages that it is virtually not possible to think of anything in threes without making the association. Hence secondary meanings of the triad, such as the three theological virtues that Filocolo envisioned after a superinfusion of grace and baptismal wash, or such as the Lord's Resurrection on the third day after the Crucifixion, will assimilate to its primary sense, Trinity. Trinity is a magnetic pole that also pulls into its field, across a figural bridge from the pagan skies, Venus of the third heaven. In *Diana's Hunt* and in the *Ameto,* where Boccaccio asks Venus to perform allegorically as Trinitarian Grace,[8] 3 clearly enjoys status as a symbol both secular and sacred.

---

8. See Cassell and Kirkham, *Diana's Hunt,* 30–33, 51–52.

Although Boccaccio does not seem to send the goddess of love down in that guise for the *Filocolo,* she does point to the Trinity in certain signs of her appearances. Both Fiammetta's court on thirteen questions of love and the goddess's thirteen epiphanies in 301 chapters across the central three books of the romance (2.1–4.49) imprint love with a variant number whose values, arithmetic and symbolic, are higher than 3. That variant, 13, translates as a 1 and a 3 to the more powerful formula of Three-in-One.

Numbers clone into multiplied meanings. Through resemblance by analogy, a single digit implies all the things that come in that quantity— good and bad alike—or whatever falls into a corresponding ordinal position. For Boccaccio, 3 could refer to the three persons of the Trinity; the three theological virtues; and the third day after the Crucifixion, the day of Christ's Resurrection. Beyond these typical medieval values, his numerology adds an original register of mythological symbolism, which assigns to Venus the number 3 because her "place" is the third heaven. In its larger Boccaccian semantic field, both sacred and profane, then, 3 implies "love." The number 7 filters by analogy into layers that suggest Diana and chastity, the seven planets, the seven liberal arts, the seven virtues, and, in opposition to the last, the seven vices. What numbers mean, whether *in malo* or *in bono,* in lexicons holy or secular, must be evaluated in context, with due respect for the literary content they flag and define.

The pentad, which marks canto 5 of Dante's *Inferno* as a circle of lust,[9] may in a positive aspect be the Pythagorean sum of "marriage." Boccaccio will so have it in *Filocolo* 1.5 and on Day Five of the *Decameron.* For the *Filocolo,* he coins another meaning for the number 5 when he puts it into the service of the Pentecostal church. Not until we have traversed the whole romance and can look back on its flow lines—from love fostered by Venus but tempered by Diana to family life in Christ, from the Rome of the Caesars to the Rome of the popes, from polytheism to Christianity— can we look on Pentecost in full perspective. Boccaccio's symbolic punning with the number 5, which gives it sense as both matrimony and Pentecost, is an invention that weds moral action to poetic structure in his pentagonal novel.

Carried along by broad lines of movement, vignettes in the action of the *Filocolo* capture concepts and customs linked to *Quinquagesima,* the liturgical cycle of Pentecost. The perils of Biancifiore, for example, suspend her

9. Victoria Kirkham, "Quanto in femmina foco d'amor dura!" *Letture Classensi* 18 (1988): 235–50, revised and enlarged as "A Canon of Women in Dante's Commedia," *Annali d'Italinistica* 7 (1989): 16–41.

in one situation that brings Florio riding to the rescue dressed to the teeth as a medieval knight. His costume and escutcheon transcend historical realism to accompany a hero whom Boccaccio secretly mounts under the Pentecostal banner. Thereafter, as the "Red Knight" whose shield displays six roses, Florio will continue traveling for a good part of the novel.

To save Biancifiore from the king's charge of attempted regicide, he must outfight the black-hearted seneschal Massamutino, a duel for which Venus provides the sword from her partner, Mars. But that weapon, magic though it be, is not enough. So Ascalion garbs the lad in full armorial regalia, from toe to top: hose of mail, spurs, greaves, cuisses, hauberk, gorget, cuirass, bracers, basinet with camail, and heaume. Encased in the most fashionable ensemble of the day, Florio chooses his chivalric colors from Boccaccio's closet of symbols. He will be the Red Knight, with his vest "vermilion sendal" and his breast plates covered in "vermilion samite." That is as it should be for a lover at whose side Mars, the red god, fights invisibly. The device on his buckler, "six vermilion rosettes" against a field of gold, also suits the occasion. As red is the color of love, so roses are the flower of Venus. Just six rosettes may be called for here because, according to a mythographic tradition from late antiquity, 6 was a number of Venus.[10]

Later, when Florio becomes Filocolo to search the world with five companions, he keeps the same shield, by now a sign of the band of six who quest under the aegis of Venus. Red roses again shield our hero, himself a flower by name, when they cover him in a "vermilion-rose tunic" as he hides in the basket that Sadoc uses to smuggle him up inside the Arab's Tower.[11] Outlining his plan, the castellan explains that they can proceed on a holiday soon to come.

---

10. Ascalion puts on Filocolo "una grossa giubba di zendado vermiglio," then a pair of light breastplates, "coperte d'un vermiglio sciamito"; over his left shoulder he places a small shield with a golden field, "nel quale sei rosette vermiglie campeggiavano" (*Filoc.* 2.45). For a note on this episode in its recent (and imprecise) English translation by Donald Cheney, see Victoria Kirkham, "Two New Translations: The Early Boccaccio in English Dress," *Italica* 70, no. 1 (1993): 79–89. Martianus Capella connects the number 6 with Venus in *The Marriage of Mercury and Philology* 736 (trans. Stahl et al., p. 280): "The number six is assigned to Venus, for it is formed of a union of the sexes: that is, of the triad, which is male because it is an odd number, and the dyad, which is female because it is even; and twice three makes six." Perhaps the "six low mountains" surrounding the Valley of the Ladies in the *Decameron* (6, concl.) allude to this same Neoplatonic connection between number and goddess. The mythographers knew as a commonplace that roses were the flower of Venus. See, e.g., Boccaccio's *Genealogie* 3.22: "Mirtumque arborem illi sacram statuunt et ex floribus rosam" [And they assign the myrtle to her as a sacred tree and among flowers, the rose].

11. To prepare Biancifiore for Florio's impending visit in bed, Glorizia pretends she has seen him in a dream, where he was wearing "una gonnella quasi di color di vermiglia rosa."

... di qui a pochi giorni in queste parti si celebra una festa grandissima, la quale noi chiamiamo de' cavalieri. In quel giorno, i templi di
Marte e di Venere sono visitati con fiori e con frondi e con mar-
avigliosa allegrezza.

[... a few days from now in these parts we celebrate a very great
feast, which we call the Knights' Holiday. On that day, people visit
the temples of Mars and Venus with flowers and with boughs and
with marvelous happiness.] (4.104.3–4)

That is the day when the castellan has "roses and flowers" picked from
nearby for the Admiral to send up as gifts to the most beautiful damsels in
the tower. So their strategy will be to hide Filocolo inside a basket piled
high with roses and hoist it to the harem.

The "Knights' Holiday," as we know, is Pentecost. In the popular parlance of Boccaccio's time, the feast was called *Pasqua rosata,* or "Easter of
the Roses." Attested linguistically in Italy from the twelfth century, *pasca
rosata* describes a connection between Pentecost and roses that probably
derives from a pagan cultural substratum and the feast of the *Rosalia* (*dies
rosae*). From early Christian times, roses actually did fill the churches that
day, as Boccaccio's *Filocolo* may obliquely imply with Sadoc's reference to
worshipers of "Mars and Venus." In Rome, at least as late as the seventeenth century, roses were thrown from the cupola of Santa Maria della
Rotunda while the pope said mass, to signify the coming of the Holy
Ghost in tongues of fire.[12] Maybe Boccaccio's Naples also knew that
usage, which could justify an upside-down, wrong, "Arab" perversion of
the custom: cranking roses up to a great height. Still in the nineteenth century, Tuscans understood Whitsunday roses with a vocabulary that
named the major liturgical holidays of the year, including Christmas, as
"Easters": *Pasqua di ceppo* (Yule-log Easter), *Pasqua d'uva* ("Grape
Easter," which was Easter Day), and *Pasqua di rose* ("Easter of the

---

But that is what he must have really been wearing when he landed from the basket in the
antechamber guarded by the old nurse (*Filoc.* 4.13). The lover's arrival in a basket of flowers,
an episode in other versions of the European romance as well, relates to an ancient and widespread tradition of floral imagery as a symbol of erotic passion, documented by Karl P. Wentersdorf in "Iconographic Elements in *Floris and Blancheflour,*" *Annuale Mediaevale* 20
(1981): 76–96. Cf. also William L. Calin, "Flower Imagery in *Floire et Blancheflor,*" *French
Studies* 18, no. 2 (1964): 103–11.
    12. Carlo Battisti and Giovanni Alessio, *Dizionario etimologico italiano* (Florence: Bar-
bèra, 1950–65), s.v. "pasquarosa."

Roses," or Pentecost). They were the great annual feasts, not just for worship, but for folk entertainment in rhythms associated with the foods and
customs of seasons in their passing.

Those were the days when, back in medieval romance, events of the
greatest moment occurred. Pentecost especially was a season favored for
grand assemblages. So in *Flamenca,* a Provençal jewel of the mid–twelfth
century, five messengers scour the land to assemble guests, housed in five
hundred tents, for the heroine's marriage on Pentecost. Carolingian and
Arthurian tales often schedule full-court gatherings (*court plenière*) at Pentecost, and on such occasions new knights were created. It was a chivalric
practice from which arose yet another "Easter," *Pasqua di cavalieri,* as
Giovanni Sercambi attests in the first decade of the fifteenth century.[13]
Recurrence of Pentecosts as timeposts in courtly romance doubtless reinforced Boccaccio's Pentecostal plan for the *Filocolo,* a chronology with
precedent both secular and biblical.

The "festa de' cavalieri," when Florio at last recovers Biancifiore, happens to be their birthday. Boccaccio leaves it to us to make the connection,
which is not so very difficult, since we well remember the marvel of that
double birth on the same holiday and the pretext for the children's names.
We do have to look back more closely, though, to notice that this date in
Gemini comes around exactly five times in the *Filocolo.*

(1) 1.39. The children are born "nel giocondo giorno eletto per festa
de' cavalieri, essendo Febo nelle braccia di Castore e di Polluce
insieme" [on the joyful day designated as the Knights' Holiday,
when Phoebus was in the arms of Castor and Pollux together].

(2) 2.12. Their tutor has observed Ovid's effects on his pupils and
reports the problem to his king, who puts a stop to such nonsense by sending Florio away to school. He has entered his
fifteenth year: "il sole, poi che Lucina chiamata dalla tua madre
mi ti donò, è quattordici volte ad un medesimo punto ritornato
nelle braccia di Castore e di Polluce, e è entrato nel cammino
usato per compiere la quintadecima, e è già al terzo della via, o
più avanti" [since Lucina, called by your mother, gave you to
me, the sun has returned fourteen times to the same point in the

---

13. Sercambi is cited in ibid. The fourteenth-century Italian *Rinaldo da Montalbano*
begins with a plenary court called by Charlemagne at Pentecost; see Pio Rajna, "Rinaldo da
Montalbano," *Il Propugnatore* 3 (1870): 213–41. Du Méril (*Floire et Blanceflor,* lxxv–lxxix)
cites several Old French romances that reckon Pentecost as the Knights' Holiday.

arms of Castor and Pollux, and it has entered its usual path to complete the fifteenth and is already a third of the way, or more, along].

(3) 4.12. After being stranded at Naples for five months, "essendo già Titan recevuto nelle braccia di Castore e di Polluce" [when Titan had already been received in the arms of Castor and Pollux], Florio relates a strange dream to Ascalion; that very day, while walking along the salty shore, they chance upon Fiammetta's garden.

(4) 4.91. Florio has arrived in Alexandria; one day "Venuto . . . già Titan ad abitare con Castore" [when Titan had . . . come to dwell with Castor], he resolves to embrace Biancifiore in the Arab's Tower.

(5) 5.95. We are in Cordova for Florio's coronation: "Il dolce tempo era, e il cielo tutto ridente porgeva graziose ore: Citerea, tra le corna dello stellato Tauro splendidissima, dava luce, e Giove chiaro si stava tra' guizzanti Pesci; Apollo nelle braccia di Castore e di Polluce più lieto ogni mattina nelle braccia della sua Aurora si vedea entrare; Febeia correa con le sue agute corna lieta alla sua ritondità" [It was the sweet time, and heaven, all smiling, lent gracious hours. Citherea, between the horns of the starry bull, gave light most resplendent, and Jove shone bright among the wriggling fish; Apollo, in the arms of Castor and Pollux, could be seen entering the arms of his Aurora more happily every morning; Phoebe was hurrying happily, with her sharp horns, toward her rotundity].

The sun's returns to Gemini articulate the story, marking with astrological anniversaries major turnings in the plot: the children's birth, their first separation, Florio's Neapolitan sojourn and the love debate, the prelude to their reunion (it is just a gesture, since Florio has to be satisfied with throwing his arms around the Arab's Tower), and their ascent to the throne as Christian rulers of Spain.[14]

---

14. Bruno Porcelli, in "Strutture e forme narrative nel *Filocolo*," *Studi sul Boccaccio* 21 (1993): 207–33, identifies further programmatic use of the number 5 in the *Filocolo:* five and a half years pass between Florio's return to Montoro after Biancifiore has been sold (2.10) and his coronation (5.95); there are five major "partitions" in the love story; events take place in five major locations (although Porcelli somewhat confusingly lists seven). He suggests that Boccaccio took the idea for the major divisions of the *Filocolo* into five books from a Greek romance by Xenephon of Ephesus.

Both the sun's position in Castor and Pollux and the Knights' Holiday
are, of course, synonyms for Pentecost, when tongues of fire rested on the
apostles' heads. And fire burns red, love's symbolic color. Now we better
realize why the *Filocolo* so frequently settles into hues of vermilion and
why rubious flames so often arise from its pages. Although various colors
code the characters and physical objects in their surroundings, Boccaccio
keeps returning to this rubescent palette. On the way to her execution,
after being perfidiously convicted of trying to poison King Felice, a down-
cast Biancifiore comes from prison dressed entirely in black (2.52). But the
night before, presenting the peacock at the king's birthday table, she was
festively gowned in "vermilion samite" (2.33). For Jealousy, a scrawny,
pale-faced woman sought out by Diana, dark clothes are usual (3.27).
Diana herself, perpetually virginal, prefers a "candid" tunic when she visits the House of Sleep, who dwells sluggish and recumbent on a bed of
black sheets (3.28). Mars first descends into the story riding a "red horse"
and suffused with a "red light": "l'altissimo prencipe delle battaglie, sol-
lecitato dalla sua amica [Venere], discese del suo cielo, e sopra un rosso
cavallo . . . della rossa luce di che era coperto tutto parea che ardesse"
(2.57). As Florio takes a closer look at this bigger-than-life apparition, he
sees the god "oltre alla misura degli uomini grandissimo . . . ferocissimo
nel viso, e tutto rosso" [huge beyond the measure of men, with a most
fierce face, and all red]. Mars will team invisibly with Florio to defeat Massamutino, his divinity numinous in "vermilion splendor." The ruddy
cloud, sign of heaven's favor, puts Ascalion in mind of two anecdotes from
Roman history: once, flames appeared over the commander Lucius Martius's head, as he was inspiriting troops in Spain to a victorious battle;
another time, the woman Tanaquil witnessed fire over the head of the child
Servius Tullius as he slept, auguring that slave-boy's future rule.

Io non veggio davanti a noi se non uno splendore molto vermiglio.
. . . Quale vuo' tu della tua futura vittoria più manifesto segnale?
Certo quella fiamma che apparve a Lucio Marzio sopra la testa . . .
non fu più manifesto segno del futuro triunfo. Né quella ancora che
apparve a Tulio, ancora picciolo fanciullo, dormendo, nel cospetto
di Tanaquila, fu più manifesto segnale del futuro imperio.

[All I can see ahead of us is something shining very red. . . . What
more manifest sign could you wish of your future victory? The flame
that appeared to Lucius Martius over his head . . . was no more man-

ifestly a sign of future triumph. Nor again was the one that appeared
over Tullius, as he slept in the presence of Tanaquil, more manifestly
a sign of future rule.][15] (2.58.7–10)

As for the hero Florio, ups and downs in his psyche correlate with his
clothing just as if his costumes were priestly vestments scheduled for the
liturgical year. When he departs Marmorina in search of Biancifiore, he
puts on purple (3.75), which hue of mourning, as Boccaccio the canonist
well knew, dominates church vestments during Lent. For his triumphal
entry into Rome for baptism at the Lateran, Florio wraps himself in a
cloak of gold (5.71). Mostly, though, Florio favors red. It is the color in
which illustrators of the *Filocolo* like to let us see him. Covered with vermilion samite beneath a standard of vermilion roses, he fought in the
benevolent shadow of Mars—the red god sheathed in a red cloud—to save
Biancifiore from an unjust death.[16] What had alerted him to her danger
was the magic ring she gave him (a family heirloom that had come down
to Biancifiore from Hannibal's brother, Hapsdrubal, to Alchimedes, Scipio Africanus, Quinto Lelio Africano, Giulia Topazia, and Glorizia), with
a stone, naturally, of "vermilion" (2.20). At the Admiral's Tower, Filocolo
is camouflaged by a carmine tunic as he passes in a basket of roses through
the window of Biancifiore's suite (5.113). Color coordinates extend
beyond his wardrobe and chivalric ornaments. Thus, in a motif that recalls
both the myth of Theseus and the romance of Tristan and Iseult, Filocolo's ship spreads like semaphores its canvas. As his crew weighs anchor
at Pisa on a journey for Sicily (the leg of their journey that diverts them to
Parthenope), they unfurl "bloodred sails" and head in the direction of the
"Island of Fire" (4.6).

So much fiery red finds one emblematic key in the idol of Cupid who
presides at the entrance to the most heavenly room of all the one hundred
chambers within the harem honeycomb of the Admiral's Tower.

---

15. Boccaccio's source for the two Roman anecdotes was Valerius Maximus *Factorum et
dictorum memorabilium* 1.6.2 and 4.43.7 (see Quaglio's commentary in his edition of the *Filocolo*, 794–95 nn. 3–4).

16. Grossvogel (*Ambiguity and Allusion,* 106–7) finds in the Martian cloud "a sign pointing to other signs." He argues that it should recall the cloud in book 1 of the *Filocolo* as well
as the cloud and pillar of fire in Exodus 14:24. Hence, as Grossvogel notes, Mars (like other
pagan figures in the romance) "has religious attributes with Biblical connotations." Other
accounts of the Floire and Blanchefleur legend link the lovers with red and white, respectively—connections initially related to their names. See Edmund Reiss, "Symbolic Detail in
Medieval Narrative: *Floris and Blancheflour,*" *Papers on Language and Literature* 7 (1971):
339–50.

A fronte alla porta di questa, sopra una colonna, la quale ogni uomo che la vedesse la giudicherebbe di fuoco nel primo aspetto, tanto è vermiglia e lucente, dimora il figliuolo di Venere; . . . ma egli non ha gli occhi fasciati . . . , anzi gli ha quivi belli e piacevoli, e per pupilla di ciascuno è un carbuncolo, che in quella camera tenebre essere non lasciano per alcun tempo, ma luminosa e chiara come se il sole vi ferisse la tengono.

[Before the door to the room, on a column that anyone would on first sight judge to be made of fire (so ruddy is its light), dwells the son of Venus . . . , but his eyes are not blindfolded; . . . rather, they are fair and pleasing, and each has for a pupil a carbuncle that never lets any shadows into that room; instead, they keep it as luminous and bright as if it were struck by sunlight.][17] (4.85.8)

But Ascalion's memories of Roman prodigies—flames that sprung mysteriously over a man and boy to forecast victory and empire—must remind us of the miracle recorded in Acts 2, that very first Pentecost of the Christian Church, when fire whirled from a wind and rested in tongues on the apostles' heads. The event will repeat itself in the *Filocolo,* on a smaller scale and in the peaceful setting of a courtly garden near Naples. Instead of twelve men, one woman receives the gift. Caleon watches while a "spiritlet" from the third heaven kindles this flame over Queen Fiammetta's crown. Like Ascalion, he thinks back to the lambent sign Tanaquil beheld.

. . . questa luce, lasciando ne' begli occhi i suoi vestigii, il vidi salire sopra la vostra corona, sopra la quale, come egli vi fu, insieme con i raggi parve che nuova fiamma vi s'accendesse, forse qual fu già quella che fu da Tanaquila veduta a Tulio piccolo garzone dormendo.

[. . . this light, leaving its traces in your fair eyes, I saw climb over your crown, and once there with its rays it seemed to kindle there a new flame, perhaps like the one Tanaquila once saw on the little boy Tullius as he lay sleeping.][18] (4.43.7)

---

17. Red plays an important role in other versions of the European legend as the color of the carbuncles that shine in Cupid's eyes in Blanchefleur's prison tower. See, e.g., Wentersdorf, "Iconographic Elements," for quotes from medieval lapidaries that describe the fiery color of the carbuncle and its implications as a symbol of love.

18. Smarr (*Boccaccio and Fiammetta,* 38–39) was to my knowledge the first to connect the flamelet over Fiammetta's head in the love debate with the iconography of Pentecost.

Not only does Caleon see this entrancing play of light, but he is privileged to hear it perform a perfect madrigal. "My flamelet," the little spirit sings, "reveals the power of the arrows that Fiammetta shoots from her eyes at whomsoever she pleases." Over the queen of the debate, as she rules in favor of virtue to Caleon's question about which kind of love is best, dances the spiritlet, shining as a flamelet.

That "Lady-of-the-Flamelet," who is really named Maria and whose father is king of Parthenope, duplicates the Author's beloved, also a Princess Maria and a woman who appears under fiery circumstances. To paraphrase his words in the prologue of the romance, the fateful encounter—or rather, eye contact—occurs after the fourth hour has passed on a day whose first hour Saturn rules, when sacerdotal successors to the man who humbly girt the rope are singing the office that celebrates the son of Jove's glorious birth from Pluto's despoiled kingdoms, "in a temple in Parthenope named after him who, to become deified, suffered himself to be sacrificed on the grate." Out of circumlocution, we understand that since Saturn rules its first hour, the day in question is Saturday. The sun has progressed to past the fourth hour, which would put it in the fifth. Priests in the order of Saint Francis joyfully chant mass for the risen Christ as he harrows hell. Their service takes place at a church in Naples named San Lorenzo. It is Easter Saturday. Here, in the sanctuary whose patron saint was roasted to death by fire, no sooner had our Author seen his lady than her eyes sent forth a "fiery arrow" that flew into his heart and kindled there an "inextinguishable flame."

Not just one but two "Fiammettas" come to fictional life in Boccaccio's *Filocolo.* The first, chronologically, lived at the time of Justinian; her later congener, in Angevin Naples. The Author falls in love with the latter; Caleon, his interior double, adores the earlier princess. Creating them, Boccaccio forges a genealogy that runs along a flame line. It has biblical ancestors in the apostles, classical antetypes in Lucius Martius and Servius Tullius. From history both scriptural and Roman descend two daughters, a "Flamelet" for each of the historical time frames of the *Filocolo.*[19] Links in a chain of associations—red clothing, red armor, a red ring, a red god on a red horse in a red cloud like the fire over Lucius Martius and Servius Tulius, red sails, red roses, a red Cupid with eyes of fiery carbuncles, a

---

19. Smarr, *Boccaccio and Fiammetta,* 36–39, reads this as one of many programmatic "doublings" in the *Filocolo.* The narrator's love story begins at Easter; Florio and Biancifiore have a story that belongs to Pentecost, the liturgical climax of the paschal cycle. See discussion later in this chapter.

flamelet over Fiammetta, fiery arrows in the fifth hour, a martyr grilled on a bed of fire—all these rubificient symbols point ahead to Pentecost, the feast that perfects Eastertide and commemorates a miracle of fire.

Death threatens Florio and Biancifiore in a form not commensurate with their crimes—for they are innocents—but matched to Boccaccio's legal training and liturgical motifs. At the trial hastily mounted for Biancifiore, Massamutino, who had masterminded the plot of the poisoned peacock, rises to demand of Felice verdict and sentence.

> . . . per mio consiglio dico e giudico che misurando giustamente la pena col fallo, che ella muoia: e sì come ella volle che la vostra vita per la focosa forza del veleno si consumasse, così la sua con ardente fuoco consumata sia.

> [. . . by my counsel, I say and judge that measuring justly the penalty with the fault, she must die; and just as she wished your life to be consumed by the fiery power of poison, so hers should be consumed by burning fire.] (2.38.5)

After the couple is discovered abed in the Arab's Tower, they are put out in a meadow for the same kind of public execution. Alexandria's Admiral has suitably barbaric sergeants who have tied the two naked lovers together and lowered them on a rope from the tower, against which they dangle. Boccaccio then plays with both fire and a "pending" judgment.

> I quali tanto così legati pendono, quanto nel duro petto dell'amiraglio pende qual pena tale offesa voglia dare; ma poi che con diliberato animo elesse che la loro vita per fuoco finisse, comanda che nel prato siano posati, e quivi in accesi fuochi siano sanza pietà messi.

> [Bound thus, they hang suspended for as long as it pends in the Admiral's hard heart what penalty he wants to impose for such an offense; but then, when he has deliberated and decided that their life should end by fire, he orders that they be placed in the meadow and there thrown mercilessly into burning fires.] (4.127.8)

As the poet indulges in a bit of flamboyant Gothic rhetoric, the love connection comes forward in capital letters. What this mannered, amorous alphabet signals on a second level, in allegory submerged, are flames fanned by Pentecostal winds. Lamenting for the umpteenth time her hopeless fate, Biancifiore moans:

Oimè misera, a che morte son io apparecchiata! Al fuoco! Il fuoco caccerà de' fermi petti l'amoroso fuoco. Quel fuoco che il mare, né la terra, né paura, né vergogna, né ancora gl'iddii hanno potuto spegnere, il fuoco lo spegnerà.

[Woe, miserable me, what death awaits me! By fire! Fire will drive from constant hearts amorous fire. That fire that neither sea, nor earth, nor fear, nor shame, nor even the gods could extinguish—it will be extinguished by fire.] (4.130.6)

Were this not enough, to redouble the attack, the men who light the fires to burn up the lovers are two hot-blooded Libyans whose names Boccaccio translates right in the story: Ircuscomos (Wild-haired) and Flagrareo (Burning-eyed) (4.131). Luckily, the magic ring remains in the lovers' possession, the ring with a ruby red stone that shields whomever it touches from destruction by fire. So the flames that engulf them fail to harm them, and the moment Venus dissipates the smoke, they emerge "così freschi come rugiadosa rosa colta nell'aurora" [fresh as a dewy rose plucked at dawn] (4.149).[20]

Cupid's arrows and fires of love—these are commonplaces of courtly lyricism. But like Venus and Diana in their extended range of connections, such topoi operate in Boccaccio's vernacular fiction across boundaries both profane and sacred. They lead us by association to Queen Fiammetta, who rules crowned with a flamelet, and to the warrior god, Mars, whose reddish glow Boccaccio compares with two heroes of Rome visited by flickerings over their heads. This is, obviously, a zone of Pentecostal values. Inside it fall two more "red" incidents, far apart in the *Filocolo* plotline but causally related.

Crimson stains the first, a "bloodred" episode at the center of book 1. Like Charlemagne's rear guard, a contingent commanded by his paladin Roland, the pilgrims who follow Quinto Lelio Africano meet ambush in the Pyrenees. King Felice and his "Arab" loyalists wipe out the Christian men, leaving a battlefield bathed in their blood. In language that inter-

---

20. Their survival of the fire and release from it recall the animals in *Diana's Hunt*. They are heaped to burn in a holocaust, then jump out "fresh as the lily" in the form of handsome young men.

weaves Carolingian romance and classical epic, Boccaccio makes the
ground of this defeat both an eerie place running with Lucan's gore—
"vermilion sand, furrowed with various rivulets of blood"—and a heroic
proving ground for Christian martyrdom.[21] As in Statius's *Thebaid,* where
Creon refused to allow burial of the dead who had marched with the Seven
against Thebes, here, too, all the fallen are left on the field, exposed to the
elements. Before they can be interred, some twenty years must pass. It is
no surprise that, after all that time, it takes a miracle to make possible the
burial. The *Filocolo* readily arranges this. Lively with the doings of its
pagan gods, Boccaccio's romance can just as easily orchestrate action
from a Christian heaven.

Not until late in book 5 does Boccaccio pick up this thread in his plot.
Florio and Biancifiore, now married and baptized, happen to be camped
in the very valley of the Pyrenees where Felice's guard had slaughtered the
pilgrims. They are en route to Santiago de Compostela, fulfilling the vow
that Biancifiore's parents could not. Now that time and place are ripe for
the martyrs' bone recovery, Quinto Lelio Africano and his wife, Giulia
Topazia, appear to Biancifiore in a dream vision. Dwelling among the
elect, they brighten the darkness of her sleep as souls resplendent with all
fairness of youth, clothed in those bodies they had inhabited when death
cut them down.

> . . . a Biancifiore in fulvida luce un giovane di grazioso aspetto con
> una giovane bellissima accompagnato, di vermiglio vestiti, le
> apparvero. . . . [They said] "sepera le sante reliquie dalle inique. . . .
> le vedrete tutte vermiglie rosseggiare, come se di fuoco fossero"

> [. . . to Biancifiore there appeared in a burst of light a young man of
> graceful aspect accompanied by a most beautiful young woman,
> dressed in vermilion both . . . . [They said] "Separate the holy relics
> from the iniquitous . . . . You will see them all shining vermilion as if
> they were fire."] (5.90.1–4)

The moment the vision vanishes, Biancifiore, accompanied by Florio and
Mennilio, gets up and goes out without a lantern. Like a starry night,
everywhere the valley floor shines with "rubescent relics." Describing these
remains, Boccaccio stresses their coloration and value. Within a short

---

21. *Filoc.* 1.31: "la vermiglia arena, che di varii ruscelletti di sangue era solcata." The battle takes place in 1.26, the longest chapter of book 1 and the textual location of Lelio's death.

space of two chapters recur the formulas "sante reliquie," "tutte vermiglie rosseggiare," "le vermiglie ossa," "le rosseggianti reliquie," "ossa rosseggianti," "vermiglie reliquie," "vermiglie ossa" (5.90–91). His vocabulary, with a modifier that alternates between "red" and "vermilion," shifts in its substantive between "bones" and "relics." He denotes differences between past and present, between corporal and spiritual, between life on earth and life in heaven. Long gone is the blood that streamed over a battlefield two decades before; in its place, the nocturnal landscape produces an orrery of ruddy phosphorescence. Once upon a time, pilgrims became sainted martyrs. Yesterday's bones have turned into today's holy relics. Filial piety will deliver Biancifiore's parents' "relics" to a final resting place, the city that was theirs body and soul, that Rome where Christian romance must begin and end.

Like any historical novel, the *Filocolo* flows on more than one chronological register. It is about the past; it is about the present. As in his earlier *Diana's Hunt,* Boccaccio speaks through the *Filocolo* to contemporary women of King Robert's Angevin court. A feminine collectivity whom Maria-Fiammetta figures, they must have delighted in all the pages centered on Biancifiore—a fragile young thing buffeted by the gods, a constant heroine chaste to her wedding day, a daughter respectful of her parents' memory, a wife blessed in motherhood by the son she bears, "little Lelio."[22] But starting from its original title, which erases Biancifiore and announces only a male protagonist, the *Filocolo* is a more masculine work than *Diana's Hunt.* Pitched first of all to King Robert and composed by a student of canon law, the *Filocolo* is a summa of credence in Italy in the early trecento. We hear it in Friar Ilario's theology, openly preached. We decipher it in the poet's occulted registers of liturgical symbolism. We discover it over and over in a book where daily fictional life mirrors popular religious practice—worship, prayers, pilgrimage, rituals, and miracles.

Boccaccio's focus is the cult of a single male saint, James. From distant Galicia, he works his miracles wherever he is worshiped.[23] Quinto Lelio prays in paleo-Christian Rome before an image of James, who answers the believer in a dream. Later Lelio dies with fellow soldiers in the faith on a

---

22. We hear of this child at 5.63. He is six months old at the time of Florio's baptism.

23. The Spanish elements in the *Filocolo,* based on a story inspired by the cult of Saint James, stem from Boccaccio's acquaintance with a Spanish archetype of the romance, a version of the tale related to the *Crónica de Flores y Blancaflor.* Only in this Spanish version and in the *Filocolo,* for example, is Cordova the capital of Felice's kingdom. Similarly, Boccaccio's "Montoro" (which becomes Verona) must derive from the Andalusian "Montor." See Grieve, *Floire and Blanchefleur,* 48–49, 99.

field red with blood and joins the ranks of early Christian martyrs. Christ himself promises their reward, rallying them from a cloudlet in accents that echo the Gospels, with his final words on earth.

Voi sarete oggi tutti meco nel vero tempio di Colui il cui [sic] voi andate a vedere, e quivi le corone apparecchiate alla vostra vittoria vi donerò.

[Today you shall all be with me in the true temple of Him whose place you are going to see, and there I shall give you the crowns prepared for your victory.] (1.25.10).

Many years after, it will be Lelio's turn to speak from heaven, telling Biancifiore to collect for burial their martyred bones, which a red glow will distinguish from animal and heathen remains. Those relics remind us of other objects venerated in the treasure of Saint Peter's. Pope Vigilius himself permits them to be displayed for Florio and his party: they are the veronica, which Vespasian brought from Jerusalem; the seamless tunic; the head of Saint John the Baptist; and the heads of Saint Peter and Saint Paul (5.77).

Actually, the *Filocolo* past has more than one track, because several strata of history are superimposed there. We are in a transitional Rome, an empire both pre-Christian and paleo-Christian. Boccaccio emblazons his hero and heroine with the most illustrious Roman bloodlines imaginable: they descend, respectively, from Scipio Africanus and Julius Caesar. Those ancient lineages, the quintessential pagan clans, take a great step in history to produce proud new generations that now—or soon will—believe in a new religion. Quite naturally, pagan gods—Venus, Mars, Diana, Cupid, Hymen, Iris, Juno, Jove—still populate this world of evolving beliefs. At the same time, occasional slippages in the fiction put us up into another period, where "Arab" horsemen slaughter Christian pilgrims in Iberia, and where we have characters like the Admiral of Alexandria, who keeps women stored for the sultan of Babylonia in a stronghold called the Arab's Tower. The reign of Pope Vigilius (537–55) anchors historically the *Filocolo,* which has a larger time frame running from 529 to 552.[24] This

---

24. Quaglio has meticulously reconstructed the chronology of the romance, in "Tra fonti e testo del *Filocolo*"; see especially 340–41. In the fiction, Justinian is referred to as living, and his dates were, in fact, 527–66. He was converted by Pope Agapetus during the period 533–36. Remarkably, Boccaccio's narrative is quite consistent in its internal time references, and it reflects the author's efforts to achieve a true historical setting.

cannot, however, be an era of hostile Saracens, since Muhammad was not born until later in the sixth century. The Moslems did not begin to spread until the seventh century, and not until the eighth did they conquer Spain. Was Boccaccio confused about his dates? It is more likely that the anachronism is deliberate. His purpose must have been less to re-create a remote era in realistic detail than to present a sort of universal non-Christian past. Pagan idolatry and Moslem heresy overlap as he looks back from a perspective typical of his times, a Gothic century that regarded statuettes of the gods as if they were so many little Muhammads, or "mawmets."[25]

A pope not particularly memorable dates the fiction, but we are meant to look beyond him to his greater contemporary, Justinian. Justinian, the emperor, is the personage that really accounts for timing in the *Filocolo.* Boccaccio keeps him to the wings and recalls him at one remove through his son, Bellisano, who seems to be the poet's invention. We first hear of Justinian as Filocolo, rapt in contemplation of the Christ image at San Giovanni in Laterano, is approached by a priest. The instrument of Filocolo's conversion, he is connected to Justinian through the emperor's son, called Bellisano. Boccaccio introduces him and explains how he came to the Lateran:

> . . . uno uomo antico non troppo e di bella apparenza, in iscienza peritissimo, il cui nome, secondo ch'egli poscia manifestò, era Ilario, disceso di parenti nobilissimi, d'Attene quivi con Bellisano, patrizio di Roma, e figliuolo dell'inclito imperadore Giustiniano, quivi venuto, e all'ordine de' cavalieri di Dio scritto, forse a guardia del bel luogo diputato

> [. . . a man not overly old and of handsome appearance, with most expert knowledge, whose name, as he afterwards revealed it, was Ilario, descended from most noble parents; come there [to Rome] from Athens with Bellisano, a patrician of Rome and son of the distinguished emperor Justinian, he was enrolled in the order of the knights of God, perhaps appointed as guardian of that beautiful place]. (5.52.4)

---

25. The idols representing non-Christian deities were known as "mawmets" in most European vernaculars, a generic name deriving from the name of Muhammad, the prophet of Islam. See Camille, *The Gothic Idol,* 135.

Not long after, when Filocolo eloquently imparts the truth he has learned from Ilario to his companions at their inn, we learn that Justinian is still living.

> . . . "io annunziatore dell'etterna gloria vi voglio essere." . . . E mirabile cosa fu che, secondo ch'egli disse poi, nella lingua gli corre-ano le parole meglio che egli prima nell'animo non divisava di dirle, la qual cosa superinfusa grazia di Dio essere conobbe . . . . "Gius-tiano imperadore, il quale, in uno errore con noi insieme, quello las-ciando, ricorse alla verità."

> ["I want to announce to you eternal glory." . . . And it was an amaz-ing thing, as he (Filocolo) himself said afterward, the words flowed on his tongue better than he had formed them before in his mind, which he knew to be grace from God superinfused . . . . "Justinian the Emperor, who, in one error together with us, leaving that, had recourse to the truth."] (5.59.4–7)

Why should Justinian be the exemplary convert whose experience Filocolo sees as parallel to his own? It is a subject soon remembered again, as Ilario assures Filocolo's reconciliation with his wife's family in Rome because the emperor's son, Bellisano, happens to be a relative of Biancifiore's mother. Says the priest,

> Egli è in questa città patrizio Bellisano, figliuolo di Giustiano imper-adore de' romani, il quale alla cattolica fede, come avanti ti dissi, tornò, non sono ancora molti anni passati, dirizzandolvi Agapito sommo pastor.

> [There is in this city the patrician Bellisano, son of Justinian, emperor of the Romans, who returned to the Catholic faith, as I told you before, not so many years past, when Agapetus, the supreme shepherd, directed him to it.][26] (5.64.5)

With the reference to "Agapito, sommo pastore," Boccaccio's rationale comes clearly into view. His inspiration for elevating Justinian as the model convert was in a beloved model close at hand—none other than

---

26. The same grace that inspired Giannotto to eloquence was the start of his friend Abraam's conversion (*Dec.* 1.2).

Dante. The allusion to Justinian's story, as Dante had let him tell it in *Paradiso* 6, has by now become patent.

> E prima ch'io a l'ovra fossi attento,
> una natura in Cristo esser, non piùe,
> credea, e di tal fede era contento;
>   ma 'l benedetto Agapito, che fue
> sommo pastore, a la fede sincera
> mi drizzò con le parole sue.

[And before I had put my mind to this work (of codifying the laws), one nature and no more I held to be in Christ, and with that faith I was content; but the blessed Agapetus, who was the supreme pastor, directed me to the true faith by his words.][27] (*Par.* 6.13–18)

Once again on cue from Dante, Boccaccio draws his story into the circle of a golden era—even though his Angevin loyalties ought to militate against such politics. His allegiance in poetry is really to Dante, not to any imperial dynasty. Here in Justinian is a legal authority to whom the student of church law respectfully nods; here is the archconvert who can set an example for all Europe; here is a Christian emperor illustrious in universal history.

The pagan gods, those "superfluous" characters ubiquitous until Florio's baptism, have to be present in full force to make the point that they are many, unlike the true God, who is Triune unity.[28] Over and over again, they descend into the action, or they remain above the scenes as mortals below seek to contact them through all sorts of rites. Venus, with thirteen recorded interventions in the three central books, dominates. Her eventual ally, Diana, takes action seven times. Mars, too, cooperates with Venus, a match in myth that nicely suits a marriage story.[29] In allegory of a Servian

---

27. Actually, the emperor had been guilty of a heresy rather than of complete ignorance of Christ, so Filocolo stretches the analogy.

28. Smarr (*Boccaccio and Fiammetta,* 49) also recognized this narrative movement in the *Filocolo:* "As it leads from the false pagan gods to the true Christian one, so too it leads from the epic of pagan myth to the epic of Christian history."

29. When Ascalion remarks that he has served Mars more than Venus (4.177), we are obviously to understand that he is a soldier, not a lover. For the symbolism of Mars and Venus as a marriage couple, see Kirkham, "'Chiuso parlare in Boccaccio's *Teseida.*" Boccaccio knew their mythography both *in bono* and *in malo* when he wrote the *Filocolo.* The two sides of their relationship come up in the seventh question in the love debate, as Caleon argues that Venus softens Mars (4.45), whereas Fiammetta counters with censure of their adultery (4.46).

sort, Mars first enters the picture to strengthen Florio for combat against the seneschal, lending his sword (2.42) and riding beside the youth in a ruddy cloud, "a miracle of red light" (2.71). Later, as Florio and Biancifiore are to be burned at the stake, the warrior god will muster to virile battle Ascalion, Dario, Bellisano, and others who fight the Admiral's monstrous minions, "hirsute" and "burning" Libyans (4.139). Gradually, in Mars—that red god whose aura reminded Ascalion of two fire miracles in Roman history and who patronizes the Knights' Holiday—we recognize the torchbearer of Pentecost.

Often the gods are named several in a string or mentioned as a lump sum. For example, we are told that on the night before Florio is to ride up the tower wall in his rose basket, "no god is left in heaven to whom Florio's words do not travel" (4.107). One of the fullest lists, stretched rhetorically with the device of polysyndeton, unfolds as the lovers' troubles end at last, an event worthy indeed of special thanks to higher powers. Florio places myrtle wreaths in all the temples of Alexandria.

Egli a Giunone uccide il tauro e a Minerva la vacca e a Mercurio il vitello; a Pallade le sue ulive e a Cerere frutta e piene biade, e a Bacco poderosi vini, e a Marte egli co' suoi compagni offerano le penetrate armi, e a Venere e al suo figliuolo, e a qualunque altro dio o dea celestiale o marino o terreno o infernale offera degni doni, sopra gli altari di tutti accendendo fuochi e 'l simigliante fa Biancifiore, e Ascalion e i suoi compagni, e con loro l'amiraglio e molti cittadini."

[For Juno he kills a bull, and for Minerva a cow, and for Mercury a calf; to Pallas he and his companions offer her olives, and to Ceres fruit and ripe grain, and to Bacchus mighty vines, and to Mars their pierced arms, and to Venus and to her son and to every other god or goddess whatsoever of heaven or sea or earth or hell he offers worthy gifts, lighting fires on the altars of them all; and Biancifiore does the same, and Ascalion and his companions, and with them the Admiral and many citizens.] (4.155)

From here on, as we approach book 5 of the *Filocolo,* the gods' influence drops off dramatically. It will only persist, really, in the odd parenthesis that encloses Idalogos.[30] Afterward, powerful currents pushing from the

---

30. There has long been speculation that Boccaccio wrote the fifth book of the *Filocolo* after a lapse in time. The Idalogos episode is of a nature that would have put it more naturally in an earlier book.

capital of Christendom clear them from the air. But just at this moment, they tower at a zenith. We are still very much in Egypt, both literally and metaphorically, since it is the land of a polytheistic society. We are, so to speak, at the antipodes of Rome.

God, Christ, and the saints also assert themselves in the story, to even greater effect, although they each appear only once. Saint James visits sleeping Lelio and promises him a child (1.5); Christ promises a place in heaven and crown of martyrdom to the Christian pilgrims who shed their blood (1.25); God issues a thunderous threat to Felice (5.80); Quinto Lelio returns as a spirit to the site of his unburied, sun-bleached bones and shows them, miraculously glowing red, to the child whom James long before had announced (5.90). The appearances of those who speak from a Christian heaven are few; they constitute singular events that underscore a monotheistic faith. God comes once in the whole *Filocolo* because there is only one God. So, too, the others—Christ, James, Lelio—come but one time only. All the panoply of false idols must fall, swept off their columns and written out of the leaves in the book. Many old gods must yield to the one new God. Heathen sanctuaries are transformed into houses of Christian worship; on an old Greek romance, Boccaccio builds a modern Catholic catechism.

The *Filocolo* affirms orthodox Christianity. Boccaccio recites lessons he has learned from the Bible, from lives of the saints, from the canons of church law. Much of his culture as canonist he channels through Ilario's words of instruction. As Smarr has emphasized, the Author's doubles in this novel are not just lovers, Caleon and Idalogos, those cited by romantic critics in their selective vision. He has another double in Friar Ilario, the "joyful" one whose name bespeaks how "gladly" he carries the Good News. He knows all Scripture, the whole providential history of the world, the tenets of the faith set forth in the Credo. Sermons, too, he can preach, compositions to rival and please a king who ruled nearly eight centuries later on the Angevin throne of Naples. Ilario's "great expertise in knowledge," as Boccaccio calls it, extends well beyond book learning, to popular forms of belief, manifestations like miracles and relics. In echoic rhythms, he seconds Boccaccio, who created a literary artifact inspired by the cult of Saint James and his shrine at Santiago. The canonist's characters make pilgrimages, they welcome martyrdom, they seek baptism, they witness miracles, they destroy idols, they convert the heathen. Boccaccio takes seriously here not only the church, as he always did, but its cult practices, certain of which he would later gleefully mock. We have only to recall what manner of "saints" people the first stories of the first two days in the *Decameron;* what warped paternosters lie in the repertory of the *Corbaccio* widow.

Certaldo's most famous son celebrates the coming of the Word to the world and the *translatio Ecclesiae.* Underlining and troping this movement of the Church from East to West, Ilario journeys from Greece to Rome with Bellisano, the son of Justinian. Justinian, who ruled from Constantinople, is the model convert canonized by Dante, in whose *Comedia* he had himself narrated the *translatio imperii.* By imitating Justinian's example, Florio assumes his role as a Christian king in the West, directed to a straight path by "the Good News" and baptized by the pope who sat in Saint Peter's soon after Agapetus.[31] Not only does he follow Saint James and complete the conversion of occidental Europe, but he also takes his place in an international line of secular lordship. Boccaccio's portrait of Florio's growth, education, and conversion has in it something of the medieval genre called *De regimine principum,* or "Mirror of Princes." In that sense, the *Filocolo* is the story of an ideal Christian ruler in the making, a young man to whom tutors, travel, and paternal counsel impart a curriculum complete with the seven liberal arts as well as the Christian virtues and vices in time for his dynastic succession to the throne. Indicative of Boccaccio's fondness for mystic numbers, arithmetic receives particular mention, a discipline that teaches the "holy principles of Pythagoras" (2.10).[32]

In marriage and conversion, in love and redemption, the canonist at King Robert's court found themes for an epic romance. Easter and Pentecost, days proper for baptism according to canon law, punctuate its calendar. Holy Saturday, when the Author first sees Maria, redeems individual sinners. The final feast day in the paschal cycle, Pentecost, which schedules the lives of his romantic protagonists, heralds collective salvation and universal conversion. Maria-Fiammetta could not help but be absent from *Diana's Hunt* and the *Filostrato,* both composed before the *Filocolo.* For her appearance in Boccaccio's fiction, we have to wait until the *Filocolo*

---

31. Agapetus I was pope from 535 to 536; his successor was Silverius, from June, 536, to March, 537; following Silverius came Vigilius, from 537 to 555.

32. Porcelli, in "Strutture e forme," enumerates the categories of Florio's education. Within the five-part division of the *Filocolo* into books, he finds a tripartite narrative structure marking a line of moral ascent. The progression loosely parallels the three parts of Dante's *Commedia* in its linguistic borrowings and corresponds to the three great subjects defined by Dante as worthy of poetry (arms, love, and rectitude), being a "triple *iter*" that carries Florio from war, to love, to rational maturity.

because she was invented for this, his Pentecostal novel. Her double name, duplicated in the princess courted by Caleon, brackets the novel's liturgical chronology: she is Maria for Easter weekend; for Whitsunday, a Lady-of-the-Flamelet.

Pagan deities, too, have Christian resonance. Later, in the *Genealogy of the Gentile Gods,* Boccaccio would allegorize them openly. Here he does so covertly. Both in her operations with Diana and in her pairing with Mars, Venus sheds a benevolent influence as the lady of the lovers' ascendent. She fosters love regulated by the goddess of chastity and protected by the warrior god, love that prefigures the protagonists' new life in Christian charity. The old polytheistic gods are not redundancies; they are a panoply necessary as the precondition for conversion and for a fully satisfactory resolution of the romance. They lead to its Christian denouement. In retrospect, Juno and Venus and Diana and Mars and Minerva and Mercury and Pallas and Hymen and Cupid and Bacchus and Ceres and Astrea and Pluto and Neptune and Apollo together all reinforce the power of the Word, the power of the One.

Looking back on the *Filocolo,* we see how Boccaccio has brought to life historic layers from our era of grace. Florio and Biancifiore find a new life in a new love of Christ and bring the new religion to Spain. A new Author tells their story, one whose name is filled with grace and who sails the skiff of his "booklet" over seas with "graceful" winds billowing the sails. The classic fairy tale, of lovers who conquer all and live happily ever after, has doubled its tracks to become a Christian fiction, a triumph of the Pentecostal community. It is the raconteur's fantasy as a Roman canonist.

Appendix: A Brief Chronology of the Life and Works of Giovanni di Boccaccio di Certaldo

July, 1313	Birth of Boccaccio the illegitimate son of Boccaccino da Certaldo and an unknown mother.
1327	Boccaccio moves from Florence to Naples with his father, an agent of the Bardi Bank.
1330–35	Canon law student at University of Naples.
ca. 1332–34	Earliest Latin compositions: *Elegia di Costanza, Allegoria mitologica.*
[Apr. 3, 1333]	[In the fiction of the *Filocolo,* Boccaccio falls in love with Maria-Fiammetta.]
ca. 1333–34	*Caccia di Diana.*
ca. 1334	*Filostrato.*
ca. 1336–38/39	*Filocolo.*
1338	Translation into Tuscan of Livy's third and fourth *Decades.*
1339	Four allegorical epistles in Latin ("Crepor celsitudinis," "Mavortis milex," "Nereus amphytritibus," "Sacre famis").
ca. 1339–41	*Teseida delle nozze d'Emilia.*
early 1341	Boccaccio moves back to Florence from Naples in wake of European financial crisis.
1341–42	*Comedia delle ninfe fiorentine;* first draft of *De vita et moribus domini Francisci Petracchi.*
1342	*De Canaria.*
1342–43	First draft of *Amorosa visione.*

ca. 1343–44	*Elegia di Madonna Fiammetta.*
ca. 1344–46	*Ninfale fiesolano.*
1346	Boccaccio is in Ravenna at the court of Ostasio da Polenta.
1347–48	Boccaccio visits court of Francesco Ordelaffi at Forlí.
1349–50	Birth of Boccaccio's third illegitimate child, Violante.
1347(?)–66	*Bucolicum carmen.*
ca. 1350	Conception of *Genealogia deorum gentilium.*
Aug.–Sept., 1350	Ambassadorial mission to the Romagna and to Ravenna, where he delivers ten gold florins from the city of Florence to Dante's cloistered daughter, Sister Beatrice.
early Oct., 1350	In Florence Boccaccio briefly meets Petrarch, who stops en route to Rome on pilgrimage.
1351	Receives from Petrarch Cicero's *Pro Archia.*
Jan., 1351	Boccaccio chosen by lot to serve as chamberlain of Chamber of the *Comune* of Florence.
winter, 1351–52	Ambassador from Florence to Ludwig of Baveria in the Tyrol.
Mar., 1351	Trip to Padua for visit with Petrarch.
after Mar., 1351	First redaction of *Trattatello in laude di Dante.*
Jan., 1352	Chamberlain and delegate of Florence in the ceding of Prato to Florence by Naples crown.
ca. 1350–52	*Decameron.*
May–June, 1354	Ambassadorial mission from Florence to Pope Innocent VI in Avignon.
July, 1354	Mission to Certaldo to organize citizen resistance against the captain of a mercenary company.
ca. 1355	Conception and draft of *De casibus virorum illustrium, De montibus.*
April, 1355	Petrarch receives Boccaccio's gift of a valuable old manuscript of Augustine's *Enarrationes in Psalmos.*
May–Aug., 1355	Named officer of the Condotta (to review conduct of the unruly soldiers in service of the *Comune* of Florence).

ca. 1355	*Corbaccio.*
1355	Trip to Naples; visits the monastic library at Montecassino and finds manuscripts of Varro's *De lingua latina,* Cicero's *Pro Cluentio,* the Ciceronian *Rhetorica ad Herennium,* Tacitus's *Annales* and *Historiae.*
1355–57	*De montibus* begun (corrections continue until 1374).
summer, 1357	Trip to Ravenna.
Mar., 1359	Trip to Milan, where he visits with Petrarch; they plant laurel trees together in Petrarch's garden.
June, 1359	Named ambassador from Florence to Lombardy.
1360	First draft of *Genealogia;* first redaction of *De casibus,* which Boccaccio continues to revise until the end of his life.
Nov., 1360	Pope Innocent VI legitimizes Boccaccio so that he can receive holy orders as a priest.
1360–62	Studies Greek and Homer with Leontius Pilatus.
1360	*Genealogia* probably finished, dedicated to Hugh IV, king of Cyprus.
1360	First redaction of *De casibus.*
July 2, 1361	Political turbulence in Florence; Boccaccio transfers his house in the quarter of Santa Felicita to his half brother Jacopo and removes to Certaldo.
1361	*De mulieribus* begun, continued in nine successive redactional phases up to 1375, dedicated to Andrea Acciaiuoli.
1361–62	Consolatory epistle to Pino de' Rossi.
winter, 1361–62	Trip to Ravenna; Boccaccio sends to Petrarch his *Vita sactissimi patris Petri Damiani,* based on the life of St. Peter Damian by Giovanni da Lodi.
1362	The Blessed Petroni of Siena predicts that Boccaccio will die soon if he does not give up poetry.
Oct., 1362–Mar., 1363	Disastrous trip to Naples at invitation of Nic-

	colò Acciaiuoli; discovery at Montecassino of Martial's *Liber de spectaculis.*
1363	On return from Naples, stops over in Venice to visit Petrarch in his home on the Riva degli Schiavoni.
1363	Death of his daughter, Violante.
1363	Third redaction of *Trattatello.*
1365	Another term as officer of the Condotta (to review conduct of soldiers on payroll of the *Comune* of Florence).
Aug. 21, 1365	Boccaccio makes a will.
Aug.–Nov., 1365	Ambassadorial mission to the Grimaldi Doge in Genoa and to Pope Urban V in Avignon.
1367	Second diplomatic mission to Pope Urban V, now back in Rome.
1368	Visit to Petrarch in Padua.
1369–70	Publishes his *Bucolicum carmen.*
1370	Return to Naples, where he is well received by Queen Giovanna.
1373–74	Completion of *De casibus,* dedicated to Mainardo Cavalcanti.
Sunday, Oct. 23, 1373	Boccaccio begins his public readings of the *Esposizioni sopra la Comedìa di Dante* in the Florentine church of Santo Stefano di Badia, salaried by the city.
1374	Ill health forces him to break off his Dante readings, probably around the end of January.
Aug. 28, 1374	Last will and testament.
Oct. 19, 1374	News reaches Boccaccio of Petrarch's death (July 19).
Dec. 21, 1375	Death in Certaldo.

Bibliography

Alan of Lille. *Anticlaudianus or The Good and Perfect Man*. Translated by James J. Sheridan. Toronto: Pontifical Institute of Mediaeval Studies, 1973.

——. *Plaint of Nature*. Translated by James J. Sheridan. Toronto: Pontifical Institute of Medieval Studies, 1980.

Albertazzi, Adolfo. *Romanzieri e romanzi del cinquecento e del seicento*. Bologna: Zanichelli, 1891.

Altfranzösisches Wörterbuch. Edited by Adolf Tobler and Erhard Lommatzsch. Weisbaden: F. Steiner, 1963.

Ammonizioni del Re Felice di Spagna al suo figliuolo. Nozze Zambrini-Mazzoni. Imola: Galeati, 1880.

Anselm of Laon. *Enarrationes in Apocalypsin*. *Patrologia latina* 162:1419–1586.

Antona-Traversi, Camillo. "Della realtà dell'amore di M. G. Boccaccio." *Il Propugnatore* 16 (1883): 57–92, 240–80, 387–417.

——. "Notizie storiche sull'*Amorosa visione*." *Studi di Filologia Romanza* 1 (1885): 425–44.

Apicius. *Cookery and Dining in Imperial Rome*. Edited and translated by Joseph Dommers Vehling. New York: Dover, 1977.

Aquinas, Thomas. *Commentary on the Nicomachean Ethics*. Translated by C. I. Litzinger, O.P. Chicago: Henry Regnery, 1964.

Armour, Peter. "The Love of Two Florentines: Brunetto Latini and Bondie Dietaiuti." *Lectura Dantis* 9 (1991): 11–33.

Augustine. *Sermo 219*. *Patrologia latina* 38:1088.

——. *De civitate Dei contra paganos*. Translated by William M. Green. 7 vols. Loeb Classical Library. Cambridge: Harvard University Press, 1972.

Auzzas, Ginetta. "L'inventario della 'Parva libraria' di Santo Spirito e la biblioteca del Boccaccio." *Italia Medioevale e Humanistica* 9 (1966): 1–74.

——. "I codici autografi. Elenco e bibliografia." *Studi sul Boccaccio* (1975): 1–20.

Bacchi della Lega, Alberto. *Serie delle edizioni delle opere di Giovanni Boccaccii*. 1875. Reprint, Bologna: Forni Editore, 1967.

Balduino, Armando, et al., eds. *Miscellanea di studi in onore di Vittore Branca*. 5 vols. Florence: Olschki, 1983.

————. *Boccaccio, Petrarca e altri poeti del Trecento.* Florence: Olschki, 1984.

Bandini, Domenico. "De viris claris." From *Aedilium ecclesiae florentiae (Fons memorabilium universi).* In *Le vite di Dante, Petrarca e Boccaccio scritte fino al secolo decimosesto,* edited by Angelo Solerti, 677–78. Storia letteraria d'Italia scritta da una Società di Professori, vol. 4. Milan: Dottor Francesco Vallardi, n.d.

Baránski, Zygmunt G., and Patrick Boyde, eds. *The Fiore in Context: Dante, France, Tuscany.* Notre Dame: University of Notre Dame Press, 1997.

Baránski, Zygmunt G., Patrick Boyde, and Lino Pertile, eds. *Lettura del "Fiore."* *Letture Classensi* 22. Ravenna: Longo, 1993.

Barbour, John. *The Buik of Alexander.* Edited by R. L. Graeme Ritchie. Scottish Text Society, n.s., vols. 12, 17, 21, 25. Edinburgh and London, 1921–29.

Bartholomaeus Anglicus. *Natural History (De proprietibus rerum).* Translated by H. Rackham. Loeb Classical Library. Cambridge: Harvard University Press, 1967.

Battaglia, Salvatore. "Schemi lirici nell'arte del Boccaccio." In *La coscienza letteraria del Medioevo,* 625–44. Naples: Liguori, 1965. (First published in *Archivium Romanicum* 19, no 1 [1935]: 61–78.)

————. *Giovanni Boccaccio e la riforma della narrativa.* Naples: Liguori, 1969.

Bede. *Explanatio Apocalypsis. Patrologia latina* 93:130–206.

Bembo, Pietro. *Prose della volgar lingua, Gli Asolani, Rime.* Edited by Carlo Dionisotti. Turin: UTET, 1966.

Benvenuto da Imola. *Comentum super Dantis Aldigherij comoediam.* 5 vols. Florence: Barbèra, 1887–88.

Bergin, Thomas G. *Boccaccio.* New York: Viking, 1981.

————. Introduction to *Il Filocolo,* by Giovanni Boccaccio. Translated by Donald Cheney with the collaboration of Thomas G. Bergin. New York: Garland, 1985.

Bertolini, Virginio. "Dalla 'Marmorina' del Boccaccio all'appellativo di 'Città marmorea' dato a Verona nel medio evo." In *Atti e Memorie della Accademia di Agricultura, Scienze e Lettere di Verona* 18 (1966–67): 321–32.

Bestiaire roman. Translated by E. de Solms. Paris: Zodiaque, 1977.

Bestiaris. Edited by Saverio Panaunzio. Barcelona: Barcino, 1963.

Bianciotto, Gabriel, ed. *Bestiaires du Moyen Age.* Paris: Stock, 1980.

Bibliografia degli Zibaldoni di Boccaccio (1976–1995). Edited by Dipartimento di Filologia e Storia, Università degli Studi di Cassino. Rome: Viella, 1996.

Billanovich, Giuseppe. *Restauri boccacceschi.* Rome: Edizioni di Storia e Letteratura, 1945.

————. "Petrarca e il Ventoso." *Italia Medievale e Umanistica* 9 (1966): 389–401.

Blumenfeld-Kosinski, Renate. "The Poetics of Continuation in the Old French *Paon* Cycle." *Romance Philology* 39, no. 4 (1986): 437–47.

Boccaccio, Giovanni. *Filocolo.* Naples: Sixtus Russinger Tedesco, 1478.

————. *Philocolo vulgare.* Edited by Hieronimo Squarzafico. Venice: Donino Pincio Mantuano, 1503.

————. *Le Philocope de messire Jean Boccace florentin, contenant l'histoire de*

Fleury et Blanchefleur, Divisé en sept livres traduitz d'italien en français par Adrien Sevin, gentilhomme de la Maison de Gié. Paris: Denis Jadot, 1542.

———. *Le lettere edite e inedite di messer Giovanni Boccaccio.* Edited by Francesco Corazzini. Florence: Sansoni, 1877.

———. *Rime di Giovanni Boccaccio.* Edited by Aldo Francesco Massèra. Bologna: Romagnoli, 1914.

———. *Il Filocolo.* Edited by Ettore De Ferri. 2 vols. Turin: Unione Tipografico-Editrice Torinese, 1927.

———. *Opere latine minori.* Edited by Aldo Francesco Massèra. Bari: Laterza, 1928.

———. *Filocolo.* Edited by Salvatore Battaglia. Bari: Laterza, 1938.

———. *Rime.* Edited by Vittore Branca. Bari: Laterza, 1939.

———. *Genealogie deorum gentilium.* Edited by Vincenzo Romano. 2 vols. Bari: Laterza, 1951.

———. *Boccaccio on Poetry, Being the Preface and the Fourteenth and Fifteenth Books of Boccaccio's Genealogia Deorum Gentilium.* Translated by Charles G. Osgood. 1930. Reprint, Library of the Liberal Arts, Indianapolis: Bobbs-Merrill, 1956.

———. *Rime.* Edited by Vittore Branca. Padua: Liviana, 1958.

———. *Comedia delle ninfe fiorentine.* Edited by Antonio Enzo Quaglio. In *Tutte le opere,* 2: 665–835. Milan: Mondadori, 1964.

———. *Filostrato.* Edited by Vittore Branca. In *Tutte le opere,* 2: 15–228. Milan: Mondadori, 1964.

———. *Teseida delle nozze d'Emilia.* Edited by Alberto Limentani. In *Tutte le opere,* 2: 229–664. Milan: Mondadori, 1964.

———. *Tutte le opere.* Edited by Vittore Branca. 10 vols. Milan: Mondadori, 1964–99.

———. *Esposizioni sopra la Comedìa.* Edited by Giorgio Padoan. *Tutte le opere,* vol. 6. Milan: Mondadori, 1965.

———. *De mulieribus claris.* Edited by Vittorio Zaccaria. *Tutte le opere,* vol. 10. Milan: Mondadori, 1967.

———. *Filocolo.* Edited by Antonio Enzo Quaglio. *Tutte le opere,* 1: 45–675. Milan: Mondadori, 1967.

———. *The Decameron.* Translated by G. H. McWilliam. Harmondsworth: Penguin, 1972.

———. *Amorosa visione.* Edited by Vittore Branca. In *Tutte le opere,* 3: 1–272. Milan: Mondadori, 1974.

———. *Decameron: Edizione diplomatico-interpretativa dell'autografo Hamilton 90.* Edited by Charles S. Singleton with Franca Petrucci, Armando Petrucci, Giancarlo Savino, and Martino Mardersteig. Baltimore: Johns Hopkins University Press, 1974.

———. *Trattatello in laude di Dante.* Edited by Pier Giorgio Ricci. In *Tutte le opere,* 3: 423–538. Milan: Mondadori, 1974.

———. *Decameron.* Edited by Vittore Branca. *Tutte le opere,* vol. 4. Milan: Mondadori, 1976.

————. *Decameron.* Translated by John Payne. Revised with commentary by Charles S. Singleton. 3 vols. Berkeley: University of California Press, 1982.

————. *De casibus virorum illustrium.* Edited by Pier Giorgio Ricci and Vittorio Zaccaria. *Tutte le opere,* vol. 9. Milan: Mondadori, 1983.

————. *Il Filocolo.* Translated by Donald Cheney with the collaboration of Thomas G. Bergin. New York: Garland, 1985.

————. *L'Ameto.* Translated by Judith Serafini-Sauli. New York: Garland, 1985.

————. *Amorosa visione.* Translated by Robert Hollander, Timothy Hampton, and Margherita Frankel. Hanover, N.H.: University Press of New England, 1986.

————. *Carmina.* Edited by Giuseppe Velli. In *Tutte le opere,* 5, pt. 1. Milan: Mondadori, 1991.

————. *De vita et moribus Domini Francisci Petracchi de Florentia secundum Iohannem Bochacii de Certaldo.* Edited by Renata Fabbri. In *Tutte le opere,* 5, pt. 1. Milan: Mondadori, 1991.

————. *Diana's Hunt, Caccia di Diana: Boccaccio's First Fiction.* Edited and translated by Anthony K. Cassell and Victoria Kirkham. Philadelphia: University of Pennsylvania Press, 1991.

————. *Epistole.* Edited by Ginetta Auzzas. In *Tutte le opere,* 5, pt. 1. Milan: Mondadori, 1992.

————. *Rime.* Edited by Vittore Branca. In *Tutte le opere,* 5, pt. 1. Milan: Mondadori, 1992.

————. *Corbaccio.* Edited by Giorgio Padoan. In *Tutte le opere,* 5, pt. 2. Milan: Mondadori, 1994.

————. *Genealogie deorum gentilium libri,* Edited by Vittorio Zaccaria. In *Tutte le opere,* vols. 7–8. Milan: Mondadori, 1998.

Bode, W. H., ed. *Scriptores rerum mythicarum latini tres.* 1834. Reprint, Hildesheim: Georg Olms, 1968.

Bologna, Ferdinando. *I pittori alla Corte Angioina di Napoli, 1266–1414, e un riesame dell'arte nell'età fridericiana.* Rome: U. Bozzi, 1969.

Borghi Cedrini, Luciana. *Appunti per la lettura di un Bestiario medievale: Il bestiario valdese.* Turin: G. Giappicelli, 1976.

Boshart, Jon D. "Giovanni Boccaccio's *Amorosa Visione:* A New Appraisal." Ph.D. diss., Johns Hopkins University, 1974.

Bragantini, Renzo, and Pier Massimo Forni, eds. *Lessico critico decameroniano.* Turin: Bollati Boringhieri, 1995.

Branca, Vittore. "L'atteggiamento del Boccaccio di fronte alle sue *Rime* e la formazione delle più antiche sillogi." In *Tradizione delle opere di Giovanni Boccaccio,* vol. 1, *Un primo elenco dei codici e tre studi,* 287–329. Rome: Edizioni di Storia e Letteratura, 1958.

————. "Nuove testimonianze manoscritte e nuove rime." In *Tradizione delle opere di Giovanni Boccaccio,* vol. 1, *Un primo elenco dei codici e tre studi,* 243–86. Rome: Edizioni di Storia e Letteratura, 1958.

————. "Per l'attribuzione della *Caccia di Diana.*" In *Tradizione delle opere,* vol. 1, *Un primo elenco dei codici e tre studi,* 121–43. Rome: Edizioni di Storia e Letteratura, 1958. (First published in *Annali della R. Scuola Normale Superiore di Pisa*, 2d ser., 7 [1938]: 287–302.)

———. *Tradizione delle opere di Giovanni Boccaccio*. Vol. 1, *Un primo elenco dei codici e tre studi*. Rome: Edizioni di Storia e Letteratura, 1958.

———. "Notizie e documenti per la biografia del Boccaccio." Pt. 1, "Una nuova ambasceria (1359)." *Studi sul Boccaccio* 3 (1965): 7–16.

———. "Un primo elenco di codici illustrati di opere del Boccaccio." In "Boccaccio visualizzato I," *Studi sul Boccaccio* 15 (1985–86): 121–48.

———. *Boccaccio medievale e nuovi studi sul Decameron*. 6th ed., rev. Florence: Sansoni, 1986.

———. "Implicazioni espressivi, temi e stilemi fra Petrarca e Boccaccio." In *Boccaccio medievale e nuovi studi sul Decameron,* 300–32. 6th ed., rev. Florence: Sansoni, 1986.

———. "Schemi letterari e schemi autobiografici." In *Boccaccio medievale e nuovi studi sul Decameron,* 191–249. 6th ed., rev. Florence: Sansoni, 1986.

———. *Tradizione delle opere di Giovanni Boccaccio*. Vol. 2, *Un secondo elenco di manoscritti e studi sul testo del "Decameron" con due appendici*. Rome: Edizioni di Storia e Letteratura, 1991.

———. *Giovanni Boccaccio: Profilo biografico*. 2d ed. Florence: Sansoni, 1992.

———, ed. *Boccaccio visualizzato*. 3 vols. Turin: Einaudi, 1999.

Branca, Vittore, and Pier Giorgio Ricci. *Un autografo del Decameron (Codice Hamiltoniano 90)*. Florence: Olschki, 1962.

———. "Notizie e documenti per la biografia del Boccaccio." Pt. 4, "L'incontro napoletano con Cino da Pistoia." *Studi sul Boccaccio* 5 (1968): 1–18.

Brisebarre, Jean (Jean le Court). *Le Restore du paon*. Edited by Richard J. Carey. Geneva: Droz, 1966.

Brown, Virginia. "Boccaccio in Naples: The Beneventan Liturgical Palimpsest of the Laurentian Autographs (Mss. 29.8 and 33.31)." *Italia Medioevale e Umanistica* 34 (1991): 41–126.

Brownlee, Kevin. "Jean de Meun and the Limits of Romance: Genius as Rewriter of Guillaume de Lorris." In *Romance: Generic Transformations from Chrétien de Troyes to Cervantes,* edited by Kevin Brownlee and Marina Scordilis Brownlee, 114–34. Hanover, N.H.: University Press of New England, 1985.

———. "The Practice of Cultural Authority: Italian Responses to French Cultural Dominance in *Il Tesoretto, Il fiore,* and the *Commedia*." *Forum for Modern Language Studies* 33, no. 3 (1997): 258–69.

Brownlee, Kevin, and Victoria Kirkham, eds. *Boccaccio 1990: The Poet and His Renaissance Reception*. *Studi sul Boccaccio* 20 (1991–92): 166–397.

Bruni, Francesco. *Boccaccio: L'invenzione della letteratura mezzana*. Bologna: Il Mulino, 1990.

———. "Il *Filocolo* e lo spazio della letteratura volgare." In *Miscellanea di studi in onore di Vittore Branca,* edited by Armando Balduino et al., vol. 2, *Boccaccio e dintorni,* (Florence: Olschki, 1983), 1–21.

Calin, William L. "Flower Imagery in *Floire and Blancheflor*." *French Studies* 18, no. 2 (1964): 103–11.

Camille, Michael. *The Gothic Idol: Ideology and Image-Making in Medieval Art.* Cambridge: Cambridge University Press, 1989.

Il Cantare di Fiorio e Biancifiore. See Crescini.

Caracciolo, Enrichetta. *Misteri del chiostro napoletano.* 1864. Reprint, Florence: Giunti, 1986.

Carducci, Giosuè. *Ai parentali di Giovanni Boccacci in Certaldo.* Bologna: Zanichelli, 1876.

Carey, George. *The Medieval Alexander.* Cambridge: Cambridge University Press, 1956.

Cassell, Anthony K., and Victoria Kirkham, eds. and trans. *Diana's Hunt, Caccia di Diana: Boccaccio's First Fiction.* Philadelphia: University of Pennsylvania Press, 1991.

Cazalé-Bérard, Claude. "Les Structures narratives dans le premier livre du *Filocolo* de Giovanni Boccaccio." *Revue des Études Italiennes,* n.s., 17 (1971): 111–32.

Cazalé-Bérard, Claude, and Michelangelo Picone, eds. *Gli Zibaldoni di Boccaccio: Memoria, scrittura, riscrittura.* Florence: Franco Cesati, 1998.

Cervigni, Dino. "Beatrice's Act of Naming." *Lectura Dantis* 8 (1991): 85–99.

Chaucer, Geoffrey. *The Canterbury Tales.* Edited by F. N. Robinson. Boston: Houghton Mifflin, 1961.

Cheney, Christopher R., ed. *Handbook of Dates for Students of English History.* London: Offices of the Royal Historical Society, 1945.

Cherchi, Paolo, and Michelangelo Picone, eds. *Studi di Italianistica in onore di Giovanni Cecchetti.* Ravenna: Longo, 1988.

Chiappelli, Fredi. "Discorso o progetto per uno studio sul *Decameron.*" In *Studi di Italianistica in onore di Giovanni Cecchetti,* edited by Paolo Cherchi and Michelangelo Picone, 105–11. Ravenna: Longo, 1988.

Chrétien de Troyes. *Cligès.* Edited by Alexandre Micha. Vol. 2 of *Les Romans de Chrétien de Troyes.* Paris: Honoré Champion, 1965.

———. *Erec et Enide.* Edited by Mario Roques. Vol. 1 of *Les Romans de Chrétien de Troyes.* Paris: Honoré Champion, 1966.

———. *Le Chevalier de la Charrete.* Edited by Mario Roques. Paris: Honoré Champion, 1967.

Ciampi, Sebastiano. *Monumenti d'un manoscritto autografo di messer Giovanni Boccacci.* Florence: G. Galletti, 1827.

Cicero, Marcus Tullius. *Epistolae ad familiares.* In *Epistolae,* vol. 1, edited by L. C. Purser. 1901. Reprint, Oxford: Clarendon Press, 1979. Translated by W. Glynn Williams, Loeb Classical Library, Cambridge: Harvard University Press, 1959.

Cirillo-Falzarano, Marilina, and Mei-Mei Akwai Ellerman, eds. *Studies in Honor of Dante Della Terza.* Cambridge: Harvard University Office of the University Publisher, 1996.

Clark, Willene B., and Meradith T. McMunn, eds. *Beasts and Birds of the Middle Ages.* Philadelphia: University of Pennsylvania Press, 1989.

Clubb, Thomas Chaldecott. *The Life of Giovanni Boccaccio.* New York: Albert and Charles Boni, 1930.

Comparetti, Domenico. *Virgilio nel medioevo.* Edited by Giorgio Pasquali. 1943. Reprint, Florence: La Nuova Italia, 1981.

Contini, Gianfranco, ed. *Poeti del Duecento.* 2 vols. Milan: Ricciardi, 1960.
Copeland, Rita. *Rhetoric, Hermeneutics, and Translation in the Middle Ages.* Cambridge: Cambridge University Press, 1991.
Corazzini, Francesco, ed. *Le lettere edite e inedite di messer Giovanni Boccaccio.* Florence: Sansoni, 1877.
Costantini, Aldo Maria. "Studio sullo Zibaldone magliabechiano." *Studi sul Boccaccio* 7 (1973): 21–58.
Cottino-Jones, Marga, and Edward F. Tuttle, eds. *Boccaccio: Secoli di vita.* Ravenna: Longo, 1977.
Crescini, Vincenzo. *Contributo agli studi sul Boccaccio.* Turin: Loescher, 1887.
———, ed. *Il Cantare di Fiorio e Biancifiore.* 2 vols. Scelta di Curiosità Letterarie Inedite o Rare dal Secolo XIII al XIX, vol. 89 (Disp. 233) and vol. 100 (Disp. 249). 1889. Reprint, Bologna: Commissione per i Testi di Lingua, 1969.
Crespo, Roberto. *Una versione pisana inedita del Bestiaire d'amours.* Leiden: Universitaire Pers, 1972.
Curtius, Ernst Robert. "The Author's Name in Medieval Literature." In *European Literature and the Latin Middle Ages,* 515–18. Bollingen Series 36. Princeton: Princeton University Press, 1973.
Dante Alighieri. *La commedia secondo l'antica vulgata.* Edited by Giorgio Petrocchi. 4 vols. Milan: Mondadori, 1966–67.
———. *Convivio.* Edited by G. Busnelli and G. Vandelli. Revised by Antonio Enzo Quaglio. 2 vols. Florence: Le Monnier, 1968.
———. *The Divine Comedy.* Translated with commentary by Charles S. Singleton. 6 vols. Bollingen Series 80. Princeton: Princeton University Press, 1970–75.
———. *Vita nuova.* Translated by Barbara Reynolds. Harmondsworth: Penguin, 1971.
———. *Vita nuova.* Edited by Domenico de Robertis. In *Opere minori,* edited by Domenico de Robertis and Gianfranco Contini, vol. 1, pt. 1, 1–247. Milan: Ricciardi, 1984.
———. *La divina commedia.* Edited by Umberto Bosco and Giovanni Reggio. 3 vols. Florence: Le Monnier, 1987.
Della Torre, Arnaldo. *La giovinezza di Giovanni Boccaccio (1313–1341): Proposta di una nuova cronologia.* Città di Castello: S. Lapi, 1905.
delle Colonne, Guido. *Historia destructionis Troiae.* Translated by Mary Elizabeth Meek. Bloomington: Indiana University Press, 1974.
de Looze, Laurence. "'Mon nom trouveras': A New Look at the Anagrams of Guillaume de Machaut—the Enigmas, Responses, and Solutions." *Romanic Review* 79 (1988): 537–57.
———. "Signing Off in the Middle Ages: Medieval Textuality and Strategies of Authorial Self-Naming." In *Vox Intertexta: Orality and Textuality in the Middle Ages,* edited by A. N. Doane and Carol Pasternak, 162–78. Madison: University of Wisconsin Press, 1991.
del Sera, Beatrice. *Amor di virtù: Commedia in cinque atti, 1548.* Edited by Elissa Weaver. Ravenna: Longo, 1990.
Denk, Otto. *Einfürung in die Geschichte der altcatalanischen Litteratur, von deren Anfängen bis zum 18 Jahrhundert.* Munich: M. Poessl, 1893.

de Rougement, Denis. *Love in the Occident.* Translated by Montgomery Belgion. New York: Pantheon, 1956.

De Sanctis, Francesco. "Il Boccaccio e le sue opere minori." *Nuova antologia* 14 (1870): 221–52.

———. *Storia della letteratura italiana.* 1870. Reprint, Florence: Sansoni, 1965.

Deyermond, Alan D. *The Middle Ages: A Literary History of Spain.* New York: Barnes and Noble, 1971.

Di Benedetto, F. "Considerazioni sullo Zibaldone Laurenziano del Boccaccio e restauro testuale della prima redazione del *Faunus.*" *Italia Medioevale e Umanistica* 14 (1971): 91–129.

Dizionario etimologico italiano. Edited by Carlo Battisti and Giovanni Alessio. Florence: Barbèra, 1950–65.

Dobelli, Ausonio. *Figure e rimembranze dantesche nel Decamerone.* Modena: Namias, 1897.

du Méril, Édélstand, ed. *Floire et Blanceflor: Poèmes du XIIIᵉ siècle.* Paris: P. Jannet, 1856.

Durling, Robert M. "The Ascent of Mt. Ventoux and the Crisis of Allegory." *Italian Quarterly* 18, no. 69 (1974): 7–28.

———, ed. and trans. *Petrarch's Lyric Poems.* Cambridge: Harvard University Press, 1976.

Durling, Robert M., and Ronald Martinez. *Time and the Crystal: Studies in Dante's Rime Petrose.* Berkeley: University of California Press, 1990.

Enciclopedia dantesca. Rome: Istituto della Enciclopedia Italiana, 1970–78.

Felberg-Levitt, Margaret. *Les Demandes d'amour: Edition critique.* Montreal: Ceres, 1995.

Ferreri, Rosario. *Innovazione e tradizione nel Boccaccio.* Rome: Bulzoni, 1980.

Fido, Franco. "Architettura." In *Lessico critico decameroniano,* edited by Renzo Bragantini and Pier Massimo Forni, 13–33. Turin: Bollati Boringhieri, 1995.

Il fiore. Edited by Gianfranco Contini. In Dante Alighieri, *Opere minori,* edited by Domenico de Robertis and Gianfranco Contini, vol. 1, pt. 1, 553–798. Milan: Ricciardi, 1984.

Fontanini, Giusto. *Biblioteca dell'eloquenza italiana di Mons: Giusto Fontanini . . . con le annotazioni del signor Apostolo Zeno.* 2 vols. 1706. Reprint, Venice: G. B. Pasquali, 1753.

Forni, Pier Massimo. *Adventures in Speech: Rhetoric and Narration in Boccaccio's Decameron.* Philadelphia: University of Pennsylvania Press, 1996.

Friedman, John Block. "Peacocks and Preachers: Analytic Technique in Marcus of Orvieto's *Liber de moralitatibus,* Vatican lat. MS 5935." In *Beasts and Birds of the Middle Ages,* edited by Willene B. Clark and Meradith T. McMunn. Philadelphia: University of Pennsylvania Press, 1989.

Friedmann, Herbert. *A Bestiary for Saint Jerome: Animal Symbolism in European Religious Art.* Washington, D.C.: Smithsonian Institution Press, 1980.

Fulgentius, Fabius Planciades. *Fulgentius the Mythographer.* Translated by Leslie George Whitbread. Columbus: Ohio State University Press, 1971.

Galletti, Salvatore. *Patologia al Decameron.* Palermo: S. F. Flaccovio, 1969.

Gathercole, Patricia M. "Boccaccio in French." *Studi sul Boccaccio* 5 (1968): 275–97.

———. "The French Translators of Boccaccio." *Italica* 46, no. 3 (1969): 300–9.

Geoffrey of Vinsauf. *Poetria nova of Geoffrey of Vinsauf.* Translated by Margaret F. Nims. Toronto: Pontifical Institute of Mediaeval Studies, 1967.

Ghisalberti, Fausto. "Medieval Biographies of Ovid." *Journal of the Warburg and Courtauld Institutes* 9 (1946): 10–59.

Giamboni, Bono. *Il libro de' vizi e delle virtudi.* Edited by Cesare Segre. Turin: Einaudi, 1968.

Glossa ordinaria. Edited by Walafrid Strabo. *Patrologia latina,* vols. 113–14.

Gordon, R. K. *The Story of Troilus.* 1934. Reprint, Toronto: University of Toronto Press, 1978.

Gower, M. S., and McKenzie, K. "Il bestiario toscano secondo la lezione dei codici di Parigi e di Londra." *Studi Romanzi* 8 (1912): 1–100.

Gratian. *Corpus juris canonici.* Pt. 1, *Decretum Gratiani.* Edited by Emil Ludwig Richter. Leipzig: Bernhard Tauchnitz, 1839.

Gregory the Great. *Morals on the Book of Job.* Translated by J. Bliss. Library of the Fathers of the Holy Catholic Church Anterior to the Division of East and West, vols. 18, 21, 23, 31. Oxford: John Henry Parker, 1844–50.

Grieve, Patricia. *Floire and Blancheflor and the European Romance.* Cambridge: Cambridge University Press, 1997.

Grossvogel, Steven. *Ambiguity and Allusion in Boccaccio's Filocolo.* Florence: Olschki, 1992.

Guillaume de Lorris and Jean de Meun [Jean Chopinel]. *Le roman de la rose.* Edited by Ernest Langlois. 5 vols. Paris: Firmin Didot, 1914–24.

———. *The Romance of the Rose.* Translated by Charles Dahlberg. Princeton: Princeton University Press, 1971.

Haller, Robert S., trans. and ed. *Literary Criticism of Dante Alighieri.* Lincoln: University of Nebraska Press, 1973.

Hardie, Colin, ed. *Vitae virgilianae antiquae.* Oxford: Clarendon Press, 1966.

Haseloff, Arthur. *Pre-Romanesque Sculpture in Italy.* Translated by Ronald Boothroyd. New York: Hacker Art Books, 1971.

Hausknecht, Emil, ed., *Floris and Blauncheflur: Mittelenglisches Gedicht aus dem 13. Jahrhundert.* Berlin: Weidmann, 1885.

Hauvette, Henri. *Etudes sur Boccace (1894–1916).* Turin: Bottega d'Erasmo, 1968.

———. "Notes sur des manuscrits autographes de Boccace à la Bibliothèque Laurentienne." In *Etudes sur Boccace,* 87–146. Turin: Bottega d'Erasmo, 1968. (First published in *Mélanges d'Archéologie* 14 [1894]: 87–146.)

Herzog, Hans. "Die beiden Sagenkreise von Flore und Blanscheflur." *Germania,* n.s., 17 (1884): 137–228.

Hessling, D. C., ed., *Le Roman de Phlorios et Platia Phlore.* Amsterdam: Johannes Müller, 1917.

Heyer-Caput, Margherita. "Le *questioni d'amore* del *Filocolo:* Tirocinio letterario di Giovanni Boccaccio." In *Studies in Honor of Dante Della Terza,* edited by

Marilina Cirillo-Falzarano and Mei-Mei Akwai Ellerman, 65–88. Cambridge: Harvard University Office of the University Publisher, 1996.

Hollander, Robert. *Boccaccio's Two Venuses.* New York: Columbia University Press, 1977.

———. "The Validity of Boccaccio's Self-Exegesis in his *Teseida.*" *Medievalia et Humanistica,* n.s., 8 (1977): 163–83.

———. "Boccaccio's Dante: Imitative Distance (*Decameron* I 1 and VI 10)." In *Boccaccio's Dante and the Shaping Force of Satire,* Ann Arbor: University of Michigan Press, 1997. (First published in *Studi sul Boccaccio* 13 (1981–82): 169–98).

———. *Il Virgilio dantesco.* Florence: Olschki, 1983.

———. *Boccaccio's Last Fiction: "Il Corbaccio."* Philadelphia: University of Pennsylvania Press, 1988.

———. *Dante's Epistle to Cangrande.* Ann Arbor: University of Michigan Press, 1993.

———. *Boccaccio's Dante and the Shaping Force of Satire.* Ann Arbor: University of Michigan Press, 1997.

———. "The Proem of the *Decameron.*" In *Boccaccio's Dante and the Shaping Force of Satire,* 89–107. Ann Arbor: University of Michigan Press, 1997.

Holmes, Urban Tigner. *A History of Old French Literature from the Origins to 1300.* New York: Russell and Russell, 1962.

Hopper, Vincent Foster. *Medieval Number Symbolism.* 1938. Reprint. New York: Cooper Square, 1969.

Horace. *Satires and Epistles.* Translated by Smith Palmer Bovie. Chicago: University of Chicago Press, 1959.

Hortis, Attilio. *Studj sulle opere latine del Boccaccio con particolare riguardo alla storia della erudizione nel Medio Evo e alle letterature straniere.* Trieste: Libreria Julius Dase Editrice, 1879.

Hubert, Merton Jerome, trans. *The Romance of Floire and Blanchefleur: A French Idyllic Poem of the Twelfth Century.* Chapel Hill: University of North Carolina Press, 1966.

Hugues Capet: Chanson de geste. Edited by Adélaïde Edouard Le Lièvre de La Grange. 1864. Reprint, Nendeln, Liechtenstein: Kraus Reprint, 1966.

Huot, Sylvia. *From Song to Book: The Poetics of Writing in Old French Lyric and Lyrical Narrative Poetry.* Ithaca: Cornell University Press, 1987.

Hutton, Edward. *Giovanni Boccaccio: A Biographical Study.* London: John Lane at the Bodley Head, 1910.

———. Introduction to *The Decameron,* by Giovanni Boccaccio. Translated by J. M. Rigg. Everyman's Library. New York: Dutton, 1930.

Isidore of Seville. *Etymologie sive origines.* Edited by W. M. Lindsay. 1911. Reprint, Oxford: Clarendon Press, 1971.

Jacoff, Rachel. "Intertextualities in Arcadia: *Purgatorio* 30.49–51." In *The Poetry of Allusion: Virgil and Ovid in Dante's Commedia,* edited by Rachel Jacoff and Jeffrey T. Schnapp, 131–44. Stanford: Stanford University Press, 1991.

———. *The Cambridge Companion to Dante.* Edited by Rachel Jacoff. Cambridge: Cambridge University Press, 1993.

Jean de la Mote. *Le Parfait du paon.* Edited by Richard J. Carey. University of North Carolina Studies in the Romance Languages and Literatures, no. 118. Chapel Hill: University of North Carolina Press, 1972.

Karpp, Heinrich. *Die Mosaiken in Santa Maria Maggiore zu Rom.* Baden-Baden: Bruno Grimm, 1966.

Kaske, Robert E., with Arthur Groos and Michael W. Twomey. *Medieval Christian Literary Imagery: A Guide to Interpretation.* Toronto: University of Toronto Press, 1988.

Kirkham, Victoria. "The *Filocolo* of Giovanni Boccaccio with an English Translation of the Thirteen *Questioni d'amore.*" Ph.D. diss., Johns Hopkins University, 1971.

———. "Reckoning with Boccaccio's *Questioni d'amore.*" *MLN* 89, no. 1 (1974): 47–59.

———. "Numerology and Allegory in Boccaccio's *Caccia di Diana.*" *Traditio* 34 (1978): 303–29.

———. "Renaissance Portraits of Boccaccio: A Look into the Kaleidoscope." In "Boccaccio visualizzato II," *Studi sul Boccaccio* 16 (1987): 284–305.

———. "Quanto in femmina foco d'amor dura!" *Letture Classensi* 18 (1988): 235–50.

———. "A Canon of Women in Dante's *Commedia.*" *Annali d'Italinistica* 7 (1989): 16–41.

———. "Eleven is for Evil: Measured Trespass in Dante's *Commedia.*" *Allegorica* 10 (1989): 27–50.

———. "Amorous Vision, Scholastic Vistas." In *The Sign of Reason in Boccaccio's Fiction,* 55–116. Florence: Olschki, 1993.

———. "An Allegorically Tempered *Decameron.*" In *The Sign of Reason in Boccaccio's Fiction,* 131–71. Florence: Olschki, 1993. (First published in *Italica* 62, no. 1 [1985]: 1–23.)

———. "Boccaccio's Dedication to Women in Love." In *The Sign of Reason in Boccaccio's Fiction,* 117–29. Florence: Olschki, 1993. (First published in *Renaissance Studies in Honor of Craig Hugh Smyth,* edited by Andrew Morrogh, Fiorella Superbi Gioffredi, Piero Morselli, and Eve Borsook [Florence: Giunti Barbèra, 1985], 1:333–43.)

———. "'Chiuso parlare' in Boccaccio's *Teseida.*" In *The Sign of Reason in Boccaccio's Fiction,* 17–53. Florence: Olschki, 1993. (First published in *Dante, Petrarch, Boccaccio: Studies in the Italian Trecento in Honor of Charles S. Singleton,* edited by Aldo S. Bernardo and Anthony L. Pellegrini [Binghamton: Medieval and Renaissance Texts Studies, 1983], 305–51.)

———. "The Last Tale in the *Decameron.*" In *The Sign of Reason in Boccaccio's Decameron,* 249–65. Florence: Olschki, 1993. (First published in *Mediaevalia* 12 [1989 for 1986]: 205–23.)

———. "Painters at Play on the Judgment Day (*Decameron* VIII,9). " In *The Sign of Reason in Boccaccio's Fiction,* 215–35. Florence: Olschki, 1993. (First published in *Studi sul Boccaccio* 14 [1983–84]: 256–77.)

———. *The Sign of Reason in Boccaccio's Fiction.* Florence: Olschki, 1993.

———. "John Badmouth: Fortunes of the Poet's Image." In *Boccaccio 1990: The*

Poet and His Renaissance Reception, edited by Kevin Brownlee and Victoria Kirkham. *Studi sul Boccaccio* 20 (1991–92): 355–76.

———. "The Parallel Lives of Dante and Virgil." *Dante Studies* 110 (1992): 233–53.

———. "*Purgatorio* XXVIII." In *Dante's Divine Comedy: Introductory Readings,* pt. 2, *Purgatorio.* Supplement to *Lectura Dantis* 12 (1993): 411–32.

———. "Two New Translations: The Early Boccaccio in English Dress." *Italica* 70, no. 1 (1993): 79–89.

———. "Dante's Polysynchrony: A Perfectly Timed Entry into Eden." *Filologia e critica* 20, nos. 2–3 (1995): 329–52.

———. "Morale." In *Lessico critico decameroniano,* edited by Renzo Bragantini and Pier Massimo Forni, 249–68. Turin: Bollati Boringhieri, 1995.

———. "Iohannes de Certaldo: La firma dell'autore." In *Gli zibaldoni di Boccaccio: Memoria, scrittura, riscrittura,* edited by Claude Cazalé-Bérard and Michelangelo Picone, 455–68. Florence: Franco Cesati, 1998.

———. "L'immagine del Boccaccio nella memoria tardo-gotica e rinascimentale." In *Boccaccio visualizzato,* edited by Vittore Branca, 3 vols. 1: 85–144. Turin: Einaudi, 1999.

Kirkham, Victoria, and María Rosa Menocal. "Reflections on the 'Arabic' World: Boccaccio's Ninth Stories." *Stanford Italian Review* 7, nos. 1–2 (1987): 95–110.

Kirschbaum, Engelbert. *Lexikon der Christlichen Ikonografie.* Rome: Herder, 1972.

Klapisch-Zuber, Christiane. "Zacharie, ou le père évincé: Les rites nuptiaux toscans entre Giotto et le Concile de Trente." *Annales Economie, Sociétés, Civilisations* 6 (1979): 1216–43.

———. *Women, Family, and Ritual in Renaissance Italy.* Translated by Lydia C. Cochrane. Chicago: University of Chicago Press, 1985.

Klauser, Theodor. *Frühchristliche Sarkophage in Bild und Wort.* Olten, Switzerland: Urs Graf-Verlag, 1966.

Koeppel, Emil. *Studien zur Geschichte der Italienischen Novelle in der Englischen Literatur des sechzehnten Jahrhunderts.* Strasbourg: K. J. Trübner, 1892.

Koerting, Gustav Carl Otto. *Boccaccios Leben und Werke.* Leipzig: Fues, 1880.

Krautheimer, Richard. "Introduction to an 'Iconography of Medieval Architecture.'" *Journal of the Warburg and Cortauld Institutes* 5 (1942): 1–33.

Lafont, Robert, and Christian Anatole, eds. *Nouvelle Histoire de la littérature occitane.* 2 vols. Paris: Presses Universitaires de France, 1970.

Landau, Marcus. *Giovanni Boccaccio: Sua vita e sue opere.* Translated by Camillo Antona-Traversi. Naples: Dalla Stamperia del Vaglio, 1881.

Langland, William. *Piers the Plowman.* Translated by J. F. Goodridge. Harmondsworth: Penguin, 1966.

Latini, Brunetto. *Li Livres dou Tresor.* Edited by Francis J. Carmody. University of California Publications in Modern Philology, no. 22. Berkeley: University of California Press, 1948.

———. *Il tesoretto.* In *Poeti del Duecento,* ed. Gianfranco Contini, 2: 175–277. Milan: Riccardi, 1960.

———. *Il Tesoretto (The Little Treasure)*. Translated by Julia Bolton Holloway. New York: Garland, 1981.

Le conte de Floire et Blanchefleur: Roman pré-courtois du milieu du XIIe siècle. Translated by Jean-Luc Leclanche. Paris: Honoré Champion, 1986.

Lewis, C. S. *The Allegory of Love*. 1936. Reprint, New York: Oxford University Press, 1958.

Logan, J. L. "The Poet's Central Numbers." *MLN* 86 (1971): 95–98.

Lother, Helmut. *Der Pfau in der altchristlichen Kunst*. Leipzig: Dieterich, 1929.

Macdougal, Elizabeth, ed. *Fons Sapientiae: Renaissance Garden Fountains*. Dunbarton Oaks Colloquium of the History of Landscape Architecture, no. 5. Washington, D.C.: Dunbarton Oaks, 1978.

MacFarlane, Katherine Nell. "Isidore of Seville on the Pagan Gods (*Origines* VIII.11)." *Transactions of the American Philosophical Society* 70, no. 3 (1980): 1–40.

Macrobius, Ambrosius Theodosius. *Commentary on the Dream of Scipio*. Translated by William Harris Stahl. Records of Civilization, Sources and Studies, no. 48. New York: Columbia University Press, 1952.

———. *The Saturnalia*. Translated Percival Vaughan Davies. New York: Columbia University Press, 1969.

———. *Commentarium in somnium Scipionis*. Edited by J. Willis. Leipzig: Teubner, 1970.

Malagoli, Luigi. "Timbro della prosa e motivi dell'arte del Boccaccio nel *Filocolo*." *Studi mediolatini e volgari* 6–7 (1959): 97–111.

Manetti, Giannozzo. From *Vita et moribus trium illustrium poetarum florentinorum*. In *Le vite di Dante, Petrarca e Boccaccio scritte fino al secolo decimosesto*, edited by Angelo Solerti, 680–93. Storia letteraria d'Italia scritta da una Società di Professori, vol. 4. Milan: Dottor Francesco Vallardi, n.d.

Marcus, Millicent. *An Allegory of Form: Literary Self-Consciousness in the Decameron*. Saratoga, Calif.: Anma Libri, 1979.

Martial. *Epigrams*. Translated by Walter C. A. Ker. 2 vols. Loeb Classical Library. Cambridge: Harvard University Press, 1947–50.

Martianus Capella. *De nuptiis Philologiae et Mercurii*. Edited by A. Dick. 1925. Reprint, Stuttgart: Teubner, 1969.

———. *The Marriage of Mercury and Philology*. Edited by William Harris Stahl. 2 vols. New York: Columbia University Press, 1971.

The Marvels of Rome. Mirabilia Urbis Romae. Edited and translated by Francis Morgan Nichols. Revised by Eileen Gardiner (New York: Italica Press, 1986).

Massèra, Aldo Francesco. "Le piú antiche biografie del Boccaccio." *Zeitschrift für Romanische Philologie* 27 (1903): 298–338.

Mazzatinti, G. *Un bestiario moralizzato tratto da un manoscritto eugubino del secolo XIV*. Rome: Accademia dei Lincei, 1889.

Mazzoni, Francesco. "Una presunta fonte del Boccaccio (*Filocolo, quest.* XIII; *Decameron* X iv)." *Studi Danteschi* 29 (1950): 192–96.

Mazzotta, Giuseppe. *The World at Play in Boccaccio's Decameron*. Princeton: Princeton University Press, 1986.

———. "Life of Dante." In *The Cambridge Companion to Dante,* edited by Rachel Jacoff, 1–13. Cambridge: Cambridge University Press, 1993.

McCullogh, Florence. *Medieval Latin and French Bestiaries.* Chapel Hill: University of North Carolina Press, 1960.

McGregor, James H. *The Image of Antiquity in Boccaccio's Filocolo, Filostrato, and Teseida.* New York: Peter Lang, 1991.

———. *The Shades of Aeneas: The Imitation of Vergil and the History of Paganism in Boccaccio's Filostrato, Filocolo, and Teseida.* Athens: University of Georgia Press, 1991.

McKenzie, K. "Unpublished Manuscripts of Italian Bestiaries." *PMLA* 20 (1905): 380–433.

Melczer, William, trans. *The Pilgrim's Guide to Santiago de Compostela.* New York: Italica Press, 1993.

Menocal, María Rosa. *The Arabic Role in Medieval Literary History.* Philadelphia: University of Pennsylvania Press, 1987.

Meun, Jean de [Jean Chopinel]. See Guillaume de Lorris.

Meyer, Heinz. *Die Zahlenallegorese im Mittelalter: Methode und Gebrauch.* Munich: Willhelm Fink, 1975.

Minnis, Alastair J. *Medieval Theory of Authorship.* 2d ed. Philadelphia: University of Pennsylvania Press, 1988.

Minnis, Alastair J., and A. B. Scott, with David Wallace, eds. *Medieval Literary Theory and Criticism, c. 1100–c. 1375: The Commentary Tradition.* Oxford: Clarendon Press, 1988.

Mommsen, Theodore. *Petrarch's Testament.* Ithaca: Cornell University Press, 1957.

Monteverdi, Angelo. "Un libro d'Ovidio e un passo del *Filocolo.*" In *Autori diversi: Studia Philologica et letteraria in honorem L. Spitzer,* edited by Anna Granville Hatcher and Karl Ludwig Selig, 335–40. Bern: Francke, 1958.

Moore, Olin. "Boccaccio's *Filocolo* and the Annunciation.'" *Modern Language Notes* 33 (1918): 438–40.

Morosini, Roberta. "'Per difetto rintegrare': Il *Filocolo* di G. Boccaccio." *Bollettino dell'Accademia Lucchese di Scienze Lettere e Arti* 8, nos. 3–4 (1997): 14–20.

Morrogh, Andrew, Fiorella Superbi Gioffredi, Piero Morselli, and Eve Borsook, eds. *Renaissance Studies in Honor of Craig Hugh Smyth.* 2 vols. Florence: Giunti Barbèra, 1985.

Munier, Charles. "A Propos des textes patristiques du Décret de Gratien." In *Proceedings of the Third International Congress of Medieval Canon Law,* edited by Stephan Kuttner, 43–50. Monumenta Iuris Canonici, ser. C: Subsidia, vol. 4. Vatican City: Biblioteca Apostolica Vaticana, 1971.

Muscetta, Carlo. *Boccaccio.* 2d ed. Bari: Laterza, 1974.

Muscetta, Carlo, and Paolo Rivalta, eds. *Parnaso italiano.* Vol. 1, *Poesia del Duecento e del Trecento.* Turin: Einaudi, 1956.

New Catholic Encyclopedia. 18 vols. New York: McGraw Hill, 1967.

Osgood, Charles G. "Boccaccio's Knowledge of the Life of Virgil." *Classical Philology* 25 (1930): 27–36.

———, trans. *Boccaccio on Poetry, Being the Preface and the Fourteenth and Fif-*

teenth Books of Boccaccio's Genealogia Deorum Gentilium. 1930. Reprint, Library of the Liberal Arts, Indianapolis: Bobbs-Merrill, 1956.

Oulmont, Charles. *Les Débats du Clerc et du Chevalier dans la littérature poétique du Moyen Age: Etude historique et littéraire suivie de l'édition critique des textes.* Paris: Honoré Champion, 1911.

Ovid. *Metamorphoses.* Translated by Frank Justus Miller. 2 vols. Loeb Classical Library. 1916. Reprint, Cambridge: Harvard University Press, 1961.

———. *Heroides and Amores.* Translated by Grant Showerman. Loeb Classical Library. 1914. Reprint, Cambridge: Harvard University Press, 1963.

———. *Tristia ex Ponto.* Translated by A. L. Wheeler. Loeb Classical Library. 1924. Reprint, Cambridge: Harvard University Press, 1965.

Ovide moralisé. Edited by C. de Boer. *Verhandelingen der Koninklijke Akademie van Wetenschappen.* Afdeeling Letterkunde, n.s., vol. 15 (1915).

The Oxford Classical Dictionary. Edited by N. G. L. Hammond and H. H. Scullard. 2d ed. Oxford: Clarendon Press, 1970.

Pächt, Otto, and J. J. G. Alexander. *Illuminated Manuscripts in the Bodleian Library.* 4 vols. Oxford: Clarendon Press, 1966.

Padoan, Giorgio. "Il mito di Teseo e il cristianesimo di Stazio." *Lettere Italiane* 11, no. 4 (1959): 432–57.

———. "Sulla genesi del *Decameron.*" In *Boccaccio: Secoli di Vita,* edited by Marga Cottino Jones and Edward F. Tuttle, 143–76. Ravenna: Longo, 1977.

Parkes, Malcolm B. *Pause and Effect: An Introduction to the History of Punctuation in the West.* Berkeley: University of California Press, 1993.

Paulys Realencyklopädie classischen Altertumswissenschaft. Edited by Georg Wissowa, Wilhelm Kroll, and Karl Mittelhaus. 49 vols. Stuttgart: J. B. Metzlerscher, 1894–1980.

Perella, Nicolas J. "The World of Boccaccio's *Filocolo.*" *PMLA* 76 (1961): 330–39.

Pertile, Lino. "Lettura dei sonetti CLXXXI–CCX (4 aprile 1992)." In *Letture Classensi* 22. *Lettura del "Fiore,"* ed. Zygmunt G. Baranski, Patrick Boyde, and Lino Pertile, 131–53. Ravenna: Longo, 1993.

Peterson, R. G. "Critical Calculations: Measure and Symmetry in Literature." *PMLA* 91 (1976): 367–75.

Petrarca, Francesco. *Rerum familiarium libri I–VIII.* Translated by Aldo S. Bernardo. Albany: State University of New York Press, 1975.

———. *Petrarch's Lyric Poems.* Translated by Robert M. Durling. Cambridge: Harvard University Press, 1976.

———. *Epistole.* Edited by Ugo Dotti. Turin: Unione Tipografico-Editrice Torinese, 1978.

———. *Rerum familiarium libri I–XVIII.* Translated by Aldo S. Bernardo, Saul Levin, and Reta A. Bernardo. 2 vols. Baltimore: Johns Hopkins University Press, 1992.

Petrie, Marion, Tim Halliday, and Carolyn Sanders. "Peahens Prefer Peacocks with Elaborate Trains." *Animal Behavior* 41 (1991): 323–31.

Picone, Michelangelo. "Tipologie culturali: Da Dante a Boccaccio." *Strumenti Critici* 30 (1976): 263–74.

Pisanelli, Baldassare. *Trattato della natura de' cibi et del bere.* Venice: Domenico Imberti, 1611.

Plaidy, Jean. *The Vow on the Heron.* 1980. Reprint, New York: Putnam, 1982.

Porcelli, Bruno. "Strutture e forme narrative nel *Filocolo.*" *Studi sul Boccaccio* 21 (1993): 207–33.

Price, Jocely. "*Floire et Blancheflor:* The Magic and Mechanics of Love." *Reading Medieval Studies* 8 (1982): 12–33.

Pseudo-Augustine. *Expositio in Apocalypsim B. Joannis. Patrologia latina* 35:2417–52.

Pseudo-Hugh of Saint Victor. *De bestiis et aliis rebus. Patrologia latina* 177:15–164.

Pucci, Antonio. "Proprietà di Mercato Vecchio." In *Parnaso italiano,* vol. 1, *Poesia del Duecento e del Trecento,* edited by Carlo Muscetta and Paolo Rivalta, 87–94. Turin: Einaudi, 1956.

Quaglio, Antonio Enzo. "Tra fonti e testo del *Filocolo.*" *Giornale Storico della Letteratura Italiana* 139, no. 427 (1962): 321–69.

———. "Prime correzioni al *Filocolo:* Dal testo di Tizzone verso quello del Boccaccio." *Studi sul Boccaccio* 1 (1963): 27–252.

———. "Tra fonti e testi del *Filocolo.*" *Giornale Storico della Letteratura Italiana* 140, no. 431 (1963): 321–63.

———. *Scienza e mito nel Boccaccio.* Padua: Liviana, 1967.

Rabanus Maurus. "De bestiis." In *De universo libri XXII. Patrologia latina* 111:9–614.

Rajna, Pio. "Rinaldo da Montalbano." *Il Propugnatore* 3 (1870): 213–41.

———. *Le fonti dell'Orlando furioso: Ricerche e studi.* Florence: Sansoni, 1876.

Ramat, Raffaello. "Giovanni Boccaccio, 1340–1344." *Belfagor* 19 (1964): 17–30.

Reinhold, Joachim. *Floire et Blancheflor: Etude de littérature comparée.* 1906. Reprint, Geneva: Slatkine Reprints, 1970.

Reiss, Edmund. "Symbolic Detail in Medieval Narrative: *Floris and Blancheflour.*" *Papers on Language and Literature* 7 (1971): 339–50.

Ricci, Pier Giorgio. "Per la dedica e la datazione del *Filostrato.*" *Studi sul Boccaccio* 1 (1963): 333–47.

———. "Notizie e documenti per la biografia del Boccaccio." Pt. 5, "Dominus Johannes Boccaccius." *Studi sul Boccaccio* 6 (1971): 1–10.

Richard of Fournival. *Li Bestiaires d'amours di maistre Richart de Fornival e li Response du bestiaire.* Edited by Cesare Segre. Milan: Ricciardi, 1957.

———. *Master Richard's Bestiary of Love and Response.* Translated by Jeanette Beer. Berkeley: University of California Press, 1986.

Richard of Saint Victor. *In Apocalypsim Joannis. Patrologia latina* 196:683–888.

Rigolot, François. "La 'Conjointure' du *Pantagruel:* Rabelais et la tradition médiévale." *Littérature* 41 (1981): 93–103.

Riquer, Martin de. *Caballeros andantes españoles.* Madrid: Espasa-Calpe, 1967.

Ritchie, R. L. Graeme, ed. *The Buik of Alexander,* by John Barbour. 4 vols. Scottish Text Society, n.s., vols. 12, 17, 21, 25. Edinburgh and London, 1921–29.

Roche, Thomas. "The Calendrical Structure of Petrarch's *Canzoniere.*" *Studies in Philology* 71 (1974): 152–72.

Roman van Cassamus (Middle Dutch). Edited by Eelco Verwijs. Gronigen: J. B. Wolters, 1869.

Ryding, William W. *Structure in Medieval Narrative.* The Hague: Mouton, 1971.

Santaga, Marco. *Per moderne carte: La biblioteca volgare di Petrarca.* Bologna: Il Mulino, 1990.

Santillana, Marqués de. *Paginas escogidas.* Edited by Fernando Gutierrez. Barcelona: Luis Miracle, 1939.

Sasso, Luigi. "L'*interpretatio nominis* in Boccaccio." *Studi sul Bocaccio* 12 (1980): 129–74.

Savi-Lopez, Paolo. "La novella di Prasildo e Tisbina (*Orlando innamorato I, I, XII*)." In *Raccolta di studi dedicati ad Alessandro d'Ancona,* 54–57. Florence: Barbèra, 1901.

Schnapp, Jeffrey T. "Un commento all'autocommento nel *Teseida.*" In *Boccaccio 1990: The Poet and His Renaissance Reception,* ed. Kevin Brownlee and Victoria Kirkham. *Studi sul Boccaccio* 20 (1991–92): 185–203.

Segalla di Arco, Silvio. *I sentimenti religiosi nel Boccaccio.* Bern: F. Miori, 1909.

Seidlin, Oscar. "The Lofty Game of Numbers: The Mynheer Peeperkorn Episode in Thomas Mann's *Der Zauberberg.*" *PMLA* 86, no. 5 (1971): 924–39.

Serminocci, Jacomo. *Un capitolo delle definizioni di Jacopo Serminocci, poeta senese del secolo XV.* Edited by Pasquale Papa. Nozze Renier-Campostrini. Florence: Coi Tipi dell'Arte della Stampa, 1887.

Servius. *Servii grammatici qui feruntur in Vergilii carmina commentarii.* Edited by Georg Thilo and Hermann Hagan. 2 vols. Leipzig: Teubner, 1881.

Settembrini, Luigi. *Lezioni di letteratura italiana dettate nell'Università di Napoli.* Vol. 1. Naples: Antonio Morano, 1879.

Silber, Gordon Routledge. *The Influence of Dante and Petrarch on Certain of Boccaccio's Lyrics.* Menasha, Wis.: George Banta Publishing Company, 1940.

Singleton, Charles S. "The Poet's Number at the Center." *MLN* 80 (1965): 1–10.

———, trans. and comm. *The Divine Comedy.* 6 vols. Bollingen Series 80. Princeton: Princeton University Press, 1970–75.

Skutch, Otto. "Notes on Metempsychosis." In *Studia Enniana,* 151–56. London: University of London, Athlone Press, 1968.

Smarr, Janet Levarie. "Symmetry and Balance in the *Decameron.*" *Medievalia* 2 (1976): 159–87.

———. "Boccaccio's *Filocolo:* Romance, Epic, and Religious Allegory." *Forum Italicum* 12, no. 1 (1978): 26–43.

———. "Boccaccio and the Stars: Astrology in the *Teseida.*" *Traditio* 35 (1979): 303–32.

———. *Boccaccio and Fiammetta: The Narrator as Lover.* Urbana: University of Illinois Press, 1986.

———. "Ovid and Boccaccio: A Note on Self-Defense." *Mediaevalia* 13 (1987): 247–55.

Solerti, Angelo, ed. *Le vite di Dante, Petrarca e Boccaccio scritte fino al secolo decimosesto.* Storia letteraria d'Italia scritta da una Società di Professori, vol. 4. Milan: Dottor Francesco Vallardi, n.d.

Spitzer, Leo. "Note on the Poetic and the Empirical 'I' in Medieval Authors." *Traditio* 4 (1946): 414–22.

Statius. *Thebaid.* In *Statius,* 2 vols., translated by J. H. Mozley, 1: 339–571; 2: 1–505. Loeb Classical Library. Cambridge: Harvard University Press, 1961.

Stillinger, Thomas. "The Form of Filostrato." *Stanford Italian Review* 9 (1990): 191–210.

———. *The Song of Troilus: Lyric Authority in the Medieval Book.* Philadelphia: University of Pennsylvania Press, 1992.

Storia di Napoli. 10 vols. Naples: Società Editrice Storia di Napoli, 1967–71.

Stufa, Maria Luisa Incontri Lotteringhi della. *Desinari e cene: Dai tempi remoti alla cucina toscana del XV secolo.* Florence: Editoriale Olimpia, 1965.

Surdich, Luigi. *La cornice di amore: Studi sul Boccaccio.* Pisa: ETS Editrice, 1987.

Sutton, Peter C., et al., eds. *Masters of Seventeenth-Century Dutch Genre Painting.* Philadelphia: University of Pennsylvania Press, 1984.

Symonds, John Addington. *Giovanni Boccaccio as Man and Author.* London: John C. Nimmo, 1895. Reprint, New York: AMS Press, 1968.

Tacuinum sanitatis, Codex 2396 der Österrreichischen Nationalbibliothek, Wien, Enchiridon virtutum vegetabilium, animalium, mineralium rerumque omnium explicans naturam iuvamentum nocumentum remotionemque nocumentorum eorum, Autore anonymo. Graz: Akademische Druck und Verlagsanstalt, 1985.

Taylor, A. B., ed., *Floris and Blancheflour: A Middle-English Romance Edited from the Trentham and Auchinleck Manuscripts.* Oxford: Clarendon Press, 1927.

Terpening, Ronnie H. *Lodovico Dolce: Renaissance Man of Letters.* Toronto: University of Toronto Press, 1997.

Tertullian. *The Apologetic Works.* Translated by Rudolph Arbesmann et al. New York: Fathers of the Church, 1950.

Testaferri, Ada. "Modello narrativo e semiotico nel *Filocolo.*" *Quaderni d'Italianistica* 8, no. 2 (1987): 139–48.

The Three King's Sons. Edited by F. J. Furnival. Early English Text Society, no. 67. London: K. Paul, Trench, Trübner & Co., 1895.

Torraca, Francesco. *Per la biografia di Giovanni Boccaccio.* Milan: Società Editrice Dante Alighieri, 1912.

———. *Giovanni Boccaccio a Napoli (1326–1339).* Naples: L. Pierro e figlio, 1915.

Trapp, J. B. "The Grave of Vergil." *Journal of the Warburg and Courtauld Institutes* 47 (1984): 1–31.

Traversari, Guido. *Bibliografia boccaccesca.* Vol. 1, *Scritti intorno al Boccaccio e alla fortuna delle sue opere.* 1907. Reprint, New York: Burt Franklin, 1973.

Trimpi, Wesley. "The Ancient Hypothesis of Fiction: An Essay on the Origins of Literary Theory." *Traditio* 27 (1971): 1–78.

———. "The Quality of Fiction: The Rhetorical Transmission of Literary Theory." *Traditio* 30 (1974): 1–118.

Underwood, Paul A. "The Fountain of Life in Manuscripts of the Gospels." *Dunbarton Oaks Papers* 5 (1950): 41–138.

Valerius Maximus. *Factorum et dictorum memorabilium.* Translated by Luigi Rusca. 2 vols. Milan: Rizzoli, 1972

Varagine, Jacopo da. *Leggenda aurea.* Translated by Cecilia Lisi. 2 vols. Florence: Libreria Editrice Fiorentina, 1984.

———. See also Voragine, Jacobus de.

Varchi, Benedetto. *Due lezzioni di M. Benedetto Varchi, l'una d'Amore, et l'altra della Gelosia, con alcune utili et dilettevoli quistioni da lui nuovamente aggiunte.* Lyons: Rovillio, 1560.

Varro, Marcus Terentius. *Varro on Farming.* Translated by Lloyd Storr-Best. London: G. Bell and Sons, 1912.

Velli, Giuseppe. "L'*Ameto* e la Pastorale, il significato della forma." In *Boccaccio: Secoli di Vita,* edited by Marga Cottino Jones and Edward F. Tuttle, 67–80. Ravenna: Longo, 1977.

———. "Cultura e 'imitatio' nel primo Boccaccio." In *Petrarca e Boccaccio: Tradizione, memoria, scrittura,* 77–117. 2d ed. Padua: Antenore, 1995.

———. *Petrarca e Boccaccio: Tradizione, memoria, scrittura.* 2d ed. Padua: Antenore, 1995.

———. "Sull' *Elegia di Costanza.*" In *Petrarca e Boccaccio: Tradizione, memoria, scrittura,* 118–32. 2d ed. Padua: Antenore, 1995. (First published in *Studi sol Boccaccio* 4 (1967): 241–54.)

Veruda, Roberto. *Il Filocolo e la Historia destructionis Troiae di Guido delle Colonne: Strutture e modelli della narratività boccacciana.* Florence: Atheneum, 1993.

Villani, Filippo. From *De origine civitatis Florentiae et de eiusdem famosis civibus.* In *Le vite di Dante, Petrarca e Boccaccio scritte fino al secolo decimosesto,* edited by Angelo Solerti, 671–76. Storia letteraria d'Italia scritta da una Società di Professori, vol. 4. Milan: Dottor Francesco Vallardi, n.d.

Vinaver, Eugène. *The Rise of Romance.* Oxford: Oxford University Press, 1971.

Virgil. *Aeneid.* In *Eclogues, Georgics, Aeneid,* 2 vols., translated by H. R. Fairclough, 1: 241–571; 2: 1–365. Loeb Classical Library. Cambridge: Harvard University Press, 1974.

———. *Georgics.* In *Eclogues, Georgics, Aeneid,* translated by H. R. Fairclough, 1: 79–237. Loeb Classical Library. Cambridge: Harvard University Press, 1974.

Voeux de l'epervier. Ed. G. Wolfram and F. Bonnardot. *Jahrbuch der Gesellschaft für Lothringische Geschichte und Altertumskunde* 6 (1894): 177–280. (Also published separately at Metz in 1895.)

Voragine, Jacobus de. *The Golden Legend.* Translated by Granger Ryan and Helmut Ripperger. New York: Arno Press, 1969.

Waetzoldt, Stephan. *Die Kopien des 17. Jahrhunderts nach Mosaiken und Wandmalereien in Rom.* Römische Forschungen der Bibliotheca Hertziana, vol. 18. Vienna: Anton Schroll and Company, 1964.

Wallace, David. *Chaucer and the Early Writings of Boccaccio.* Woodbridge, Suffolk: D. S. Brewer, 1985.

Ward, Marvin J. "*Floire et Blancheflor:* A Bibliography." *Bulletin of Bibliography* 40, no. 1 (1983): 45–64.

Watson, Paul F. *The Garden of Love in Tuscan Art of the Early Renaissance.* Philadelphia: Art Alliance Press, 1979.

———. "In a Court of Love: Giovanni Toscani and Giovanni Boccaccio at the

Elvehjm." *Elvehjem Museum of Art, University of Wisconsin-Madison, Bulletin/Annual Report,* 1985–86, 4–16.

———. "On a Window in Parnassus." *Artibus et Historiae* 16 (1987): 127–48.

———. "To Paint Poetry: Raphael on Parnassus." In *Renaissance Rereadings: Intertext and Context,* edited by Maryanne Cline Horowitz, Anne J. Cruz, and Wendy A. Furman, 114–41. Urbana: University of Illinois, 1988.

Weaver, Elissa, ed. *Amor di Virtù: Commedia in cinque atti, 1548,* by Beatrice del Sera. Ravenna: Longo, 1990.

Wentersdorf, Karl P. "Iconographic Elements in *Floris and Blancheflour.*" *Annuale Mediaevale* 20 (1981): 76–96.

Wetherbee, Winthrop. *Chaucer and the Poets: An Essay on Troilus and Criseyde.* Ithaca: Cornell University Press, 1984.

———. "History and Romance in Boccaccio's *Teseida.*" In *Boccaccio 1990: The Poet and His Renaissance Reception,* edited by Kevin Brownlee and Victoria Kirkham. *Studi sul Boccaccio* 20 (1991–92): 173–84.

Wheaton, Barbara Ketcham. "How to Cook a Peacock." *Harvard Magazine,* Nov.–Dec., 1979, 63–65.

Whiting, B. J. "The Vows on the Heron." *Speculum* 20 (July, 1945): 161–78.

Wilkins, Ernest Hatch. *The Making of the Canzoniere and Other Petrarchan Studies.* Rome: Edizioni di Storia e Letteratura, 1951.

———. "Boccaccio's First Octave." *Italica* 33, no. 1 (1956): 19.

———. "The 1527 *Philopono.*" In *The Invention of the Sonnet and Other Studies in Italian Literature,* 139–45. Rome: Edizioni di Storia e Letteratura, 1959.

———. "Variations on the Name *Philocolo.*" In *The Invention of the Sonnet and Other Studies in Italian Literature,* 139–45. Rome: Edizioni di Storia e Letteratura, 1959.

———. *A History of Italian Literature.* Revised by Thomas G. Bergin. Cambridge: Harvard University Press, 1974.

Wilpert, Joseph, and Walter N. Schumacher. *Die Römischen Mosaiken der Kirchlichen Bauten vom IV–XIII Jahrhundert.* Freiburg: Herder, 1976.

Witthoft, Brucia. "The *Tacuinum sanitatis:* Studies in Secular Manuscript Illumination in Late Fourteenth-Century Lombardy." Ph.D. diss., Harvard University, 1973.

Zambrini, Francesco. *Le opere volgari a stampa dei secoli XIII e XIV.* 4th ed. Bologna: Zanichelli, 1878.

Zardi, Antonio. *Albertino Mussato: Studio storico e letterato.* Padua: Angelo Draghi, 1884.

Index

301

Plates

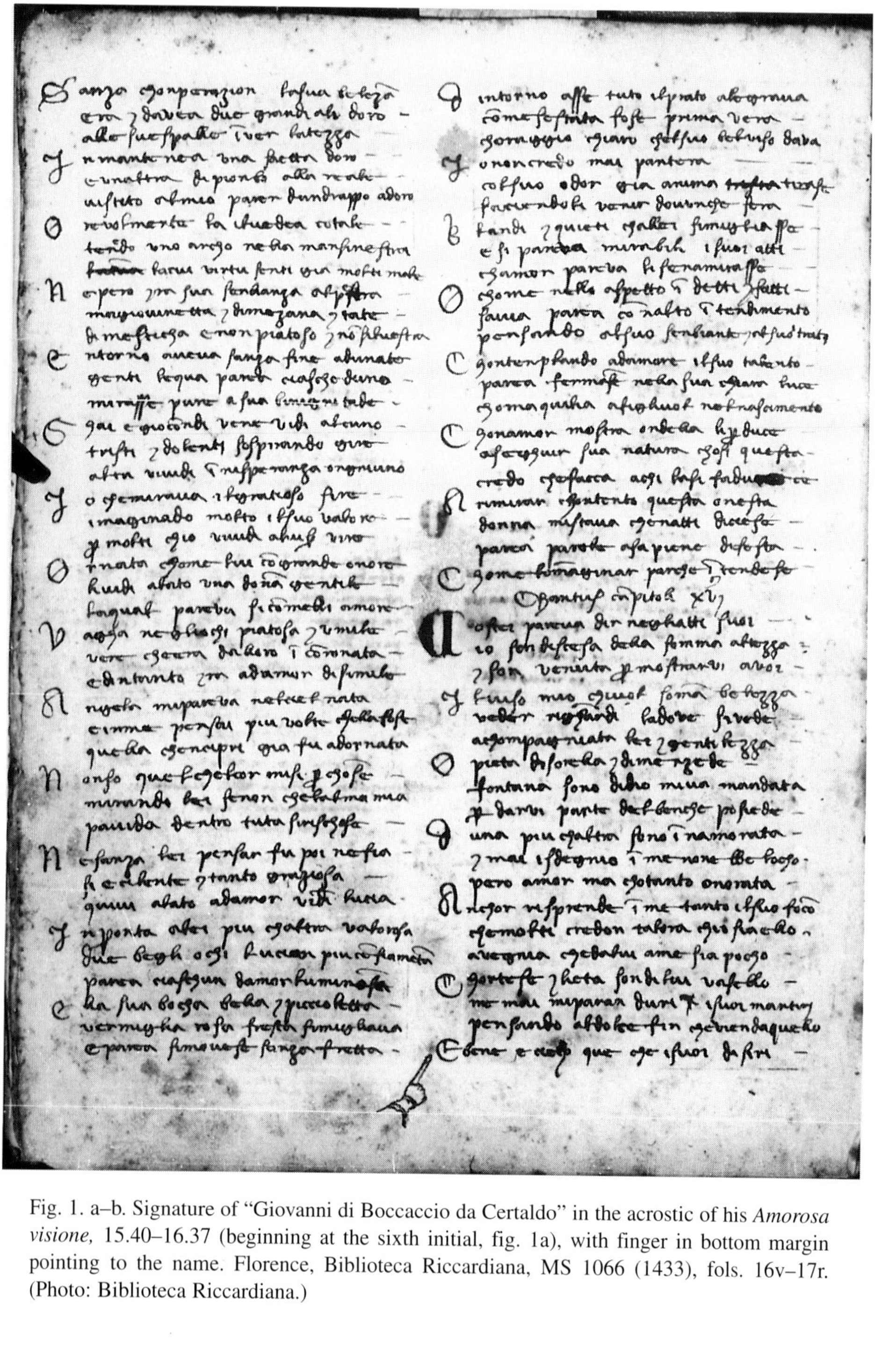

Fig. 1. a–b. Signature of "Giovanni di Boccaccio da Certaldo" in the acrostic of his *Amorosa visione,* 15.40–16.37 (beginning at the sixth initial, fig. 1a), with finger in bottom margin pointing to the name. Florence, Biblioteca Riccardiana, MS 1066 (1433), fols. 16v–17r. (Photo: Biblioteca Riccardiana.)

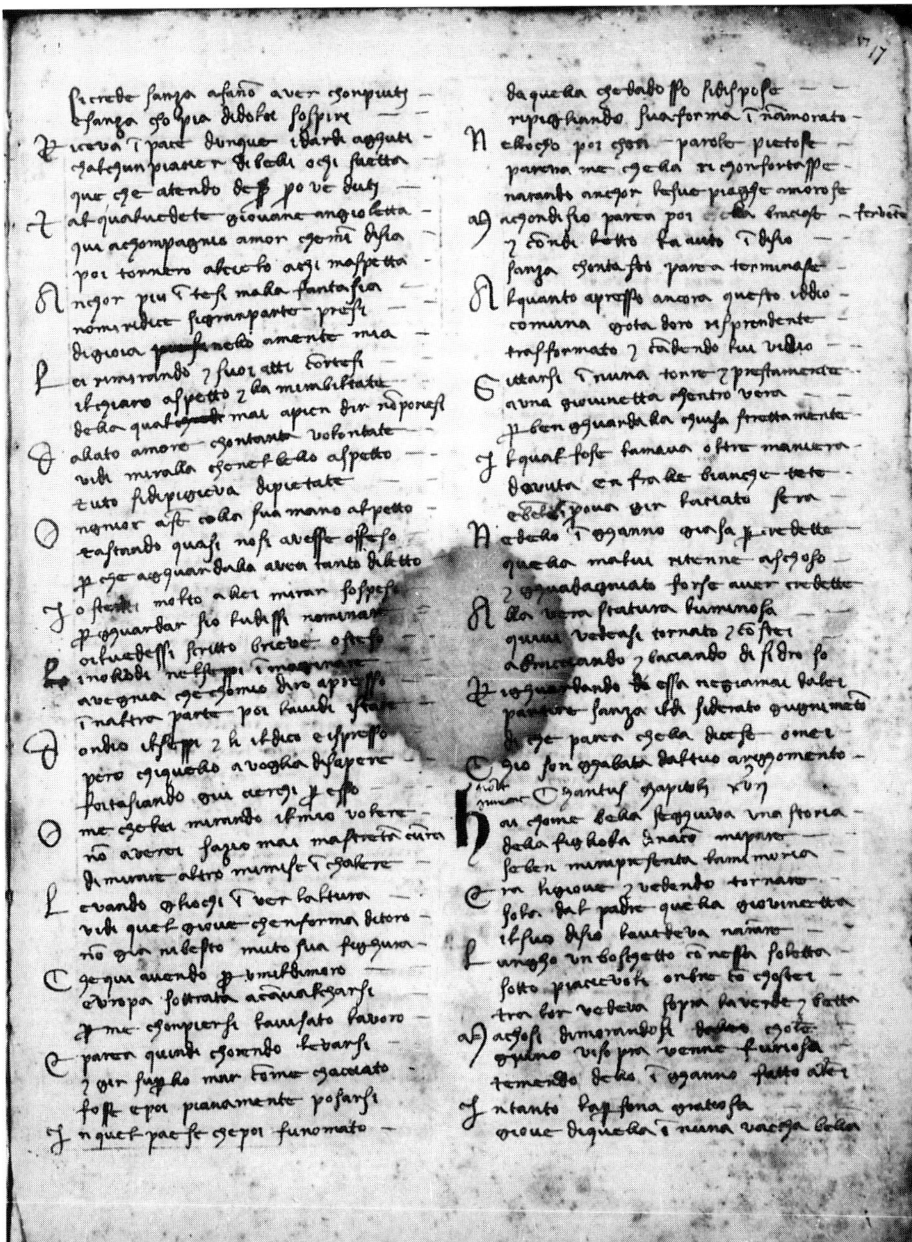

Fig. 2. Juno in her peacock-drawn chariot descends from heaven to visit the pope. *Filocolo,* incipit of book 1. The Bodleian Library, Oxford, MS Canon Ital. 85 (fifteenth century), fol. 1r. (Photo: The Bodleian Library.)

Fig. 3. Venus visits Cupid on Cyprus. *Filocolo,* incipit of book 2. The Bodleian Library, Oxford, MS Canon Ital. 85, fol. 25r. (Photo: The Bodleian Library.)

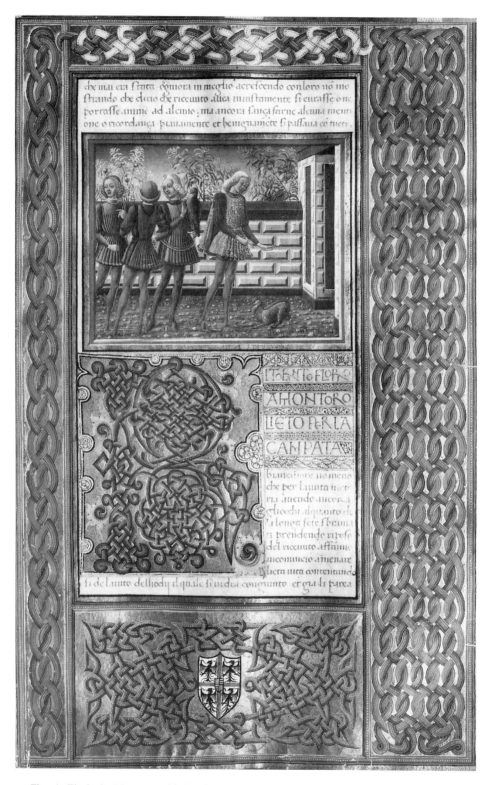

Fig. 4. Florio in Montoro with hunting dog and falcon. *Filocolo,* incipit of book 3. The Bodleian Library, Oxford, MS Canon Ital. 85, fol. 67r. (Photo: The Bodleian Library.)

Fig. 5. Filocolo and companions depart in search of Biancifiore. *Filocolo,* incipit of book 4.
The Bodleian Library, Oxford, MS Canon Ital. 85, fol. 114v. (Photo: The Bodleian Library.)

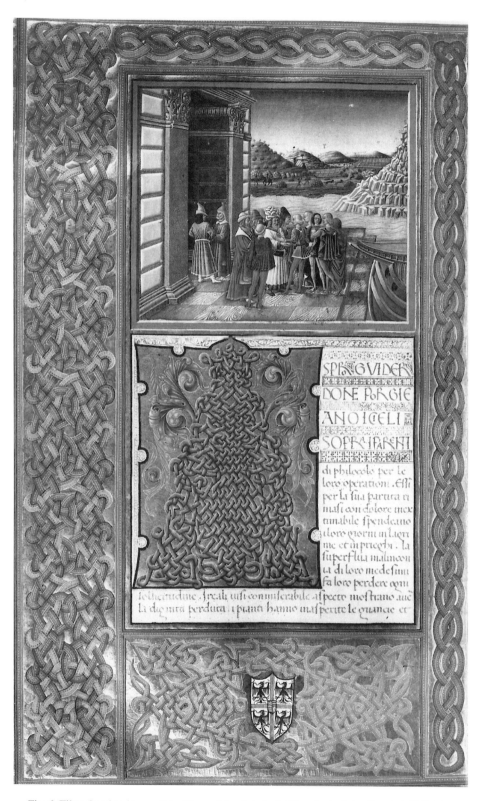

Fig. 6. Filocolo takes leave of the Alexandrian Admiral. *Filocolo,* incipit of book 5 (5.2). The Bodleian Library, Oxford, MS Canon Ital. 85, fol. 190v. (Photo: The Bodleian Library.)

ragione di non amarti giamai. ma dignamente odiarti. Et se ella morisse potendola tu aiutare gran vergogna ti sarebbe. e veramente mai viuere li cto non douresti. Dunque leuati su non vincha il sonno la debita sollici-tudine. pero che mai niuno pigro guadagnera i graciosi doni.

Ca. lvii. Di quel che florio uidi nel sogno τ come da mar-te fu suigliato.

VIII

El piciolo spacio che Florio qui adormentato stette gli fu la fortuna molto graciosa. pero che a lui parea cosi dormen-do chon le sue forze hauere liberata Bianchafiore da ogni pericolo. Et con lei essere in vno piaceuole giardino pieno

Fig. 7. Mars awakens Florio and takes him under his tutelage. *Filocolo* 2.57. From an edition printed in Naples by Sixtus Russinger Tedesco in 1478, fol. 59v. Woodcut by a northern artist. By permission of the British Library. (Photo: British Library.)

Iana che delí alti regní conofceua là míferia i che bíázafiore éra ue
nuta p lopatione di lei ífemedefima fi ríputo effere uédícata del nó
riceuuto facríficío tépo le fue íre có gíufto freno elle fáce orecchie
piego a diuotí priegí di bíázafiore & li foi feãní lafciatí a q̃lí dí Venere fe
nádo & cofi diffe. O Venere fono allí tue orechíe puenutí i pietofi prieghí
della tua bíázafiore come alle mee. certo fi rifpofe Cítherea· & gía dí q̃ mí
uolea moucre p ádare a porgerle il dímádato cóforto. Ma tu che níua tua
íra uoglí féza uédetta da te cacíare. lafcía ormai le fopchíeuole offefe. z pdo
na al difauéturato fallo alla inocéte gíouene. acío chío nó había cagíone dí
q̃tamiare i toí chuorí có piu afpreza. tu nó meno dí me fe teũta daíntaf co
fteí. po che bone cb ella haggía mecho il chuore a te có le opatóne a feruító
& ora a te come a me foccorfo nella pféte aduerfita dímáda· Adũque diffe
Díana· ãdiamo le míe íre fono paffate e ̧ba cópaffíone d̃ foí malí porto nel
petto porgíamo lí il domádato cóforto· a chui uencre diffe· Io la ueggío fo
pra le falate ũde uíta da ágofcíofi piáti foaueméte dormíre z effere portata
uerfo il mío móte· al q̃le luogo fpero chel fuo difío ácora faro có letícia ter
· míare· auegna cb féza idugío effef nó po p q̃llo cb p adíetro hai adoperato

Fig. 8. Diana joins Venus in heaven; henceforth the two goddesses work as allies to protect
Biancifiore. *Filocolo* 3.52. From an edition printed in Naples by Sixtus Russinger Tedesco in
1478, fol. 104v. Woodcut by a northern artist. By permission of the British Library. (Photo:
British Library.)

Fig. 9. *Monumental Crucifixion with Pope Honorius III and His Father Confessor, Fra Jacobus.* Rome, San Giovanni in Laterano, fresco, first quarter of the thirteenth century, lost. Recorded in a manuscript copy of the seventeenth century. Vatican City, Biblioteca Apostolica Vaticana, MS Barb. Lat. 4423, fol. 1. (Photo: Vatican Library.)

Fig. 10. Giovanni Toscani, *Scene in a Court of Love: Filocolo's Parable. Filocolo* 4.19–22 (the f rst question in the love debate). Tempera and gold on panel, 1425. 14 5/8″ x 18 3/16″. Copyright © Elvehjem Museum of Art, University of Wisconsin-Madison. Gift of Samuel H. Kress Foundation, New York. (Photo: Elvehjem Museum of Art.)